TRADITIONAL COUNTRY SKILLS

Traditional COUNTRY SKILLS

A Practical Compendium of American Wisdom and Know-how

EDITED BY SHEILA BUFF

The Lyons Press

GUILFORD, CONNECTICUT

An imprint of The Globe Pequot Press

Copyright © 2001 by The Lyons Press

The Lyons Press is an imprint of the Globe Pequot Press.

Designed by Cindy LaBreacht
Printed in the United States of America

10 9 8 7 6 5 4 3 2 1

Library of Congress Cataloging-in-Publication Data

Traditional country skills : a practical compendium of American wisdom and know-how / edited by Sheila Buff.
    p. cm.
  Includes bibliographical references (p.).
  ISBN 1-58574-155-8
  1. Agriculture—United States—Handbooks, manuals, etc. 2. Farms, Small—United States—Handbooks, manuals, etc. 3. Country life—United States—Handbooks, manuals, etc. I. Buff, Sheila.

S501.2 .T73 2001
630'.973—dc21   2001022450

DEDICATION

This book is dedicated to the Farmers of America; the noblest race of men God's sun ever shone upon; a race headed by George Washington and Thomas Jefferson; a race that made the Republic, and that has the future of American freedom and prosperity in its keeping.

CONTENTS

INTRODUCTION

When Thomas Jefferson wrote in 1782, in his *Notes on the State of Virginia*, that "those who labor in the earth are the chosen people of God, if ever he had a chosen people, whose breasts he has made his peculiar deposit for substantial and genuine virtue," over 90 percent of the American populace lived and worked on farms.

A century later, the Jeffersonian ideal of the sturdy, self-sufficient American farmer had undergone radical change—and the farmers of the period stood poised on the brink of yet more radical change. In 1880, the American population had topped 50 million. Nearly 23 million people, or 49 percent of the population, were gainfully employed in agriculture. They worked on some 4 million farms averaging 153 acres apiece. A decade later, in 1890, the population had grown to nearly 63 million, largely from huge numbers of European immigrants. About 26 million people, or 43 percent of the population, worked on farms. The number of farms had risen, however, to over 4.5 million. By 1900, when the American population was nearly 76 million, 29 million people, or only 38 percent of the population, worked on farms. The number of farms, however, had risen to over 5.7 million, averaging 147 acres.

The American farm population would reach its historic peak in 1920, when there were over 6.4 million farms and more than 31 million people living on them. After that, increased mechanization, low farm income, and better opportunities elsewhere combined to drain young people off the farms. Today, just over a century later, the American population is over 250 million, yet the farm population is under 5 million, or about 2.6 percent of the labor force. The number of farms is just over 2 million, averaging over 450 acres. Of these farms, fewer than half are family owned; the rest are part of the vast acreage of corporate farms.

As the numbers show, from the end of the Civil War to around 1900, American agriculture grew at an accelerating pace. The total number of farms, the acreage under cultivation, and the value of farm property nearly doubled in this period.

A driving force behind agricultural expansion was the Homestead Act of 1862, which granted 160 acres of public land to any settler who farmed it for five years. The Homestead Act was a major incentive to westward expansion across the Great Plains and into California.

The effect of the Homestead Act can be seen most dramatically in the opening of the Great Plains to settlement. In 1870, all of Kansas, Nebraska, and the Dakotas had perhaps 50,000 farms; in 1900, the buffalo and Native Americans were gone, and nearly 400,000 farms covered the grasslands.

Even as the American farm population was doubling, however, the urban population was tripling. And even as demand for farm products was growing, manufacturing was becoming the true lifeblood of America. By 1890, the total value of manufactured goods outstripped the total value of agricultural products.

Mechanization and industrialization were felt on the farm as well. Improved farm machinery such as the mechanical reaper and mechanical mower greatly increased efficiency and made farm labor less backbreaking. Sewing machines, cream separators, and pumps in the kitchen reduced the labor demands on farm women. In the 1830s, it took some eleven man-hours of hand labor to produce a ton of hay; in 1900, it took only about ninety minutes. Mechanization meant that crops could be planted, cultivated, and harvested at the optimum times, which led to higher yields and higher quality. A good farmer could make his farm pay.

In 1900 the great revolution in mechanized farming from the widespread use of gasoline-powered tractors and trucks was still a few years off. The great golden age of American farming—the brief period of high prices and farm prosperity that lasted from roughly 1900 to 1920—was yet to come.

Starting in the 1870s, better transportation and communications networks let the farmers' crops reach their markets more efficiently. The development of a far-reaching rail network, the widespread availability of the telegraph and the telephone, and an improved rural mail delivery system all brought farmers' products to the outside world.

They also brought the outside world to the farmer. The small mail-order firm begun in 1872 by Aaron Montgomery Ward soon grew into a rural institution. Montgomery Ward catalogs, crammed with over 10,000 items ranging from horse rugs to carpeting, brought consumer goods to the farmer. Jefferson's self-sufficient farmer, producing most of his modest needs on his own farm, had been replaced by a specialized farmer who sold his products—wheat, fruit, chickens, eggs, butter, cheese, milk—for cash, hired outside labor, and purchased machinery, seeds, and livestock. By 1900, only 60 percent of what a farmer consumed came from his own farm.

As farming became more industrialized, more specialized, and more part of a cash economy, farmers needed knowledge. Their needs were first recognized in 1862 by two important pieces of legislation. The College Land Grant Act allotted public lands for the construction of agricultural colleges; this was augmented in 1890 by the Morrill Act, which gave annual federal payments to the land grant colleges. Additional legislation in 1862 formed the federal Department of Agriculture (it was elevated to cabinet status in 1889). The extremely influential agricultural extension programs that were part of the land grant colleges and the state experimental stations encouraged scientific farming.

Accompanying—and stimulating—the growth of agricultural training and research were scores of agricultural newspapers and journals. With names such as *New England Farmer, Southern Agriculturalist, Working Farmer,* and *Plow,* weekly or monthly farm papers flourished in the latter half of the nineteenth century. The oldest farm publication in the United States, *Prairie Farmer,* was founded in 1841 by a young easterner named John S. Wright who had moved to Chicago, then in its formative years as a marketing center for grain, livestock, and other farm products. Wright became known as the Prophet of the Prairies for his crusading efforts on behalf of scientific agriculture and such social issues as the need for improved rural schools.

Another well-known farm paper was *American Agriculturist,* which exists, in modified form, to this day. The great success of this paper was due primarily to its early owner, Orange Judd. Born in 1822 near Niagara Falls in New York, Orange Judd graduated from Wesleyan University in Connecticut in 1847. In 1853, he became the joint owner and editor of *American Agriculturist* and went on to expand his empire with a number of other farm journals and papers, including a German-language version of *American Agriculturalist, Hearth and Home,* and *The Thresherman.* In 1870 he donated the money to build the Orange Judd Hall of Natural Science at Wesleyan, the first college building in the country for undergraduate science. (It still stands and today houses the psychology department.) *American Agriculturist* was later purchased in 1922 by Henry Morgenthau Jr., who became chairman of the Federal Farm Board under Franklin Roosevelt in 1933 and then served as secretary of the treasury from 1934 through 1945. (The Morgenthau Plan, which would have turned Germany into a strictly agricultural nation after World War II, was scrapped in favor of the Marshall Plan.) Orange Judd became the editor of *Prairie Farmer* in 1882 and stayed on until 1888. Today both *Prairie Farmer* and *American Agriculturalist* are still published by Farm Progress, a leading agricultural publisher.

Orange Judd began a major book publishing program in the late 1870s. The titles he commissioned and published covered a vast number of farming topics, ranging from treatises on raising specialized crops such as asparagus and celery to general works on broad topics such as profitable dairy operations. Although Judd died in 1892, the publishing operation continued into the 1920s. Other publishers also put out agricultural titles to meet the high demand. These books, designed to inform farmers about new and better ways to run their farms, form the basis of this volume.

A fascinating aspect of all the farm journals and books of the period is their presumed audience. Without ever directly stating it, the authors assume that their readers are literate white men who own and operate reasonably prosperous family farms of at least fifty acres. Left out of the discussion entirely are the sizable number of tenant farmers, sharecroppers, and farm laborers who did not own their land and formed a large and neglected pool of rural poverty. Left out for the most part are women; left out entirely are the many African-American farmers of the period. Even so, the agricultural periodicals and books of the latter half of the nineteenth century are a fascinating window into the past. Despite the gathering speed of agricultural change, they still show us clearly the simpler rhythms of rural life more than a century ago.

TRADITIONAL COUNTRY SKILLS

PART I: Structures

CHAPTER 1

BARNS AND OUTBUILDINGS

The elegantly simple wooden barn symbolizes the farm. The classic red-painted, tin-roofed barn of the picture postcard, however, achieved its remarkable blend of form and function only in the late 1860s and early 1870s—and the tall, cylindrical silo right next to it became a standard part of the picture only by the turn of the century.

Earlier barn designs, including the elegant Dutch-style barn with its broad gable roof, had developed regionally, especially in New York, New Jersey, Pennsylvania, and Ohio by the eighteenth century. This style often included a pent roof, an overhang above the wide central door. Dutch barns had notably heavy timbers. The overall design was of a wide central space flanked by columned aisles. The central area was entered through a wide wagon door placed on the narrow end of the barn; smaller stock doors opened onto the aisles.

Even so, until the 1860s, many farms lacked what we think of now as the basic barn: a large wooden structure on at least two levels, with stall space for animals below and a large loft for hay and grain storage above. Until the 1860s or so, farms more often had a collection of small, low structures designed primarily for sheltering animals. Hay was usually stored outdoors in ricks or haystacks; shocked grain was often left standing in the fields and brought in as needed to be threshed. Additional small outbuildings were tacked on as needed or as the farmer could afford around the edges of the farmyard. The resulting clutter of sheds was not only highly inefficient but also raised the risk of fire.

As farming practices changed, the basic two- or three-decker form of the barn, also known as the bank barn, became highly popular. Based on the Dutch design, the bank barn gets its name from the way it was ingeniously built against a hillside whenever possible. Where no hill was convenient, an earthen bank, or ramp, was built up to the second level. Either way, two levels of the barn could be easily entered from outside. Animals could be led into the lower level, while loaded wagons could bring hay, grain, and so on directly to the upper level.

THREE-STORY BARNS

Three-story barns, or "three-deckers," as they are sometimes called, when conveniently arranged, are decidedly the most economical, both of material in building, and of labor and care in management. The accompanying plan has been pre-

Fig. 1.—ELEVATION OF BARN.

pared in response to several requests for a barn-plan to accommodate a small farm, and not to cost more than $1,500 to $2,000.

It is rarely or never worth while to attempt to build a three-story barn upon level ground, but where a descent can be used having a slope of 18 inches in 10 feet for a space of 50 or 80 feet, it will do very well. A bridge, or a walled approach to the barn floor is often dangerous. Access by a self-sustaining sodded earth bank, sloping off gradually to the general surface, is decidedly preferable. A good cellar is seldom to be had without considerable digging, and the wall against the bank must be a substantial one of concrete, or of stone, or brick, well laid in cement, and guarded from the action of water by surface channels and underdrains. The cellar ought to be at least 9 feet high, the floor grouted and cemented water-tight, and should be accessible from the south. Being used for manure, convenience of loading carts requires it to be reasonably high. The feeding or cattle floor is not necessarily so high; 7 feet in the clear is as low as one ever ought to be, and 8 feet is about right. This floor should be accessible from each end, and well lighted. The openings for the manure to be thrown into the cellar, and for the liquid manure to flow through, must be where the liquid will not rot the beams. The floor should be laid of well-seasoned inch-and-a-half plank, merely tacked down at first if not perfectly dry, especially if the barn can stand through one summer before it is used. In this case the floor can be re-laid permanently in autumn, after this extra seasoning, and the

seams caulked and pitched. The thrashing floor should be not less than 12 feet wide, the doors opening nearly the full width, and 10 feet high. From the sill to the plate cannot well be less than 14 feet, and the barn should be framed to dispense with the great cross-beams so much in the way of the horse-forks (see figure 5). The side beams, connecting the inner posts with the outer frame, should be level with the top of the great door. We commend a feature which we have long known to work well, namely, laying a corn floor upon the tie-beams of the roof. In this barn such a floor would afford 18 × 40 feet of space for spreading out corn to cure, in the hottest place to be found. Such a loft will hold easily 1,000 bushels of corn in the ear. The corn is lifted in tubs attached to the common horse-fork rigging. The corn sheller is placed here, and the shelled corn run down by a shute.

In building such a barn economically, it is expected of course that the farmer will do a good deal of the labor with his own men and teams, at times when other work does not press. He will dig the cellar and grade the ground for the approach and for the barn-yard. He will haul all the stones, sand, cement, and lime, for the wall, and, perhaps, mix the mortar and lay the walls himself. He will cut and hew the timber, haul to the saw-mill and back again, and assist in the framing and raising. It depends, therefore, a good deal on the part of the country in which the barn is to be built, what timber, as well as what foundation, can be economically used. The barn can be built near New York with bought materials and hired labor, for $2,000.

DESCRIPTION OF THE BARN.—The barn is 30 × 40 feet inside measure, and the plans are drawn to a scale of $1/16$ of an inch to the foot. Fig. 2 is a plan of the main floor. On the left, space is taken for the shop and the grain room. The former, a room 10 × 14, has a large double window and a single

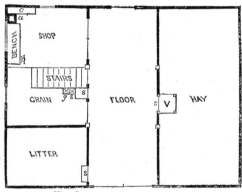

Fig. 2.—PLAN OF MAIN FLOOR.

one. The double doors make it possible to run a wagon or carriage into the shop, for painting or other repairs. There is a carpenter's bench and a closet for tools. The chimney passes through this room, and a fire can be made if necessary. The grain room should be supplied with bins, and there should be two or three shutes for different kinds of grain or

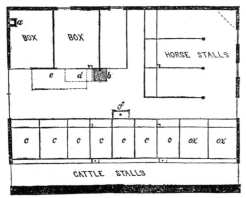

Fig. 3.—PLAN OF CATTLE FLOOR.

meal. These are shown at *g s*, fig. 2, and are intended to be of canvass, after passing through the floor, so that they may be turned to one side and out of the way. These rooms need not be more than 7 or 7 1/2 feet high. From the thrashing floor, two shutes, or trap doors communicate with the floor below—one near the stairs for cut hay, etc. one near the litter bay, through which bedding may be thrown down at the rear of the cows, while the ventilator is also used as a shute, and through it, long hay is thrown down, falling in the passage-way between the horse stables and the cow mangers. This ventilator (*V*) is 3 × 3 feet square, and extends from the cattle floor out through the roof of the barn.

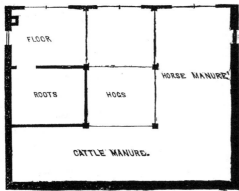

Fig. 4.—PLAN OF BARN-CELLAR.

The plan of the cattle floor (fig. 3) needs little explanation. The stairs at *e* are hinged and may be turned up and fastened, so that a cart can be driven, or backed under them, to dump a load of green fodder upon the floor, or one of muck to be thrown through the trap door *f* to the pigs. The feed-box *d* is movable. Near the end of the barn, where the horse and ox stalls are, the shed for wagons, carts, tools, etc., is supposed to be placed. At *b* a hydrant and water-trough is placed. One corner of the horse stable may be partitioned off

for nice harness, etc., if desired. In the cellar plan, fig. 4, a root cellar is provided, also a floor where steaming apparatus may be set up. Here the "working hogs" are to be kept, and either shut off from the manure, or allowed to range over it, and given the range of the barn-yard besides, if that be desirable. This cellar is accessible to carts or wagons through

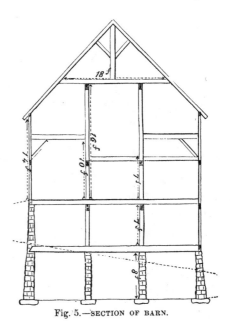

Fig. 5.—SECTION OF BARN.

three 8-foot doors, and it is lighted by windows in these doors, and by other in the ends. The ground of the barn-yard slopes the cellar, and the water is collected in a tank to be pumped through a hose over the manure whenever it gets too dry, or too hot. Fig. 5 represents a cross-section of the barn, and shows the framing and slope of the ground.

A GOOD FARM BARN

The following plan (figure 16) is of a simple and inexpensive barn. The size is forty by fifty-five feet; it has a large shed attached for cattle. The fifteen-foot barn floor, see figure 17, is of good medium width; if wider the room would not be wasted. On the left are the horse stalls, five feet wide. There might be five stalls four feet wide, but for a large horse the width ought to be about five feet. The whole space given to horses is fifteen by twenty feet. Beyond, the floor widens seven feet, and the rest of the left side is devoted to cattle stalls, twenty-five feet, giving room for six cow and ox stalls, and two passage ways, one of which may be closed and made a stall for a cow. The seven-foot space affords abundant room for hay cutter, feed box, and accompaniments, located close to both cattle and horses; and if cattle are fed in the shed on feed prepared in the feed box, a passage at the rear conducts conveniently to their mangers. A three-foot square trunk ascends, from over the seven by twenty-five-foot space in front of the cow stalls, to the roof, securing abundant ventilation, and affording a shute, through which hay, or straw, may be readily dropped from the mow; or corn cobs, and other matters, from the granary.

The right side of the barn floor is occupied by a hay bay. There is a tight ceiling of matched boards over the stables, at

Fig. 16.—ELEVATION OF BARN.

a hight of eight feet. The posts are sixteen feet to the eaves. The roof is what is usually called half-pitch, more lasting than if flatter. A substantial, tight floor is laid upon the straining beams of the roof. This may be extended, if desired, through the entire length of the barn, or only from one end to over the barn floor. In it is a large trap door directly over the thrashing floor. A small gable with a door in it, over the great doors, affords communication with the front of the barn, so that grain in bags or barrels may be raised or lowered as well here as through the trap door. This floor is the gra-

nary or corn loft, easily made rat proof, close under the roof, and consequently very hot in sunshiny, autumn weather. Corn in the ear is easily hoisted by horse power from the wagons and, if spread on the floor not more than a foot thick, it will cure much sooner and more perfectly than in cribs. This grain floor is reached by a stairway from the floor over the stables; under the stairs is a shute, or shutes, for conducting the shelled corn, etc., to the feeding floor. This arrangement requires strong posts and roof framing, but not stronger than for a slate roof of a less pitch, for such a roof will support double the weight likely to be placed on the floor. Not only is the roof constructed to bear the weight of the slates, but of two feet of snow, and the force of high winds in addition. The weight of grain will only give increased steadiness, a large part being borne by the posts, the floor preventing all racking. The shed is thirty by forty feet, with twelve-foot front, and eight-foot rear posts, open in front, and having windows in the back. At the rear, a passage way four feet wide communicates with the cow stable in the barn, and forms the feeding alley to the loose boxes in the shed. Cattle will not suffer in such a shed, left entirely open, in the severest winter weather, but it is best to close the front by boarding, and doors, having large windows for light and air. The pigpens are placed contiguous to the barn yard, so that the swine may be allowed the free range of the compost heaps, at least in their own corner. In the hog house is a steam boiler; and a pipe, boxed and packed in sawdust, and laid underground, crosses the yard to the feeding floor, for steaming and cooking the fodder for the cattle. By this arrangement the swine are located at a considerable distance from the granary and root cellar. But this is not a serious inconvenience, and it is best to remove any source of danger from fire as far as possible.

The root cellar is seven feet deep under the hay bay, on the right side of the barn. There are two shutes from the floor to the cellar, and there is a stairway as indicated. Besides, access is had by a cellar way, on the eastern side.

This plan may very readily be reduced, to say thirty by forty-two feet, making the floor, twelve feet, the bay, fifteen feet, four horse stalls, eighteen feet, and four cow stalls, twelve feet, in a line across the left side—the floor being fifteen feet wide in front of the cow stable, and other contractions made in the same proportions.

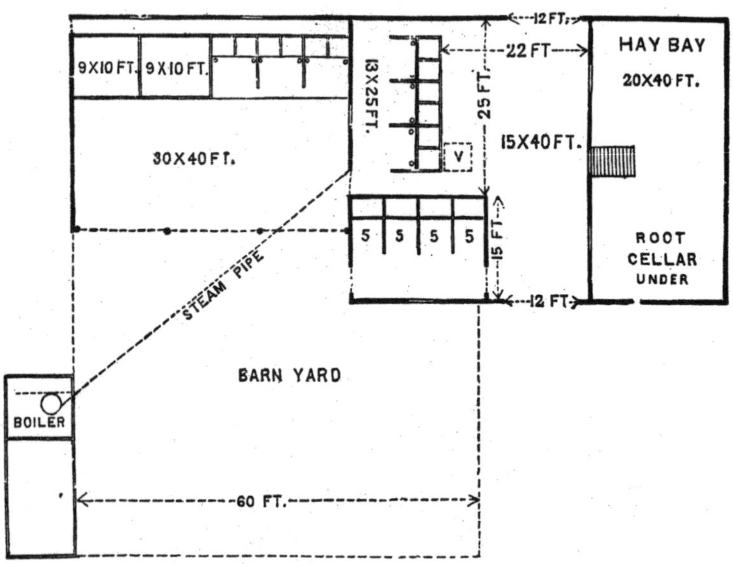

Fig. 17.—PLAN OF BARN FLOOR AND BARN YARD.

ANOTHER BARN FOR MIXED FARMING

Very many farmers desire a barn for mixed husbandry, for storing hay and grain, for keeping stock, and all the labor-saving implements, with a good root cellar in a convenient place, and a yard for manure. The following plan, figure 18,

Fig. 18.—ELEVATION OF BARN AND STABLE.

shows such a barn. Its cost ranges from one thousand five hundred to two thousand five hundred dollars, according to the price of materials and the amount of finish put upon the work. In most places, where stone for the lower story and lumber can be cheaply procured, one thousand five hundred dollars will be sufficient to build a barn fifty feet square, including everything needed.

A PLAN FOR A SMALL BARN

There are many small farmers, villagers, gardeners, etc., who wish only barn room enough for a single horse and carriage, and a cow. To such, the requirements are cheapness and durability, combined with convenience; and with these points in view a plan, figure 24, is given of a small barn, designed by Prof. G. T. Fairchild, late of the Michigan

Fig. 24.—A SMALL CHEAP BARN.

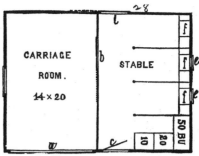

Fig. 25.—GROUND PLAN OF BARN.

Agricultural College. The engraving gives a view of the barn from the front; while plain in its construction, it is pleasing in outline. The first floor, figure 25, is twenty by twenty-eight feet, and eight feet between joints. A large sliding-door, a, nine feet wide, admits the carriage with the horse attached, which, when unhitched, is led through the sliding door, b, into the stable. The small stable door, c, opens by hinges inwards, while the back door, d, opening to the manure yard, moves upon rollers. Two small windows, e, e, give sufficient light to the stable. The hay racks and feed boxes for the stalls are shown at f, f, f, each having a hay shute leading from the floor above. The grain bins are neatly arranged under the stairway, these being three in number, ranging in capacity from fifty to ten bushels. The second story, or hay loft, figure 26, is six feet from floor to plates, and

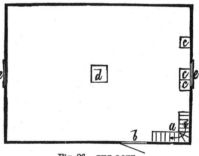

Fig. 26.—THE LOFT.

gives ample room for the storage of hay and straw. The stairs are in one corner, a, and out of the way; b, the door for the admittance of hay and straw; c, c, c, ends of the hay shutes; d, ventilator; e, e, windows. The ventilator serves the purpose of a shute for throwing down the straw used for bedding. It has a number of openings for this purpose at various hights, including one at the bottom for cleaning out the dust, chaff, etc., which are constantly accumulating in the loft.

The cost of this barn will vary according to the locality and the price or lumber, etc. The estimate for it in Michigan was three hundred dollars, above the foundation, with two coats of paint; but in most States the lumber would cost more than in Michigan, and the estimate would be correspondingly increased.

The basic design of the bank barn met the first and foremost consideration for any farmer: it was economical. It was also easy to build, cost little to maintain, and was efficient, which meant that labor expenses were reduced. The basic barn was also easy to expand; extensions, sheds, and lean-tos could be built on later. In the New England building tradition, the barn was often connected to the house by a series of smaller sheds and storage areas, sheltering the farmer from the weather.

In 1870 the construction cost for a quite substantial three-story barn was estimated at around $1,500 to $2,000—a not inconsiderable sum for that time. A smaller two-story barn could be built for about $500. The major expenses were lumber, shingles, hardware (nails, spikes, and so on), concrete and gravel for the foundation, and labor. The costs were lower, of course, if the farmer could provide most of his own labor. Digging the foundation, for example, was a job that could be done in the slower winter period.

Another way the farmer could save on costs was to provide his own lumber. Even if the wood came from the farmer's own woodlot, however, it had to be felled, trimmed, and sawed. Few farmers had the machinery or expertise for this. Sawyers with portable steam-powered sawmills were usually brought in. Preparing enough lumber for a good-size barn could take six weeks or more.

THE BASIC BARN

The basic three-decker barn had a basement, or ground, floor, a feeding or cattle floor (second floor, sometimes called the barn floor), and a main floor (the third floor or hay loft). Typical dimensions for a moderate-size three-decker barn might be thirty-six by forty-eight feet. The basement floor would be ten feet high, while the feeding floor might be a bit lower at eight feet. The loft often reached eighteen feet at the peak. A really substantial barn for a large farming operation could be considerably larger—over ninety by fifty feet square and reaching sixty feet high at the peak.

The roof was generally shed-style and made of tin or shingle (shingles were more expensive but provided scope for decoration). A shed roof was simple to construct, although it meant there was less storage room in the loft than if a gambrel, or hipped, roof were used.

Hogs and sheep were often housed in pens on the basement floor. This area was also used to handle manure from the cattle floor above. Root cellars and the cutters and boilers for preparing root feeds were here as well. The cattle floor was reached by a broad, sloping earthen bank or hill leading to a wide door on the broad side of the barn. Cattle stalls and horse boxes were here; chutes and trapdoors from the main floor above made it easy to pitch down hay and straw. The main floor was really the top floor—a spacious loft area designed to store hay, straw, and corn and other grains. Older barns from the days before threshing machinery also included threshing floors here. The main floor was reached from inside the barn by stairs. A crane arrangement and a sliding door in the side of the barn made it easy to lift hay bales and grain sacks to the third floor; later, elevators (really conveyor belts) powered by stationary gas or steam engines were used.

The three-floor barn with a feeding floor was designed for farmers with a fair amount of livestock—a small dairy herd and four horses, say. The smaller farmer, with only a cow or two and two or three horses, needed only a typical two-decker barn, with animal housing on the ground floor and hay and grain storage in the loft.

The prairie barn of the Midwest needed to be very large to accommodate the hay and grain storage necessary for getting livestock through long, cold winters. These barns had more in common with the old Dutch-style barn: gambrel roofs for large haymows, doors in the gable end, and stock in aisles.

THE DAIRY BARN

Dairy farmers had a number of important requirements for a barn. Mostly, it needed to be large. A dairy barn had to shelter the herd and provide room for milking, as well as have space for cleaning and storing the dairy equipment. The barn also had to store the huge amounts of hay and grain needed to feed the herd. A convenient system for handling the copious amounts of manure created by a dairy herd was essential. In dairy barns, the cows were generally kept on the basement floor, usually in a row of stanchions, not stalls, although opinion and methods on this important matter differed considerably. The main floor had horse stalls but was primarily a hayloft.

A WESTCHESTER CO., N.Y., DAIRY BARN

The general style of one of the best dairy barns is shown in the four illustrations which follow. It belongs to Mr. Edward

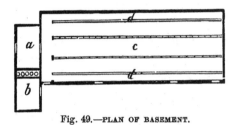

Fig. 49.—PLAN OF BASEMENT.

Fig. 50.—SECTION.

B. Brady, of Westchester Co., N. Y. Figure 51 represents the elevation of the barn. It is situated upon the side of a hill, in which the basement stable is placed. This basement is of stone, and nine feet high. The barn is twenty feet high above the stables, eighty feet long, and twenty-eight feet wide. The yard is surrounded with a stone wall, and a manure pit is dug under the center of the building, large enough to back a wagon into. The basement has four doors, and is amply lighted and ventilated. The floor is divided in the center by a wide feed passage, upon each side of which are stanchions to hold the cows. There are no troughs, but the feed is placed upon the floor before each cow. The stanchions are made of oak, are self-fastening by means of an iron loop, which is lifted by its bevelled end as the stanchion is closed—falling over and holding it securely. The space between the stanchions for the cow's neck, is six inches. Each cow has a space of three feet, and

there are no stalls or partitions between them. The floor, upon which the cows stand, is four and one-half feet wide. To the rear is a manure gutter, eighteen inches wide, and six inches deep, and behind the gutter a passage of three feet and six inches—in all giving a space of fourteen feet from the center of the feed passage to the walls upon either side. This is shown in the plan, figure 49, in which *a* is the grain pit, *b*,

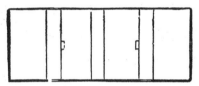

Fig. 52.—PLAN OF FLOOR.

the spring house, *c*, the feed passage, and *d* the manure gutters. The same is seen in cross section in figure 50. The barn floor, shown in figure 52, has four bays and three floors. Two of the floors have sliding doors, opening into the barn yard, and spacious windows above them, as seen in figure 51. Shutes are made in the floors, by which hay is thrown down into the feed passage. These also serve for ventilation, in connection with the cupolas upon the roof.

Fig. 51.—A WESTCHESTER CO., NEW YORK, DAIRY BARN.

Fig. 57.—VIEW OF DAIRY BARN.

VARIOUS CATTLE STANCHIONS

In the engraving figure 8, one of the stanchions is shown open, and the other two closed. The pieces *d, e, f, g,* and *h,* are immovable, *a, b, c,* being the movable stanchions. The device consists of three strips, two inches wide, and three quarter inch thick, fastened to one upright piece by means of two bolts, *d* and *b;* the length of the strip is regulated by the distance between the stanchions. Bolts are also used at *a* and *c,* the bolt at *c* passing through a small block, two inches thick, which assists in moving the upright piece. A similar block, *e,* is also placed on the movable stanchion, upon which the block at *c* rests when the stanchion is closed.

The fastening *f,* and the piece *c,* are so arranged as to fall in place at the same time. It will be seen that the animal not

Fig. 8.—SELF-CLOSING CATTLE STANCHION.

only fastens herself in place, but she is doubly secured by the pieces *f* and *c.* (The block at *e* may be omitted if desired, and the device be used with the fastening *f* only.) A badly hooked

cow is often the result of careless hired men, and such carelessness is obviated by the use of the above arrangement. A cow takes her place in the open stanchion, and in trying to get at the feed below, presses against the lever *a,* brings *c* to place, and closes the stanchion.

The engraving, figure 9, shows how every farmer who uses stanchions can arrange to close all the cows in at the same time. The two-inch strip *g,* is planed on all sides, and made to move easily in the loops *e, d,* which are of heavy galvanized iron, bent below so as to allow the strip to slide, and are attached to the immovable stanchions by screws. The hard wood pins *a, b, c,* extend about two inches through, so as to catch the movable stanchions. A lever is fixed at *h,* and attached to the movable strip. This device is comparatively inexpensive, and can be attached to all kinds of movable stanchions, generally used for fastening cows. Even after it is put on the stanchions, it need not be used unless desired. It has the advantage in being separate from every stanchion.

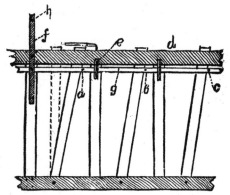

Fig. 9.—DEVICE FOR CLOSING CATTLE STANCHIONS.

One, two, or more animals may be closed in by hand and the balance with this device. It in no way interferes with the necks of the cows, and saves a great many steps. If a person reaches over in front of the cows, to close them in by hand, he is in danger of being struck in the face with a horn. The above device removes this danger. It is simple and cheap.

The use of permanent neck-chains, locked on around the necks of breeding animals and young blooded stock, affords an excellent means of fastening the animals in their stalls. A chain and snap are attached to the stall, by which, the snap being caught into the ring of the neck chain, the animals are fastened. A better way is shown in the accompanying sketch of a cow stable. Two round stanchions are placed three feet apart for each stall, and are the only indications of subdivisions or stalls in the stable. A chain about eighteen inches long having a snap at one end, is attached by a ring to each stanchion. Both chains are made fast to the ring in the "necklace," and should have very little slack. If the stanchions are of hard wood, and smooth, the rings will slide easily up and down, but should not come within a foot of the floor. The cows will have free motion of the head to

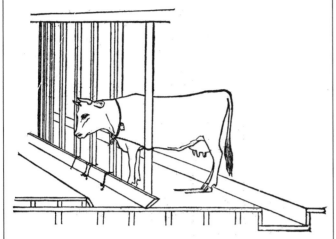

Fig. 10.—CHAIN CATTLE STANCHION.

either side, can lie down and get up easily, but have very little motion forward and back, hence will keep on the platform and keep clean. They are besides kept perfectly devoted each to her own affairs, as she cannot reach over to either neighbor, to quarrel or to steal her forage.

STALLS BETTER THAN STANCHIONS

The only point in favor of stanchions is that they take up less room than stalls, but the increase in milk is a reward for allowing more space and convenience to each cow. The cut shows one kind of stall. The rack, *a*, is of hardwood 30 inches high, with the slats wide enough so the cow can thrust her nose through up to her eyes.

The bottom of the rack is 18 inches wide, extending into the stall toward the cow. The feed box, *b*, slides through an opening in the stall on the barn floor. It can be drawn into the feedway, cleansed out and a new feed put in without being disturbed by the cow. The halter strap, *c*, is just long enough to allow the cow to lie down comfortably. The gutter, *d*, is 8 inches lower than the stall floor. When she lies down she will put her head under the rack in kneeling and when

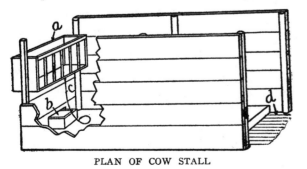

PLAN OF COW STALL

she gets up, she will move backward so that she can look through the rack. The length and width of stall can be made to suit the cows. Small breeds, like Jerseys and Ayrshires, will need about 6 inches less each way than Holsteins and Shorthorns.

GOOD TIES FOR COWS

The merits of stanchions and other forms of cow ties have been debated by dairymen for a long time. The mass of experience is in favor of the tying arrangement which will

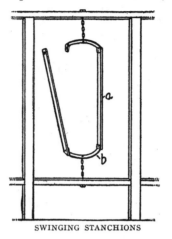

SWINGING STANCHIONS

give the cow the most freedom of movement. The old-fashioned solid stanchion fails in this respect. In many cases it is difficult for the cow to lie down or get up with her head fast in one of these stanchions.

The heavy swinging stanchions have advantages over this, but it also must be criticised in many cases, because of its weight and of the consequent lack of freedom on the part of the cow. A very light swinging stanchion is the best type of that form. It is easy to fasten, as the cows will in most cases put their heads in position as they go into the stall. There is not so much danger of the dairyman being struck by the horns of the cow in fastening these stanchions. Many modern barns are equipped with this kind.

The chain tie is favored in many sections. This consists simply of a crosschain with considerable slack, attached to a ring at each end which runs over a perpendicular iron rod about 18 inches long. In the center of this chain is a loop with a snap which goes around the cow's

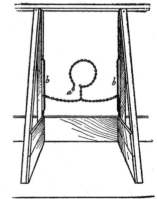

NECK CHAIN

neck. This arrangement gives the greatest freedom, and allows the cow to lie down and get up without difficulty. If light partitions are used between the heads of the cows no difficulty will be experienced in their striking each other with their horns. This is by far the least expensive of cow ties, and is at the same time one of the most satisfactory.

THE MODEL BARN

The pages of the agricultural journals and books of the time held up the barns of successful farmers across the country as examples, with detailed elevations and discussions of the ornamentation and paint schemes. The designs of these model barns varied considerably. In general they incorporated each farmer's favorite ideas and labor-saving devices; the sometimes elaborate ornamentation applied by gentlemen farmers to model barns on their demonstration farms was easily ignored. These barns should be seen as ideals and models to be followed and adapted by the ordinary farmer on a less extravagant basis.

THE BARN OF
MR. DAVID LYMAN

Among the many large and expensive barns now scattered through the country, there are few more thoroughly satisfactory to old school farmers with broad ideas, than one built by the late Mr. David Lyman, of Middlefield, Connecticut. Mr. Lyman required a very large barn for his farm purposes simply, and built one, a front view and interior plans of which are here given. The elevation of the building, figure 1, shows entrances to its two main floors; there is a basement below.

THE UPPER, OR HAY FLOOR.—This floor is shown in figure 2; all the hay, grain, and straw are stored here. It maintains the same level throughout. Two thrashing floors cross the building, and are entered from the high ground on the west by a very easy ascent. The main entrance crosses over an engine room, seen in figures 1 and 3. This room is built of stone, arched above, and is roomy as well as secure.

By means of a hay fork and a number of travellers, the hay is taken from the loads and dropped in any part of the immense bays. The forks are worked by one horse, attached to a hoisting machine, of which there are two, placed near

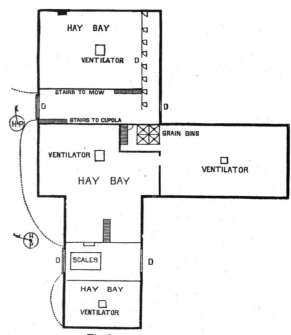

Fig. 2.—PLAN OF HAY FLOOR.

the great doors during the haying season, as indicated by the letters marked *H, P*, in the plan, figure 2.

On the main floor are bins for grain and ground feed, provided with shutes connecting them with the feeding floor. There are hay scales, also—a fixture in one of the floors—which afford the means of being very accurate in many things, in regard to which guess work is ordinarily the rule. The great ventilators, so conspicuous in figure 1, pass from the feeding floor to the roof, and are furnished with doors at different elevations, quite to the top of the mow, thus forming convenient shutes to throw down hay or straw. A long flight of stairs passes from the principal barn floor to the cupola, from which a magnificent view is obtained of the whole farm and surrounding country.

Fig. 1.—PERSPECTIVE ELEVATION OF MR. DAVID LYMAN'S BARN—FROM THE NORTH WEST.

THE FEEDING FLOOR is entered by several doors. Two double doors open upon a spacious floor in the rear of the horse stalls, which extends through the middle of the main barn. The northwest corner, figure 3, is occupied by a large harness and tool room, with a chimney and a stove. On the

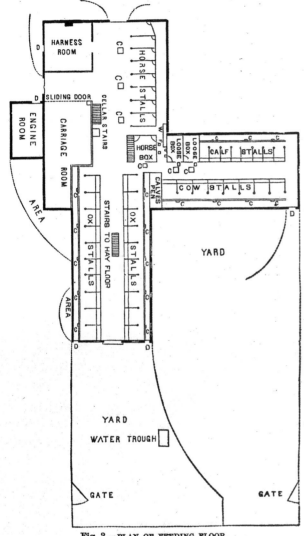

Fig. 3.—PLAN OF FEEDING FLOOR.

right of the front entrance is the carriage room, which is closed by a sliding door, or partition. There is room on the open part of this floor, behind the horse stalls, and adjacent, to drive in three wagons at a time, and let the horses stand hitched. Between the ox stalls in the south wing, is a ten-foot passage way through which carts with roots or green feed may be driven, the stairs in the middle being hinged at the ceiling and fastened up. The stalls are seven feet wide, and arranged to tie up two cattle in each. A gutter to conduct off the urine runs along behind each range of stalls, and there are well secured traps, one in about every fifteen feet, through which the manure is dropped to the cellar. The letter *C*, wherever it occurs in figure 3, indicates a trap door of a manure drop. The

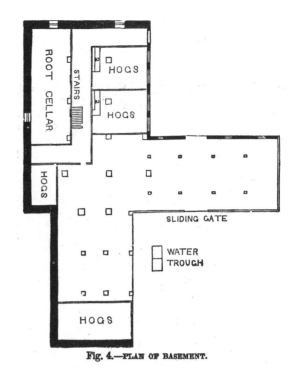

Fig. 4.—PLAN OF BASEMENT.

letter *D* is placed wherever there are doors which, in the engraving, might be taken for windows.

The cattle pass to the yards through doors in the ends of the wings. The south yard is nearly upon a level with the floor, sloping gradually away toward the south and east; but the large barn yard is on the level of the manure cellar, and an inclined way gives access to the yard on the east side, from the cow stalls. Three roomy, loose boxes are provided, one for horses, and two as lying-in stables for cows. Near the points marked *W*, and *F*, stands the hydrant for flowing water, and the trough for mixing feed, and here, too, the shutes for grain and cut feed discharge from the floor above.

VENTILATION AND LIGHT.—Four immense ventilating trunks, four feet square, rise from the feeding floor straight to the roof. These are capped by good ventilators of the largest size, and cause a constant change of air in the stables, the draft being ordinarily sufficient to be felt like a fresh breeze, by holding the hand anywhere within a few feet of the openings. This keeps the air in the whole establishment sweeter and purer than in most dwellings. The windows on all sides of this floor are of large size, with double sashes, hung with weights.

THE BARN CELLAR.—This is arranged for hogs, roots, and manure. The fixed partitions in the cellar are only two, one enclosing the root cellar, and the other, outside of that, shutting off a wide, cemented passage way, extending from the door at the northeast corner, around two sides of the root cellar, as shown in figure 4. The rest of the cellar is occupied by the manure, and hogs are enclosed in different parts of the cellar, according to convenience.

Fig. 5.—MR. LAWSON VALENTINE'S BARN, "HOUGHTON FARM," MOUNTAINVILLE, N. Y.

SIZE OF BARN.—The building covers more than one-fifth of an acre of land, and thus there is over three-fifths of an acre under a roof. The main barn is fifty-five by eighty feet. The wings are each fifty-six feet long, the south one being thirty-five wide, and the east wing thirty-one and one-half feet wide. The four leading points sought for and obtained were: first, economy of room under a given roof, second, plenty of light, third, plenty of air, and ventilation which would draw off all deleterious gas as fast as generated, and fourth, convenience to save labor. Saving of manure, and many other things were of course included. The windows are all hung with pulleys, and are lowered in warm days in winter, and closed in cold days. This is important.

Fig. 9.—PERSPECTIVE VIEW OF MR. KYLE'S BARN.

Fig. 14.—A MISSOURI BARN.

THE ROUND BARN

Round barns were first suggested in the mid-1700s. George Washington had one on his estate at Mount Vernon, and the famous stone round barn built by the Shakers in Hancock, Massachusetts, survives to this day, a sturdy and elegant example of Shaker construction. The round barn didn't really start to catch on until the 1880s, however, when new ideas about farm efficiency began to be widely promoted by agricultural colleges and field stations in the Midwest. By 1900, round barns, octagonal barns, and even pentagonal barns were all suggested as being more cost-effective and efficient than the standard rectangular barn. The round barn was particularly recommended for dairy farming. The idea was that a central silo made it easier and cheaper to store, handle, and distribute the feed. The domed, self-supporting roof saved interior space by eliminating supports and providing a large, unobstructed hay loft. A round barn ninety feet in diameter could comfortably accommodate a hundred dairy cows in stalls around the perimeter. According to the Kansas State Board of Agriculture's biennial report for 1911 to 1912, the lumber costs of a round barn with a diameter of 60 feet and encompassing 117,669 cubic feet were $799.96; the lumber costs for an equivalent plank frame barn 36 by 78 feet and encompassing 117,138 cubic feet were $1,023.27.

Despite the claims of cost savings and increased efficiency, the round barn never really overcame the innate conservatism of farmers. Even so, many were built, mostly in the Midwest. A surprising number remain today, some lovingly preserved and many in an advanced state of decay.

A PRACTICAL ROUND BARN

There is no economy in building a round barn, that is, strictly round. The barn here illustrated has 26 sides nearly 12 feet long, making a barn 94 feet in diameter. The sills, plates and roof in a strictly round barn are very expensive, and the work will not last as well as when built as shown. The

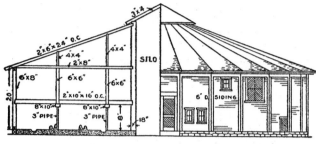

CROSS-SECTION OF BARN

floor space of the first floor is nearly the same as if round, and the hay loft is very little smaller. If the building is round, the walls should be lathed with metal lath, over rough boxing, and plastered with two coats of portland cement. In fact, this finish is to be preferred in building any shaped barn, as it requires no paint and practically no repairs.

The floor plan of the barn shown is self-explanatory. It has stalls for 40 milch cows, three bull pens, two hospital stalls, pen for baby beef that will accommodate about 2 1/2 cars of calves, stalls for seven horses, including the two box stalls, and the feeding room and silo. The silo is 16 × 34 feet,

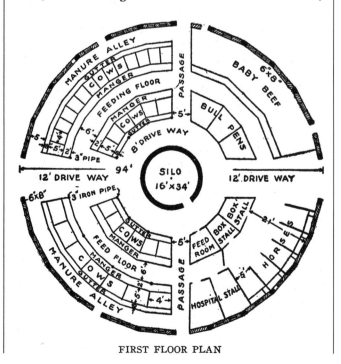

FIRST FLOOR PLAN

will hold about 140 tons of silage, and requires about ten acres of average corn to fill.

The hay loft has 166,500 cubic feet of space, and deducting the silo and bins for ground feed will hold 300 tons of loose hay. The ground feed is stored in hopper-shaped bins above the feed room, and drawn down through small spouts as wanted. The hay is handled with hay forks, and to locate the trolleys as near the roof as possible, trap doors are left in the loft floor, and hay hoisted from the driveways. A circle trolley may be installed, as two straight ones. Several large hay doors are also built in the outside walls above the loft floor. The silo, the floors of the cow stalls, including the gutters and mangers, also the 8-foot driveway around the silo, are of cement, and, while it is intended to install litter and feed carriers, it is also intended to drive around the entire barn, or the feed floor with a cart if desired. The interior arrangement of first floor may, of course, be changed in several ways, and the cows faced in the opposite direction, etc., or stalls and other equipment arranged for different stock.

AN ILLINOIS ROUND BARN

The barn, as shown, has about the same floor space as a barn would have 36 feet wide and 180 feet long. The ventilation is always much better in the round barn, the work of caring for and feeding may be accomplished with less labor, there are never any drafts on the stock, the building may be built for less money, and is much stronger. As shown, the barn has a stone foundation, the roof is covered with asbestos roofing felt, and the walls covered with 6-inch drop siding. Everything is of the best, and all exposed woodwork painted two coats. This building would cost about $4700 without the cow stanchions. Where home labor is used, and the lumber can be secured for less than $30 per thousand, the barn may, of course, be erected for less.

SILOS

Today the silo forms an integral part of our mental picture of a typical farm. In 1900, however, the silo was just starting to catch on.

A silo is a tall, airtight, cylindrical structure designed to create and store silage—fermented feedstuff (usually corn or alfalfa) for feeding livestock. It is a remarkably efficient and economical feeding method, because the entire plant—in the case of corn, the stems, leaves, and ears—is used. Silage is very nutritious, and dairy cows in particular are very fond of the slightly sour flavor. The silage plant is harvested at its peak protein level (before it has become too fibrous), then chopped and stored in the silo. Under airtight conditions, the silage ferments and keeps well for several months. Losses to rodents and spoilage are minimal.

A typical silo is anywhere from ten to eighteen feet in diameter and thirty to fifty feet high. Silage is added by using an elevator to carry it to the top; the fermented silage is removed from the bottom.

Silage was in use in the United States by the 1880s. It wasn't until the end of the nineteenth century, however, that agricultural colleges started heavily promoting the use of silos and silage made from whole-plant corn. Even then, the standard tower silo wasn't necessarily the norm; the pit silo, which could easily be dug by any farmer, was often recommended. In the end, though, the pit silo is far more labor-intensive. A tank or tower silo, filled from the top using a gas- or kerosene-powered elevator and emptied from the bottom, was far more efficient.

EUROPEAN METHODS AND EXPERIMENTS.

Corn fodder is largely depended upon as food for stock over a great extent of country, and its used might be made well nigh universal, as no forage plant is so easily grown as corn. Could it be preserved fresh and green for six months or more, instead of being cured and used in a dry state, its value would be greatly increased. That it may be so preserved has been shown by experiment, and the process is claimed to be easy, and very profitable. Of late years, a great number of French, Belgian and German farmers have adopted the plan, and some extensive stock feeders have used it largely with the most favorable results. Several communications by prominent farmers and professors of agriculture in farm schools, have been made to the "Journal of Practical Agriculture" of Paris, from which the following facts have been condensed, and by the aid of the illustrations, the methods in use, with the cost, may be learned. In figures 221, 222, and 223, are shown the pits or silos, as they are filled with the cut corn fodder, then covered with earth and pressed down with its weight; finally the cut fodder shrinks to less than half the bulk it had at first. The pits are about seventy-five feet long, nine feet wide above, six feet wide at the bottom, and six feet deep. The sides and ends are built up of masonry laid in cement. In these pits the corn stalks are laid evenly in layers about eight inches in thickness, after having been cut and exposed to the sun for two

Fig. 223.—ENSILAGE PIT AFTER SIX MONTHS.

or three days. During this time the stalks lose by exposure to the sun, two-fifths of their weight when first cut. A quantity of salt is scattered over every layer equal to about sixty-six pounds for each pit. The three pits hold about eighty tons (seventy-five thousand kilos), of green fodder. The fodder is heaped up as shown in figure 221, to a hight of six feet above the surface of the ground, and then covered with earth to a thickness of two or three feet. Seven months after, one pit was opened and the fodder was found in perfect condition except for an inch or two upon the surface and the sides, where it was black and decayed. Its color was yellow, its odor agreeable, but the stalks had lost all their sweetness, and had acquired some degree of acidity. Twenty-four beeves were then fed about nine hundred pounds daily of the preserved fodder, or nearly forty pounds per head on the average, which was equal to about sixty pounds of fresh green fodder. The fodder was

Fig. 221.—PIT BEFORE COVERING.   Fig. 222.—PIT AFTER COVERING.

Silo.

eaten with great relish, and only some portions of the larger and harder stalks were left, the corn having been cut when ripe, and being of a large growing variety known as the giant maize.

SILAGE consists of green crops stored in pits or in air-tight rooms above the ground. This compartment in which the food is stored is called a silo.

All crops may be used for making silage, but green corn is the one generally used. Silos above ground may be built of stone, concrete, brick, or other material. When wood is used, it is best to have double walls, and the space between them should be filled with straw or some non-conducting substance. Silage is excellent for milch cows, and every farmer should have a supply for them. The Romans and some of the early Europeans were familiar with the uses of silage over two thousand years ago. In this country it has been known since 1875.

Installing a silo was an important capital investment for a farmer, but it was well worth the expense. Silage was highly nutritious, which meant better yields from dairy cattle. It replaced some grain in the feed, which saved both money and time. Finally, silage largely replaced root feeding. Because roots such as turnips and carrots had to be crushed and were usually steamed, this too saved a huge amount of labor. It also meant that some land no longer had to be used for root crops—it could be used for hay, corn, or pasturage instead.

A HOMEMADE FEED CUTTER

An old lawn mower can be arranged to make a fairly satisfactory straw or feed cutter. One must rig up a hopper, as shown in the sketch, and attach the mower to the lower end of it so that the straw or grain will just strike the knives where the grass usually comes into the mower. A crank and a belt arrangement makes it easy for one man to feed and turn the cutter. This is a good use for a lawn mower in the winter time when it is not working outdoors.

WORKING THE LAWN MOWER

SAW ROOT CUTTER

Those who have cut roots in the winter time with a butcher knife or hatchet will fully appreciate something better for a root cutter. A Wisconsin farmer has found a serviceable homemade lever cutter very efficient for all roots. For hard ones, like rutabagas, it is about the best thing available. His is made out of an old hand saw, sharpened on the back,

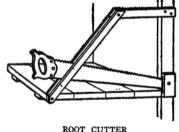

ROOT CUTTER

fastened by means of a bolt passing through a hole punched at the small end, and held by a guide formed of two pieces of wood secured upright, so as to have a slit for the saw to work in. This contrivance is a success, and with a little practice the roots may be cut very rapidly. See accompanying illustration. The cutter may be mounted upon the wall wherever it will be most convenient. The bench or platform should be at about the height of a common table.

HOMEMADE CABBAGE CUTTER

A cheap and easily made cabbage and root cutter is shown in the drawing. Take two 12-inch boards and nail them strongly together. With dividers mark around a circle, then saw out and mark in quarters. Cut four slots 7 inches long on a slant, as shown by dotted lines, so the cabbage will fall through easily. Next cut two circles 4 inches in diameter. Nail one to the large wheel on the back and leave the other loose on the shaft to act as a bearing.

Make a frame to admit the wheel, leaving 2 inches clear, and just wide enough so the knives do not strike the side.

Make a top over the wheel and put a hopper on the opposite side from the crank. The knives are 8 inches long and can be made from an old bucksaw and ground down sharp, with a bevel on one side. Screw these on the wheel at a slant according to the thickness the cabbage is wanted. A square hole should be cut through the center of the wheel for the shaft.

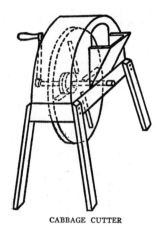

CABBAGE CUTTER

BARN CONVENIENCES

Windows were a crucial aspect of any barn design. In the days before electricity, fire from lanterns was a constant hazard. Windows let in light and also provided ventilation, features particularly important in dairy barns. In general, however, barn windows are small, adding to the overall impression of massiveness given by the structure. Additional air circulation was provided by ventilators or sometimes decorative cupolas on the roof. Lightning rods were widespread by 1900. Windvanes, though usually far less decorative or whimsical than the faked antiques and modern reproductions of today would suggest, were a common adornment. Wide, well-constructed sliding or hinged doors, with a variety of ingenious fastening devices, were essential. Equally essential and ingenious were mouse and rat traps and a wide range of labor-saving contrivances.

LIGHT NEEDED IN BARNS

Here and there we see an old-style barn, built by our grandfathers, the only window being a single row of panes over the large door. Through this comes all of the light admitted to the barn, except what comes through the open cracks between the boards. When a barn of this kind is filled with hay it is comfortably warm, but very dark; by midwinter the hay, being half consumed, leaves the walls unprotected. With the light come in also the cold wintry winds to chill the cattle. Our fathers built some barns warmer, covering the walls with shingles or the cracks with narrow battens. The light being thus shut out, it was necessary to have windows; so they put in just enough to enable them to see to feed their cattle. It was left for our generation to build barns that are tight, comfortable, and well-lighted. But even at present many farmers do not realize the importance of light in a cattle barn. Experiments show that a herd of milch cows not only keep in better health and condition by having plenty of light, but they give more milk. Every barn should be provided with abundant light and sunshine on the side where the cattle stand. The practice, which is far too prevalent, of keeping cows in a dark and damp basement is not a good one. They can not have the sunshine and pure air so necessary for good health. Windows that are exposed may be protected for a trifling sum by covering them with wire netting. The day of windowless barns has passed; but some of our new barns would be improved by a few more windows.

LANTERNS IN THE BARN

It is estimated that nine-tenths of all fires are caused by carelessness. Never light a lamp or lantern of any kind in a barn. Smokers may include their pipes and cigars in the above. The lantern should be lighted in the house or some outbuilding, where no combustibles are stored. A lantern which does not burn well, should never be put in order in the hay mow. There is a great temptation to strike a match and relight an extinguished lantern, wherever it may be. It is best to even feel one's way out to a safe place, than to run any risks. If the light is not kept in the hand, it should be hung up. Provide hooks in the various rooms where the lights are used. A wire running the whole length of the horse stable, at the rear of the stalls, and furnished with a sliding hook, is very convenient for night work with the horses. Some farmers are so careless, as to keep the lamp oil in the barn, and fill the lantern there, while the wick is burning. Such risks are too great, even if the buildings are insured.

HANG UP THE LANTERN

Here is a good idea for hanging a lantern over the barn floor. Get two pulleys with screw stems, and screw one in beam over

PULLEY-HUNG LANTERN

head, the other at top of post. Have a bracket lower on the same post. Take a piece of small but strong cord, and at one end fasten a snap and pass the other end through the pulleys. Put your lantern on the snap and draw it high enough so it will be out of reach of forking hay, and you can see all over the

barn floor. You can raise the lantern high enough to pitch hay from the top of the mow with no danger of turning the light over and burning the building and contents.

The end of the cord opposite the lantern may be fastened with a snap, or more length may be allowed for adjusting the height of the lantern, and the cord may be secured by a hitch or a few turns around a button or two spikes driven halfway in and bent over in opposite directions.

FASTENING HEAVY DOORS

There is little difference in the effectiveness of these two locks for heavy doors. The left-hand device is extremely

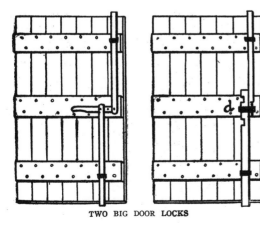

TWO BIG DOOR LOCKS

Tubular or Barn Lantern.

To Burn Kerosene.

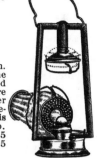

55775 Our New Clipper Lift is a thoroughly serviceable lantern in every respect, strongly made and nicely finished; the oil pot is retinned to prevent leakage; the burner being locked makes it an absolutely safe lantern: the lift movement is simple and efficient; the globe is very easily removed, making it without doubt the easiest handled lantern on the market.
Price........$0.35
Per dozen... 3.95

55777 Hinge Tip Tubular Lantern. The globe is removable from the guards within which it is held, and when the globe and globe plate are thrown back leaves the burner exposed, to trim wick, lift or remove the burner: the globe is securely locked in position at top.
Each.......................$0.35
Per dozen.......... .... 3.95

55779 Side Spring or Square Lift Lantern with new inside guard and locked glass flange and burner; the side spring securely locks the globe up when raised, and firmly holds the globe on to the glass flange when lowered. No rust can ever form to cause the lift to stick or work hard. This lantern has a patent one piece tube without elbows or joints, extra large oil pot, retinned to prevent leakage; a well-made and easy working lantern.
Each............... ....$0.39
Per dozen....... . ... 4.45

55785 Cold Blast or Storm Lantern; is made on the same principle as street lamps, with wind break, and is a very desirable lantern where there are strong drafts or wind; it is especially adapted for use in mills and other places where there is considerable dust, as the burner will not clog up; it has a number 2 burner and takes a one inch wick, which throws a large and brilliant light; a good all around lantern, one that is sure to give good satisfaction.
Price................. ....$0.85
Per dozen................. 9 25

55786 Solid Brass Side Spring Safety Tubular Lantern, perfect in every detail; no rust can ever form to cause the lift to stick or work hard. The glass flange is securely locked so that the burner cannot become detached without first unlocking the glass flange; the globe is removable without taking off the guard.
Each...................... ....$1.00
Per dozen.....................10.80

Tubular Dash Lanterns.

55787 Safety Tubular Dash Lantern, with patent globe lifting attachment that holds globe up while trimming or lighting by turning one side of the thumbpiece on lifting attachment; has spring fastening on back for dash boards; it can also be hung on a nail and makes a good barn lamp; burns kerosene and makes a big light.
Each.................... ...$0.50
Per dozen................. 5.60

quick and handy; the other very neat and substantial. The lock to the left has both bars pivoted to a lever handle, which is pivoted to the door midway between the ends of the arms. Moving the lever handle up moves both arms out of slots above and below the doors. The fastening may be also worked from the inside by cutting a slot through the door and setting a pin in one of the arms, so that it can be moved in the slot.

The right-hand fastening is worked by raising the lower arm so that the notch incloses the middle staple at *d*. Then the upper arm can be pulled down. Both arms stay firm and snug whether the door is shut or open.

HOLD THE BARN DOORS SHUT

A latch that will hold double doors shut is shown in the cut. This is put on the inside of the door that is closed first. It is

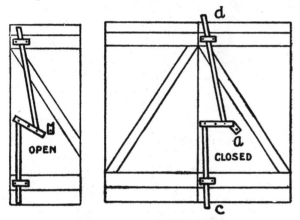

LATCH FOR DOUBLE DOORS

made of hardwood 4 inches wide and 1 inch thick. To open the door, turn the piece, *a*, to the right and pull down on the crosspiece which is fastened to the door by a bolt in the middle. This will raise the latch, *c*, and lower the latch, *d*, as shown in the cut to the right.

Open your doors to a fine day,
but make yourself ready for a foul one.

Prosperity is the thing in the world
we ought to trust the least.

FASTENING THE STABLE DOOR

A handy stall door fastener is shown in Figure 1. It consists of a piece of oak or other hard wood 4 inches wide by $7/8$ inch thick and 2 inches longer than the width of the door. It is fastened to the door by a $3/8$-inch bolt through the middle and it

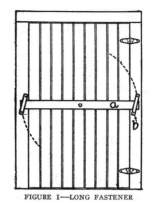

FIGURE 1—LONG FASTENER

works like a button. Cleats, *b*, are sawed out and fastened to the door jamb on each side to hold the fastener in place.

Another handy fastener that can be worked from either side of the door is shown in Figure 2. There are three upright pieces, *a*, two of which are on the door and one on the door jamb or casings. Another piece, *b*, slides through these and holds the door shut. A pin, *c*, goes through the bolt and through the door to open or shut it from the opposite side. The bolt is kept shut by the spring, which can be made from a piece of hickory, or other tough hardwood, whittled down to the proper thickness. The spring feature is the chief advantage, and a very important one it is, of this excellent fastener. It is also a good point that the fastener works nicely from the opposite side of the door.

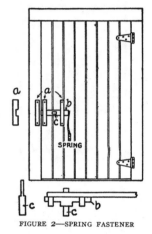

FIGURE 2—SPRING FASTENER

STAIRS FOR THE BARN

A lot of time is saved if one has handy stairs which can be used for throwing down hay as well as a passageway. These steps are made of light material and instead of putting on a

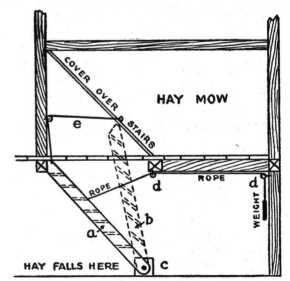

CROSS-SECTION WITH STAIRS

lower step, use a block, *c*, and attach the stringers of the stairs to it at each end with a pin. A rope passes over the pulleys at *d*, to a weight, which allows the stairway to be held upright while the hay is being put down. The rope, *e*, is handy to pull the stairs into position.

A BARN WINDLASS

It is easily made of iron pipe or a bar fastened to the ladder or other suitable support by means of eyebolts or stout staples,

WINDLASS

as shown at *a* in the drawing. It may be used for raising grain, wagon boxes and other heavy things to the upper part of the barn, and, if desired, may be rigged with block and falls, so as to increase the power without increasing the effort. A loose bolt placed in a hole will prevent unwinding. The picture shows how simple this device is. Every farmer knows how useful a barn windlass may be.

GRAIN BOX EASY TO EMPTY

The trouble with most grain boxes is to get out the last third of the grain. Bending over the edge jackknife fashion is neither pleasant nor healthful. A box or bin may be made with half its front on hinges, so that it can be let down and all the contents scooped out without difficulty. The bin may be made from a piano box with a partition in the middle for two kinds of grain.

EASILY CONSTRUCTED GRAIN BINS

Grain bins with compartments for different kinds of feed are handy in barn or stable. By procuring a number of dry-goods boxes, all of the same size and shape, and nailing them together side by side, so that they will appear as one, the bin is easily made. The cover should extend the entire length of the bin, and though leather hinges will answer, it is better to attach it with iron ones, for then, with a good staple and hasp, the contents can be kept under lock and key if desired.

A CONVENIENT BARN TRUCK

No dairyman can afford to ignore that which will lighten his labor in any way whatever. Be his stable ever so conveniently constructed, he has enough to do. Hence the importance of his considering a feeding truck or car if he does not have one. Made of good lumber, the only iron about it need be the handle at each end, by which to push or pull it along the feeding alley in front of the cows which are to be fed, and the small

Climax Rat Trap.

45306 A Self-Setting Rat Catcher. Convenient bait box, novel tilting platform. This trap is made with a bait box that is supplied through a lid at the top. It holds the bait alluringly to the rat, yet he cannot readily withdraw it through the fine meshes. The trap is made of heavy double crimped steel wires which cannot be displaced or broken. The trap will maintain its original shape and can be shipped compactly and will always reach destination in good condition. Size of trap, 20 inches long, 8 inches wide, 7 inches high. Price, each.................$1.00
Per dozen 10.50

Combination Rat and Mouse Trap.

45307 This is made of retinned wire cloth and may be used to catch either mice or rats. When set for mice, the end is closed, the mice entering at the hole inside the trap; small wire door drops behind them that can be easily opened by the mice on the outside but not from inside; as one mouse will act as a decoy for another, quite a number may be caught at once. When rats are to be caught it is set as seen in cut. Weight, 1 lb. 13 oz. Each $0.35
Per dozen....................................... 3.60
N. B.—Rat traps are often sprung by mice who go out between the wires and leave no track behind them. This trap will catch them every time.

Rat Traps.

45308 National Rat Traps Weight, 1 lb. 3 oz Each... ......$0.25
Per doz $2.70

Genuine Marty's French Trap for Catching Rats Alive.

45309 The Marty trap is made only in France, and was patented in the United States in December, 1893. It is a wonderful effect trap, and is used by the leading hotels, public institutions and market houses. Many testimonials proving that they will catch their full capacity night after night as long as the rats hold out. No. 3, family size, 17 inches long, capacity, 20 rats. No. 1, hotel and stable size, 27 inches long, capacity, 50 rats. No. 3. Each..... ....$0.75
Per dozen................. .... 7.20
No. 2. Each................ .... 1.75
Per dozen................................ ....20.00

trucks on which it is mounted. The wheels procured, any good blacksmith can make these, so that the truck is by no means difficult to construct. The box body should be about 2 feet wide, 20 inches deep and 4 1/2 feet long. Silage can be conveyed in it from the silo to the mangers very readily. If the silo is some distance away, it will save much hard work.

IMPROVED GRAIN BIN

A very convenient grain-bin is illustrated in figure 24. The lid or top is raised as usual; then, when desirable, the front top board, which is hinged at the bottom, and hooked inside at the top, is unlocked and let down. This gives convenient access to the bin both in filling and in emptying—enabling one to take out the last remnants of grain or meal.

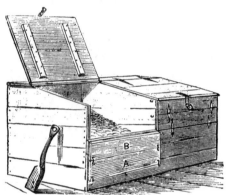

Fig. 24.—CONVENIENT GRAIN BIN.

Not every thrifty farmer felt the need to paint his barn. Many were perfectly content to let the boards weather to a beautiful silvery gray. In the early nineteenth century, farmers in New England and the mid-Atlantic regions who did paint their barns often chose red. This was not a conscious design statement or even a tradition. Red paint, made from iron oxide, was cheap and easy to get. White barns became popular in the 1870s. Why? There's no good explanation. Possibly the sanitation practice of whitewashing the interior of the barn each year was simply carried to the exterior. It's also possible that the growth of dairy farming at this time led to the association of white with milk, or perhaps the idea was to project an image of sanitation and efficiency. Hex signs, found on Pennsylvania Dutch barns to this day, were a traditional ethnic form of decoration. Faded examples of the famous Mail Pouch chewing tobacco ads and other ads painted on the sides of barns, forerunners of the roadside billboard, can still be seen here and there. Most date from the first quarter of the twentieth century. The incentive to the farmer for allowing the sign was usually an offer to paint the whole barn—an offer most cash-strapped farmers found hard to refuse.

ROOT CELLARS

Root crops were an important winter food for both the farmer and his animals. In particular, beets, mangel-wurzels, carrots, and even potatoes were grown as animal fodder. Root feeding was labor intensive, because the roots needed to be washed and chopped. As silos became more popular, root feeding declined.

Regardless of who was destined to eat the roots, storing them successfully required a root cellar—a cool, dark place with good ventilation near the barn or house. The best design for root storage generated a surprising amount of discussion. In the agricultural journals and books of the 1880s and onward, the merits of root cellars versus root pits versus root houses were variously debated, and some of the recommendations were quite elaborate.

ROOT CELLARS
AND ROOT HOUSES

The leading features of a good root cellar are: cheapness, nearness to the place where the roots are consumed, dryness, ventilation, and, above all, it should be frostproof. If a hillside is handy, it can aid much in securing all of these important points. First make an excavation in the hillside, in size according to the desired capacity of the cellar. Erect in this

Fig. 232.—CROSS SECTION OF ROOT CELLAR.

excavation a stout frame of timber and planks, or of logs, which latter are often cheaper. Over this frame construct a strong roof. Throw the earth, which has been excavated, over the structure until the whole is covered, top and all, to a depth of two feet or more. A door should be provided upon the exposed side or end. This door may be large enough to enter without stooping. Or it may be simply a "man hole," which is better than a regular door, so far as protection from frost is concerned, but not so convenient for putting in and taking out roots. Sometimes, when the bank is a stiff clay, such houses are built without constructing any side walls,

Fig. 240.—PRAIRIE ROOT CELLAR.

the roof resting directly on the clay. A cross section of such a root cellar is shown in figure 232. In such cases, the facing, or front, of the cellar may be built up with planks, logs, or stones, as circumstances determine.

Figure 240 shows a root pit for use in the open prairies, where shelter is scarce, and the means of building are not abundant. An excavation is made in the ground six or seven feet deep and as wide as may be suitable to the length of the poles with which it is to be covered. The length will be according to the necessities of the builder. It is covered with rough poles, over which some coarse hay is thrown. The sod, which should be cut from the surface in strips with the plow and an axe, is then laid closely on the top, and earth is heaped over the sod. A man hole at one corner, or, if it is a long cellar, in the middle, is constructed with small poles and about two feet high. A ladder or row of steps is made from this to the bottom. The man hole when not used is filled with straw or hay, which is thrown upon a loose door or boards resting upon the logs, and a stone or log is laid upon the straw to keep it from being blown away. Openings may be made along the side opposite to the entrance through which the roots or potatoes may be shovelled or dumped. These openings may be closed with sods and earth during the winter.

ROOT WASHERS

A convenient washer for potatoes and roots, consists of a kerosene barrel hung in a frame, as shown in figure 89. Two

Fig. 89.—ROOT WASHER.

openings are made in one side of the barrel—a large one, two staves wide, and a small one only one inch wide. The pieces cut out are used for lids, both of which are fastened with hinges and buttons, and are made to fit tight by having thick cloth tacked around their edges. A bushel of potatoes or roots are placed in the barrel, with two or three buckets of water, the lids are closed and buttoned, and the barrel is slowly turned. If they are very dirty, open the small aperture, and by turning the barrel back and forth allow the water and

Fig. 90.—VEGETABLE WASHER.

mud to run out. Add clean water and turn again. They will soon be cleansed, when the large aperture may be opened, and the roots or tubers emptied into a basket. The fastenings at each end of the barrel can be made by any blacksmith, and they should be bolted on with one-quarter or three-eighths inch bolts. With this simple contrivance a man can wash a large quantity of roots in a day without catching cold or a chill. If kept out of the sun, such a contrivance will last a lifetime. In figure 90 is shown a potato and vegetable washer for household use. The ends of the cylinders are cut out of inch

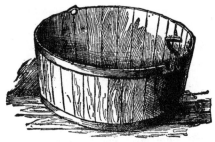

Fig. 91.—TUB FOR WASHER.

board and are twelve inches in diameter. The shaft runs through and has collars, to which the ends of the cylinders are fastened to hold them firm. Strong, tinned wires are fastened from end to end, as seen in the engraving. Five of these are fastened together, and form the lid to the aperture through which articles are admitted. The end of the lid is fastened by means of a loop, which springs over a button. The vegetables to be washed are placed in the cylinder, the box is half filled with water, and by turning the crank, or by moving it back and forth, they are quickly cleansed. Narrow wooden slats may be used instead of wire, if desired. An ordinary tub, or a half barrel, arranged as seen in figure 91, may be used instead of the box.

ROOT PULPERS AND CUTTERS

Those who feed beets, turnips, carrots and other roots, find it necessary to reduce them by some cheaper method than cutting by hand with a knife. An excellent machine for pulping roots is shown in figure 85. It may be made by any carpenter in two days, at a cost of

Fig. 85.—ROOT PULPER.

about six dollars. The plan of the machine is given in the engraving. It is simply a square or oblong box, with a spiked cylinder fitted in it, the cylinder having a square gudgeon at one end, to which a handle is fitted. To save expense the heavy wheel and handle attached, of a fodder cutter, may be taken off and used on the root pulper, as the two will rarely be used at the same time. The cylinder is closely studded with sharp, chisel-pointed spikes. These teeth are made of one-quarter inch square bar iron, and are three inches long; the sharp

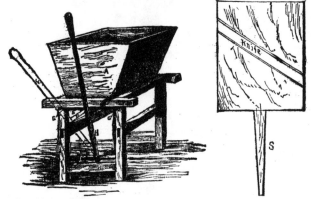

Fig. 86.—HOME-MADE ROOT-CUTTER.   Fig. 87.—ROOT-CUTTER SLIDE.

edges are worked out on an anvil, and are chilled by immersion in cold salt water when red hot, the other end being cut with a screw thread. To secure strength, and to make the machine work with more ease, the cutters are screwed in so far as to leave only half an inch or a little more projecting. A still cheaper form is illustrated in figure 86. At *A* is seen the hopper which is without a bottom. The slide, figure 87, contains a two-edged knife, and runs in the grooves, *G, G*, in the top of the frame, close to the bottom of the hopper. Near the bottom of the frame is a roller, *R*, into which is fitted the handle, *H*. This is connected with the slide by the rod, *R*. The knife should be about four inches wide and one-quarter inch thick, be placed diagonally in the slide, leaving half an inch space between it and the bottom of the slide. When using the apparatus all that is necessary is to move the handle to and from the hopper. It works easily and quickly, is durable, and with fair usage is not likely to get out of order.

ICEHOUSES

In the days before refrigeration, ice, where available, was important to the farmer. The primary use was in the dairy, where ice was valuable for cooling milk and keeping butter fresh—an important consideration where the sale of butter provided a steady source of scarce cash income. Ice was also important in warmer weather for preserving other farm products such as eggs, fresh meat, and fruits and vegetables. Where practical, ice was even valuable as a salable product, although most farmers harvested and stored ice primarily for home use.

The ideal icehouse was carefully designed to insulate the cut blocks of ice. For extra insulation, they were often sunk partially below ground or built into hillsides. Good drainage at the base of the icehouse was crucial. Drains would let in warm air, however, so a well-made icehouse had a foundation about two feet deep filled with gravel or sand. It was extremely important to make the floor of the icehouse as airtight as possible; warm air coming in through the floor would melt the ice very quickly.

Good ventilation at the top of the house was equally important, as were deep eaves to shade the sides of the house from warming sunlight. The building was double-walled, with the space between the exterior and interior walls filled with an insulating material such as straw or sawdust. Finally, the whole building was whitewashed to reflect heat. Sawdust, chaff, or straw was packed in between the blocks of ice within the house as well.

A well-made icehouse could keep ice successfully from one winter to the next. On prosperous farms, a spring room or dairy was attached to the icehouse, with vents to let in cool air. Elaborate icehouses with cooling chambers underneath were sometimes built, but most farmers found that a simple icebox would suffice for daily use.

ICE-HOUSE AND SUMMER DAIRY COMBINED

Perfect control of the temperature of the dairy is a great step gained towards making the best butter. It is only by means of ice, or very cold spring water that we can keep the most desirable temperature in very warm weather.—During most of the year there is little difficulty in maintaining sufficient coolness. In winter the problem is how to keep a dairy warm enough and not get it too hot. This is the battle with the weather that we wage almost the year round. In former years we have given numerous plans for ice-houses, both large and small, with cool rooms or refrigerators attached. We have lately had our attention called to the desirableness of a combination of the dairy and ice-house, and present the following plan which we deem entirely practical.

Fig. 1.—ELEVATION OF ICE-HOUSE AND DAIRY.

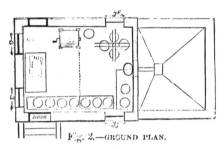

Fig. 2.—GROUND PLAN.

The plan proposes an ice-house above ground and a dairy half below; the ice room half covering the dairy, and the rest of the dairy being covered by a cool room, which forms the entrance to the ice-house. The exterior walls of the ice-house are of wood, those of the dairy are of stone. The floor of each room is laid in cement with a slope sufficient to

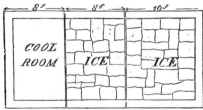

Fig. 3.—PLAN OF UPPER PART OF ICE-HOUSE.

carry off the water. The drainage of the ice-house is collected and made to pass by a pipe, into a vessel in the dairy, where the end of the pipe is always covered with water. The water is allowed to flow through shallow troughs in which milk pans may be set. The amount of water would not be large, but it will be cold and ought not to be wasted.

Fig. 4.—SECTION OF ICE-HOUSE AND DAIRY.

The building represented in the perspective elevation, fig. 1, is 28 feet long by 14 wide. The ice-room seen in figs. 2 and 3, is 10×12 feet on the ground, and about 12×16 feet, including the space above the dairy. The sides of the building are 9 feet above the ground, and the hight of the dairy 7 feet in the clear. The outside walls of the ice-house are made of 2-inch plank, 10 inches wide, set upright, having inch-and-a-half planks nailed on the inside, weatherboarded

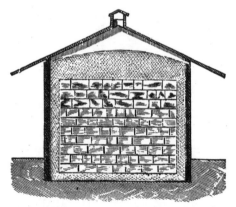

Fig. 142.—SECTION OF AN ICE HOUSE FILLED.

neatly on the outside, and filled with spent tan-bark or other dry, non-conducting substance. The partition wall between the dairy and the ice-house, and between the cool room and the ice-house, is half the thickness, and not filled. Thus

Fig. 148.—VERTICAL SECTION OF ICE HOUSE.

forming closed air spaces between the studs. These spaces communicate with the dairy, by little doors near the floor and so currents of cold air may be established and perfectly regulated, entering the dairy on the side towards the ice-house. These, with a ventilator V, at the top of the room for carrying off the warmest air, will surely

cause the temperature to be easily governed. This description, with the engravings, sufficiently illustrate the idea to enable any good builder to carry it out.

Fig. 149.—SMALL ICE HOUSE COMPLETE.

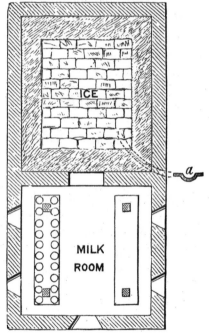

Fig. 158.—ICE HOUSE AND MILK ROOM.

Fig. 159.—ANOTHER ICE HOUSE.

LOCATION AND BUILDING

The location should be where the ice can be removed and delivered with the least amount of labor; however, it is very important that the icehouse should be located in the coolest place, in as dry a place as possible, and always above ground. The lowest layer of ice should always be at least 6 inches above the outside level of ground.

The size of the building must be determined by the amount of ice used during the year. For instance, a dairy farm upon which 35 cows are kept, and from which the milk is sold, needs an icehouse 16 × 16 and 14 feet high. If the

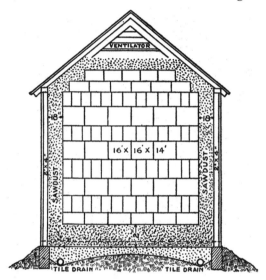

CROSS-SECTION OF ICEHOUSE

cream is to be sold and skim milk fed to the calves, immediately from the separator, an icehouse 14 × 14 and 12 feet high is of sufficient size. In both cases we make allowance for the use of 25 pounds of ice per day during the summer months for household purposes. For a man who keeps about 20 cows and sells the milk, an icehouse 14 × 14 and 12 feet high is of sufficient size; however, in no case should an icehouse be smaller than 12 × 12 and 10 feet high, because the outside surface is too great, compared with the volume, and, therefore, too much ice is wasted in proportion to the amount used.

The building should be as near the shape of a cube as possible, for the cube contains the greatest amount of volume with the least amount of surface exposed other than circular forms. It is not always practical to build as high as we build square, owing to the amount of labor and the inconvenience of storing the ice; therefore, the dimensions given are really the most practical.

If the icehouse is not built upon a sandy surface and where rapid drainage is natural, it is necessary to cut a space

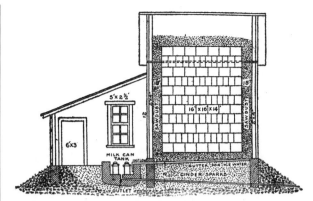

A GOOD COLD COMBINATION

to a depth of 12 to 18 inches, where the icehouse is to be located, lay a tile drain to drain this, and fill it with sand or finely crushed stone. Put a 6-inch foundation of concrete of the size you wish to build your icehouse in this pit, and fill around the outside.

FREEZING ICE IN BLOCKS

Where a pond or stream is not handy from which to get the year's supply of ice, blocks can be frozen in forms with comparatively little labor. A supply of pure water is essential. The forms are best made of galvanized iron of any size desired. A convenient size is 16 inches wide, 24 inches long and 12 inches deep inside measure. The sides and ends should be made to taper 1/4 inch, so that the frozen block will drop out easily. The top of the mold should be reinforced with wire for the sake of strength and durability.

With a dozen or 20 forms one can put up quite a supply of ice during the winter. The forms should be set level on joists or boards and placed a few inches apart. Fill them nearly full with pure water and let them freeze, which they will do in one or two days and nights in suitable weather. When frozen solid, turn the forms bottom side up and pour a dipper of warm water on them, which will release the cake of ice. The form can then be lifted off, the ice put away in the icehouse and the form filled with water again.

HOMEMADE ICE MOLDS

Dry Cold Air Refrigerators.

Our sales of refrigerators last season were way beyond our expectation, and we were compelled to disappoint some of our customers. This year we are prepared for a still larger increase in the trade and feel confident we can at all times make prompt shipments, as we have ample stock of dry hardwood lumber, with the latest improved machinery, the best of dry kilns, and the most skilled workmen. We **Guarantee** our refrigerators to give **Perfect Satisfaction**. The capacity of the factory is over two hundred complete refrigerators per day.

Points of Superiorty—Scientific Insulation.

The walls of the refrigerators are constructed as follows. First, the outside case; second, a layer of wool felt; third, a dead-air space; fourth, a charcoal sheathing; fifth, inside case; sixth, a charcoal sheathing which is non-odorous, waterproof and a first class insulator; seventh, a zinc lining, making complete seven walls to preserve the ice. The result is a great saving of ice and lower temperature than can be obtained in other refrigerators.

Ice being placed on the false bottom in the upper compartment, the air under the false bottom becomes very cold and heavy, and falls through the opening into the provision chamber below, forcing the warm air up through the flues, where it strikes the ice, is condensed and cooled. Our refrigerators will keep crackers and ginger snaps crisp and dry. We advise our patrons to buy as large a refrigerator as possible, to get the benefit of **cold storage.** Each size has a special design of great beauty.

The Metallic Ice Rack.

Is a very important feature of our goods, as the under side acts as a moisture condenser, while the arched center prevents the moisture from dropping through the opening into the provision chamber below. The **shelves** are made of heavy galvanized iron with wide slats and rolled edges, making them very strong.

This cut shows style of our single door refrigerator.

44003 Hardwood, Antique finish, empire style. Richly carved panels and ornaments; single door. Holds 35 lbs. ice.; Length, 26½ in.; Depth, 18in.; Height, 40 in. Price, each........$7.26

44004 Same as No. 44003, except that it holds 30 lbs. of ice. Has porcelain lined water cooler. The faucet is nickel plated and the tumbler holder bronzed. We do not advise the use of melted ice for drinking water, as it is frequently impure and always has condensed on its surface the smells from the food below, so we get rid of it as soon as possible and provide a separate place for drinking water. Price each......... 9.05

44005 Hardwood Antique Finish, richly carved panels and ornaments. Flap in front lifts up for waste pan; single door. Size of opening of provision chamber 17½ in. high, 16½ in. wide, 11½ in. deep.

Holds lbs. ice.	Length.	Depth.	Height.	Price, each.
40	28 in.	20 in.	44 in.	$8.36

44006 Same as No. 44005, except that it holds 35 lbs. of ice. Has porcelain lined water cooler. The faucet is nickel plated and the tumbler holder bronze. Price each...............10.34

44007 Solid Ash, Antique Finish, elegant hand carved ornamentation; single door. **Size of** opening of provision chamber 18 in. **high,** 20½ in. wide, 13¾ in. deep; single door.

Holds lbs. ice	Length.	Depth.	Height.	Price.
45	32	21½	46½	10.12

44008 Same as No. 44007 except that it holds 40 pounds of ice, has porcelain lined water cooler with nickel plated faucet and bronze tumbler holder. Price, each........................$12.10

44009 Solid Ash, Antique Finish, hand carved, raised ornaments. This refrigerator is deep enough to hold two rows of dishes, one behind the other; single door. Size of opening of provision chamber 20 in. high, 21¼ in. wide, 17¼ in. deep.

Holds Ice.	Length.	Depth.	Height.	Price.
40 lbs.	33 in.	24½ in.	49 in.	$11.66

44010 Same as No 44009, except that it holds 35 pounds of ice, has porcelain lined water cooler, flap in front, lifts up for water pan. Price, each...................... $14.10

44011 **Solid** Ash, Antique Finish, rich hand carvings, **double doors,** movable flues. Size of opening of provision chamber 18¼ in. high, 22½ in. wide, 13½ in. deep. Holds 45 lbs of ice. Length 34 in.; depth 22 in.; height 47 in.

This cut shows style of our double door refrigerators.

Price, each..12.32

44012 Same as No 44011 except that it will hold 40 pounds of ice, has porcelain lined water cooler. All goods are warranted to give perfect satisfaction. Price, each..........................$14.30

44013 Solid Ash, Antique Finish, elegant hand carving, double door, patent arch center, false bottom, and interior circulation of pure, dry, cold air. Size of opening of provision chamber 20 in. high, 25 in. wide, 14½ in. deep. Our Best Family Size.

Holds ice.	Length.	Depth.	Height.	Price, each.
70 lbs.	36½ in.	23 in.	50 in.	$14.10

44014 Same as No. 44013, except that it holds 60 lbs. of ice. Has porcelain lined water cooler Price, each..16.28

44015 Solid Ash, Antique Finish, double doors. This style has a partition between the doors, making two separate provision chambers. A most excellent family size. Size of opening of each provision chamber 20½ in. high, 13½ in wide, 17½ in. deep.

Holds ice.	Length.	Depth.	Height.	Price.
125 lbs.	41½ in.	25½ in.	52 in.	$16.72

44016 Same as No. 44015, except that it holds, 115 lbs. ice. Has porcelain lined water cooler. The large ice chamber affords room for bottles, pitchers, etc...................................19.20

44017 Solid Ash. Four Doors, Antique Finish, rich hand carvings. Ice doors open in front; size of opening, 14x29 inches. Two provision chambers below. Size of each provision chamber, 23½ in. high 13 in. wide, 19 in. deep.

Holds ice.	Length.	Depth.	Height.	Price.
150 lbs.	41½ in.	26 in.	60 in.	$18.92

44018 Same as No. 44017, except, that it holds 140 pounds ice, has porcelain lined water cooler, Price, each...................................21.34

Sideboard Style Refrigerators.

As we furnish refrigerator sideboards on orders it requires from 7 to 10 days before we can ship.

44019 Same as No. 44003, with the addition of a sideboard top. It has beveled plate glass mirror, 12x18, and convenient shelf on which things can be placed when the cover is raised; 72 inches high. Price, each..............................$11.88

44020 Same as No. 44005, with the addition of a sideboard top, beveled plate glass mirror 12x18 inches. Height, 75 inches. Price, each..........13.30

44021 Same as No. 44011 with the addition of a sideboard top. The glass is bevel plate, 16x20 inches. Price, each..............................19.00

Hardwood Ice Chests, antique ash finish. Made double with inside boxes with lining between. This makes them triple walled and the best ice boxes in the market. They are lined throughout with zinc and furnished with metal shelves. We have an opening in the back for ventilation. We cannot guarantee them not to sweat, as we do our Dry Air Refrigerators.

	Length.	Depth.	Height.	Price.
44022	30 in.	18 in.	25 in.	$4.50
44023	33 in.	20 in.	27 in.	5.50
44024	36 in.	22 in.	31 in.	6.75
44025	40 in.	24½ in.	34 in.	8.25
44026	44 in.	29 in.	36 in.	10.50

Table of shipping weights for the Dry Cold Air Refrigerators and Ice Chest:

Catalogue No.	Weight.	Catalogue No.	Weight
44003	120 lbs	44015	265 lbs
44004	125 "	44016	275 "
44005	145 "	44017	300 "
44006	150 "	44018	310 "
44007	170 "	44019	145 "
44008	175 "	44020	170 "
44009	170 "	44021	210 "
44010	175 "	44022	100 "
44011	180 "	44023	130 "
44012	185 "	44024	160 "
44013	200 "	44025	200 "
44014	210 "	44026	250 "

CHAPTER 2

FENCES AND GATES

Few subjects were of as much concern to the farmer as good fences and sturdy, easy-to-handle gates. Fences marked boundaries, but their primary purpose was to control livestock. Fences kept livestock safely enclosed where they belonged and kept them safely out of where they didn't belong.

Before North America was settled, timber shortages in Europe had led to the creation of a variety of fencing methods, including hedges, ditches, and stone walls. But the early American colonists faced no such restraints. They made a variety of fences out of wood, such as the famous split-rail fence. European commentators often criticized what seemed to them an extravagant waste of timber, but to settlers intent on clearing away the woods, wooden fences made perfect sense. A split-rail fence was quick and easy to erect. It also used the plentiful and cheap material that was at hand, didn't require metal, and didn't require any specialized building skills or complex maintenance. Problems arose, however, when wood was in shorter supply, as it eventually became in New England, or practically nonexistent, as it was on the Great Plains. The invention of barbed wire in 1888 made fencing a much simpler, if less elegant, proposition.

RAIL FENCES

The earliest settlers made ramshackle zigzag rail fences from the timber they cut to clear their fields. Metal was scarce and expensive, so these fences were held together with stakes, braced with rocks, and sometimes tied with vines. Logs of chestnut, oak, cedar, white pine, or juniper were preferred for their ease of splitting and durability. Alternatives to rail fences included a range of improvised fencing made from various combinations of stumps, brush, rocks, and even sod on the Great Plains.

As time went by, many of the primitive old fences were later replaced with more solid rail-and-post construction held together with metal bolts, brackets, or wire. Even later, barbed wire would be added on top; sometimes the old fence was torn down entirely and replaced with barbed wire.

A FENCE OF
"STAKES AND RIDERS"

A very common method with the "worm" or "Virginia" rail fence is to drive slanting stakes over the corner in saw-horse style, and lay the top rail into the angle thus formed. The

Fig. 6.—A STAKE AND RIDER FENCE.

stakes, resting on the rails and standing at angle, brace the fence firmly. But the feet of the stakes extending beyond the jagged corners formed by the ends of the rail are objectionable. This is remedied in part by putting the stakes over the middle of the panel—at considerable distance apart—and laying in them long poles horizontally. In this case the stakes should be set at such an angle as to prevent their moving sidewise along the top rail, which should be a strong one. These stakes and long riders are frequently used to raise the hight of low stone walls. Figure 6 shows a fence nearly all

Fig. 7.—A POLE FENCE.

composed of stakes and riders, which is straight and requires fewer rails than a worm fence. First, crotched stakes, formed by the forks of a branching tree limb, a foot or more long, are driven a foot or so into the ground at a distance apart corresponding to the length of poles used. The bottom poles are laid into these, and two stakes, split or round poles, are driven over these and the next poles laid in. Then two more stakes and another pole, and so on as high as the fence is required. This will answer for larger animals, and be strong and not expensive. For swine, and other small live-stock, the crotch stakes may be replaced by blocks or stones, and the lower poles be small and begin close to the ground.

A POLE FENCE

A fence which is cheaply constructed in a timbered region, and calls for no outlay whatever, besides labor, is illustrated at

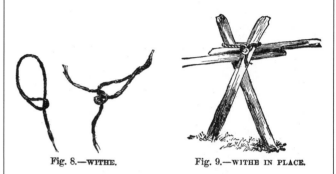

Fig. 8.—WITHE.   Fig. 9.—WITHE IN PLACE.

figure 7. The posts are set in a straight line, having previously been bored with an inch augur to receive the pins. When they are set, the pins are driven diagonally into the posts, and the poles laid in place. It would add much to its strength, if the poles were laid so as to "break joints." A modification of this fence is sometimes made by using withes instead of pins to hold the poles in place. The withe is made of a young sapling or slender limb of beech, iron-wood, or similar tough fibrous wood, with the twigs left on. This is twisted upon itself, a strong loop made at the top, through which the butt is slipped. When in place, the butt end is tucked under the body of the withe.

OTHER PRIMITIVE FENCES

In the heavily timbered parts of the country, where the settlers a few years ago were making farms by felling and burning the huge pine trees, a fence was constructed like the one shown in figure 14. Sections of trees, about four and a half feet long and

Fig. 14.—LOG POSTS.

often as thick, were placed in line and morticed to receive from three to five rails. This style of fence could be used by the

Fig. 15.—STUMP FENCE.

landscape gardener with fine effect for enclosing a park or shrubbery.

In the same regions, when a farmer has pulled all the stumps from a pasture that slopes toward the highway, the

Fig. 16.—WICKER FENCE.

stumps may be placed in line along the road with the top ends inside of the field. The gaps between where the stumps can not be rolled close together, are filled with brushwood. A portion of this fence is shown in figure 15.

Fig. 17.—BRUSH FENCE.

Where other material is costly, or not to be obtained, the wicker fence, constructed of stakes and willows, is much used. In the far West it is to be seen in every town, generally built on a small embankment of earth from one to two feet deep. In this climate, with occasional repairs, it lasts from ten to fifteen years. Figure 16 shows the style of construction.

Throughout the forest regions is found the staked and ridered brush growing on the line where the fence is constructed. Figure 17 illustrates a few rods of brush fence—such fencing being met with in our Southern States.

A PRAIRIE SOD FENCE

A sod fence, beside its other value, is a double barrier against the prairie fires which are so sweeping and destructive to new settlers, if unobstructed, for a wide strip is cleared of sods, the fence standing in the middle of it. A very convenient implement for cutting the sod is shown at figure 23. It is made of planks and scantling, the method of construction being clearly shown. The cutting disks are four wheel-coulters from common breaking plows, all attached to an iron shaft sixteen inches apart. They are set to cut three or four inches deep. This is run three times along the line of the fence, making nine cuts, the cutters being held down by a man riding on the rear of the apparatus. Then with a breaking

Fig. 23.—SOD CUTTER.

plow one furrow is turned directly in the line of the fence, completely inverting the sod, the team turned to the right, and a second or back furrow is inverted on top of the first. Additional furrows are cut, diminishing in width to five or six inches on the outer side, as shown in the diagram, figure 24. After the two inner sods are turned, the rest are carried by hand, wheelbarrow or a truck, (figure 20), and laid on the sod wall, care being used to "break joints" and to taper gradually

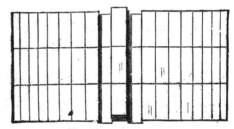

Fig. 24.—THE SOD CUT.

to the top. If a more substantial fence is wanted, a strip thirty-two inches wide may be left as a part for the fence, the first two farrows inverted upon the uncut portion, so that their edges just touch. The sod fence is then continued to the summit just twice as thick as it would be by the process just described. After the fence is laid, a deep furrow should be run on each side, throwing the earth against the base of the fence. A very effective and cheap fence is made by laying up a sod "dyke" as above described, three feet high, then driving light stakes along the summit, and stringing two strands of barbed wire to them.

STONE FENCES

The rural landscape of New England and the mid-Atlantic states is laced with ancient stone fences marking the ghostly boundaries of long-abandoned fields and pastures. Covered with lichens, tumbling down, and ripped open for roads, these old fences are reminders of the heartbreaking amount of sheer physical toil it took to turn the rocky soil into productive farmland. They are also a stark reminder of exactly why so many farmers from these regions were gone by the early 1800s, leaving behind rocky hilltop farms for the richer soils of western New York, western Pennsylvania, and the Western Reserve (now Ohio).

Building a functional stone fence was more a matter of persistence than skill. These fences were actually composites that were part wood and part stone (the wooden parts are long gone from the remnant fences seen today). In the simplest form, a furrow was plowed as a guideline. The stones from the field were piled onto sledges and dragged to the perimeter. They were stacked to about four feet high, and the fence was topped with a couple of wooden rails—high enough to keep the pigs and cows in or out, as the case may be. A stone wall high enough to serve the same function would have required a lot more labor to reach the same useful height. To make a more elaborate composite fence, fence posts were sunk, the stones were stacked to a convenient height, and boards or rails were added above them. Ruler-straight fences were not needed. Stone fences tend to meander a bit in general and often swerve to avoid large obstacles.

Simple stone fences were remarkably durable and functional. Taller stone fences reaching five feet high were a more complicated undertaking, requiring a much higher skill level. The average farmer had little need for such solid construction and couldn't usually spare the cash to have one built.

BUILDING A STONE FENCE

A permanent stone fence should be built from four to five feet high, two feet wide at the base and one foot at the top, if the kind of stones available allow this construction. If a higher fence is desired, the width should be correspondingly increased. The surface of the soil along the line of the fence should be made smooth and as nearly level as possible. The hight will depend upon the situation, the animals, the smoothness of the wall (whether sheep can get foot-holds to climb over), and the character of the ground along each side.

Fig. 19.—LAYING UP A STONE FENCE.

If the earth foundation be rounded up previously, sloping off to an open depression or gully, less hight will be needed. Such an elevation will furnish a dry base not heaved by frost like a wet one. Without this, or a drain alongside or under the wall, to keep the soil always dry, the base must be sunk deeply enough to be proof against heavy frosts, which will tilt and loosen the best laid wall on wet soil. The foundation stones should be the largest; smaller stones packed between them are necessary to firmness. The mistake is sometimes made of placing all the larger stones on the outside of the wall, filling the center with small ones. Long bind-stones placed at frequent intervals through the wall add greatly to its strength. The top of the fence is more secure when covered with larger close-fitting, flat stones. The engraving shows a wooden frame and cords used as a guide in building a substantial stone fence. Two men can work together with mutual advantage on opposite sides of the stone wall.

REINFORCING A STONE WALL

A stone wall which affords ample protection against sheep and hogs, may be quite insufficient for horses and cattle. The

Fig. 21.—STONE WALL REINFORCED.

deficiency is cheaply supplied in the manner indicated by the illustration, figure 21. Round poles or rails are used, and if the work is properly performed, the fence is very effective.

A COMPOSITE FENCE

The fence illustrated at figure 22 is quite common in some parts of New England. A ridge is thrown up by back-furrowing with a plow, and both that and the ditches finished by hand with a shovel. Light posts are easily driven through the soft earth, and a board fence, only three boards high, made in the usual manner. Then the stones, as they are picked up in the field, are hauled to the fence and thrown upon the ridge. This clears the field, strengthens the ridge, prevents the growth of weeds, and assists in packing the earth firmly around the bottom of the posts.

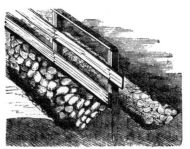

Fig. 22.—COMPOSITE FENCE.

BOARD FENCES

Where stone fences weren't a practical necessity, or where rail fences needed to be replaced with something more substantial, board fences were built. These required split or sawn boards, uniform fence posts, plenty of nails, and even paint, which made them expensive in terms of both material and labor.

MAKING FENCE POSTS

There is quite an art in splitting logs into posts. Every post should have some heart wood, which lasts the longer, for two reasons: That there may be durable wood into which to drive the nails, and without it some of the posts, composed entirely of sap-wood, will rot off long before others, making the most annoying of all repairing necessary. If the log is of a size to make twelve posts, split along the lines of figure 146, which will give each post a share of heart wood. This will make a cross section of the posts triangular, the curved base being somewhat more than half of either side. This is a fairly well shaped post, and much better than a square one having little or no heart wood. Although the log may be large enough to make sixteen or eighteen posts, it is better to split it the same way. It should first be cut into halves, then quarters, then twelfths. If it is attempted to split one post off the side of a half, the wood will "draw out," making the post larger at one end than the other—not a good shape, for there will be little heart wood at the small end. When the log is too large to admit of it being split in that way, each post may nevertheless be given enough heart wood by splitting along the lines, shown in figure 147. First cut the logs into halves, then quarters, then eighths. Then split off the edge of each eighth, enough for a post—about one-fourth only of the

Fig. 146.   Fig. 147.

wood, as it is all heart wood, and then halve the balance. A good post can be taken off the edge, and yet enough heart wood for the remaining two posts remain.

Board fences required a fair amount of maintenance, such as replacing sagging or rotted boards, straightening fence posts tilted by frost heave and heavy snow, and painting. On the other hand, well-made board fences were solid, functional, attractive, and created an air of prosperity about the farm. They were also, on the whole, less likely to injure valuable farm animals.

BUILDING BOARD FENCES

In building a board fence, always start right, and it will be little trouble to continue in the same way. Much of the board fencing erected is put together very carelessly, and the result is a very insecure protection to the field or crops. A fence-post should be set two and a half or three feet in the ground, and the earth should be packed around it as firmly as possible. For packing the soil there is nothing better than a piece of oak, about three inches square on the lower end, and about six feet long, rounded off on the upper part to fit the hands easily. Properly used, this instrument will pack the soil around a post as it was before the hole was dug. In putting on fence boards, most builders use two nails on the ends of each board, and one in the middle. Each board should have at least *three* nails at the ends, and *two* in the middle, and these nails should never be less than ten-pennys. Smaller nails will hold the boards in place for awhile, but when they begin to warp, the nails are drawn out or loos-

Fig. 25.—PROPERLY CONSTRUCTED BOARD FENCE.

ened, and the boards drop off. This will rarely be the case where large nails are used, and a much stiffer fence is secured. Many fence builders do not cut off the tops of the posts evenly, but this should always be done, not only for the improvement that it makes in the looks of the fence; but also for the reason that there should always be a cap put on, and to do this, the posts must be evened. The joints should

Fig. 26.—A DURABLE BOARD FENCE.

always be "broken," as is shown in the engraving, figure 25, so that in a four-board fence but two joints should come on each post. By this means more firmness and durability is secured, there being always two unbroken boards on each post to hold it in place, preventing sagging. On the face of the post immediately over where the rails have been nailed on, nail a flat piece of board the width of the post and extending from the upper part of the top rail to the ground.

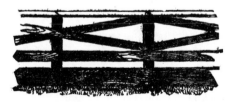

Fig. 27.—A NEAT FARM FENCE.

Figure 26 shows a slight modification, which consists in setting the posts on alternate sides of the boards, securing additional stability. The posts are seven feet long, of well seasoned red cedar, white oak, chestnut, or black locust, preference being accorded to order named. The boards are

sixteen feet long, fastened with ten-penny steel fence nails. The posts for a space of two and a half feet from the lower end are given a good coat of boiled linseed oil and pulverized charcoal, mixed to the consistency of ordinary paint, which is allowed to dry before they are set. When the materials are all ready, stretch a line eighteen inches above the ground, where it is proposed to build the fence. Dig the post holes, eight feet apart from the centers, on alternate sides of the line. The posts are set with the faces inward, each half an inch from the line, to allow space for the boards. Having set the posts, the boards of the lower course are nailed on. Then, for the first length, the second board from the bottom and the top board are only eight feet long, reaching to the first post. For all the rest the boards are of the full length, sixteen feet. By this means they "break joints." After the boards are nailed on, the top of the posts are sawed off slanting, capped, if desired, and the whole thing painted. A good coat of crude petroleum, applied before painting, will help preserve the fence, and save more than its cost in the paint needed.

We see another style of board fence now and then that is rather preferable to the ordinary one; it looks better than the old straight fence. It saves one board to each length; and by nailing on the two upper boards, as shown in the illustration 27, great extra strength is given. These boards not only act as braces, but ties also, and a fence built on well set posts, and thoroughly nailed, will never sag or get out of line until the posts rot off.

REINFORCING A BOARD FENCE

The old method of topping out a low board fence is shown at figure 38. Since barbed wire has become plenty, it is more usual to increase the height of the fence by stringing one or

Fig. 38.—STRENGTHENING A BOARD FENCE.

two strands of that on vertical slats nailed to the tops of the posts. Yet, in cases where there are plenty of sound rails left from some old fence, or plenty of straight saplings, the old method is still a very cheap and convenient one.

LIVE FENCES

Live fences, plantings of fast-growing, thorny, durable trees such as Osage orange (also known as bois d'arc), honey locust, and buckthorn, were tried with some success in the 1860s and 1870s, especially on the prairies. Once barbed wire became readily available, however, the live-fence idea was basically abandoned, although not before buckthorn had turned into an invasive pest on the prairies and crowded out native vegetation.

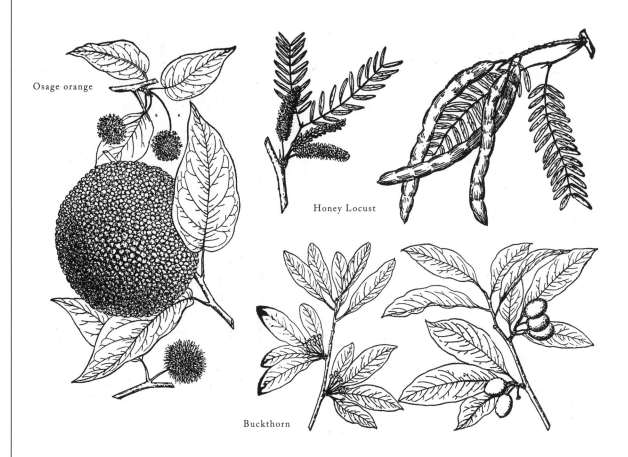

Osage orange

Honey Locust

Buckthorn

BARBED WIRE FENCES

The invention of barbed wire was a major milestone that almost magically solved fencing problems for farmers and ranchers. Barbed wire is generally made from two strands of fence wire twisted together, with wire barbs (cut on a slant to give them sharp points) wound around one or both wires at regular intervals, generally every four to five inches. The beauty of barbed wire is not just the barbs, which keep livestock from pressing too hard against the fence. The twisted double strand also makes the wire strong and able to expand and contract without breaking.

The basic concepts of barbed wire were patented in the United States in 1867, but it wasn't until 1874 that Joseph Glidden of De Kalb, Illinois, invented a practical machine to manufacture it. So quickly was it adopted that within fifteen years, barbed wire had transformed the open range of the West into fenced pastureland.

Barbed wire had overwhelming advantages. First and foremost, it was cheap. It was also very effective, though not without drawbacks—valuable livestock, especially horses, could be injured by the barbs. Barbed wire was easy to put up, easy to move as needed, and very durable. Maintenance was very simple, consisting mostly of tightening sagging strands and fence posts and occasionally splicing broken wire.

By 1876, some 1,500 tons of barbed wire were produced, enough for 3,000 miles of single-strand fence. By 1886, those figures were 135,000 tons, enough for 270,000 miles of fencing.

Glidden soon had many competitors, all producing their own variants on the basic concept and creating a fertile field for later collectors, who now seek different examples. In general, all variants on barbed wire used two wires and barbs with either two or four points, although a number of specialty wires were made.

Barbed wire was attached to fence posts with metal staples. To prevent injury to livestock, it was important to build the fence high enough, usually with five or six strands, so that the animals couldn't get a leg over it. To save costs or take advantage of existing fencing, composite fences were often built, with rails or boards on the lower portion and two or three strands of barbed wire on the top.

Barb wire, like the harvester, the sowing machine, and most other valuable inventions, has attained its present form from very crude beginnings. The original barb wire consisted of

Fig. 58.—THE KELLY BARB WIRE.

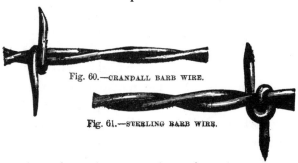

Fig. 59.—HORSE-NAIL BARB.

double-pointed metallic discs, strung loosely upon plain wire. The next step was to twist this with another wire, as shown in figure 58.

Another crude beginning was the "horse-nail barb," which consisted of a common horse-shoe nail bent around a plain wire, and the whole wrapped spirally with a smaller wire, as shown in figure 59. Various forms of two-pointed and four-pointed barb wire are manufactured, the principal difference being the shape of the barbs and the manner of coiling them around one or both of the strands. A few of the leading styles are illustrated herewith. Figures 60 and 61 show two varieties of two-pointed barb wire.

Fig. 60.—CRANDALL BARB WIRE.

Fig. 61.—STERLING BARB WIRE.

Of the numerous styles of four-pointed wire, three typical forms are illustrated in figures 62, 63, and 64.

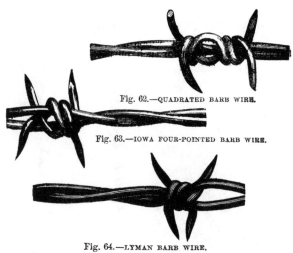

Fig. 62.—QUADRATED BARB WIRE.

Fig. 63.—IOWA FOUR-POINTED BARB WIRE.

Fig. 64.—LYMAN BARB WIRE.

The Glidden patent steel barb wire is made in three styles, as shown in figures 65, 66, and 67. Figure 65 shows the two-point wire, in which, like the others, the barb is twisted around only one of the wires. Figure 66 shows the "thick-

Fig. 65.—GLIDDEN PATENT STEEL TWO-POINT.

set" which has barbs like the other, but set closer together for such purposes as sheep folds, gardens, or other places, which require extra protection. The four-point barb wire, figure 67,

Fig. 66.—GLIDDEN PATENT STEEL " THICK SET."

Fig. 67.—GLIDDEN PATENT FOUR-POINT.

has barbs of the same form as the two other styles, that is a sharply pricking barb attached to one of the wires of the

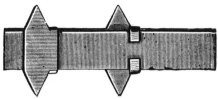

Fig. 68.—BRINKERHOFF STEEL STRAP AND BARB.

Fig. 69.—ALLIS PATENT BARB.

fence strand, upon which the other wire is twisted, holding the barb firmly in place. The barb is at right angles to the wire, and does not form a hook, but a straight short steel

Fig. 70.—BRINKERHOFF FENCING TWISTED.

Fig. 71.—TWO STRAND TWISTED WIRE FENCING.

thorn. A sharp point which inflict an instantaneous prick repels an animal more safely than a longer and duller barb.

STEEL FENCE STAPLES

For fastening barb wires to the post nothing has been found so satisfactory as staples made for the purpose from No. 9 steel wire. They are cut with sharp points to drive easily into

Fig. 72.—1¼-INCH STAPLE.   Fig. 73.—1¾-INCH STAPLE.

Fig. 74.—SQUARE TOP STAPLE FOR BRINKERHOFF FENCING.

the posts, and are of different lengths, from one inch and a quarter to one and three-quarters. Figures 72 and 73 show the usual staples for wire, and figure 74 a staple made specially for strap fencing.

HOW TO SET BARB WIRE FENCE

The timber for posts should be cut when the sap is dormant. Midwinter or August is a good time to cut post timber. They should be split and the bark taken off as soon as possible after cutting the timber. For end posts, select some of the best trees, about sixteen inches in diameter, from which take cuts eight and a half feet in length, splitting them in quarters for brace posts. They should be set three feet in the ground,

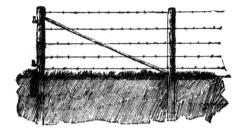

Fig. 75.—WELL-BRACED BARB-WIRE FENCE.

which is easily done with a post-hole digger. When setting the brace posts, take a stone eighteen inches to two feet long, twelve inches wide, and six inches thick, which is put down against the post edgewise, on the opposite side to the brace, as seen in figure 75, putting it down about even with the surface of the ground. This holds the post solid against the brace. A heart-rail, ten feet in length makes a good brace. Put one of the long posts every sixteen or twenty rods along the line of fence, as they help to strengthen it, and set lighter and shorter posts along the line about sixteen feet apart.

Fig. 76.—A WIRE FENCE WELL BRACED.

After the posts are set, two or three furrows should be turned against them on each side, as it helps to keep stock from the wire. Such a fence should be built of a good height. It is better to buy an extra wire than have stock injured. There is no pulling over end posts or sagging wire.

To make an extra solid wire fence, brace the posts, as shown in figure 76, on both sides, in order to resist the tension in either direction. Every eighth post should be thus braced, and it makes a mark for measuring the length of the fence, for eight posts set one rod apart, make eight rods, or a fortieth of a mile for each braced post. The braces are notched into the top of the posts, just below the top wire, and a spike is driven through both the brace and the post. The braces abut upon large stones which give them great firmness.

Fig. 77.—DEVICE FOR UNROLLING WIRE.

Fig. 79.—A SULKY WIRE-HOLDER.

FENCE WIRE REEL

Here is a device on which one can wind barbed wire that is much better than an old barrel. The reel is mounted on a truck made of old buggy wheels with short shafts. The cart may be drawn along by a man while a boy steadies the reel to keep it from unwinding too rapidly. For winding up wire, the

WIRE REEL ON WHEELS

machine is best pushed just fast enough to keep up with the wire as it is being wound on the reel. A crank placed upon the reel proves serviceable in winding up.

WIRE STRETCHERS

For stretching barb wire there are various implements in the market, and other quite simple and effective devices can be

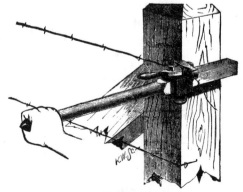

Fig. 84.—THE CLARK STRETCHER.

Fig. 85.—THE "COME ALONG" STRETCHER.

made on the farm. Figure 84 shows the Clark stretcher and the manner of using it. Another stretcher, called the "Come Along" stretcher, figure 85, is used not only for tightening the wires, but also for handling it, in building or moving fences.

The useful wire stretcher, figure 86, consists of a mowing machine knife-guard, bolted to a stout stick; one curved, as

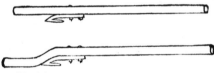

Fig. 86. HOME-MADE WIRE STRETCHERS.

shown in the lower engraving, is preferable to a straight one, as it will not turn in the hand. When using it, the wire is held firmly in the slot, and may be easily stretched by applying the stick as a lever.

BUILDING WIRE FENCES ON UNEVEN GROUND

One of the great perplexities about building wire fences on rolling ground, is how to make the posts in the hollows remain firm, for the pull of the wire in wet weather, or when the frost is coming out, lifts them and causes the wire to sag, and they cease to be an effective barrier. Posts should not be

Fig. 96.—FENCE ON UNEVEN GROUND.

used in the lowest depressions, but in their place at the lowest spots a heavy stone should be partially sunk into the ground, about which a smooth fence wire has been wrapped, as seen in figure 96. When the fence is built, the fence wires are brought down to their place and the wire about the stone is twisted first about the lower wire, then the next, and so on to the top. This prevents the wire from raising, and does away with all trouble of the posts being pulled out by the wires. In fencing across small streams the same plan is successful.

COMBINED WIRE
AND BOARD FENCE

A very cheap fence is made of two boards below and three strands of barb wire. To make the fence pig-proof without

Fig. 97.—MANNER OF BRACING END-POST.

the boards, five strands of wire, three inches apart, would be required at the bottom. Two common fencing boards will occupy the same space, when placed three inches apart, and cost less. But for the upper part of the fence, wire is much cheaper than boards. The most considerable item in this greater economy is the saving of posts. The wire requires a post every sixteen feet; hence half the posts are saved. A stout stake, driven midway between the posts, holds the center of the boards in place. These stakes need extend only eighteen inches above ground.

DOG-PROOF FENCES

Figure 104 shows a sheep-yard fence, built of wire and boards, as a safeguard against vicious dogs. It consists of ordinary posts, and three lengths of boards, with an equal

Fig. 104.—A FENCE AGAINST DOGS.

number of barb-wires for the upper portion and a single strand placed near the ground. The sheep are in no danger of injuring themselves with such a fence, and it is an effective barrier to blood-thirsty dogs.

Figure 105 shows a cheaper fence for the same purpose. It has one strand of barb wire below the boards, which prevents attempts of dogs to dig under it. For fencing sheep against dogs, the "thick-set" barb wire is the most effective of any.

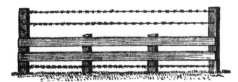

Fig. 105.—A CHEAPER FENCE.

GATES

Good fences were useless without good gates. In the days of simple split-rail fences, rails or bars were simply laid across an opening and held in place, usually by passing the ends through holes in a fence post. To pass through the fence, the bars had to be taken down and then put up again, a time-consuming and laborious operation. Gates were considerably more efficient.

GOOD BARS
FOR THE FARM

It is an important matter to the farmer that his farm should be well equipped with good, substantial bars. Some farmers go to as much trouble in a year's time in moving a poor gate or bars back and forth as they drive in and out of fields, and in chasing cattle about, as making dozens of such bars as are represented here. Use round poles about 2 1/2 or 3 inches in diameter. Set two good-sized posts one on either side of the barway, and to each one, an equal distance apart, nail large horseshoes, allowing the round part to stand out far enough from posts to admit the bar poles easily.

BAR WITH HORSESHOE CATCH

A good farm gate needed to be at least fourteen feet wide to let livestock or a standard wagon through. It had to be sturdily built and securely fastened—farm animals, especially cows, were notorious for being able to open gates and escape from pastures into fields. Measures had to be taken to keep the gate from sagging, which made it very hard to open and also left an opening through which livestock could escape.

There is but one right way to brace a gate, and many wrong ones. The object of bracing is to strengthen the gate, and also to prevent its sagging. Gates sag in two ways; by the moving to the one side of the posts upon which the gates are

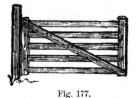

Fig. 177.

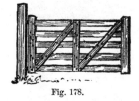

Fig. 178.

hung, and the settling of the gates themselves. Unless braced the only thing to hold the gate square is the perfect rigidity of the tenons in the mortises; but the weight of the gate will loosen these, and allow the end of the gate opposite the hinges to sag. It is plain that a brace placed like that shown in figure 177 will not prevent this settling down. The only opposition it can give is the resistance of the nails, and these will draw loose in the holes as readily as the tenons in the mortises. A brace set as shown at figure 178 is not much better, as the resistance must depend upon the rigidity of the

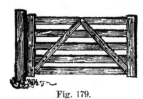

Fig. 179.

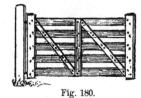

Fig. 180.

upright piece in the middle, and the bolts or nails holding it will give way enough to allow the gate to sag. The method shown in figure 179 is fully as faulty, while the form shown in figure 180 is even worse. It seems strange that any one should brace a gate in these ways, but it is quite frequently seen attempted. The only right way to brace a gate is shown

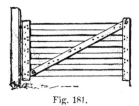

Fig. 181.

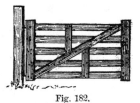

Fig. 182.

in figure 181. The gate may be further strengthened as shown in figure 182. Before the gate can sag, the brace must be shortened; for as the gate settles, the points *a* and *b* must come closer together, and this the brace effectively prevents.

Fig. 183.

Fig. 184.

The posts should be set in such a way that they will not be pulled to one side and allow the gate to sag. The post should be put below the line of frost, or else it will be heaved out of position; three feet in the ground is none too deep.

KEEPING A GATE FROM SAGGING

The average farm gate is heavy, and after a little time it sags. When they get this way it takes a strong man to open and shut one. Here is a remedy. Get a wheel, either big or little, from an old piece of machinery, and bolt it to the front end of

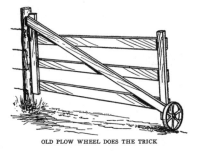

OLD PLOW WHEEL DOES THE TRICK

the gate in such a way that the gate will be held level. Now the smallest child can open the gate for you. Try it, for it is a saver—saves your patience, your back and the gate.

AN EASILY OPENED GATE

Take an old buggy wheel and fasten it as shown in the drawing to the gates that are opened often. The piece of board indicated by *c* drops between the spokes of the wheel and holds the gate either open or closed. A child can easily operate the heaviest gate with this attachment.

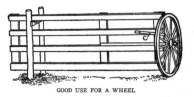

GOOD USE FOR A WHEEL

A vast array of ingenious gate hinges, gate fasteners, self-closing gates, and clever designs for special purposes were developed over the years.

A STRONG AND NEAT GATE

The posts, *a, a,* figure 192, of oak or other durable wood, are eight inches square, and stand five and one half feet above the ground. The posts, *b, b,* three and one third inches thick, four and three quarter feet long, are mortised to receive the slats, *c, c,* which are of inch stuff, three inches wide and ten feet four and three-quarter inches long. They are let into

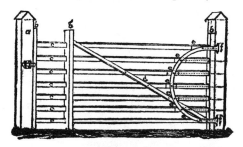

Fig. 192.—A WELL-MADE GATE.

posts, *b, b,* at the distance marked in the engraving. The slats, *d,* are three inches wide, and one inch thick, and are placed opposite each other on front and back of the gate as braces; *e, e,* are simply battens to make a straight surface for the hinges, *f, f;* all except the upper and lower ones are very short and carried back to the post. The hinges, made by a blacksmith from an old wagon tire, are one and one-half inch wide, three-sixteenth inch thick, and are fastened by light iron bolts through the battens at *e,* and to the rear post.

The above describes a cheap, light, durable gate, which in over twenty-three years' use has never sagged, though standing in the thoroughfare of three farms, and also, for years past, used for access to a sawmill. It is made of the best pine. The hinge is an important point. It is not only cheap and easily made, but acts as a brace for the gate at every point, and thus permits the gate to be light made. With this hinge sagging is impossible. A gate of this kind will rot down first.

SELF-CLOSING GATES

Every self-closing gate should be provided with a drop or spring catch, a suitable bevel for it to strike against and notch to hold it. Gates opening into the garden or out upon the street, should be so hung that they will swing either way. Figure 195 shows a hinge and slide for such a gate. In opening the gate from either side, the arm of the upper hinge slides upon the iron bar, raising the gate a little as it swings around. When loosed, it slides down without help, and

Fig. 195.—HINGE AND SLIDE FOR GATE.   Fig. 196.

closes by its own weight. Figure 196 shows another form of the iron slide, suitable for a wide gate post, and more ornamental than the plain slide in figure 195.

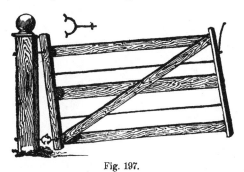

Fig. 197.

Figure 197 shows a very good and common hanging. The upper hinge consists of a hook in the post and a corresponding eye in the hinge-stile of the gate. The lower hinge is made of two semi-circular pieces of iron, each with a shank, one of which is shown above the gate in the engraving. They are made to play one into the other. This style of hanging may be used on any ordinary kind of gate, but is specially useful for a small street gate opening into a door-yard.

LIFTING GATES

There are various forms of gates not hung on hinges at all, but either suspended from above to lift, and provided with counterweights, or made in the form of movable panels. Figure 202 represents a gate for general use, which is peculiarly well adapted to a region visited by deep snows in winter. The post, firmly set, extends a little higher than the length of the gate. In front of this and firmly fastened to it at bottom and top, is a board at sufficient distance from the post for the gate to move easily between them. An iron bolt

Fig. 202.—GATE SHUT.

through the large post and the lower end of the tall, upright gate bar, serves as a balance for the gate to turn on. A rope attached to the bottom of the gate runs over the pulley and has a weight of iron or stone that nearly balances the gate. The opened gate is shown in figure 203.

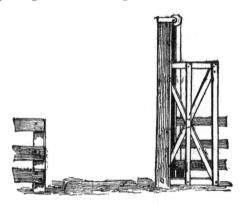

Fig. 203.—GATE OPEN.

Figure 204 shows a gate balanced in a similar manner, and arranged so it can be opened by a person desiring to drive through, without leaving the vehicle. It is suspended by ropes which pass over pulleys near the top of long posts,

Fig. 204.—A "SELF-OPENING" GATE.

and counterpoised by weights upon the other ends of the ropes. Small wheels are placed in the ends of the gate to move along the inside of the posts, and thus reduce the friction. The gate is raised by means of ropes attached to the center of the upper side of the gate, from which they pass up to pulleys in the center of the archway, and then out along horizontal arms at right angles to the bars which connect the tops of the posts. By pulling on the rope, the gate, which is but a trifle heavier than the balancing weights, is raised, and after the vehicle has passed, the gate falls of itself. In passing in the opposite direction, another rope is pulled, when the gate is raised as before.

WEST INDIA FARM GATES

The illustrations, figures 219 and 220, show two forms of gates used on the island of Jamaica. These gates are twenty-one feet long, each, and cannot possibly sag, even if any number of small boys swing on them.

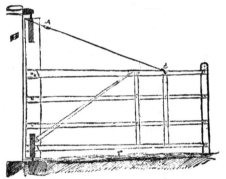

Fig. 219.—WIDE FARM GATE.

GATE HINGES OF WOOD

It is often convenient and economical, especially in newly settled regions, where blacksmiths and hardware stores are not at hand, to supply hinges for gates, to make them of wood. The simplest and most primitive form is shown in figure 221. A post is selected having a large limb standing out nearly at right angles. A perpendicular hole in this secures the top of the rear gate standard. The foot rests in a stout short post, set against the main post. A small gimlet hole should extend outward and downward from the lowest side or point in the hole in the short post, to act as a drain, or the water collecting in it would be likely to soon rot both the standard and the short post itself. Another form is to hold the top by a strong wooden withe. A third form is illustrated in figure 222, in which the top of the standard passes through a short piece of sawed or split plank, spiked or pinned upon the top of the post.

Fig. 221.   Fig. 222.

DOUBLE-LATCHED GATES

Figure 231 represents a substantial farm gate with two latches. This is a very useful precaution against the wiles of such cattle as have learned to unfasten ordinary gate-latches. The latches work independently of each other, the wires, *b, b*, being fastened to the hand lever *a*, and then to the latches *e, e*. A roguish animal will sometimes open a gate by raising the latch with its nose, but if one attempt it with this,

Fig. 231.—A DOUBLE-LATCHED FARM GATE.

it can only raise one latch at a time, always the upper one, while the lower one remains fastened. As soon as the animal lets go, the latch springs back and catches again. A hog cannot get through, for the lower latch prevents the gate from opening sufficiently to allow it to pass. A cow will find it difficult to open the gate, because she cannot raise the gate high enough to unlatch it. The latches *e, e*, work up and down in the slides *c, c*, and when the gate is fastened they are about half-way between the top and bottom of the slides.

Figure 232 shows another form of double latches, which are closed by absolute motion, instead of depending upon their own weight. There are two latches fastened to a jointed lever, so that when the upper end or handle is pushed back-

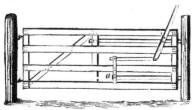

Fig. 232.—A GATE FOR ALL LIVE STOCK.

ward or forward, the latches both move in the same direction. The construction of the gate, and the form and arrangement of the latches and lever, are plainly shown.

GATES OF WOOD AND WIRE

One of the cheapest and most popular styles of farm gate is made of plain or barbed wire, supported by wooden frames. Figure 237 shows a very neat form of combination gate.

Fig. 237.—A NEAT GATE OF SCANTLING AND WIRE.

A GOOD AND CHEAP FARM GATE

Figure 238 shows a gate of common fence boards and wire, which can be made by any farmer. The longer upright piece, seven feet long, may be made of a round stick, flattened a little on one side. The horizontal bars are of common fence boards cut to the desired length, and the shorter, vertical piece may be made of scantling, two by four inches. Three wires, either plain or barbed, are stretched at equal intervals between the upper and lower bar. A double length of wire is extended from the top of the long upright to the opposite lower corner of the gate. A stout stick is inserted between the two strands of this diagonal brace, by which it is twisted until it is sufficiently taut. If the gate should at any time begin to sag, a few turns brings it back.

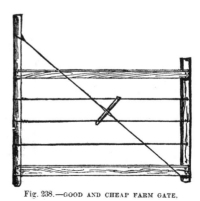

Fig. 238.—GOOD AND CHEAP FARM GATE.

GOOD GATE LATCHES

Some cows become so expert, they can lift almost any gate latch. To circumvent this troublesome habit, latches made as shown in figure 246 will fill this bill exactly. It is a piece of iron bar, drawn down at one end, and cut with a thread to screw into the gate post. A stirrup, or crooked staple, made as shown, is fitted by a screw bolt and nut to the bar. A small bolt must be driven in to keep the stirrup from being thrown over. A projecting slat on the gate, when it is shut, lifts the stirrup and holds the gate. This latch is too much for breechy cows, and they are never able to get "the hang of it."

Fig. 246.—GATE LATCH.

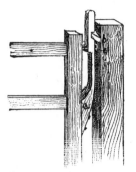

Fig. 247.—SPRING GATE CATCH.

In figure 252 is represented a style of gate latch in use in some Southern States. It possesses marked advantages, for certain purposes, over others. It holds to an absolute certainty, under all circumstances, and by allowing the latch pin to rest on the bottom of the slot in the post, it relieves the hinges and post from all strain. The latch may be formed by a common strap-hinge, made to work very easily, and the pin should be either a strong oak one or an iron bolt or "lag screw."

Fig. 252.—GATE LATCH.

Figure 253 shows a latch which cannot be opened by the most ingenious cow or other animal. The latch of wood slides in two iron or wood bands screwed to the gate. It is moved by a knob between the bands, which also prevents it from going too far. The outer end is sloping and furnished with a notch. It slides through a mortise, and the drop-pin, which plays vertically in two iron bands, is lifted by the slope on the latch, and drops into the notch. It can be opened only by lifting the drop-pin, and sliding back the latch at the same time.

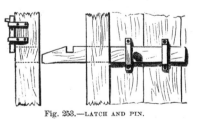

Fig. 253.—LATCH AND PIN.

Figure 254 shows a very ingenious and reliable form of latch. The curved tail must be thin enough and sufficiently soft to admit of bending, either by a pair of large pincers or a hammer, just so as to adapt it to the passage of the pin bolted through the front stile of the gate. As the gate closes, the latch lifts out and the tailpiece advances. The catch-pin cannot possibly move out, unless the whole end of the gate moves up and forward.

Fig. 254.—GATE LATCH.

RUSTIC GATES

A picturesque rustic gate is shown in figure 213. The fence and posts are made to correspond. Its manner of construc-

Fig. 213.—ORNAMENTAL GATE.

tion is clearly shown in the illustration. The vases on the top of the posts may be omitted, unless time can be taken to keep them properly watered.

A very neat, cheap, and strong rustic gate is shown in figure 214. The large post and the two uprights of the gate are of red cedar. The horizontal bars may be of the same or other wood. The longer upright is five and a half feet long, the shorter one four and a half feet. The ends of the former are cut down to serve as hinges, as shown in the engraving. Five holes are bored through each of the upright pieces, two inches in diameter, into which the ends of the horizontal bars are inserted and wedged securely. For the upper hinge a piece of plank is bored to receive the gate, and the other end reduced and driven into a hole in the post, or nailed securely to its top. A cedar block, into which a two-inch hole has been bored, is partially sunk in the ground to receive the lower end of the upright piece. A wooden latch is in better keeping with the gate than an iron one.

Fig. 214.—LIGHT RUSTIC GATE.

CHAPTER 3

WATER SUPPLY

A steady supply of water was and is of crucial importance to any farmer. Ideally, in earlier days houses, stables, and barns were situated near year-round flowing streams. The water was brought by wooden pipes to troughs for animals and into a cistern or barrel next to or inside the house for household use. The traditional rain barrel next to the house was another convenient source of water for household use and watering the kitchen garden.

The ideal was far from common, however, and even year-round streams sometimes dried up in droughts. The solution was a well. Early wells were hand dug and operated by the traditional bucket on a windlass or by a wooden pump made from a hollowed log. As a safety measure and to keep debris out of the well, well curbs, or enclosures, were used; pump platforms served the same purpose.

WINDLASS AND TITLING BUCKET

As ordinary pumps draw water only thirty-three feet perpendicularly, and practically only about thirty feet from the

Fig. 122.—IMPROVED WINDLASS.

water surface, force-pumps or windlasses are required, for wells thirty or more feet deep. The common windlass with stop ratchet serves a fair purpose, but requires the bucket to be let all the way down by turning the crank backward. Various forms of brakes have been devised. Figure 122 shows the construction and operation of one.

SECURING THE WELL-BUCKET

One who has much experience with well-buckets, will find they are often set down outside of the curb, and not always in a clean place. In this manner the water in the well may be fouled with clay, if with nothing worse. Every person should be very careful to avoid anything that may in any degree tend to impair the purity of the water in a well. One way to secure this

Fig. 124.

end is to have the bucket always in a safe place. This may be done by fixing a cord or a chain to the beam over the pulley, or to the stirrup of the pulley, and fastening a hook to its lower end, upon which the bucket should always be hung when not in use. This arrangement for the well-bucket is made plain by figure 124.

WELL-CURB OF STAVES

Figure 123 is a very strong and durable curb made of staves. A cooper can make it, setting up the staves, which are one and one-quarter inch thick, as for a barrel, using three iron hoops. The shaft of the windlass is also of iron, to which a wooden cylinder is fastened by a couple of bolts driven through the wood and iron. In making the windlass, fashion the wood to the right size, and then split open the cylinder, cut a place for the shaft, fit it in, and then drive bands over the ends.

Fig. 123.—A " BARREL " WELL-CURB

CURB WITH A BUCKET SHELF

Another device for keeping the bucket clean is shown in figure 125. An iron plate of suitable size is held on the end of an arm fastened at right angles to an upright iron rod. The bottom of this rod rests upon an iron projecting from the corner of the curb, and the top is held in place by an eye-rod. The filled bucket is raised high enough so that the plate is placed directly under it. Let up on the windlass when the bucket is secure on the plate, and it may be swung to one side without straining the back, or danger of slipping when it is icy.

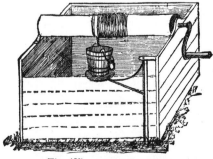

Fig. 125.—A BUCKET SHELF.

COVERED WELL-CURBS

Figure 126 is a desirable covering for a well-curb.

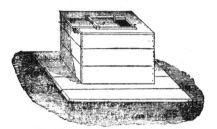

Fig. 126.—A WELL-CURB COVERING.

A VENTILATED PUMP PLATFORM

Here is a way to keep the well clean and pure at all times. Make the frame of the platform of 2 × 4's allowing a space 2 to 6 inches between the top and bottom parts of the sides.

HELPS TO KEEP WATER PURE

This space is covered on the inside with a fly screen to keep out dirt and insects, and outside of this with a larger meshed screen to keep out large vermin. This gives good ventilation to the well, which never becomes foul. In the winter cover the platform with straw and snow.

A NON-FREEZING PUMP

One of the simplest methods of preventing a pump from freezing is shown in figure 129. The pump is boxed from the platform to six inches or more above the spout, the box being made large enough to admit of a packing of sawdust or spent tan bark between it and the pump-stock; or the pump-stock can be well wrapped with heavy hardware paper and then

Fig. 129.—PUMP PROTECTOR.

boxed tightly, which will effectually keep out almost any ordinary degree of cold. It is well to have the platform double-boarded, running each layer of boards in opposite directions, and mounding up well around the platform with earth, to still further protect against cold.

HOOK FOR CLEANING WELLS

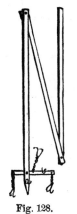

Every farmer who has open wells, knows how difficult and tiresome a task it is, to extricate articles which have fallen into them, but figure 128 shows a contrivance which has been used successfully.

HOW TO BUILD A CISTERN

Fig. 128.

Every part around the surface of a cistern should be made close. The beams which support the floor should be bedded in the wall, or shoulder of the cistern, and covered with lime or cement mortar, leaving a smooth surface all around the first floor. This should then be covered

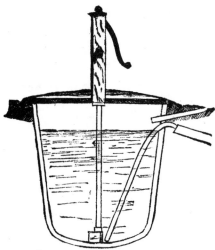

Fig. 137.—FROST-PROOF CISTERN.

with a second floor, raised eight or ten inches on a frame of two by ten joists, made of cedar or chestnut. The earth should be packed closely against this frame, and the top floor

should extend a few inches beyond the frame all around. The cistern is then frost and vermin proof. Another important point is to get rid of the sediment that gathers at the bottom of every cistern. This is done by carrying the overflow pipe to the bottom of the cistern on a line with the inlet pipe, and thus forming a current which disturbs the sediment and carries it to the overflow. This is shown in figure 137, also the arrangement of the draw-pipe, which should have a fine wire strainer on the end, and should rest upon a support near the bottom of a fine strainer, at least two feet high. A piece of one-quarter inch mesh of galvanized wire gauze, bent into a pipe a foot in diameter, and covered with thick flannel cloth, doubled, makes a filter for the water.

FILTER FOR CISTERN WATER

The problem of keeping water in a cistern clean is most easily solved by not allowing it to get dirty, as can be done by the device shown in the drawing below. Two barrels, each with a

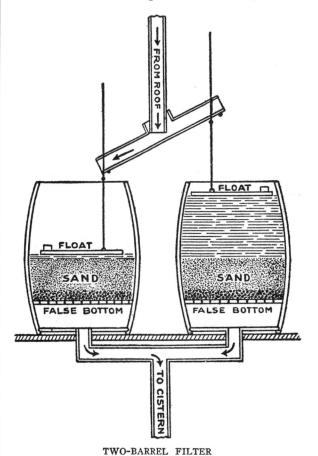

TWO-BARREL FILTER

perforated false bottom, are set side by side beneath the water spout from the roof and connected with a pipe leading to the cistern. Above the false bottoms fine gravel and then sand are packed to the depth of 8 or more inches. On top of the sand rest stout floats as large as can be let down into the barrels. From near the margin of the floats two heavy wires extend vertically upward about 2 feet to engage loosely near their centers with a tilting spout by means of knobs on both the ends of the spout and the wires.

When the barrels are empty the floats rest on the sand. As the water begins to pour in one barrel it strikes the float, but is prevented from gouging a very deep hole at the outside of the barrel by striking a strip of wood about 1 inch high, 2 inches wide and 1 foot long. This spreads the flow. A layer of gravel at this place would also help prevent gouging. If the flow is too great to filter away readily, the float will rise and the knob on the wire will engage with the spout, which will be tilted until the flow will suddenly start into the other barrel. If the delivery pipe to the cistern be large enough there should be no danger of either barrel overflowing. When the sand becomes dirty a few minutes will serve to remove it and put in fresh. This will insure clean water in the cistern, and greatly reduce the number of times the disagreeable job of cleaning out the cistern must be done.

DOG POWER FOR PUMP

This sketch shows an arrangement for making use of the dog for carrying water. It simply consists of a wheel 8 feet in diameter and 18 inches wide, with room enough inside for the dog to walk around, where he acts as a tread power, which causes the pump to revolve. In southern California there are a number of these dog-power pumps, which cost less than $15. A good-sized dog can easily earn his living in an arrangement of this kind.

DOG POWER PUMPING DEVICE

By the 1870s portable well-drilling equipment was in widespread use. The earliest well-digging rigs were hand- or horse-powered; by the 1880s steam-powered rigs using boring augers were common. These rigs were often operated by threshermen, who already had steam traction engines, as a way to keep busy in the off-season.

Well-digging machines could reach depths of a hundred feet and bore holes as wide as twelve inches. The more usual standard was twenty to thirty feet, the depth from which a hand pump could lift water. By the 1870s, cast-iron hand pumps were in widespread use.

Anti-Freezing Well Pump.

43936 With 4 feet set length as in cut. This is a light but durable pump for use in well of ordinary depth. The set length is wrought iron and connected under spout. Prices are for pump with iron cylinder. Average weight, 60 lbs.

No.	Cylinder.	For pipe.		Price.
1	2¼ in.	1 in.	each	$2.95
2	2½ in.	1¼ in.	each	3.15
3	2¾ in.	1¼ in.	each	3.25
4	3 in.	1¼ in.	each	3.40

Anti-Freezing Force Pump.

WITH 4 FOOT SET LENGTH.

43938 This is a good medium priced force pump, with air chamber in top of stock. It is adapted for wells about 30 feet deep, but with the cylinder placed within 15 to 20 feet from the bottom it will do good work in wells 50 to 60 feet deep. Prices are for pumps with iron cylinders. Average weight, 85 lbs.

No.	Clylinder.	For pipe.	Price.
3	2¾ in.	1¼ in.	$4.95
4	3 in.	1¼ in.	5.00
5	3¼ in.	1¼ in.	5.30
6	3½ in.	1½ in.	5.80

Anti-Freezing Force Pump.

WITH 4 FOOT SET LENGTH.

43940 This is a good strong force pump, with air chamber on spout. It is especially adapted for use around gardens, yards and stables, and when located near the house is quite efficient protection against fire. When used as a lift pump, the cap on the air chamber should be unscrewed. With the cylinder properly placed, the pump will work to advanage in wells up to 75 feet deep. Prices are with iron cylinder. Average weight, 100 lbs.

No.	Cylinder.	For pipe.	Price.
3	2¾ in.	1¼ in.	$5.30
4	3 in.	1¼ in.	5.35
6	3¼ in.	1¼ in.	5.85
5	3½ in.	1½ in.	6.10

Double Acting Force Pump.

43941 The easiest double acting pump on the market. It can be used either in deep or shallow wells by attaching the lower cylinder for deep wells, or detaching the lower cylinder for shallow wells, as shown in cut. For wells 25 feet deep or less the lower cylinder is not required. In deeper wells it must be placed near the bottom of the well and connected to upper cylinder with pipe and rod. This pump is supplied with brass lined cylinder, rubber valve seat, strainer and hose attachment.

No	Cylinder	For pipe	Price for shallow well	Price for deep well
2	2½ in.	1¼		$8.10
4	3 "	1¼	$8.00	8.50

Anti-Freezing Windmill Pump.

WITH 4-FOOT SET LENGTH.

43942 This is a substantial pump for wind mill or hand use. The flat rods fit the top tightly, thus preventing stones and dirt from falling into the pump. It is adapted for either open or dug wells not exceeding 30 feet in depth, but with the cylinder placed within 15 to 20 feet from the bottom, it will do the work in a 75 foot well. Price is with iron cylinder Average weight, 80 lbs.

No.	Cylinder.	For Pipe.	Price.
2	2½ in.	1¼ in.	$3.60
3	2¾ in.	1¼ in.	3.70
4	3 in.	1¼ in.	3.90
5	3¼ in	1¼ in.	4.10
6	3½ in.	1½ in	4.20

Windmill Force Pump.

ANTI-FREEZING, WITH 4-FOOT SET LENGTH.

43944 A very desirable tank pump. The windmill top gives it a direct vertical motion to the plunger, thus wearing the cylinder evenly. It is provided with a brass stuffing box, hose coupling and back outlet. When used as a lift pump, loosen the screw in the air chamber. It has a cock spout, so that water can be forced in tank or discharged at spout. The length of stroke is 6 in. and the average weight is 95 lbs.

No.	Cylinder.	For Pipe.	Price.
2	2½ in.	1¼ in.	$5.80
3	2¾ in.	1¼ in.	5.90
4	3 in.	1¼ in.	6.00
5	3¼ in.	1¼ in.	6.20
6	3½ in.	1½ in.	6.45

We can furnish above pump without cock spout for 50 cent lsess.

Windmill Force Pump.

ANTI-FREEZING, WITH IMPROVED VERTICAL DISTRIBUTING VALVE.

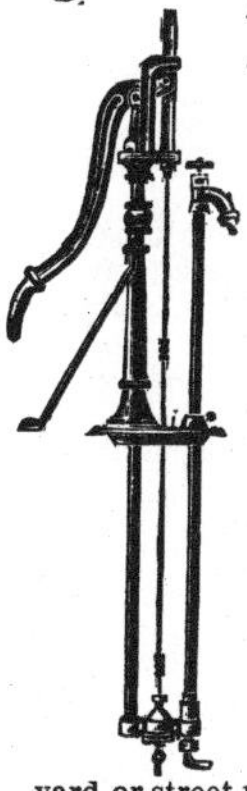

43945 One of the most popular windmill pumps made and can be used in either open, drilled or tubular wells. Its construction insures a heavy stream of water; it is easy of operation, durable and handsome in appearance. Price includes three way cock, hose coupling, and lower elbow coupling. Average weight, 55 pounds.

Price, with 6 inch stroke, each..$7.85
Price, with 10 inch stroke, each 8.65

Hand Force Pump.

EXTRA HEAVY.

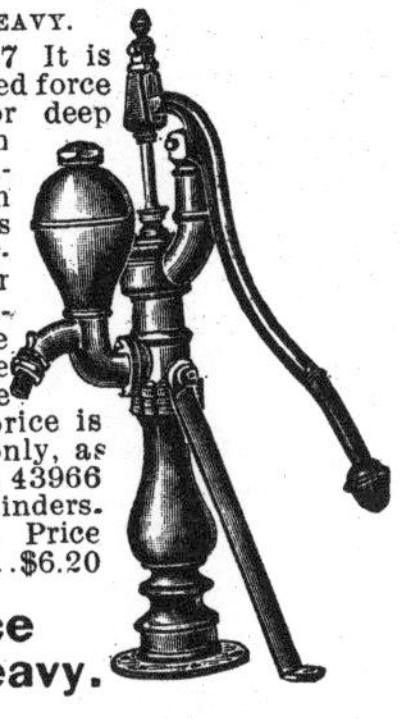

43947 It is an improved force pump for deep wells with air chamber on spout. It is very desirable for yard or street use. To prevent freezing, a drip hole should be drilled in the pipe 3 or 4 feet below the base of the pump. The price is for the pump standard only, as shown in cut. See cut No. 43966 and 43968 for price of cylinders. Average weight, 110 lbs. Price with 7 inch stroke, each...$6.20

Windmill Force Pumps, Extra Heavy.

43950 A very strong, solid pump with double braces, and is adapted for hand or windmill use. It is used mostly for very deep wells, and where a pump receives hard usage. The price is for pump standards only, as shown in cut. See Nos. 43966 and 43968 for cylinders. 6 in. stroke, height 55 in., for pipe 1½ in.

Price $9.60

10 in. stroke, height 59 in., for pipe 2 in.

Price...... .....$10.20

Hydraulic Ram.

Irrigating Lift Pump.

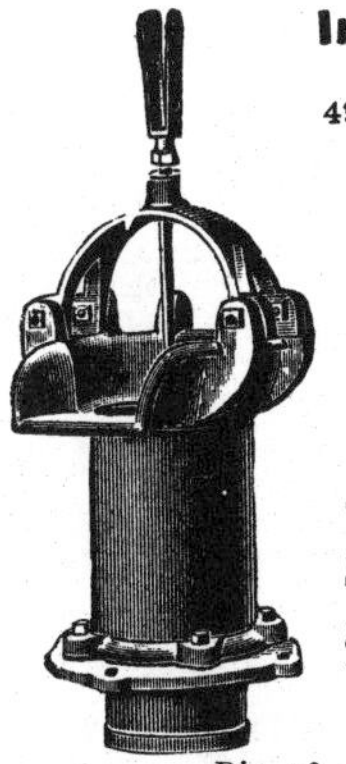

43952 This pump is capable of raising a large quantity of water by means of a wind mill or other power having a vertical motion. The No. 4, has a 10-inch stroke, 8½-inch cylinder, and a capacity of 2½ gallons per stroke. A wind mill having 40 revolutions per minute would raise with this pump 100 gallons per minute, 6,000 gallons per hour, 144,000 per day, supposing the wind to be blowing steadily at the proper speed. Four acres of land could be irrigated per day with such an outfit at the rate of 36,000 gallons to the acre. This pump is not suitable for lifting over 25 feet vertically. In deeper wells would suggest the use of our *Irrigating Cylinders.*

No.	Dia. of Cylinder	Capacity Per stroke.	Price. each.
2	6	1½ gal.	$10.75
4	8½	2½ gal.	12.25

Irrigating Cylinders.

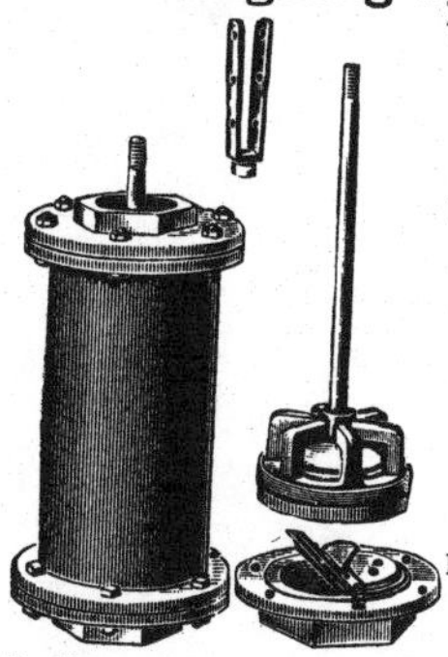

43953 This is a new iron cylinder which was recently designed for pumping large quantities of water from either shallow or deep wells.

It can be operated by wind mill or other power and is adapted for any stroke up to 12 inches. When used as a lift pump only, no pump head is required, it is only necessary to place a TEE at end of discharge pipe, which will allow the water to flow to the irrigating ditches.

Prices are for cylinder complete, with forked rod coupling, for wood rod as shown in cut.

Inside Dia.	Length.	Stroke.	Fitted for	Cap for Stroke.	Price.
6 in.	18 in.	12 in.	3 in.	1¼ gal.	$ 6.75
8 in,	18 in.	12 in.	4 in.	2¼ gal.	10.25
10 in.	18 in.	12 in.			13.80

Spiral Earth Augers.

43955 For boring wells. Strong and well made. Prices given are for either style shown in cut.

Size.	Price, each.
2½ in.	$2.75
3 in.	3.10
4 in.	4.25
5 in.	6.10
6 in.	11.20

Pitcher Spout Pumps.

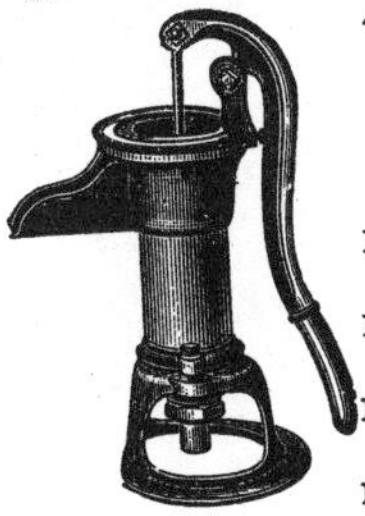

43959 This pump is extra heavy and well finished, polished cylinders and patent closed top, which prevents the water from flying up when pumped; is anti-freezing, and fitted for 1¼ inch pipe; either lead or iron.

No. 1, 2½ inch bore. Weight, 21¼ lbs., for 1-inch pipe. Price, each........ .....$1.05

No. 2, 3-inch bore. Weight 23½ lbs., for 1¼-inch pipe. Price, each $1.20

No. 3, 3½-inch bore. Weight, 26¾ lbs., for 1¼-inch pipe. Price, each....... .....$1.25

No. 4, 4-inch bore Weight, 31 lbs., for 1½-inch pipe. Price, each..............$1.45

Average weight, 30 lbs.

43960 Pitcher Spout Pump, with closed top and spout; can be used either right or left handed and is fitted with couplings for iron or lead pipe.

No. 1, 2½-inch cylinder; weight, 21 lbs., for 1 inch pipe. Price, each...............$1.25

No. 2, 3-inch cylinder; weight, 23 lbs., for 1¼ inch pipe. Price, each........... 1.35

No. 3, 3½-inch cylinder; weight, 26 lbs., for 1¼ inch pipe. Price, each 1.50

No. 4, 4-inch cylinder; weight 31 lbs., for 1½ inch pipe. Price, each..................... 1.75

Average weight, 35 pounds.

Standard Wrought Iron Pipe. Black and Galvanized.

FOR STEAM, GAS AND WATER.

The following prices are for pipe coupled and threaded in random length; that is, in pieces as they come from the mills, which range from 16 feet to 20 feet each. When ordering pipe cut to exact lengths, always make allowance for cutting and threading.

Prices subject to change of market without notice. Orders will be filled at all times at correct market rates.

43964 Black Iron Pipe.
43965 Galvanized Iron Pipes.

Size inside diameter	Black. Price per foot.	Galvanized, Price per foot.	For cutting extra threads per cut.	Approximate weight, per foot. Pounds.
⅛ in.	$0.02½	..	$0.04	.24
¼ in.	.03	$0.03¼	.05	.42
⅜ in.	.03	.03½	.04	.56
½ in.	.03¼	.04½	.04	.84
¾ in.	.03½	.05	.05	1.12
1 in.	.05	.07	.05	1.67
1¼in.	.06	.09	.06	2.24
1½in.	.07½	.12	.08	2.68
2 in.	.10	.14	.10	3.61
2½in.	.15	.22	.10	5.74
3 in.	.18	.28	.15	7.54
3½in.	.24	.35	.20	9.00
4 in.	.26	.45	.30	10.64

Iron Well Cylinders.

43966 Always state for what size pipe you wish cylinders fitted. In case you mention no size we will send them for 1¼ inch pipe. The 10 and 12 inch cylinders have 6-inch strok, and the 14-inch cylinder has an 8-inch stroke.

Diameter.	10 inches long.	12 inches long.	14 inches long.
2 in	$0.85	$1.00	$1.35
2¼ in......	.93	1.35	1.45
2½ in......	1.00	1.40	1.50
2¾ in......	1.10	1.45	1.60
3 in......	1.20	1.60	1.75
3¼ in......	1.25	1.75	1.85
3½ in......	1.30	1.85	2.00
4 in......	1.50	2.10	2.45

Seamless Brass Well Cylinder.

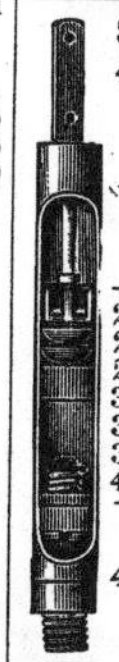

43967 Made with seamless brass body, iron caps and plunger. The 10-inch cylinders have 6-inch stroke; the 12 and 14-inch cylinders have 8-inch stroke.

Diameter.	10 in. long. Each.	12 in. long. Each.	14 in. long. Each.
2¼ in.........	$2.20	$2.50	$2.70
2½ in.........	2.40	2.60	2.85
2¾ in.........	2.60	2.70	2.90
3 in.........	2.70	2.85	2.00
3¼ in.........	2.90	3.00	3.15
3½ in.........	3.10	3.20	3.35
4 in.........	3.85	4.10	4.20

Tubular Well Cylinders.

43968

43968 This cylinder is used chiefly in deep wells, and is intended to slip inside of the pipe after the well is completed. It can be fastened at any point desired and is easily withdrawn for repairs. Prices given are for brass body cylinders and valves complete as shown in cut. Not made smaller than for 2-inch pipe.

Sizs, 2-inch. Each....... .. ..$2.40
" 2½-inch. Each.......... .... 4.00
" 3-inch. Each....................... 5.75

43970 Foot Valve and Strainer, for 1¼ inch pipe. Weight, 2 pounds, 15 ounces. Each.......... .... $0.45

43971 Foot valve for 1½ inch pipe; weight, 4½ lbs. Each $0.55

Drive Well Points.

43972 Made of wrought iron pipe, perforated and galvanized; covered with a brass jacket of No. 60 GAUZE. This is the point in common use; we can furnish points with finer GAUZE for quicksand, etc. Prices on same will be furnished on application.

Diameter.	Length.	Each.
1¼ in.	24 in.	$0.95
1¼ in.	30 in.	1.10
1¼ in.	36 in.	1.30
1¼ in.	42 in.	1.50
1½ in.	30 in.	1.35
1½ in.	36 in.	1.70
2 in.	36 in.	2 30
2 in	48 in.	3.30

43974 Lead pipe. Price per pound............$0.06½

We can furnish lead pipe any size at the above price. In ordering always give the diameter and length wanted, not the weight.

Average weight, per foot, 1 inch, 2 lbs., 8 oz.
Average weight, per foot, 1¼ inch, 3 lbs.
Average weight, per foot, 1½ inch, 4 lbs.

43975 Sheet Lead. Price, per pound..........$0.06½

Rubber Bucket Chain Pumps.

43981 Rubber Bucket Chain Pump, complete for well 10 feet deep..............$3.50
43982 Rubber Bucket Chain Pump, complete for well 12 feet deep.... ....$3.60
43983 Rubber Bucket Chain Pump, complete for wells 18 feet deep..............$4.00
43984 Rubber Bucket Chain Pump, complete for wells 18 feet deep..............$4.35
43985 Rubber Bucket Chain Pump, complete for well 20 feet deep.... ....$5.50
We would not advise the use of chain pumps for deeper wells than 20 feet.

43986 Rubber Buckets for chain pumps.
Each........................$0.08
Per dozen... .. .. .69

Wood Pumps.

Made of good selected stock, neatly painted and decorated Outside measurement of pumps is 6x6 inches with 3½-in bore.

43987—

Length.	Price with plain cylinder.	Price with porcelain lined cylinder.
6 feet....	$2.50	$3.25
7 "	3.75	3.50
8 "	3.00	3.75
10 "	3.50	4.25

43988 Wood Suction Pipe. Steam tested—to fit above pumps: 4x4-in. pipe, 1¾-in. bore, 3½ tenons at 8c. per ft.
Price is for wood pipe in 12 ft. lengths and under.

M. W. & Co's Improved water Purifying Pumps, the buckets passing down into the water full of air aereates and purifies it. It always furnishes the water from the bottom of the well, as no water enters the cups until they begin to rise at the bottom. No suckers or valves or wooden tubing to rot or get rusty; buckets are made of galvanized iron; only good for dug wells.

43993 Complete for 10 foot well........................$6.00
43994 Complete for 15 foot well...................... 7.00
43995 Complete for 20 foot well...................... 8.20
43996 Complete for 25 foot well...................... 9.30
43997 Complete for 30 foot well................. 10.53

WINDMILLS

The self-governing vaned windmill was perfected in 1854 and began to come into widespread use in the 1870s. By the 1880s, windmills on tall pipe towers had become a common feature of the rural landscape, especially on the windswept Great Plains. They remained popular for decades. A typical windmill with an eight-foot wheel generated about three-quarters horsepower; a larger twelve-foot wheel could get up to about one and a half horsepower. By the early 1900s, gasoline-powered pump jacks were used to raise water when the wind died away.

TO THE FARMERS OF AMERICA

And all Whom it may Concern:

THE EMPIRE WIND MILL MANUFACTURING CO.

OF SYRACUSE, N. Y.

Solicit your careful attention to their SELF-REGULATING, STORM-DEFYING WIND MILL, as a LABOR SAVING POWER for farm purposes, particularly for Pumping Water.

All allow this to be one of the most tedious performances connected with farm labor, and hundreds of farmers might and would keep more stock, could they be watered by a living spring at the surface of the ground.

This can now be brought about, for long and patient effort has overcome the most serious objections to Wind Mills, as heretofore constructed, and this most economical power in the world is made available; so we are fully prepared to sell, erect and warrant our machines, and adapt them to all possible situations, so as to give entire and lasting satisfaction.

Send for circulars, containing further information and testimonials, and after that, if you still doubt, write us:

I. The depth of your well.

II. The least depth of water ever known in it.

III. The height above the platform of the well to where you wish the water discharged.

IV. The lateral or side distance, if any.

V. The amount or quantity of water wanted, or at least the number of cattle to be supplied.

VI. The height at which the Mill must be erected to secure a free current of air, with all other particulars—and see if we will not give you a fair chance to TEST the Mill on your own premises till you become satisfied we have told you the truth.

Price of Mills at the Factory:

	No. 0.	No. 1.	No. 2.	No. 3.	No. 5.	No. 6.
	$75.00	100.00	150.00	300.00	700.00	1200.00
Boxing,	2.50	3.00	3.50	5.00	12.00	25.00

Pumps from $5.00 upwards. Pipe, &c., at manufacturers' list prices. WE CAN GIVE YOU WHAT YOU NEED.

Address,

EMPIRE WIND MILL MFG. CO.

SYRACUSE, N. Y.

NOTE.—I have seen several of the above named Wind Mills at work, and many testimonials highly recommending them, from Railway managers, using them at their water stations, as well as from farmers, manufacturers, and others. I have full confidence in recommending them to all stock breeders and farmers needing such machines, as an economical and highly valuable labor-saving apparatus,
L. F. ALLEN.

By the early years of the 1900s stationary gasoline engines replaced some windmills as power for the pump, but it wasn't until rural electrification in the 1930s that most windmills were replaced with electric pumps. Although today there are no American windmill manufacturers, many of these durable artifacts—sturdy survivors of decades of blizzards and tornadoes—remain in use filling stock tanks.

By 1900, wells, pumps, cisterns and filters were well understood. The importance of water purity was widely grasped, and much effort was expended in making wells and cisterns clean and safe. A labor-saving indoor hand pump in the kitchen was now commonplace. Prosperous farms near large towns, where parts and plumbers could be found, often had hot and cold running water throughout the house.

WATER SUPPLY FOR FARMHOUSE

Farmers can have running water, hot or cold, in their dwelling houses at a cost of fifty dollars and up, depending upon the size of the house and the kind of equipment needed. This makes possible the bath and toilet room, protection from fire, the easy washing of windows and walks, the sprinkling of lawns, the irrigating of gardens, and all the other conveniences which a few years ago were thought possible only in cities, where big water systems were available. This is one of the things that makes farm life attractive. It lessens the work in the house, insures a fine lawn and garden, reduces danger from fire, adds greatly to the comfort and convenience in every direction.

The way to secure this is to install a water supply system, with a pressure tank in the basement. This pressure tank is so arranged that by pumping it full under strong air pressure the water is forced all over the house, and is available for the bathroom, toilet room and the garden or fire hose. The water is distributed about the house exactly as it is in city homes, by means of galvanized iron pipes. Where a small building is to be supplied and the amount of water to be used is not large, the system can be installed for $50. For the average house $90 is a better figure. Where the house is large, and where considerable amounts of water are needed for the lawn and garden, and possibly also for washing carriages, automobiles and horses, a larger system should be installed, costing up to $150.

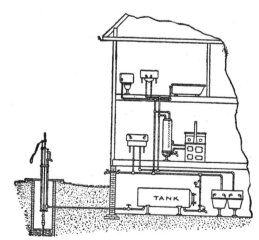

HOUSE WATER SYSTEM

PART II:
Agricultural Machinery

CHAPTER 4

TILLING

Tillage—preparing the soil for seeding—was of paramount importance to the farmer. The goal of tillage was to produce soil that was broken up into a uniform texture to a uniform depth, which varied according to the nature of the soil and the desired crop. Tillage also plowed under weeds as well as manure and manure crops such as clover, which added to the soil's fertility. By the 1800s, farmers were also well aware that proper tillage was important for retaining moisture in the soil. Tillage methods such as contour plowing also helped reduce erosion from wind and water.

PLOWS

The plow is the most basic of tillage implements. Iron-tipped wooden plows were used from antiquity until well into the 1800s. Plows made entirely from chilled iron, which was very hard and durable, were first developed in both England and the United States in the early 1800s, but they didn't start to catch on until the 1820s. Farmers were often resistant, clinging to the superstitious belief that pulling so much iron through the soil would somehow poison it. The clear superiority of the chilled iron plow eventually won out.

A crucial advance in plow design came in 1837, when John Deere built a steel plow from an old saw in Grand Detour, Illinois. Although Deere was not the first to experiment with the concept of a steel plow, his design was the most successful. It arrived just as American farmers were in urgent need of a stronger plow to break through the heavier soils of the Midwest. Deere's firm quickly became and remained one of the leading farm implement manufacturers.

From ancient times until the late 1800s, the farmer walked behind the plow to guide it. The first sulky or riding plow, a wheeled plow with a seat for the farmer, came along only in the 1860s. The design was unpopular. Farmers were justifiably concerned about adding to the draft of their horses and by the expense and complexity of the new style. In 1875, however, an improved design made sulky plows more practical, and by the mid-1880s a number of designs were being manufactured. The gangplow, with two or more moldboards, also came into use in the 1880s. Sulky plows usually required two or three horses; gangplows were pulled by four. The disk plow was just starting to come into use by the turn of the century; its true value would become apparent only when tractors became routine.

PATENT CYLINDER PLOW,

WITH SKIM, OR SUBSOIL ATTACHMENT.

THIS Plow derives its name from the form of the mold-board, which is a segment of a perfect cylinder, with its ends cut in the style of ordinary mold-boards. Its lines are thus always horizontal to the surface of the land, and consequently it turns the furrow-slice with the same uniformity as a wheel on its axle, and with the least possible friction. The friction is still further reduced by the peculiar arrangement of the share and land side, which, combined with its other improvements, reduces the draught from one-fourth to one-third less than that required by the best class of Plows now in general use.

For lightness of draught, simplicity of construction, ease of holding, and certainty of turning all soils of any required depth and width, it far surpasses any other Plow.

All the sizes are capable of turning either flat or lap furrows, of any required lap, by using shares suited to various widths, all of which can be supplied; and every furrow may be left concave on the under, and convex on the upper side, which gives the lightest and most friable condition to the soil, admitting of easy and thorough pulverization by a light harrow or cultivator.

This front plow can be raised or lowered to turn any required depth of upper furrow, or it can be removed entirely, at the pleasure of the operator.

We have 137 distinct sizes and varieties of Plows on our Price List, and most of the larger ones are arranged with fin or wrought cutters, wheels and draft rods, as may be desired. They are cast iron, polished and half polished, steel, wrought iron, &c., embracing everything required for sward and fallow plowing, cultivating, deep trenching, subsoiling, &c.

☞ Send for Price List for particulars.

R. H. ALLEN & CO.,

P. O Box 376.   189 *and* 191 *Water Street, New York.*

Steel and chilled cast-iron walking plows are built in a great variety of styles to meet a wide variety of soil conditions. Fig. 24 illustrates and names the parts of a general-purpose walking plow. Other types of walking plows are similarly constructed.

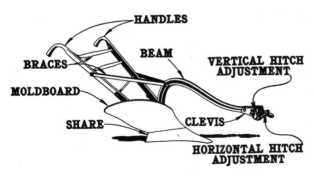

Figure 24—Common type of walking plow with important parts named.

FIG. 43—A MODERN CHILLED WALKING PLOW WITH JOINTER AND GAUGE WHEEL

THE CHILLED PLOW

In many places, especially in the eastern United States, many of the plows used are of chilled cast iron. A chilled plow with an interchangeable point is shown in Fig. 43. Chilled plows are very hard, but will not scour in all soils. The share can only be ground to an edge when dull, or it may be replaced at a small cost.

FIG. 33—THE MODERN STEEL WALKING PLOW WITH STEEL BEAM AND MOLD-BOARD FOR STUBBLE OR OLD GROUND

THE MODERN STEEL WALKING PLOW

Fig. 34 shows the modern steel walking plow suitable for the prairie soils. The parts are numbered in the illustration as follows:

1. Cutting edge or share. The *point* is the part of the share which penetrates the ground, and the *heel* or *wing* is the outside corner. A share welded to the landside is a *bar* share, while one that is independent is a *slip* share.

2. Moldboard: The part by which the furrow is turned. The *shin* is the lower forward corner.

3. Landside: The part receiving the side pressure produced when the furrow is turned. A plate of steel covers the

FIG. 34—AN UNDER VIEW OF THE MODERN STEEL PLOW, SHOWING ITS CONSTRUCTION

landside bar, furnishing the wearing surface. When used for old ground, the plow is usually constructed with the bar welded to the frog, forming the foundation to which the other parts are attached. Landsides may be classed as high, medium, and low.

4. Frog: The foundation to which are attached the share, moldboard, and landside.

5. Brace.

6. Beam: May be of wood or steel. The beam in a wooden-beam plow is joined to the plow by a beam standard.

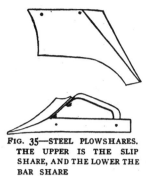

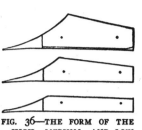

FIG. 35—STEEL PLOWSHARES. THE UPPER IS THE SLIP SHARE, AND THE LOWER THE BAR SHARE

FIG. 36—THE FORM OF THE HIGH, MEDIUM, AND LOW LANDSIDES FOR WALKING PLOWS

7. Clevis, or hitch for the adjustment of the plow.

8. Handles: The handles are joined to the beam by braces.

THE MODERN SULKY PLOW

The name sulky plow is used for all wheel plows, but applies more particularly to single plows, while the name *gang* is given to double or larger plows. Fig. 38 illustrates the typical sulky plow, and reference is made to its various parts by number:

1. The moldboard, share, frog or frame, and landside is called the plow *bottom*. Most sulky plows are made with inter-

---

70452 M. W. & Co.'s Full Chilled Plows. In all sections where chilled plows are used, our plows will be readily recognized, and our price on plows and repairs appreciated. See the following prices;

Plows—Continued.

	Turns furrow, inches.	Depth of furrow.	Weight, pounds.	Price.
A Right	8	4½	50	$3.60
B Right	10	5	65	4.80
10 Right	11	5½	70	5.25
13 Right or left	11	6	80	6.00
19 Right or left	12	6½	100	6.25
20 Right or left	14	7	112	6.50
E1 Right or left	14	7	125	6.75
40 Right or left	16	9	130	6.75
Price of jointer				1.50
Lead wheel and standard				1.00

70453 Price of repairs for the Oliver Chilled Plows, warranted to fit any of the chilled plows we send out.

Be sure and state whether plows or shares are wanted to turn furrow to the right or to the left.

		Right.	Standard.	Moldboard.	Lan'side	Shares, plain
A	"		$0.95	$0.95	$0.30	$0.20
B	"		1.13	1.32	.45	.20
10			1.50	1.50	.45	.25
13	Right or left		1.68	1.68	.50	25
19	"		1.68	1.88	.56	25
20	"		1.68	2.10	.56	25
E1	"		1.88	2.25	.56	25
40	"		1.88	2.25	.56	.25

Jointer Points, 15c. Moldboards, 40c.

70454 Breaking Plow, solid cast steel mold board; share unhardened, but of high natural temper, wood beam furnished with gauge wheel, rolling coulter, patent three-horse adjustable clevis, extra share.

Size, inches	12	14	16
Weight, lbs.	130	148	155
Each	$10.00	11.00	13.00

70455 Sod Breakers, steel beam, 2 shares, 2 fine cutters, gauge iron. 12 in. $5.75; 14 in. $6.00; 16 in. $6.25.

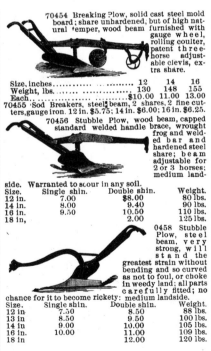

70456 Stubble Plow, wood beam, capped standard welded handle brace, wrought frog and welded bar and hardened steel share; beam adjustable for 2 or 3 horses; medium landside. Warranted to scour in any soil.

Size.	Single shin.	Double shin.	Weight.
12 in.	7.00	$8.00	80 lbs.
14 in.	8.00	9.40	90 lbs.
16 in.	9.50	10.50	110 lbs.
18 in,		2.00	125 lbs.

0458 Stubble Plow, steel beam, very strong, will stand the greatest strain without bending and so curved as not to foul, or choke in weedy land; all parts carefully fitted; no chance for it to become rickety; medium landside.

Size.	Single shin.	Double shin.	Weight.
12 in	7.50	8.50	88 lbs.
13 in	8.50	9.50	100 lbs.
14 in	9.00	10.00	105 lbs.
16 in	10.00	11.00	109 lbs.
18 in		12.00	120 lbs.

70460 Brush or Timber Land Plow, also used as a road plow, works well in all kinds of land. Strong and durable, all steel.

11 inch, 83 lbs. $7.75	13 inch, 100 lbs.....$ 9.00
12 inch, 88 lbs...... 8.12	

Subsoil Plows.

70461 Indispensable for fruit culture and deep cultivation; should be used on every farm.

Weight 90 lbs.
Cast points......................$8.00

Light All-Steel Plows.

70463 Designed for either stubble or light sod, doing both kinds of work in the most perfect manner; very light draft; scours in any soil. Is also adapted to the cultivation of corn, cotton, and fruit orchards. This plow does decidedly more work than its width of cut would indicate. Has a curved steel standard and cap, an extra steel share furnished with every one of these plows.

	Price.
Pony, 7 inch share, 10½ moldboard, 38 lbs.	$3.00
A. O.. 8 inch share, 11 moldboard, 42 lbs.	3.50
B. O., 9 inch share, 12 moldboard, 50 lbs.	4.25
C. O., 9 inch share, 14 moldboard, 60 lbs.	5.00
D. O., 9½ inch share, 15½ moldboard, 65 lbs.	5.50

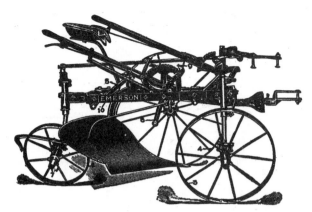

FIG. 38—THE MODERN FOOT-LIFT BEAM-HITCH SULKY PLOW WITH STEEL PLOW BOTTOM

changeable bottoms, so it is possible to use the same carriage for various classes of work by using suitable bottoms.

2 and 3 are the *rear* and the *front furrow wheels*, respectively. These wheels are set at an angle with the vertical in order that they may carry to better advantage the side pressure of the plow due to turning the furrow slice.

4. The largest wheel traveling upon the unplowed land is spoken of as the *land wheel*.

5. The connections between the plow beam and the frame are called the *bails*.

6. A rod called the *weed hook* is provided to collect the tops of high vegetation.

7. Practically all wheel plows are now provided with *inclosed wheel boxes*, which exclude all dirt and carry a large supply of grease. The inclosed wheel box has a collar which excludes the dirt at the axle end of the wheel box, and has the other end entirely inclosed with a cap. The grease is usually stored in the cap, which is made detachable from the hub.

8. Wheel plows are now generally provided with a *foot lift*, by which the plow is lifted out and forced into the ground.

9. For plowing in stony ground, it is necessary to set the plow to float, so that in case a stone is struck the plow will be free to be thrown out of the ground without lifting the carriage, otherwise the plowman will be thrown from his seat and the plow damaged.

10. The various parts of the sulky plow are usually attached to the *frame*, and this is an important part in the construction of the plow. Not all sulky plows, however, are made with a frame.

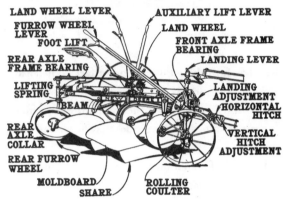

Figure 29—Two-bottom foot-lift gang plow with important parts named.

FIG. 39—THE MODERN GANG PLOW

FIG. 46—A DISK GANG PLOW TO BE OPERATED BY HORSE POWER

HITCHING WALKING PLOWS

The proper adjustment of the hitch is the most important factor in the operation of a plow. The kind of work a walking plow will do, its draft, and its handling qualities depend to a great extent upon the correct relation between power and load.

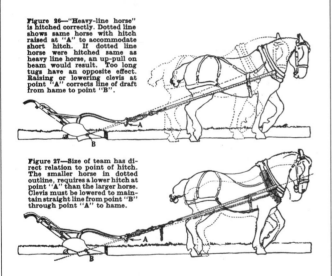

Figure 26—"Heavy-line horse" is hitched correctly. Dotted line shows same horse with hitch raised at "A" to accommodate short hitch. If dotted line horse were hitched same as heavy line horse, an up-pull on beam would result. Too long tugs have an opposite effect. Raising or lowering clevis at point "A" corrects line of draft from hame to point "B".

Figure 27—Size of team has direct relation to point of hitch. The smaller horse in dotted outline, requires a lower hitch at point "A" than the larger horse. Clevis must be lowered to maintain straight line from point "B" through point "A" to hame.

By following a few simple rules, the most inexperienced can adjust his plow to run right. The most important rule to observe is this: the point of hitch should be on a straight line drawn from center of load to the center of power when plow is at work.

Fig. 26 shows the effect of long and short tugs on the work of a plow and the adjustments necessary to get correct working position of the hitch. Fig. 27 illustrates the changes necessary in the vertical or up-and-down hitch to accommodate horses of different sizes. The correct vertical hitch of walking plows is necessary to smooth running, correct depth, and the comfort of man and beast.

The horizontal adjustment of walking-plow hitches is comparatively easy, provided the doubletree is about the right length and the share is properly set. If a right-hand plow is not taking enough land, the clevis may be moved one or two notches to the right; if taking too much land, an adjustment of one or two notches to the left will bring the desired results. A left-hand plow is adjusted in an exactly opposite manner.

PLOWING

Plowing on rough ground, with horses which are fit for anything else, is, at best, a painful necessity. There is occasionally to be found a stylish carriage team, or a pair of fast trotters which will work like oxen at the plow; but generally horses of spirit will become impatient under the frequent interruption caused by stones, or by the frequent turning necessary in small fields, while the harness generally used for this work is neither comfortable nor complete. In large fields, free from obstructions, horses may very properly be used, as they are more pleasant to work with than oxen; but in rough work the latter are preferable, being by temper and structure much better adapted to such work than horses.

Horses are frequently driven to the plow with the single line, or with a pair of lines fastened to the outer rings of each horse's bit, the inside rings being connected by a short line passing from one to the other. This will do very well for quiet, well-trained animals, in good ground; but with horses at all inclined to be unruly or impatient, or working in soft or stony ground, we should use the same sort of reins as in driving on the road, thus giving a fair hold of each horse's head.

Horses used for this work should be taught to stop instantly at the word, to start promptly and together, and to

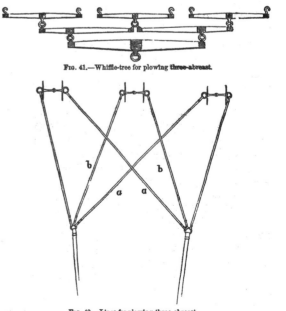

FIG. 41.—Whiffle-tree for plowing three-abreast.

FIG. 42.—Lines for plowing three-abreast.

pull evenly. The team should be brought quickly around at the turns and headlands, and made to take their places as actively as possible for the new furrow; but they should not be started, if at all blown, until they are fully ready to go to the end of it without stopping, unless, indeed, it be a very long, or a very hard one.

It is the opinion, apparently a good one, of the best farmers of the present day, that no two horses are strong enough to turn such a furrow as is necessary for the proper cultivation of the soil, and they recommend that three or four be used. Assuming this to be the case, it should be remembered that three horses working abreast will pull nearly as much on a plow as will four geared in the ordinary way,—that is, the third horse, from being fastened within three or four feet of the plow, would have nearly as much power to draw it as would two horses drawing it from a distance of from fifteen to twenty feet.

Fig. 41 represents the best form of whiffle-tree for three horses plowing abreast. Fig. 42 is an arrangement for the lines for plowing with such a team, which will be found effective for horses which are inclined to pull irregularly, before being sufficiently broken, but as soon as they understand it, the lines marked *a* and *b* may be dispensed with. Indeed, intelligent horses will soon learn to work entirely without lines.

The satisfactory performance of a riding plow depends to a great extent upon correct hitching. If both horizontal and vertical hitch adjustments are correct, the plow will run smoother, pull lighter, and do a better job of plowing than when carelessly hitched.

Fig. 34 illustrates the correct up-and-down adjustment on the vertical clevis. The correct hitch at "A" is the place where "A" is in a true line between "B" and point of hitch at the hame. When plowing deep or using tall horses, hitch at "A" should be higher than when plowing shallow or using small horses. When hitching horses strung out, the hitch at "A" must be lower than when using four horses abreast.

Figure 34—Illustrating the correct vertical hitch for riding plows. Straight line from center of draft, "B", to center of power at hame, passes through point of hitch at "A".

HARROWS

Once the land was plowed, the harrow was used to pulverize the soil further and smooth it out. This important step broke up lumps and removed air pockets. Before the seed drill came into widespread use, the harrow was also used to cover the seeds after they had been dropped into the soil.

The earliest harrows were branches or small trees either dragged directly over the soil or attached to a simple wooden frame and then dragged. Brush harrows remained in use for a surprisingly long time.

By the 1880s, a number of harrow designs were in use. The most common was a simple smoothing harrow with iron teeth in a wooden or iron frame; the angle and depth of the teeth were adjustable. The spring-tooth harrow was designed for use on rocky or stubbly ground; when the teeth caught on an obstacle they sprung back and released. The disk harrow was a row of circular blades, usually fourteen or sixteen inches in diameter. Disk harrows were heavy and became widely used only after tractors replaced horses.

A BRUSH
HARROW

For the cultivation of various kinds of crops, one of the most useful implements made on the farm, and one which properly constructed, lasts a lifetime, is a smoothing and brush harrow, figure 54. It should be made of rather heavy stuff, so that the weight, as it is dragged along, will be sufficient to break the lumps and level the soil. This harrow can be used with good effect in covering newly planted seed, and in all cases where a disc or tooth harrow would be too heavy or wide-spread, a brush harrow, like that herewith represented, will be found to be a good substitute.

Fig. 54.—BRUSH HARROW.

AN IMPROVED HARROW FRAME

Figure 55 shows a very cheap and excellent harrow frame intended for grass seeding; also for working corn and potato land while the crop is young and small. For this purpose, a harrow should be light, broad, have a large number of fine

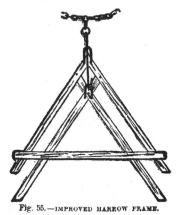

Fig. 55.—IMPROVED HARROW FRAME.

teeth sloping backward, and should be so arranged that it will draw level and not lift at the front. The owner and inventor of this harrow claims that he has secured all these. The special point of this harrow is the hitching device. This consists of a hooked bar which works in two stirrups, one to draw by and the other to permit the draw-bar or chain to rise

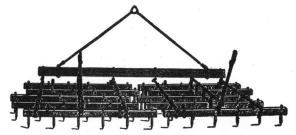

FIG. 50—A WOOD-BAR LEVER SMOOTHING HARROW. A CHEAPER HARROW IS MADE WITH FIXED TEETH AND A WOODEN FRAME

and fall, as the harrow passes over the ground that is not quite level. This is an important end to secure. The harrow is not patented, and any farmer is free to make one.

It will not be possible to illustrate all these forms of harrows. The common *smoothing harrow* is not shown, but a

FIG. 51—A CURVED KNIFE-TOOTH HARROW OR PULVERIZER

lever harrow with wooden bars is shown in Fig. 50. Wooden-frame harrows can be used to better advantage in trashy ground when they are provided with a tooth fastener so

FIG. 52—A RIDING WEEDER

arranged that the teeth will slope backward when drawn from one end. Such teeth may be spoken of as *adjustable*. A curved knife-tooth harrow, sometimes spoken of as a *pulverizer*, is illustrated in Fig. 51. This crushes clods and brings the soil into uniform structure very satisfactorily. The weeder has rather long teeth and is an excellent implement for destroying small weeds, and also to form a dust mulch and a fine tilth. The cultivator tooth has the point flattened, and is curved so as to penetrate the ground more readily. Often it is aided in passing over obstacles by being held in place with a *spring*.

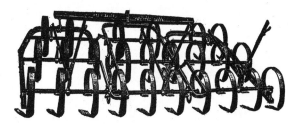

FIG. 53—A SPRING-TOOTH LEVER HARROW

THE SPRING-TOOTH HARROW

This harrow is illustrated in Fig. 53. When the teeth are caught on any obstacle they spring back and are released, this fact making it a very useful implement for stony ground. It is also an excellent pulverizer.

SPIKE-TOOTH HARROWS

Fig. 64 shows a popular style of spike-tooth harrow. The operation and adjustment of a harrow of this type are comparatively simple, there being no field adjustment other than setting the slant of the teeth with the levers provided. This adjustment is governed entirely by field conditions.

Each tooth of this harrow is held between the two notched, semi-oval frame bars by the heavy bolt which creates a tension, thereby locking the tooth to position and preventing the nut from coming loose. When one side of the tooth becomes worn, the nut may be loosened and the tooth turned to present a new cutting edge. Teeth may also be removed for sharpening.

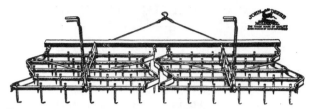

Figure 64—Spike-tooth harrow, with detail above showing how tooth is locked between bars.

Harrows.
Shipped second-class freight.

We sell a fine line of harrows, both wood and steel frames, with ridged, adjustable and spring teeth. See our Agricultural Implement Catalogue for descriptions and illustrations.

70368 Three Section Vibrating Harrow, oak beams and spools, 45 half inch square steel teeth; nine beams in three sections. Draw bar connected with chains.

We furnish extra teeth to either of the above harrows at 3½ cents each. Teeth are ½-inch steel, 9 inches long; no other size furnished. Sections have 4 bars, 20 teeth to a section.

	Feet.	Weight.	Price.
A 194, 1 section, 20 teeth, cuts	3½	50 lbs.	$ 2.50
A 195, 2 sections, 40 teeth, cuts.	7	100 lbs.	5.00
A 196, 3 sections, 60 teeth, cuts	10½	150 lbs.	7.50
A 197, 4 sections, 80 teeth, cuts.	14	200 lbs.	10.00

Our Adjustable Frame Lever Harrow.

The rails are made of channel steel, very light and very strong. The teeth can be easily taken out to change the teeth or reverse them, but cannot come out in ordinary use. This harrow has bars passing on the under side of the beams, which makes it very strong and forms a truss that makes the frame rigid.

Teeth can be set slanting at any angle or perpendicular, as desired, and can be reversed.

Three sections to any one of our harrows costs one-half more than two sections. Four sections cost twice as much as two sections. Drawbar furnished to match number of sections ordered.

	Feet.	Weight.	Price.
A 186, 1 section, 32 teeth, cuts	5	100 lbs.	$ 4.25
A 187, 2 sections, 64 teeth, cuts	10	200 lbs.	8.50
A 188, 3 sections, 96 teeth, cuts	15	300 lbs.	12.75
A 189, 4 sections, 20 teeth, cuts	20	400 lbs.	17.00

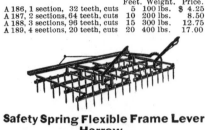

Safety Spring Flexible Frame Lever Harrow.
Shipped second-class freight.

70371 The teeth to this harrow can be set at any angle. By means of the safety springs, however, the teeth will give back to clear roots, stones and other obstructions.

This harrow can be changed so as to dispense with the spring when occasion requires, and then operates precisely like No. 70369. To do this a pin is changed from hold in front of casting to hole through the casting, thus giving the operator both styles of harrows.

	Feet.	Weight.	Price.
A 183, 1 section, 32 teeth, cuts	5	105 lbs.	$ 4.75
A 184, 2 sections, 64 teeth, cuts	10	210 lbs.	9.50
A 185, 3 sections, 96 teeth, cuts	15	315 lbs.	14.25
A 185½, 4 sect's, 128 teeth, cuts	20	425 lbs.	19.00

70372 Our Disk Harrows are made to turn to or from the center; can be spread to cultivate corn. Seeder box for sowing grain attached if desired, but must be ordered with harrow.

Shipped second-class.

	Price.
No. 36, 12—16-inches disks, cut 6 feet; weight, 350 lbs	$20.00
No. 37, 14—16-inch disks, cut 7 feet; weight, 400 lbs	22.00
No. 38. 16—16-inch disks, cut 8½ feet; weight, 425 lbs.	25.00
No. 39, 12—20-inch disks, cut 6½ feet; weight, 400 lbs	22.00

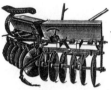

70373 Combined Disk Harrow and Broadcast Seeders.

12—16-inch disks, cuts 6½ feet	$36.50
12—20-inch disks, cuts 6½ feet	38.50

70374 Spring Tooth Harrow, practically adapted to stony and stumpy ground or tough sod. The spring tooth will cultivate the ground thoroughly. Now furnished with steel frame in place of wood. Average weight, 200 lbs.

16 Tooth	$11.50	20 Tooth	$14.50
18 Tooth	12.50	24 Tooth	17.00

For description and price of iron frame and lever spring tooth harrows, see our Agricultural Catalogue.

ROLLERS

A smooth, even surface was the goal of all tillage. Either before or after harrowing, depending on conditions, rollers were used to crush clods and smooth the soil. Rollers were heavy and clumsy, which made them hard on the horses and hard on the edges of the fields where the rollers were turned. Simpler devices made of planks, weighted down as needed with scrap iron or flat rocks, were used on smaller farms.

A CHEAPER TRIPLE ROLLER

Figure 48 shows a much simpler form of triple farm roller, made chiefly of wood. It is in three sections, each about two feet long, such a one being much easier on the team than when made solid or in merely two sections. A good oak or maple log, as nearly cylindrical as possible for ten or twelve feet, can be cut in the woods, the bark peeled off, and the log sunk under water for several weeks, when it is to be dried out under cover. If seasoned with the bark on, the worms are apt to work on it. Saw off the pieces of the required length, strike a center and work them to a uniform size, and then bore holes for the journals. The best way is to have a pump-maker

bore entirely through the pieces an inch and three-quarter hole. Then hang them on a round bar of iron or steel, an inch and a half in diameter, as a loose spindle. The brace-irons can be made of stout old tire by the nearest blacksmith, and four of them, securely bolted into place, will be sufficient. Keep under cover when not in use.

Fig. 48.—FARM ROLLER.

A DOUBLE LAND ROLLER

The cheap home-made roller shown in figure 49 consists of two sections of a round log, dressed smooth, and fitted in a frame. The frame is made of four by four oak, bolted together firmly. The logs are each eighteen inches in diame-

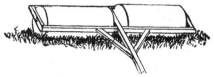

Fig. 49.—A HOME-MADE ROLLER.

ter, and three and one-half feet long, one being set three inches ahead of the other in the frame. The pins for the rollers are one and a quarter inch thick, round for four inches at one end, and square for twelve inches; this end is pointed, and is driven into an inch hole, bored in the end of the log. The tongue is braced with strong iron braces, and a seat may be fitted partly over the rear of the frame, and balance the weight of the tongue, and relieve the horses' necks.

Field Rollers.
Second-class freight.

70376 The Sherwin Field Roller, made of solid butt-cut white oak logs; weight is in the rolls, not in the box, to bring extra strain on the bearings: turns as easily as a wagon; each roll acts independently.
2-horse, 8½ ft., weight, 1,500. Price $20.00
$5.00 less where parties furnish their own log rollers
70378 Star Section Land Roller, iron disks for the ends, around which are bolted heavy oak staves; draft low, direct from heavy iron shaft on which roller revolves; 7½ ft. long, 30 inches in diameter: weight. 750 lbs. Each...$17.00
70380 Star flexible, three sections, land roller, constructed like 70378, but mounted like 70376. Price.............. .... 22.00
Grass Seed Attachment, extra................... 6.00

THE COMMON PLANKER

The common planker, although a home-made tool, is a very valuable implement for crushing clods and smoothing the surface. It is not inclined to push surface clods into the soil like the roller, but will catch them and pulverize them. The

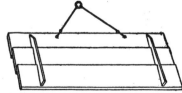

FIG. 63—THE COMMON PLANKER, A SERVICEABLE TOOL USUALLY MADE ON THE FARM

planker does not adapt itself well to any unevenness of the surface and does not pack the soil like the roller.

USEFUL CLOD CRUSHER

The illustrations, figures 51 to 53, present different views of a home-made implement to be used as a clod crusher or for other purposes. The runners are of oak plank, two inches thick, six feet long and eight inches wide, each rounded off at

Fig. 51.—CLOD CRUSHER IN OPERATION.

one end, and notched on the upper edge, as shown in the engravings. The cross-pieces are of similar material, three feet long and seven inches wide, spiked in place. The outer edges of the cross-pieces are faced with band-iron. A staple with ring is driven from the inside of each runner, near the

Fig. 52.—BOTTOM OF CLOD CRUSHER.

front, and the chain by which it is drawn is run through the ring. In this form it serves a very good purpose as a clod crusher. If additional weight is desired, large stones may be placed between the runners.

To fit it for use as a sled, it is inverted, a box of inch boards made five feet ten inches long, three feet broad, and nine inches deep. The lower edges of the sideboards are notched to fit the projections of the crosspieces. Inch boards are nailed across the bottom to close the spaces between the latter. Staples are driven into the sides of the runners to receive hickory stakes, which hold the box in place. For use in winter the thills are attached by iron straps bolted on, as shown in figure 53. When the runners become worn, the bottoms are planed off and strips of oak pinned on. The box may be replaced by a rack for drawing hay or other bulky stuff.

Fig. 53.—CLOD CRUSHER AND SLED.

CULTIVATORS

The original cultivator was the simple hoe. Animal-powered cultivators didn't come into use until the 1850s. The number of manufacturers and models blossomed in the 1880s and onward. From simple one-row walking cultivators the offerings grew to include two-row cultivators, riding cultivators, shovel cultivators, straddle-row cultivators, and more. The one-horse single- and double-shovel cultivators were used primarily by market gardeners. Larger models were used for corn, cotton, and grain crops.

Stalk cutters were used to level the dried stalks left in corn and cotton fields after harvesting.

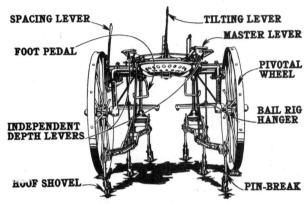

Figure 110—One-row riding cultivator. This cultivator is shown with other types of equipment in Figure 112.

FIG. 64.—FIVE- AND ELEVEN-TOOTH ONE-HORSE CULTIVATORS. EACH HAS A LEVER FOR VARYING THE WIDTH, AND ALSO GAUGE WHEELS. ONE HAS A SMOOTHING ATTACHMENT

FIG. 65—A TONGUELESS FOUR-SHOVEL CULTIVATOR WITH WOODEN GANGS. THE SHOVELS ARE NOT IN PLACE

THE ONE-HORSE CULTIVATOR

The one-horse cultivator is used largely in gardening and for cultivating corn too high to be cultivated with the straddle-

row cultivator. It may be provided with almost any number of teeth from 5 to 14. The teeth may vary from the harrow tooth designed for producing a very fine tilth, to the wide reversible shovels used on the five-tooth cultivators. Also a spring tooth may be used similar to those used on the spring-tooth harrow.

FIG. 66—A RIDING BALANCE-FRAME FOUR-SHOVEL CULTIVATOR WITH HAMMOCK SEAT AND STEEL GANGS

FIG. 67—A COMBINED WALKING AND RIDING SIX-SHOVEL CULTIVATOR WITH STRADDLE SEAT AND TREADLE GUIDE. THE HANDLES TO BE USED WHEN WALKING ARE NOT ATTACHED

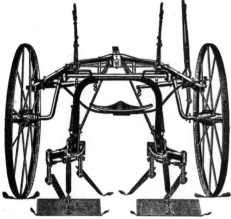

FIG. 68—A RIDING SURFACE CULTIVATOR

FIG. 69—A TWO-ROW CULTIVATOR, GUIDED WITH A LEVER

FIG. 70—A DISK CULTIVATOR

STALK CUTTER

An implement in general use in corn and cotton regions and which should be mentioned here is the stalk cutter. Its pur-

pose is to cut cotton and corn stalks when left in the field into such lengths as not to interfere with the cultivation of the next crops. The implement primarily consists in a cylinder with five to nine radial knives. It is rolled over the stalks, cutting them into short lengths. Stalk hooks are provided which gather the stalks in front of the cylinder. Two types are found upon the market, the spiral and the straight knife cutters. The spiral knife cutter carries practically all of the weight of the machine on the cylinder head while in operation, the side wheels being raised and the cylinder head brought in contact with the ground. Straight knife cutters have the cylinder head mounted in a frame, and when placed in operation are forced to the ground with spring pressure. The latter machine is much more pleasant to operate, as it rides more smoothly. Some cutters are equipped with reversible knives with two edges sharpened. A stalk cutter attachment is made for a cultivator carriage. The implement in general may be had as a single- or double-row machine.

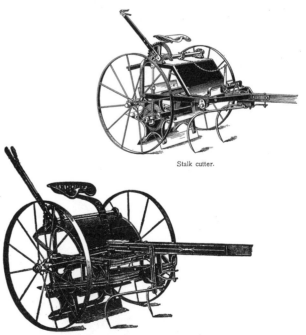

Stalk cutter.

FIG. 73—A SINGLE-ROW STALK CUTTER

CHAPTER 5

PLANTING

Once the soil was prepared, the farmer moved on to the crucial step of planting. Grain and vegetables such as turnips and carrots were grown from seed sown directly into the soil. The age-old method for hand planting, still in use well into the 1800s, was to drop the seed in hills and cover it with soil using a hoe. Broadcasting the seeds onto a plowed field and then covering them with soil using a harrow was a step up from hand planting. The next step in mechanization was the seed drill, a machine that created a furrow of the appropriate depth, dropped in the seed, and covered it again. By the 1880s, seed drills were in widespread use.

SEEDERS

Handheld and horse-drawn broadcast seeders were quite useful for smaller farms and for seeds that were not row crops—forage grasses such as alfalfa, clover, and timothy, for example. The drawback of the hand seeder is that the seeds are not distributed uniformly, a problem that was also true, though to a lesser extent, for larger seeders.

THE HAND SEEDER

The hand seeder with rotating distributer consists of a star-shaped wheel which is given a rapid rotation either by gearing from a crank or by a bow, the string of which is given one wrap around the spindle of the distributing wheel. Fig. 74 shows a seeder of this order. A bag is provided with straps which may be carried from the shoulders and the distributing mechanism placed at the bottom. The use of this seeder is confined to small areas, and the uniformity of its distribution of the seed is not the best.

FIG. 74—A CRANK HAND SEEDER. SEEDERS OF THIS KIND ARE ALSO OPERATED WITH A BOW

THE WHEELBARROW SEEDER

The wheelbarrow seeder is used to some extent for the sowing of grass seed, and seems to be the survivor of this type of seeder, which was at one time used extensively in England. A

FIG. 75—A WHEELBARROW SEEDER

vibrating rod passes underneath the box and by stirring causes the seed to flow out of the openings on the under side of the seed box.

AGITATOR FEED

A broadcast seeder is still upon the market not provided with a force feed, but having what is known as an agitator feed.

This feed is composed of a series of adjustable seed holes or vents in the bottom of the hopper, and over each is an agitator or stirring wheel to keep the seed holes open and pass the seed to them. The agitator feed, although cheaper and more simple than others, is not so accurate as the force feed described later.

Fig. 77 illustrates a broadcast seeder with an agitator feed and cultivator gangs attached. This seeder is usually used without any covering device; however, it may be procured with the cultivator gangs or with a spring-tooth harrow attachment.

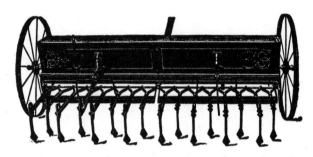

FIG. 77—AN AGITATOR-FEED BROADCAST SEEDER WITH CULTIVATOR COVERING SHOVELS. THIS IS A WIDE-TRACK MACHINE

The Little Giant Broadcast Hand Seed Sower.

70361 With this seeder, when properly used, you can distribute wheat 56 feet to a round, flaxseed 36 feet, clover seed 36 feet, timothy 27 feet, oats 36 feet. It will also sow rye, barley, millet, Hungarian corn, or any grain or seed that can be sown broadcast. This seeder has a light centrifugal wheel at the bottom, 11 inches in diameter, that is revolved rapidly in opposite directions by means of a bow, scattering the seed with great velocity. Weight 3 pounds. Price, each..................$1.50

The Niagara Broadcast Seeder.
Shipped first-class freight.
A Positive Force Feed.

70362 The "Niagara" combines all the latest improvements in sowers. The machine is attached to an end gate that fits any wagon. Attach sprocket to left hind wheel, put on link chain and go ahead. Save grain and seed by sowing it evenly. Time is money. Early seeding is what tells. Don't spend your time with the old style seeder when four times the amount of seed can be evenly distributed with the "NIAGARA." Weight, 125 lbs. Price..................$9.00

The New Five-Hoe One-Box Grain Drill.

70363 The New Five-Hoe One-Box Grain Drill. Used principally for drilling between corn rows, or putting in grain with one horse. Part of the holes can be stopped, which makes it an excellent corn, bean or pea drill; also for beets and other coarse seed. Weight, 140 lbs. Price $14.00

The Granger Seeder.
All seeders shipped first-class freight.

70364 The Granger Broadcast Hand Seeder, for sowing all kinds of grain and grass seed; sows on an average of 6 acres per hour at a common walking gait. The bag and hopper will hold about 22 quarts. Weight, 5½ pounds. Price..........$3.25
70364½ The Improved Calhoun Broadcast Hand Seeder; weight, 5½ pounds (retail price, $5.00). Our price, each..$3.00

The Cyclone Hand Seeder.

70365 This is somewhat simpler and cheaper made than the Granger, but works on the same general plan. It will sow with ease to the operator 60 acres of grain or grass seed per day. Has a shake feed, and sows perfectly accurate. Weight, 4 lbs. Price $2.25

70366 Wheelbarrow Clover and Grass Seeder

The box is 14 feet long and is carried so close to the ground that the wind has no effect on the seed; 20 to 30 acres can be sown per day; weighs 40 pounds and runs light. Price, complete, clover and grass seeder..................$7.00

Cahoon's Broadcast Seed Sower,
For Sowing All Kinds of Grain and Grass Seed.

The unprecedented success of this Seeder the past year is without a parallel in the history of Agricultural Implements. It has probably received more First Premiums at State Fairs in the fall of 1869, than was ever awarded any other machine of any name or nature, in one year. Joseph Harris, author of Walks and Talks in *American Agriculturist,* says: "I like the Cahoon Seeder very much indeed." There is one continuous voice of praise ringing in our ears from all parts of the country.
We warrant the Hand Machine to sow 50 acres of wheat in 10 hours, and the Horse Power Machine to sow 120 acres in the same time, and the work to be done with greater precision and accuracy than it can be done by any other means whatever. No farmer who has an acre of grain to sow yearly can afford to do without one of these Seeders.
Price of Hand Sowers, $10.00; Horse Power, $50.00. Send for Circulars, and name of Agent near your residence.
D. H. GOODELL & CO.,
Sole Manufacturers, Antrim, N. H.

SEED DRILLS

An early type of seed drill for grain and turnips was patented by the great English agronomist and inventor Jethro Tull in 1731. American patents for seed drills start in 1799, but the first practical designs started appearing in the 1840s. In 1851 the force-feed device was patented. This was a major improvement—the seeds were augered from the seed box by a seed cylinder, instead of dropping through a slide that was adjusted for the type and amount of seed. The force feed distributed the seed much more accurately and evenly.

A flurry of new designs in the late 1860s and early 1870s made the grain drill much more flexible. The types and amounts of seed the drills could handle, and improvements in the methods for placing the seeds at the right depth and covering them with soil, brought more manufacturers into a growing market. Once mastered, the basic design of the grain drill remained more or less unchanged until the 1930s and the advent of faster tractors that could carry larger equipment.

THE SHOE DRILL

The shoe drill came into use about 1885 and has many advantages over the hoe drill. In fact, it was used almost entirely until the more recent development in the nature of the disk drill. Fig. 83 illustrates a shoe drill with high press

FIG. 84—A STANDARD SINGLE-DISK DRILL WITH A PRESS-WHEEL ATTACHMENT. THE STEEL RIBBON SEED TUBES ARE ALSO SHOWN

FIG. 83—A LOW-DOWN PRESS DRILL WITH SHOE FURROW OPENERS

wheels. The shoes are pressed into the ground with either flat or coil springs, which permit an independent action and prevent to a certain extent clogging with trash. It is claimed that flat springs do not tire as readily as coil springs, but coil springs seem to be almost universally used.

DISK DRILLS

Disk drills are the more recent development and consist of two classes: those with single- and double-disk furrow openers. In the single-disk type the disk is formed much like those used on disk harrows. Some form of heel or auxiliary shoe is provided to insert the grain in the bottom of the furrow made. It is desirable that the passage for the seed be so arranged that there can be but little chance for it to become

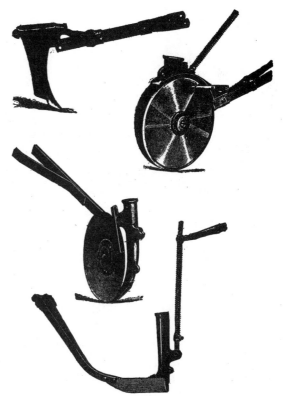

FIG. 85—THE HOE, DOUBLE-DISK, SINGLE-DISK, AND SHOE FURROW OPENERS USED ON DRILLS. THESE ARE OFTEN MADE INTERCHANGEABLE

clogged with dirt. The furrow opener that allows the seed to come into direct contact with the disk is not to be advised, but an inclosed boot should be provided to lead the seed into the bottom of the furrow. Some ingenuity is displayed by different makers in securing the desired results in this respect. In some drills the grain is led through the center of the disk. The single-disk may be given some suction, and therefore has more penetration than any other form of disk opener, fitting it especially for hard and trashy ground. The single disk has one objection, and that is that it tends to make the ground uneven, since the soil is thrown in only one direction.

The double-disk furrow opener has two disks, or really coulters, as they are flat and their action is much like that of the shoe. One disk usually precedes the other by a short distance. The double-disk has not the penetration of the single-disk, but will not ridge the ground as the single-disk does. They often have another bad feature in that they allow dry dirt to fall on the seed, and hence prevent early germination. The single-disk drill does more to improve the tilth of the ground than any other furrow opener. The fact that a slight ridge is left in the center of the furrow with the double-disk is considered by some an advantage, as the seed is better distributed; in fact, two rows are planted instead of one.

FIG. 86—A STANDARD SINGLE-DISK DRILL WITH COVERING CHAINS

FIG. 87—A FIVE-DISK DRILL FOR DRILLING BETWEEN CORN ROWS. THE CENTER FURROW OPENER IS A DOUBLE DISK

CORN PLANTERS

Handheld corn planters that dropped the seeds into a hill and covered them were among the earliest uniquely American tools. This tool, or a simple hoe, was used by small farmers until the late 1800s. In the 1850s, however, the traditional method of row planting for corn was giving way to the new idea of check planting. By seeding the corn into properly spaced hills, check fields could be cultivated both lengthwise, as row fields were, and crosswise. This was a significant improvement in keeping down the weeds. The spread of check field cultivation and improvements in mechanical corn planters went hand in hand over the next decades.

By the 1870s, on small farms, hand corn planters had been largely replaced by one-row walking corn planters, which could also double for seeding cotton. On larger farms, two-row and larger corn planters became popular, especially as the mechanisms for counting out the right number of kernels and spacing them properly were perfected in the late 1850s.

CORN PLANTERS

Accurate planting has more to do with the yield of corn and other row crops than any other mechanical factor. If hills are crowded, barren stalks and small ears result. If hills are missed, or if less than the desired number of seeds are dropped, time and land are wasted.

The illustrations opposite picture the results of accurate and inaccurate planting when three stalks per hill is ideal for

soil conditions. In poor soils, two stalks per hill is sufficient, while in very rich loam soils four stalks will do well. The inaccurate spacing of drilled corn will result in the same losses as pictured on page 77.

A, three kernels in each hill produce a perfect stand and yield three good ears.

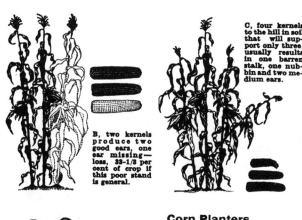

B, two kernels produce two good ears, one ear missing— loss, 33-1/3 per cent of crop if this poor stand is general.

C, four kernels to the hill in soil that will support only three, usually results in one barren stalk, one nubbin and two medium ears.

Corn Planters.

Shipped first-class freight.

70357 Champion Hand Corn Planter; has pumpkin seed attachment. Glass slide shows just how many kernels are ready to drop in next hill. Every miss hill can be avoided; no blank hill with this planter; weight, 4½ lbs. Price........$1.50

The "Chatauqua" Corn, Bean and Seed Planter.

70358 We believe one of the best hand corn, bean and seed planters. The cuts explain its operation. It is guaranteed to do good work. Automatic. The simple act of stepping forward from this position will plant the seed without any attention on your part. Weight, 4½ lbs. Price, each........$1.25
70359 The well known Eagle corn planter, with extra revolving disks Price .each.......$1.25

Triumph Corn Planter.

70360 Kent's Patent Triumph Hand Corn Planter; can be used on sod or plowed ground. Weight, 4½ lbs. Price, each.................. ....$0.75

FIG. 88—A HAND CORN PLANTER. THE CORN IS DRAWN FROM UNDER THE SEED BOX BY A SLIDE UPON CLOSING AND OPENING THE HANDLES

CORN DRILLS

Fig. 90 shows a type of one-horse corn drill used in small farm districts. It is very simple to operate. The drop is the same as shown and described in connection with the two-row planter.

Figure 90—One-row corn drill.

CORN DRILLS

Although most planters may be set to drill corn, the corn drill remains a distinct tool and is used to a large extent in certain localities of the country. Fig. 98 shows a single-row drill which differs but little from others except that an extra

FIG. 98—THE SINGLE-ROW CORN DRILL

knife is provided in front of the seed tube. Various covering devices in the way of shovels and disks are provided. Drills are now made to take two rows, and even four, when made as an attachment to a grain drill.

Cotton planter.

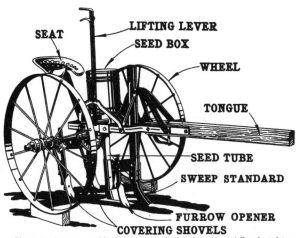

SEAT
LIFTING LEVER
SEED BOX
WHEEL
TONGUE
SEED TUBE
SWEEP STANDARD
FURROW OPENER
COVERING SHOVELS

Figure 96—One-row combination cotton and corn planter especially adapted to planting on beds or in furrows. A sweep can be attached to heavy beam for sweeping off tops of beds when planting.

THE MODERN PLANTER

Although most planters are called upon to do about the same work, they differ much in construction. The essentials of a

FIG. 89—A MODERN CORN PLANTER WITH LONG CURVED FURROW OPENERS, VERTICAL CHECK HEAD, AND OPEN WHEELS

FIG. 96—A CORN PLANTER WITH DOUBLE-DISK FURROW OPENERS, OPEN WHEELS, AND HORIZONTAL CHECK HEADS

good, successful planter have been set forth as follows: (1) It must be accurate in dropping at all times; (2) plant at a uniform depth; (3) cover the seed properly; (4) convenient and durable; and (5) simple in construction.

CHAPTER 6

HARVESTING

As American farms grew larger and more productive through mechanization, the need for efficient harvesting machinery grew more intense. Harvesting took place in a short, concentrated period; older methods couldn't harvest the new, larger grain fields quickly enough. Any implement that speeded the process and used less labor would be helpful, while a machine that automated the process even partially would be invaluable. Starting with Cyrus H. McCormick's reaper in the 1830s, many inventors took up the challenge and devised harvesting equipment that became increasingly sophisticated. The grain binder, introduced in the 1870s, made harvesting even more efficient. First perfected in 1915, the combined reaper/thresher, or combine, was the final step in mechanization.

THE REAPER

The first major advance over the age-old hand sickle or scythe for reaping grain was the cradle scythe, or cradle. This American invention was probably introduced sometime in the last quarter of the eighteenth century. The scythe handle, or snath, was lengthened and fingers were added to catch the cut grain.

Attempts at mechanized reapers were recorded in the early 1800s, but the success that revolutionized agriculture came in 1831, when Cyrus H. McCormick perfected his reaping machine. Another inventor, Obed Hussey of Baltimore, had invented a working reaper at almost exactly the same time. McCormick didn't get around to filing for a patent until 1834; Hussey filed his in 1833. The battle for precedence—and royalties—raged in the courts for decades, and the discussion continues to the present day.

The reaper revolutionized the way America farmed. The vast wheat and corn fields of the Midwest and prairie states were far too large to be harvested by traditional methods. McCormick's original sickle-and-reel reaper design, brilliant in its simplicity, gave way by the 1870s to the self-rake reaper. The revolving rakes on the reaper swept the cut grain off the platform (also called a table) and into piles for gathering. Because the grain was pushed behind the reaper, instead of to the side, the self-raking reaper let the reaper continue cutting even if the binder fell behind.

FIG. 104—THE AMERICAN CRADLE. THE TOOL USED FOR REAPING UNTIL AFTER THE MIDDLE OF THE NINETEENTH CENTURY

Hussey's first machine was indeed a very crude affair. It consisted of a frame carrying the gearing, with a wheel at each side and a platform at the rear. The cutter was attached to a pitman, which received its motion from a crank geared to the main axle. The cutter worked in a series of fingers or guards, and perhaps

approached the modern device much closer than any reaper had up to this time.

McCormick's machine was provided with a reel and an outside divider. The knife had an edge like a sickle and worked through wires which acted for the fingers or guards

FIG. 107—HUSSEY'S REAPING MACHINE (AMERICA, 1833)

Buckeye Harvester Reaper. Front View.

The Johnston Harvester Company's Wrought Iron Harvester.

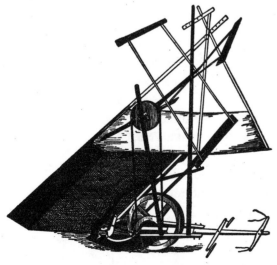

FIG. 108—M'CORMICK REAPING MACHINE (AMERICA, 1834)

The Johnston Harvester Company's Self Raking Single Reaper.

of Hussey's machine. The machine was of about 4 1/2 feet cut and was drawn by one horse. The grain fell upon a platform and was raked to one side with a hand rake by a man walking.

The Johnston Harvester Company's Self Raking Reaper and Mower.

CHAIN RAKE SELF DELIVERY REAPER.

SWEEP RAKE SELF DELIVERY REAPER ON THE ROAD.

THE SELF-RAKE REAPER

The modern self-rake resembles the early machine very much, and improvement has taken place only along the line of detail. The machine has a platform in the form of a quarter circle, to which the grain is reeled by the rakes, as well as

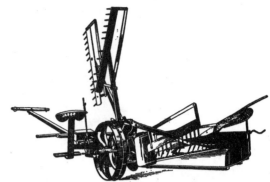

FIG. 109—A MODERN SELF-RAKE REAPER

removed to one side far enough to permit the machine to pass on the next round. The cutting mechanism is like that of the harvester. The machine is used to only a limited extent owing to the fact that the grain must be bound by hand. The reaper is preferred by some in the harvesting of certain crops, like buckwheat and peas. It is usually made in a 5-foot cut, and can be drawn by two horses, cutting six to eight acres a day.

Reaper.

GRAIN BINDERS

The reaper was a major improvement, but all it did was cut the grain and leave it in tidy piles in the field. Laborers were still needed to walk behind the reaper, gather up the sheaves, and bind them by hand. The development of the grain binder in the 1870s cut back considerably on this backbreaking labor. The grain binder combined the sickle-and-reel arrangement of the reaper with a conveyor belt that carried the cut grain to a gear-driven knotter, which tied the stalks together into a small bundle. The bundle was dropped from the rear of the binder onto the ground. Workers following the binder gathered the bundles and shocked them for further drying or, if the grain was uniformly ripe, loaded the bundles into wagons to be taken for threshing.

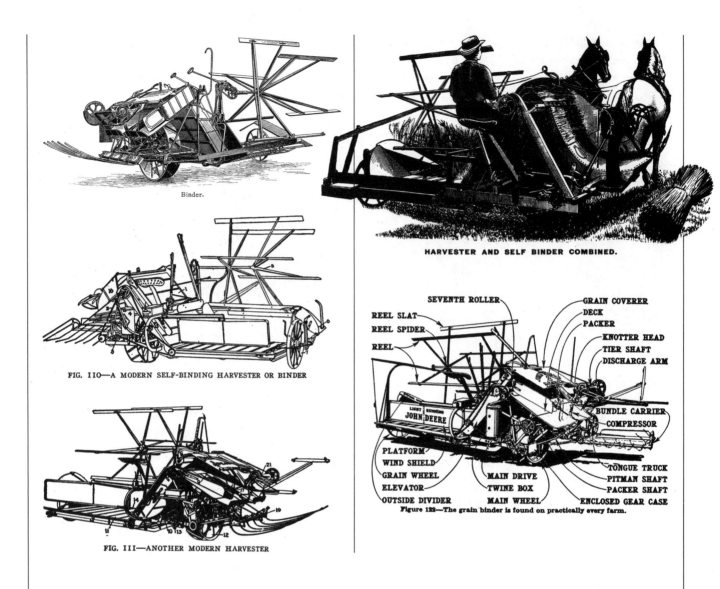

Binder.

HARVESTER AND SELF BINDER COMBINED.

FIG. 110—A MODERN SELF-BINDING HARVESTER OR BINDER

FIG. 111—ANOTHER MODERN HARVESTER

SEVENTH ROLLER

REEL SLAT
REEL SPIDER
REEL

GRAIN COVERER
DECK
PACKER
KNOTTER HEAD
TIER SHAFT
DISCHARGE ARM

LIGHT RUNNING JOHN DEERE

BUNDLE CARRIER
COMPRESSOR

PLATFORM
WIND SHIELD
GRAIN WHEEL
ELEVATOR
OUTSIDE DIVIDER

MAIN DRIVE
TWINE BOX
MAIN WHEEL

TONGUE TRUCK
PITMAN SHAFT
PACKER SHAFT
ENCLOSED GEAR CASE

Figure 122—The grain binder is found on practically every farm.

GRAIN HEADERS

In arid or semiarid regions where grains such as wheat would ripen in the field very evenly and not require shocking, heading was a more efficient method of harvesting. The grain header cut off just the grain head and left the straw standing; mowers then went over the field later to cut the straw. The machines used the same sickle-and-reel mechanism as the grain binder, but they didn't have the knotter mechanism for tying grain bundles. As these machines were pushed (not pulled) by the horses, the reel rotated and the sickles cut off the grain heads, which were carried by a conveyor belt into the wagon being driven alongside.

HEADER.

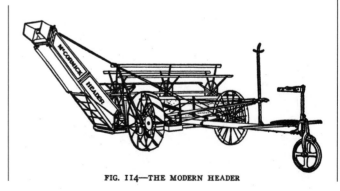

FIG. 114—THE MODERN HEADER

THE HEADER

The header is a machine arranged to cut the standing grain very high, leaving practically all of the straw in the field. The cutting and reeling mechanisms of the header are much like those of the harvester, but the machine differs decidedly in the manner of hitching the teams for propelling it. It is pushed ahead of the horses and guided from the rear by a rudder wheel. The headed grain is carried by canvases up an elevator and deposited in a wagon with a large box drawn along beside the machine. The header usually cuts a wide swath from 10 to 20 feet, and requires 4 to 6 horses to operate it. With it, 20 to 40 acres may be harvested in a day. An attachment is sometimes placed upon the header to bind the cut grain into bundles, in which case the grain is cut lower. This attachment must necessarily be very highly geared, but does very satisfactory work. A machine with a binder attachment is called a *header binder*.

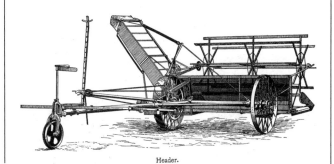

Header.

HARVESTING CORN

The corn harvest was one of the last frontiers of farm mechanization. Hand-cranked or belt-driven corn shellers were used starting in the 1860s to remove dried corn from the cob. Husking the ears was done by hand, an onerous task made slightly easier by special husking gloves.

In the late 1800s, as farmers came to realize the value of corn silage as animal fodder, a variety of machines were developed to make harvesting the corn, stalk and all, easier. Given that in 1882 there were only about a hundred silos in the country, it's not surprising that it took until after the turn of the century for ensilage cutters to come into use that chopped the standing corn and loaded it into wagons. Mechanical corn huskers and shredders of various sorts were developed in the 1890s. These machines separated the ears from the stalks, husked the ears, and shredded the stalks for silage. The rollers on these machines were extremely dangerous—hands, arms, and even lives were lost when workers got caught in the machinery. It took a surprisingly long time for safety features to be added. Practical corn pickers that removed the ears and left the stalk standing didn't become a reality until the 1930s, and the corn combine arrived only in the 1950s.

A CORN HUSKING RACK

Many who husk their corn by hand find it very tiresome to sit on the floor or ground in a cramped position. A rack made as shown in the drawing will hold two or three shocks and gives a better place for the husker to sit. Place the stalks cross-wise of the bench in front of you.

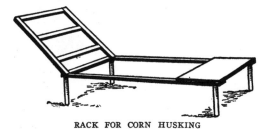

RACK FOR CORN HUSKING

FIG. 171—A ONE-HOLE HAND SHELLER

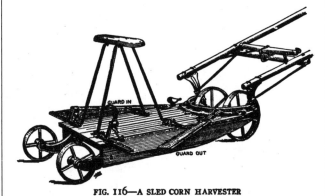

FIG. 116—A SLED CORN HARVESTER

FIG. 117—THE VERTICAL CORN HARVESTER

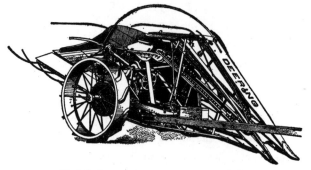

FIG. 118—THE HORIZONTAL CORN HARVESTER

Success Corn Harvester.

70546 On The Success Corn Harvester, the cutting wings are pivoted to the center of the harvester and are readily and quickly thrown in under the platform with the levers, by the operators while in motion, standing on the platform, and thus close them quickly to pass gallow hills, or obstructions, or to prevent an accident to man or horse. This is a safety and advantage possessed by no other.

No. 3 with levers, no wheel....................$16.50
No. 4 with both levers and wheel, like cut..... 18.00

FIG. 120—THE CORN PICKER-HUSKER

Corn picker and husker.

HUSKERS AND SHREDDERS

CONSTRUCTION—The husker and shredder is a combined machine to convert the coarse corn fodder, stalk and leaves, into an inviting feed for farm animals, and at the same time deliver the corn nicely husked to the bin or the wagon. By this means the entire corn crop is made use of and the fodder put into better shape for feeding.

The usual arrangement of the husker and shredder is illustrated in Fig. 170. The fodder is first placed upon the *feeding table*, from which it is fed, the butts first, to the feed or snapping rolls. Many of the machines are manufactured with self-feeders much like those for the threshing machine. Owing to the loss of hands and arms in feeding the early machines, provision is now made whereby it will be almost impossible for accidents of this nature to happen.

As the stalks pass through the snapping rolls the ears are squeezed off and allowed to fall upon a conveyor, which carries them to the husking rolls, or they may fall upon the husking rolls direct. Here the husks are pulled off and are carried to the wagon or bin. When the stalks leave the snap-ping rolls they pass over cutting plates and immediately are cut into small particles by the shredding head. This shredded fodder is then conveyed to the elevator, which may be either a carrier or pneumatic stacker. As the shredded fodder passes through the machine it passes over beaters, which agitate the fodder so that all shelled corn falls out and is conveyed to the wagon.

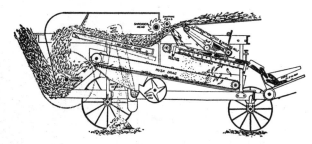

FIG. 170—SECTIONAL VIEW OF A HUSKER AND SHREDDER

THRESHERS

Well into the 1800s, the method used to thresh (or *thrash,* as it was often written then) grain wasn't all that different from that used thousands of years earlier. Handheld flails were used to beat the grain from the straw; chaff was then removed from the grain by winnowing.

A breakthrough concept for mechanizing the labor-intensive work of threshing came in 1837, when the Pitts brothers of Maine came up with the concept of an elevated conveyor belt, or "endless apron," to carry the grain through toothed rollers that shelled the grain from the head, separated the grain from the straw, and separated the grain from the chaff and dirt. The threshing machine was operated by a horse-powered sweep, a steam engine, or sometimes by water power. Instead of the seven or eight bushels of wheat a day that a good worker with a hand flail could process, the new steam-operated machines could thresh five hundred to a thousand bushels.

The Pitts brothers and others, including George Westinghouse, made continual improvements to the basic thresher concept well into the 1850s. In the 1870s a new design concept, the vibrating belt, became popular. The grain stalks passed through rollers and then were carried along a vibrating open belt. The grain fell through the belt into a pan underneath; as it fell, a fan blew away the chaff and dirt. The straw continued on to a fan housing that blew it into a straw pile. The straw was later used as livestock bedding, mulch, or compost.

As threshers got bigger and more complex, they could no longer be operated by horsepower. Before the widespread use of gasoline engines, most threshers were designed to be run by stationary steam engines belted to the machinery. The great age of the massive self-contained steam-powered thresher started around 1890 and continued into the 1930s. These massive machines were generally owned by a custom operator who moved the machine—and its associated horses, teamsters, and laborers—from farm to farm in the harvesting season.

Today, farm lore and thresher reunions have put a nostalgic spin on the old steam thresher days. The reality was somewhat different. Threshing was hot, dusty, backbreaking work even with a steam-powered thresher. The steam engineer set the thresher up near the field, but the grain had to be brought to it. Bundle haulers went out into the field and loaded the shocks into horse-drawn wagons. When the wagon got to the thresher, the bundles had to be pitched down into the bundle feeder of the thresher. The grain elevator at the end of the thresher emptied the grain into sacks or wagons. Either way of handling the grain required additional manual labor.

The work of threshing wasn't confined to the fields. Farm wives were expected to provide sleeping accommodations for the gangs of workers and cook three meals a day for them, a hugely demanding task.

THE BUFFALO PITTS THRESHER AND CLEANER.

THE PITTS AGRICULTURAL WORKS,
JAMES BRAYLEY, PROPRIETOR

In a large portion of the world the primitive or simplest implements of husbandry are still retained. The plow now used generally in the Roman States, and indeed throughout Italy, is but a slight improvement on that used there two thousand years ago. In many countries the cereal crops are still harvested with a sickle, and the grain threshed, or rather tramped out, by horses and oxen.

The laborious method of threshing by flail was common until a comparatively recent period, and many of our readers will vividly remember the time, when, with the dawning of light on a winter morn, they repaired to the paternal barn to thresh. There was merry music in the well-timed strokes of the flail, and its use for a limited time was a healthful exercise, peculiarly adapted to the development of the muscles of the arm, but when one followed it day after day for weeks or months, it became excessively fatiguing, and the last flooring was always gladly welcomed.

Threshing finished, "cleaning up" commenced; a slow and laborious process. The time was, even in this country, when the mixed husks and grain were separated by throwing them up in the air, a shovelful at a time, trusting to the wind to blow the chaff away—and in some countries this primitive method is still followed—but winnowing machines or farming mills were soon invented and very generally adopted.

No mechanical inventions have so much aided in the development of the resources of our country as those relating to labor saving agricultural machinery, and in no depart-ment of manufacture has more rapid advancement been made. Prominent among the many labor saving machines for farmers' use is the Buffalo Pitts Thresher and Cleaner.

During the days of the old system of flail threshing, eight bushels of grain was considered a good days work for a man. Then followed the labor of cleaning up, which was not inconsiderable. If such processes were in use to-day, it would be simply impossible to market the present grain crops of the country, for the reason that the combined force of all the agricultural laborers in the United States, working steadily from the end of one harvest till the beginning of the next, could scarcely thresh and clean the production. In addition to the immense amount of manual labor saved by threshing machines, they effect a great saving of capital. The construction of all the barns and threshing floors on and in which to beat out the grain by hand, would involve an expenditure of many millions of dollars. In the grain producing regions of the West and Northwest, it is a small farm that has not eighty acres of cereals, while there are scores of farmers who count their acres sown to wheat by thousands, and thousands of others who have hundreds, not to mention the vast areas in barley, rye and oats.

The Buffalo Pitts Threshers and Cleaners may be driven by water, steam or horse power. They are made several different sizes, varying from twenty-four inch cylinder to forty inch cylinder, and will thresh and clean, fit for market, from three hundred to three thousand bushels of grain per day, the capacity of course varying with their size. Those of our readers who are agriculturists need not be told that this celebrated machine is a model of perfection, nor for them need we describe its operation, or note how well it does its work, for its reputation has extended over all this land, and the better class of farmers in foreign countries are not unfamiliar with its many points of merit. Still there are those for whose information we deem it well to state that among the many distinguishing excellencies of the Buffalo Pitts Thresher and Separator, are: It threshes clean; it extracts all the kernels from the head of every straw that passes through it; it does not mash or crack the berry but delivers it in a perfect state; it perfectly separates the grain from the chaff and delivers it in bags ready for market, saving entirely the labor incident to recleaning.

The machines are made of the very best materials, only the finest qualities of iron and steel are used, and the wood work is made of carefully selected woods, free from knots and checks and thoroughly seasoned. Only skilled labor is employed in the construction. Each different part of the machine is made by men who work continuously on that one part, by which the greatest possible degree of accuracy is obtained, and every part of each is an exact duplicate of the corresponding part in every other machine of the same size and class, thus rendering it easy in case of accident to replace the broken part.

Particular attention is paid to making changes necessary to adapt these machines to the grains of foreign countries.

The Pitts Double Pinion Horse Powers were specially invented for use with the threshing machine but are adapted for all purposes for which horse powers can be used. They are manufactured in large quantities at these works, and are in great demand. They are made with the same careful attention that is bestowed upon the thresher, varying in sizes from four to twelve horses. The various parts are all made in duplicate and extras can always be obtained.

Many thousands of the Buffalo Pitts Threshers and Cleaners, and Horse Powers, are in use in all parts of the country. Consequently there is a steady demand for extras or repairs. To meet this demand several parties in different sections of the States have embarked in their manufacture by means of patterns which are taken from genuine casings perhaps, but which are necessarily imperfect. In some cases too, owners of machines, parts of which are worn or broken, take the imperfect pieces to the nearest country foundry and have new castings made from the worn or broken ones. Such repairs, however, can never work true. There is but one way to obtain perfect duplicates, and that is to purchase them from the Pitts Agricultural Works or its duly accredited agents.

Mr. Brayley, with a view of assisting those who may need extras has published a neat pamphlet of about forty pages, in which are engravings of every separate part of all the threshing machines and powers manufactured by him; each engraving being numbered. The engravings are followed by lists of the names of the parts, with their numbers and the page upon which the engraving may be found also noted. By reference to this catalogue any one can, without chance of mistake, order the exact article desired, which will be shipped the day on which the order is received, and which, when put in place, will always exactly fit.

As will be seen from our engravings, the Pitts Thresher and Cleaner was awarded the medal of honor at the Paris Exposition, that being but one of the very many awards it has received from Industrial Exhibitions, Institutes and Fairs.

For descriptive circulars, price lists or any further information desired, address James Brayley, Proprietor Pitts Agricultural Works, Buffalo, N.Y.

WORKS ESTABLISHED 1836.
G. WESTINGHOUSE & CO.,
MANUFACTURERS OF
THRESHING MACHINES,
SCHENECTADY, NEW YORK

There are two styles of Grain Threshing Machines now in use, known respectively as the "Vibrator" and the "Endless Apron." The Endless Apron style of machine was the first made, the Vibrator being of more recent invention, and, as is claimed, a simpler and more perfectly operating machine than those made after the original plan.

The Westinghouse Threshing Machine to which we desire to call the reader's attention, but which we cannot describe in the limited space at our disposal, belongs to the Vibrator class, but is in many respects different from and superior to other Vibrator machines. One of the most important features of this machine is the Improved Bar Cylinder and Concaves. This cylinder is so constructed that the spikes do not work loose and are far less liable to break than in other cylinders. The Concaves are made of the same kind of bars as the cylinder, and are easily changed to any position required for the different kinds of grain.

For a long time these machines have been in advance of others in their separating capacity, and late important improvements without an increase of machinery, has added materially to this desirable qualification. For perfection in cleaning all kinds of grain they are not surpassed.

The Powers furnished with these machines possess every desirable feature for obtaining the full value of the force applied, and are durable and easily handled.

View of THRESHING MACHINE,

Manufactured by G. Westinghouse & Co., Schenectady, New York.

The aim of the firm has been to make the very best machine, and with this end in view, improvements such as have suggested themselves have been made from year to year, during the past twenty years. To those who are acquainted with these machines, the improvements made speak for themselves, but for the information of those who are not, it is well to say that during the entire threshing season, at least one member of the firm is in almost constant attendance upon and witnessing the operations of their machines in different sections of the country, learning the wants of every community, and the appliances and conditions necessary for most successfully handling the different varieties of grain, including Flax, Grass and Clover Seeds, and each year brings out some new feature that seems desirable.

There are machines in the market sold for a less price than the Westinghouse Threshers are sold for, but as this firm produces nothing but first-class work, they do not attempt to compete with cheaply made and inferior articles, and we believe that, as a rule, the best made and most substantial machines, although costing more at first, are by far the cheapest in the end. And we have no hesitancy in asserting that in all essential and desirable qualities requisite to first-class Threshing Machines, the Westinghouse Vibrator Thresher and Cleaner, or Separator has no superior, if an equal, in the market.

During the year 1874, the works were destroyed by fire, but new and better ones have replaced them, and the firm with perfected and increased facilities are now prepared to turn out a larger number of and better made machines than ever before.

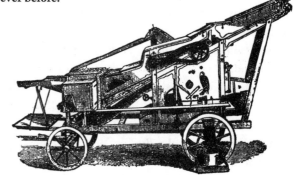

FIG. 155—THRESHING MACHINE OF 1867

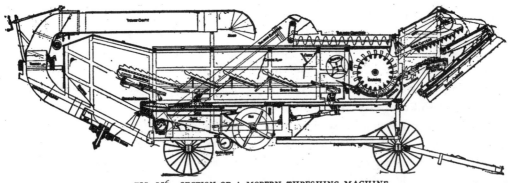

FIG. 156—SECTION OF A MODERN THRESHING MACHINE

CHAPTER 7

HAY

The census of 1900 reported some 59 million acres devoted to hay, and another 120 million acres as pastureland. In total, over 22 percent of improved land was given over to the hay crop, while hay and pasturelands together made up about 43 percent of the total acreage in improved lands. The value of the hay crop for 1899 was estimated at approximately $485 million, exceeded only by the corn crop.

Clearly forage crops, such as hay or pasture, were extremely important to American agriculture. Forage crops in general fell into three main categories: perennial grasses such as timothy, Kentucky bluegrass, Bermuda grass, orchard grass, and others; annual forage plants such as broomcorn or foxtail millet; and leguminous plants, including clover, alfalfa, field peas, and vetches. Leguminous (pod-producing) plants had the very valuable extra quality of enriching the soil by fixing nitrogen in the form of nitrates. In general, leguminous plants have deep roots, which help break up hard soils and improves the humus.

Hay was essential as animal fodder and bedding; the soiled hay was an important source of manure for fertilizer. (Straw, which consists of the stalks left after grain such as wheat has been removed, was also used as animal bedding where it was available.) Because hay is very bulky, it was grown and used almost entirely on the farm—it wasn't much of a cash crop.

HOME TESTING

Many of the more common grass-seeds, such as timothy, orchard-grass, and millet, can be tested for germination at home. The simple home-tester shown in Fig. 15 can be made and used by any one.

FIG. 15—HOME-MADE SEED-TESTER
A, Closed; *B*, Open

Mix the seed thoroughly and count out 100 or 200 seeds just as they come, making no selection. Put them between a fold of cotton flannel or some similar cloth, taking care not to let the seeds touch one another. Lay the cloth on a plate, moisten it well, but do not saturate it, cover with another plate, and keep in a warm room where the temperature will not go above 86° F. The cloth should be moistened from time to time, and the sprouted seeds counted and removed every day.

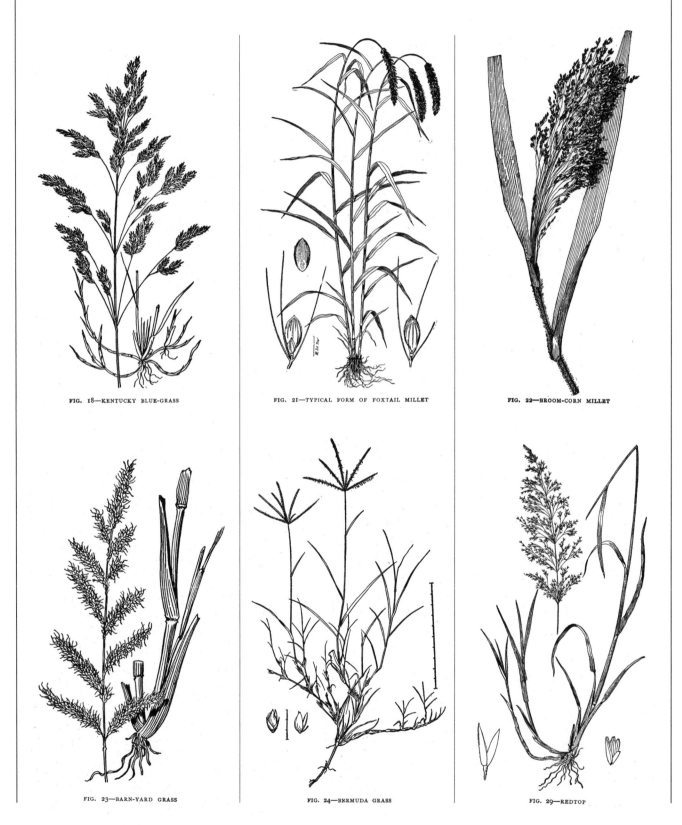

FIG. 18—KENTUCKY BLUE-GRASS

FIG. 21—TYPICAL FORM OF FOXTAIL MILLET

FIG. 22—BROOM-CORN MILLET

FIG. 23—BARN-YARD GRASS

FIG. 24—BERMUDA GRASS

FIG. 29—REDTOP

MOWERS

Until well into the nineteenth century, hay was laboriously harvested by hand using scythes and cradles. Horse-drawn mowing machines, some of which doubled as grain reapers, began to appear in the late 1850s. By the 1860s, two distinct mower types had emerged: side-cut, with a hinged cutter bar, and direct cut, with the mower bar between the wheels. By 1900, the basic mower had been perfected and was available from a wide range of manufacturers.

Buckeye Harvester Mower, on Uneven Ground.

Buckeye New Model Mower. Front View.

Buckeye Harvester Reaper. Rear View.

IRON FRAME MOWER WITH MANUAL DELIVERY REAPING ATTACHMENT.

IRON FRAME MOWER FOR ONE HORSE.

IRON FRAME MOWER FOR TWO HORSES.

MOWING ATTACHMENT FOR CHAIN RAKE REAPER.

ONE HORSE, OR PONY CLIPPER MOWER.

ONE HORSE, OR PONY
CLIPPER MOWER

A Gold Medal, (*the highest premium*,) was awarded to this machine, by the New York State Agricultural Society, at their great trial in Auburn, in July, 1866, when 59 Mowers and Reapers were offered for competition.

This is the only really practical One-Horse Mower in the market. It is constructed on the same general principle as the Two-Horse Machine, and is easily drawn and worked by one horse. It is capable of cutting three-quarters of an acre per hour with ease, without distress to the team, even in the hottest weather.

The Clipper Mowers were introduced by us in 1863. Although they at once took the first place among this class of machines, they have since been modified from year to year, as each successive season's experience in the

TWO HORSE CLIPPER MOWER.

field showed any point susceptible of improvement, and they now rank among harvesting machines as our modern light steel Tools, Plows, etc., do in comparison with the old fashioned and heavy implements of the past generation.

They are built on the system of *interchangeable parts*, a system that has not in full, been heretofore applied to the construction of any Mower. The like parts are *exact duplicates* of each other, and will fit any and all machines of the same size. By this method, we are able to secure *exact uniformity* in all our machines, and all will work *equally well* in the field, whether put together at our manufactory or by our Sub-builders.

MODERN MOWERS

Types.—Modern mowing machines are of two types, the side-cut mower and the direct-cut mower. The cutter bar of the former is placed at one side of the drive wheels or truck, while in the latter it is placed directly in front of the drivers.

FIG. 122—A MODERN TWO-HORSE MOWER

The mower consists essentially in (1) the cutting mechanism, comprising a reciprocating knife or sickle operated through guards or fingers and driven by a pitman from a crank, (2) driver wheels in contact with the ground, (3) gearing to give the crank proper speed, and (4) dividers to divide the cut grass from the standing.

The one-horse mower is usually a smaller size of the two-horse machine, fitted with shafts or thills instead of a tongue. It is made in sizes of 3 1/2- or 4-foot cut, and is used principally in the mowing of lawns, parks, etc.

The two-horse mower is commonly made in 4 1/2- and 5-foot cuts, although 6-, 7-, and 8-foot machines are manufactured. The latter are spoken of as wide-cut mowers and are usually of heavier construction than the standard machines (Fig. 122). From 8 to 15 acres is an average day's work with the 5- or 6-foot machines.

HAY RAKES

The mowed hay was left in swaths where it fell to dry in the sun. Once the hay was cured, it had to be raked into windrows for easy collection. The horse-drawn hay rake was developed simultaneously with the mower. Equipped with a spring-tooth raking mechanism, hay rakes soon fell into two groups: the self-dumping rake (dumping was accomplished by a hand lever) and the side-delivery rake. As hay loaders and hay presses came into wider use, the side-delivery rake became the preferred machine. The side-delivery rake made a thinner, lighter windrow that was easily handled by the hay loader.

Hay tedders, machines designed to stir up the hay in a heavy swath for more even drying, were somewhat controversial among farmers. Many didn't see the need for this extra step, especially after side-delivery mowers became popular. By 1900, hay tedders were fading from the scene.

RAKES

Development.—The introduction of the mower created a demand for something better and with a greater capacity than the ordinary hand rake. As long as hand methods prevailed in the cutting of the grasses there was little need for anything better than the hand rake. The first horse rake was revolving. It did very satisfactory work when carefully handled. But later in the steel tooth rake was found a much better tool. To Walter A. Wood Company, of Hoosick Falls, New York, is given the credit for bringing out the first spring-tooth rake. Differing from the modern tool, it was made almost entirely of wood except the teeth. The early rakes were dumped entirely by hand, but later an internal

FIG. 125—A STEEL SELF-DUMP RAKE FOR TWO HORSES. THE TONGUE MAY BE SEPARATED INTO THILLS FOR ONE HORSE. THE TEETH HAVE ONE COIL AND CHISEL POINTS

ratchet was provided on the wheels, which engaged a latch operated by the foot, and which carried the rake teeth up and over, thus dumping the load. The early rakes were almost universally provided with thills. Finally arrangements were made whereby the thills could be brought together and a tongue made for the use of a team instead of one horse.

Self-dump rakes are always provided with a lever for hand dumping. Rakes are made from 8 to 12 feet in width. In the purchase of a rake the important things to look for are ease in operation, strength of rake head and wheels. Often the wheels are the first to give way. Some wheels are very bad about causing the hay to wrap about the hub. The wheel boxes should be interchangeable so they may be replaced when worn.

Side-delivery rakes.—The side-delivery rake was brought about by the introduction of the hay loader, the loader creating a demand for a machine which would place

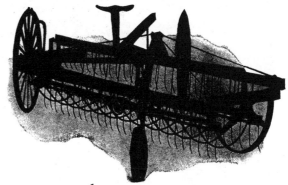

FIG. 126—ONE-WAY SIDE-DELIVERY RAKE

the hay in a light windrow. The first of these machines was manufactured by Chambers, Bering, Quinlan Company, of Decatur, Illinois.

The side-delivery rake takes the place of the hay tedder to a large extent. The method of curing hay, especially clover, by raking into light windrows shortly after being mown, has

FIG. 127—THE ENDLESS APRON OR REVERSIBLE SIDE-DELIVERY RAKE

proved very successful. A first-class quality of hay is obtained and in an equal length of time. It is claimed that if the leaves are prevented from drying up, they will aid very greatly in carrying off the moisture from the stems. Green clover contains about 85 per cent of water. When cured, only about 25 per cent is left. The leaves draw this moisture from the stems, and if free circulation of air is obtained the hay will dry quicker than if this outlet of the moisture for the water was cut off by letting the leaves dry up. Many of the one-way side-delivery rakes may be converted into tedders by reversing the forks and the direction of their movement. The standard width for side-delivery rakes is eight feet. They are drawn by two horses.

HAY TEDDERS

Hay tedders.—Where a heavy swath of hay is obtained, some difficulty is experienced in getting the hay thoroughly cured without stirring. To do this stirring the hay tedder has been

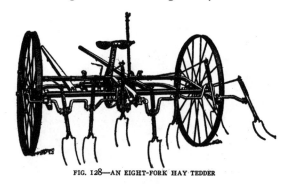

FIG. 128—AN EIGHT-FORK HAY TEDDER

devised. Grasses, when cut with a mower, are deposited very smoothly, and the swath is packed somewhat to the stubble by the passing of the team and mower over it. The office of the tedder is to reverse the surface and to leave the swath in such a loose condition that the air may have free access and thus aid in the curing.

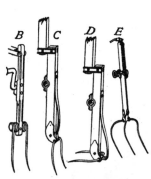

FIG. 129—TYPES OF TEDDER FORKS WITH COIL AND FLAT RELIEF SPRINGS. *D* SHOWS THE SPRING OF *C* SPRUNG

The hay tedder consists of a number of arms with wire tines or fingers at the lower ends. These are fastened to a revolving crank near the middle and to a lever at the other end. The motion of the cranks causes the tines to kick backward under the machine, thus engaging the mown hay, tossing it up and leaving it in a very loose condition.

SULKY RAKES

The sulky, or dump rake, shown in Fig. 188, is in common use in practically every section of the country. While it is easy to operate and adjust, many farmers work at a disadvantage when a slight adjustment would produce much better results.

The first requirement for good work is proper hitching. The rake shown in Fig. 188 is designed to work with the tongue 31 inches from the ground, measuring underneath at the front end. If this position is not maintained, the rake teeth will set at an improper angle, resulting in inferior work. If the tongue is too high, the teeth will have difficulty in clearing the hay after dumping; if too low, the teeth may fail to gather all of the hay.

Adjustments. Slight pressure on a foot trip lever causes the dump rods to engage in the wheel ratchets resulting in dumping of the rake. After the rake teeth have cleared the hay and started downward, they may be forced down quicker and held in position on the ground by pressure on the foot lever. An adjustment is provided at the hinge in this lever by which the wear can be taken up. If an adjustment is not made when the hinge becomes worn, the rake will be dumped with difficulty.

The height to which the teeth rise when the rake is dumped is controlled by adjusting a snubbing block bolt, located on the frame to the rear of the seat spring. If the rake rises too high and consequently does not get back to work as

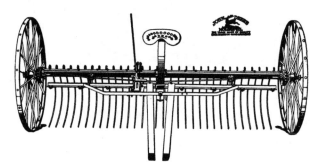

Figure 188—The sulky rake is used in practically every section of the country.

soon as it should, the block bolt must be screwed out of the block one or more turns. Turning the block bolt down permits the rake to rise higher when dumped.

If the rake repeats when it is dumped, the tension on trip spring is insufficient to hold the dump rod out of the wheel ratchets. More tension is produced by turning down the nut on the trip spring bolt.

When the wheel ratchets or dump rods become worn, the wheels and rods can be reversed, giving double wear.

Hay Rake.

All Hay Rakes and Hay Tedders shipped first-class.

70492 The Revolving Horse Hay Rake, turned head and teeth. Weight, 70 lbs., 18 teeth.

Weight, 80 lbs. Price $4.00

70493 The Reliable Lock Lever Sulky Rake, steel wheels, poles and shafts. 20 teeth, 8 foot wide. Weight, 250 lbs. Price.....$13.00 With 24 teeth, 10 feet wide; weight, 275 lbs. Price.... $14.00

70494 The Superior Self Dump Hay Rake, 9ft. Furnished with combination pole and shafts, 20 teeth, 8 feet wide, steel wheel. Price .. .$18.00 10 feet wide, with 24 teeth. Price $20.00 Weight, 350 lbs.

Hay Tedder.

0499—The Perfection Hay Tedder. Price, 6 forks. $23.00 Weight, 450 lbs. Price, 8 forks, $28.00 Weight, 500 lbs.

HAY LOADERS

Moving hay from the field to the barn was one of the most laborious operations on the farm. This labor-intensive, unpleasant step was partially mechanized in the 1880s by the invention of the hay loader. The loader was pulled along behind the wagon. Hay from the windrow was carried up into the hayrack (a type of specialized wagon), where it was then distributed by hand to make an even load.

The old-fashioned haystack was not entirely a thing of the past by the turn of the century. It was useful when the hay crop was larger than could be stored in the barn, and it was an efficient way to feed grazing animals in the field. Hay stackers or hay derricks were basically large, mechanized pitchforks; the simpler models could also be used to load hay into a wagon. More elaborate mechanisms were designed to move hay from the wagon into the barn.

NELLIS'
ORIGINAL
HARPOON HORSE HAY FORK,
AND FIXTURES.
PITTSBURGH, PA.

The Harpoon Horse Hay Fork was originally invented by Mr. Edward L. Walker, and patented by him September 6th, 1864. The fork devised by Mr. Walker was far in advance of any that had preceded it; the principle was a good one, but the instrument itself was comparatively crude, and susceptible of great improvement. The first really valuable improvement on the original fork was made by Mr. Seymour Rogers, of Pittsburgh, Pa., and by him patented January 24th, 1865; subsequently, May 29, 1866, this patent was re-issued. Mr. Seymour Rogers being at that time a member of the firm of D. B. Rogers & Sons, of Pittsburgh, which firm, deeming the Harpoon Fork a meritorious implement, purchased the first patent from the original inventor, and, adding the improvements patented by Mr. Seymour Rogers, began their manufacture on a large scale, confident that they were perfect in every respect, and sanguine of their great success. Undoubtedly the principle of the Harpoon Fork as made by

them was correct, and, when properly made, the fork was capable of doing more and better work in a given time than any other, and, indeed, the merits of other horse forks seemed to have been combined in this; but unfortunately there was a deficiency in the mechanism, and so great was the defect that nearly all the forks first put on the market were returned to have the tripping device reconstructed. This defect seriously interfered with the success of the fork, its many good points were lost sight of in the one defect, and

NELLIS' PATENT STACKER.

the Harpoon Horse Hay Fork, instead of being generally recognized as an improvement entitled to a prominent place in the front rank of labor-saving agricultural implements, was consigned by its former admirers to a dark corner in the back ground, where it remained until it passed into the hands of its present owner, Mr. A. J. Nellis.

Mr. Nellis, after a long series of costly experiments, made many improvements, and the Forks manufactured by his firm have met with unqualified success. The patents of the Nellis Original Harpoon Horse Hay Fork are dated as follows: September 6, 1864; re-issued December 18, 1866; January 24, 1865; re-issued May 29, 1866; March 20, 1866; December 18, 1866; August 13, 1867; November 9, 1867; January 11, 1870; January 18, 1870; October 21, 1873; June 30, 1874; July 21, 1874. Most of these patents for improvements were issued to Mr. Nellis, and they are all owned and controlled by him; they cover every thing embraced in the single or double harpoon principle, all harpoon forks not manufactured by them, or by his license, are infringements on his patents for which makers, sellers and users are each liable. Messrs. Nellis & Co. grant no license for their manufacture.

Since the patents previously noted were issued, further and valuable improvements have been made, and it is now generally recognized as equal to any if not superior to all other Horse Forks. It is believed to be the greatest labor-saving agricultural instrument, in comparison with its cost, and is certainly the last one a farmer would think of dispensing with. It is warmly endorsed by over 100,000 farmers who use it, and after practical tests it has received seventy-six State Fair First Premiums in seventy-six months, a record of success which we think none can excel.

In addition to the Fork but a fitting connection to it for the convenience of the farmer, and worthy of special mention, is the Nellis grapple and Nellis' patent method for moving and stacking hay. The cut at the bottom of page 95 represents Nellis' patent stacker, the patent covering an improvement in pulleys and for their arrangement. The right to use this arrangement will be given to all purchasers of Nellis' Forks and Fixtures. This method of stacking requires four poles—poles A A about 35 feet in length, and poles B about 25 feet long. Now fasten these poles together at the small end by rope or chains (see G G in cut), fasten swivel pulley and two-wheeled pulley at E, first passing rope through same; raise poles B, and secure them in an upright position by means of guy H and pin I, letting the poles lean a little forward (these poles B can also be used on front of barn); then tie (or fasten with floor hook) pulley at F. This done, pass your hoisting rope through the fork pulley (or small S hook pulley) then through dead eye pulley C, which is tied at G, on long poles; then tie this end of rope to neck of fork pulley and graduating cord at last named place also; now, by hitching your horse, you can raise your poles A A, and secure them by guy rope H and pin I, letting them lean

Nellis' Harpoon Fork.

Nellis' Grapple.

Nellis' Harpoon Fork.

Nellis' Grapple.

NELLIS' PATENT METHOD OF CONVEYING HAY, STRAW, Etc.

slightly towards poles B. Now with graduating cord pull your fork pulley down, put horse fork in S hook pulley, attach your trip cord, and you are ready for operation.

This arrangement enables you to make your stack of any desired height or length, and renders easy the attainment of an important object when stacking, which is, to keep the centre of the stack solid, as the fork deposits its load in the centre or at any desired point of a long stack, at the disposal of a man on the stack, who, by this arrangement, is enabled to do the work of from two to three men, in from one-fourth to one-third of the time required by or in the old method of stacking; a fair trial of which must convince one of the correctness of this principle

To load hay from stack back to wagon: Take pulley F, and fasten at bottom of either long poles. Fasten end of rope to pole at point formerly occupied by pulley F. Loosen the end of the rope from the fork and pass through pulley F. Loosen the end of the rope from the fork and pass through pulley at bottom of long pole, and hitch now to this end. This operation will run your material successfully back to your wagon.

This stacking principle can be readily adopted inside of barn to unload into bays or mows either side of the wagon way, and the point C answering to any desired point in the roof over the mow. (See cut on page 96.) The adoption of this method enables one to convey the material to be unloaded in any direction and distance desired, and with the Nellis Grapple for putting up pulleys, the direction for running the hay can be changed with little, if any inconvenience or delay, as it can be done between forkfuls. It is deemed indispensable by all farmers who have become familiar with its convenience.

HAY LOADER

Development.—The hay loader has been upon the market for some time, but only during recent years has there been any great demand for the tool. The Keystone Manufacturing

Company, of Sterling, Illinois, began experimenting with the hay loader as early as 1875. The machine is designed to be attached to the rear of the wagon, to gather the hay and elevate it to a rack on the wagon.

Endless apron loaders.—The hay is elevated in this type of loader on an endless apron or carrier after it has been gathered by a gathering cylinder. The main advantage of this type of loader is that it does not handle the hay as roughly as the fork loaders. This is an important feature in handling alfalfa and clover, as there is a tendency to shake out many of the leaves, a valuable part of the hay. Due provision must be made, however to prevent the hay from being carried back by

FIG. 131—AN ENDLESS APRON OR CARRIER HAY LOADER

the carrier returning on the under side. The apron or carrier usually passes over a cylinder at the under side, which has teeth to aid in starting the hay up the carrier.

Provision must be made to enable the gathering cylinder to pass over obstructions and uneven ground. For this reason the gathering cylinder is mounted upon a separate frame and the whole held to the ground by suitable springs. The loader has a great range of capacity. All modern machines will load hay from the swath or the windrow, and the carrier will elevate large bunches of hay without any difficulty.

MACHINES FOR FIELD STACKING

Sweep rakes.—Where a large amount of hay is to be stacked in a short time, the sweep rake and the hay stacker will do the work more quickly than is possible by any other means. The sweep rake has straight wooden teeth to take the hay either from the swath or windrow, and is either drawn between the two horses or pushed ahead. When a load is secured the teeth are raised, the load hauled and placed upon the teeth of the stacker and the rake backed away.

There are three general types of sweep rakes: (1) the wheel-less, with the horses spread to each end of the rake;

FIG. 132—A TWO-WHEEL SWEEP RAKE. THE TEETH ARE RAISED BY THE DRIVER SHIFTING HIS SEAT

(2) the wheeled rake, with the horses spread in the same manner; and (3) the three-wheel rake, with the horses

FIG. 133—A THREE-WHEEL SWEEP RAKE. THE DRIVER IS AIDED IN LIFTING THE LOADED TEETH BY THE PULL OF THE HORSES

directly behind the rake and working on a tongue. The latter are the more expensive. They offer advantages in driving the team, but are a little difficult to guide (Figs. 132 and 133).

Hay stackers are made in two general types: the overshot and the swinging stacker. In the overshot the teeth carrying

FIG. 134—A PLAIN OVERSHOT HAY STACKER

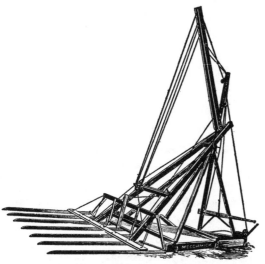

FIG. 135—THE SWING HAY STACKER. NOTE THE BRAKE AT THE REAR END FOR HOLDING THE ROPE

the load are drawn up and over and the load is thrown directly back upon the stack, the work being done with a horse or a team of horses by means of ropes and suitable pulleys (Fig. 134).

The swinging stacker permits the load to be locked in place after it has been raised from the ground to any height and swung to one side over the stack. When over the stack, the load may be dumped and the fork swung back and lowered into place. The latter stackers are very handy, as they may be used to load on to a wagon. They have not as yet been built strong enough to stand hard service.

HAY LOADERS

One of the greatest labor- and time-saving machines for the farmer is the hay loader. It displaces hand-pitching—one of the hardest and most tiresome jobs on the farm—speeds up hay making, and cuts production costs. The hay loader is needed on every farm where the hay is loaded in the field and put directly into the

Figure 189—Single-cylinder hay loader with carrier extension in lowered position.

barns or hauled to stacks. Ten to fifteen acres of hay justify the purchase of a hay loader.

The ideal combination of equipment is the side-delivery rake and the hay loader. With these two, highest quality hay can be produced at the lowest cost.

Types of Loaders. There are four distinct types of hay loaders—the single cylinder, the double cylinder, the combination raker-bar cylinder, and the raker bar. Each has its following and each has features that make it particularly adaptable to certain conditions.

The single-cylinder loader (Fig. 189) is used only for loading from the windrow. In handling hay from windrows, such as made by the side-delivery rake, it rakes its full width and delivers all of the hay onto the rack.

The floating gathering cylinder on the double-cylinder loader makes this type adaptable to loading hay from the swath as well as the windrow. When properly set, it will do better work in rough fields than either the single cylinder or raker-bar loader. Its good work in picking hay from the swath makes it especially popular in some sections.

The combination raker-bar cylinder loader (Fig. 191) combines the most desirable features of both the double-

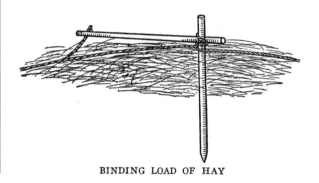

Figure 191—Combination raker-bar cylinder loader with the more important parts named.

Labels: HINGED ADJUSTABLE GATE · GATE ADJUSTING ROD · SOLID STEEL DECK · RAKER BARS · COMPRESSOR SPRINGS · TRIP ROPE · JOHN DEERE · GATHERING CYLINDER · HITCH POINT · PIVOTING TONGUE TRUCK · DRIVE CHAINS · RAKE DRUM ECCENTRIC

cylinder and the raker-bar types, and threatens to displace the latter. The operation is similar to that of the double-cylinder loader. The floating cylinder rakes over its entire width, regardless of ground conditions, and the raker bar insures smooth elevation.

Raker-bar loaders operate on an entirely different principle than cylinder loaders. A series of bars to which are fastened malleable rakes elevate the hay from swath or windrow with a lifting or pitching motion, the result of an oblong stroke of the raker bars.

BINDING PINS FOR HAY

Every person moving hay ought to have a set of binding pins. They are made in a minute and serve an excellent purpose for a lifetime. The sketch shows a rope stretched over the top of a load of hay or straw. The upright pin is worked down into the load and the other twisted in the rope and turned around the upright until the load is tightly bound. Then a small rope that is kept tied in end of the horizontal pin is tied to the binding rope and the pressure is held. Each pin is 3 1/2 feet long. One is sharpened and the other has a 1/2-inch hole bored through one end. Old fork handles are just the thing to make them of. One pin only may be made and a fork used to bind in the manner shown after the load is on.

BINDING LOAD OF HAY

HAY PRESSES

By the 1860s, patents were being granted on an ingenious variety of hay presses that squeezed hay down into easily manageable bales. (Oddly, calling this equipment a hay baler began only in the 1940s, when the process became considerably more automated.) Hay presses were powered by horses operating sweeps or from steam or gasoline engines. Early models were stationary, but wheeled presses that could be transported directly to the field quickly appeared. A fairly small hay press operated by two workers and one or two horses could handle several tons of hay in a day.

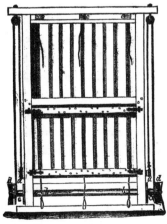

Fig. 159.—FRAME OF HAY PRESS.

HOME-MADE HAY PRESS

The press shown in figures 159, 160, and 161 may be made wholly of wood, hewn to the right size, and put together with wooden pins. The frame, figure 159, is four feet long inside of the posts, and three feet wide. The height is eight feet. The movable bottom is raised by ropes which pass over pulleys or rollers, if no iron is to be used, and are wound upon the rollers at the bottom. This roller is moved by bars to be inserted in mortises cut in the roller, similar to the manner used in moving a windlass, or a capstan on shipboard. A movable door is made to fit the bottom of the press on one side, for the purpose of removing the bale after it is pressed.

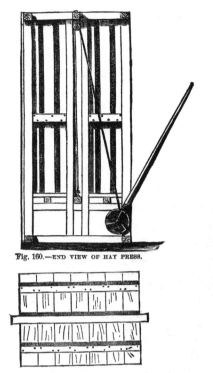

Fig. 160.—END VIEW OF HAY PRESS.

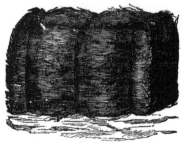

Fig. 161.—MOVABLE BOTTOM.

The bale is bound with a strong cord, pieces of which are placed on the bottom and others on the top, as shown in figure 159, and the ends are fastened when the bale is pressed as tightly as possible. It is then reduced to two and one-half feet in thickness, and eight of these bales will make a ton. The hay is easily transported in wagons when baled, and the press

Fig. 162.—HAY BALE.

can be moved from one meadow to another as the hay is cut and pressed, or it will be more convenient at times to drive the cattle to the hay rather than move the hay to the cattle. Figure 160 shows the end view of the press, figure 161, the movable bottom, and figure 162, the pressed bale. When the iron can be procured without great expense, it might be well to use the pulleys and slotted wheels as here shown, but otherwise these parts may be made of wood.

Box presses are used very little at present, being superseded by the continuous machines of larger capacity. The box press consists in a box through which the plunger or

compressor acts vertically, power being furnished either by hand or by a horse. The box, with the plunger down, is filled with hay; the plunger is then raised, compressing the hay

FIG. 143—A FULL-CIRCLE HORSE HAY PRESS ON TRUCKS FOR TRANSPORTATION

into, usually, the upper end, where it is tied and removed. The machine is then prepared for another charge.

Horse-power presses are either one-half circle or full circle. In the half-circle or reversible-lever presses the team pulls the lever to one side and then turns around and pulls it to the other side. The hay is placed loose in a compressing box, compressed at each stroke and pushed toward the open end of the frame, where it is held by tension or pressure on the sides. When a bale of sufficient length is made, a dividing block is inserted and the bale tied with wire.

In the full-circle press the team is required to travel in a circle. Usually two strokes are made to one round of the team. Various devices or mechanisms are used to obtain power for the compression. It is desired that the motion be fast at the beginning of the stroke, while the hay is loose, and

FIG. 144—A HAY PRESS FOR ENGINE POWER AND EQUIPPED WITH A CONDENSER TO THRUST THE HAY INTO THE HOPPER

slow while the hay is compressed during the latter part of the stroke. The cam is the most common device to secure this; however, gear wheels with a cam shape are often used. The rebound aided by a spring is usually depended upon to return the plunger for a new stroke; but a cam motion may be made use of to return the plunger. It is to be noted that some machines use a stiff pitman and push away from the power, while others use a chain and rod and pull the pitman toward the power or reverse the direction of travel of the plunger. A horse-power machine has an average capacity of about 18 tons a day. A cubic foot of hay before baling weighs 4 or 5 pounds when stored in the mow or stack. A baling press increases its density to 16 or 30 pounds a cubic foot. Specially designed presses for compressing hay for export secure as high as 40 pounds of hay a cubic foot.

HAY TOOLS

A variety of mechanized devices such as hay carriers, hayforks, and hay slings were used to get the hay into the barn and move it around once it was there. All operated using some variation on the idea of a steel or cable track that ran the length of the hay loft. Pulleys on trucks ran along the track; grapple forks, harpoon forks, and slings attached to the pulley carried hay bales or heavy loads of hay.

HAY CARRIER FOR HORSE FORK

Figure 154 shows an ingenious device for returning a horse hay-fork from the hay-mow to the loaded wagon. It consists of a wire rope, *C*, stretched from the end of the track, *A*, to a wooden cylinder, *B*, four inches in diameter and sixteen inches long, around which a few turns are given. Two short stakes, *D, D,* cut from a four-by-four scantling and driven slantingly into the ground, hold the roller in position. A grooved pulley, *E*, runs freely on the wire, and from its axis is suspended a fifty pound weight, *F.* The rope, *G*, runs over the pulley, *H*, which is firmly attached to the lower side of the track. The wire-rope is made of three wire clothes-lines twisted together. When in use, the upper end of the cord is

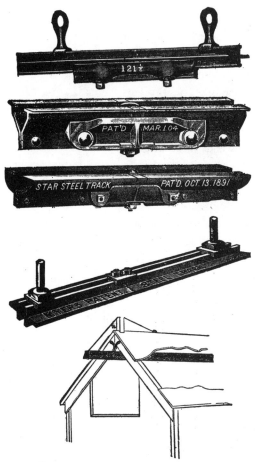

Fig. 154.—IMPROVED HAY-CARRIER.

FIG. 136—TYPES OF STEEL AND WOOD HAY CARRIER TRACKS

attached to the rope which carries the fork. It is thus carried up with the loaded fork, and brings it back by gravitation when empty.

Tracks.—A large variety of tracks is to be found upon the market to-day—the square wooden track, the two-piece wooden track, the single-piece inverted T steel track, the double steel track made of two angle bars, and various forms of single- and double-flange steel tracks. Wire cables are used in outdoor work.

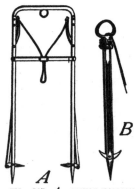

FIG. 137—*A*, DOUBLE-HARPOON HAY FORK. *B*, SINGLE-HARPOON HAY FORK

Various forms of track switches and folding tracks are to be found upon the market. By means of a switch it is possible to unload hay at one point and send it out in many different directions. In circular barns it is possible to arrange pulleys in such a way that the carrier will be carried around a circular track.

Forks are built in a variety of shapes and are known as single-harpoon or shear fork, double-harpoon fork, derrick forks, and four-, six-, and eight-tined grapple forks. To replace the fork for rapid unloading of hay, the hay sling is used. The harpoon forks are best adapted for the handling of long hay, like timothy. For handling clover, alfalfa, and the shorter grasses, the grapple and derrick forks are generally used. The derrick fork is a popular style for field stacking in some localities. Harpoon forks have fingers which hold the hay upon the tines until tripped. The tines are made in lengths varying from 25 to 35 inches, to suit the conditions. The grapple fork opens and closes on the hay like ice tongs. The eight-tined fork is suitable for handling manure.

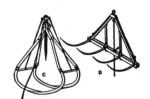

FIG. 138—*C*, A FOUR-TINED GRAPPLE FORK. *D*, A DERRICK FORK

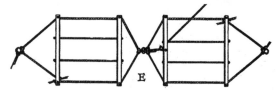

FIG. 139—A HAY SLING. THE SPRING CATCH BY WHICH THE SLING IS PARTED IS ABOVE *E*

The hay sling consists of a pair of ropes spread with wooden bars and provided with a catch, by which it may be separated at the middle for discharging a sling load. The

sling is placed at the bottom of the load, and after sufficient hay has been built over it for a sling load, another sling is spread between the ends of the hay rack and another sling load is built on, and so on.

FIG. 140—A TWO-WAY FORK HAY CARRIER. TO WORK IN THE OPPOSITE DIRECTION, THE ROPE IS SIMPLY PULLED THROUGH UNTIL THE KNOT ON THE OPPOSITE END IS STOPPED BY THE CARRIER

Carriers.—Carriers are made to suit all of the various forms of tracks and are made one-way, swivel, and reversible.

FIG. 141—A DOUBLE-CARRIAGE REVERSIBLE SLING CARRIER. DESIGNED FOR HEAVY SERVICE

FIG. 142—A LIGHTER SLING CARRIER LOADED WITH A SLING LOAD OF HAY

Horse Hay Pitching Apparatus.

Shipped as second-class freight.

No farmer who has ever used the Horse Hay Fork for unloading hay, either in the barn or on the stack, will ever go back to pitching by hand. Those who neglect to adopt it are wasting time and money every year. The best Double Harpoon Fork we sell for 63 cents, and good Pulleys for 15 cents each.

70498 Standard Double Harpoon Hay Fork, all iron and steel and very durable. The best fork in the market; standard size, regular length of tines from cross bar, 25 inches; known and used everywhere; weight, 18 pounds.
Price............................$0.63

70500 Extra Long Tined Double Harpoon Hay Fork, for loose straw, etc.; longer than needed for hay; tines 32 inches from cross bar. Weight, 20 lbs
Price, each............... $1.30

70502 Four - Tine Grapple Hay Fork. Weight, 40 lbs. Price.......... $4.25

70504 Six-Tine Grapple Horse Hay Fork. Weight, 55 lbs. Price......$5.25

70505 Fourteen Tined Combined Hay and Manure Grapple Fork, 8 tines are removable. For handling hay in connection with our stacking outfit. This fork will load or handle manure with the greatest facility. Weight, 87 lbs. Price......$9.25

Harpoon Hay Forks.

70506 The Improved Single Harpoon Hay Fork. Weight, 7 lbs. Price............................$1.75

The Milwaukee Improved Reversible and Double Swivel Wood Track Hay Carriers.

All hay tools shipped as second class freight. These carriers will run on 4x4 or 3x4 or 2x4 track, and will work either way from the stop without change —as it will pass the stop to right or left as well.

70508   70510

70508 Is reversed by threading the rope through and attaching horse to the other end of rope. Milwaukee Improved Reversible Hay Carrier. Weight, 27 lbs........... ....$3.00

70510 Leader Double Swivel Hay Carrier, is reversed by merely swinging the pulleys around, leaving fork and horse attached. Weight, 30 lbs. Price........ .... 3.50

CHAPTER 8

MANURE

Well into the 1900s, the terms *manure* and *fertilizer* were almost interchangeable. Today *manure* refers mostly to animal waste; unfortunately, only among organic farmers is the term still synonymous with *fertilizer*.

Earlier farmers used the animal droppings and soiled hay and straw from the stables as a free, natural fertilizer—indeed, most wished they had more. According to Department of Agriculture estimates from around 1905, the annual value of a single horse's manure was $27; a cow produced manure worth $19, while a hog produced manure worth $12. In general, the value of manure was estimated at anywhere from $2 to $7 a ton. At a time when a good wage for a city worker was $20 a week and farm laborers often earned only a dollar or two a day, the value of animal manure to the farmer was very real.

Handling the manure was one of the more unpleasant and labor-intensive farm jobs. By the 1880s, the manure spreader had come into widespread use. A simple manure spreader was a wagon with a beater on the back to break up the manure before it was dropped onto the soil and then plowed in. More elaborate manure spreaders had an apron or conveyor belt that carried the manure to the beater.

PREPARING AND HANDLING FERTILIZERS

When hauling manure it is usual to drop it in heaps, and leave it to be spread by a man who follows soon after. There are several methods of dumping the manure, but the most satisfactory is to use a manure hook, as shown in figure 186. The bottom of the sled or wagon should be formed of loose planks, each with its end shaved down to form handles. The side and end pieces of the box, though closely fitting, are not fastened together, so that they can be removed one at a time. One side or an end board is first taken out, and with a manure hook a sufficient amount of the load removed for

Fig. 186.—A MANURE HOOK.

the first heap. The manner of unloading the manure from the box above described, is shown in figure 187. The other side and ends are afterwards taken off, and finally the bottom pieces are raised and the sled or wagon is soon emptied. In dropping the heaps, they should be left, as nearly as may be, in straight rows, and of a size and distance apart

Fig. 187.—A MANURE WAGON BOX.

determined by the amount of manure to be spread. If they are placed regularly one rod from another each way, and eight heaps are made from a load, there will be twenty loads per acre. In spreading such heaps the manure is thrown eight feet each way, and the whole ground is covered. It is important that the spreading be done in a careful and thorough manner, each portion of the surface getting its proper share of the manure. It is important also that all lumps be broken up.

70600 Kemp's Manure spreader. Most successful machine for the purpose intended. Retail price, $85.00 to $135.00, as to size and capacity. Full information to intending purchasers.

FIG. 146—A RETURN APRON SPREADER, SHOWING THE APRON UNDERNEATH, AND ALSO A GEAR AND CHAIN DRIVE TO BEATER

FIG. 151—A MANURE SPREADER WITH AN END BOARD TO BE PLACED IN FRONT OF THE BEATER

A style of horse-drawn spreader in common use is shown in Fig. 224. It has three beaters. The upper and main beaters shred the manure; the spiral beater deposits it evenly over the entire width, making a well-defined line beyond the drive wheels.

The manure is carried back to the beaters by a steel slat conveyor, the speed of which is controlled by the feed lever

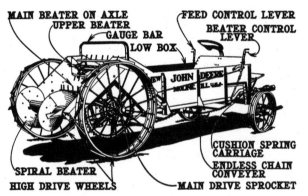

Figure 224—A horse-drawn manure spreader.

from the driver's seat. From five to twenty loads can be spread per acre, according to the setting of the feed lever.

The operator must be sure to keep the feed lever forward, in neutral, whenever the machine is not in gear or whenever the beaters are not operating. If the feed lever is left in operating position when starting to the field with a load, the conveyor forces the load back against the beater, resulting in breakage in some part of the feed mechanism. The feed lever should be thrown into neutral also when turning sharply while spreading.

With the control lever, the operator shifts the main drive chain so that it is in contact with the large drive sprocket. The three beaters are driven by two chains, both of which are set into action by the drive sprocket. The beaters should not be put into gear in this manner while the machine is in motion. The control lever should be moved to the rear only when the spreader is standing still.

Green manures were crops planted in fields for the purpose of fertilizing the ground. Crops such as clover and other legumes were good for returning nitrogen to the soil; other crops, such as buckwheat and alfalfa, were simply plowed under, where they rotted and enriched the soil. The ideal green manure crop grows quickly in cool weather and produces a lot of organic material. Green manure crops were sowed in the fall after the harvest or in the early spring before it was time to plant. In addition to their fertilizing qualities, green manures also smothered weeds and left the fields in good condition for planting.

AGENTS OF NITRIFICATION

These are soil bacteria that penetrate the roots of alfalfa, beans, clover, peas, and other leguminous plants and form knotlike enlargements which are called tubercles. These bacteria have the power of fixing the free nitrogen of the air circulating in the soil, and thus they enable the plant to live in soils in which the stock of nitrogen salts has been exhausted. These bacteria have been cultivated artificially by the government experts in the employ of the United States Department of Agriculture, and may now be shipped anywhere to farmers who wish to inoculate the soils of their fields with such nitrifying agents.

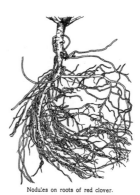

Nodules on roots of red clover.

PART III:
Crops

CHAPTER 9

VEGETABLES

Market gardening, or truck farming, became an important source of income to farmers starting in the 1880s. The reasons were improved transportation to and large demand from urban centers. The perfection of the tin can in the 1870s led to increased demand for vegetables from commercial canners. Tomato growers received a big boost from the perfection of commercial techniques for bottling ketchup starting in the 1880s.

Profits from vegetable growing could be substantial. Spinach, for instance, sold in the 1870s for around $3 a barrel, with an average acre yielding two hundred barrels. Because spinach is an early spring crop sown in late winter, the land could then be replanted to celery, cabbage, or other vegetables by May.

Root crops, including potatoes, beets, carrot, and turnips, were grown as much for winter fodder for animals as for human consumption. By the 1880s, the sugar beet had become a main crop, largely replacing imported sugarcane as a source of table sugar. Other valuable vegetable crops included cabbage, cauliflower, broccoli, lettuce, and tomatoes.

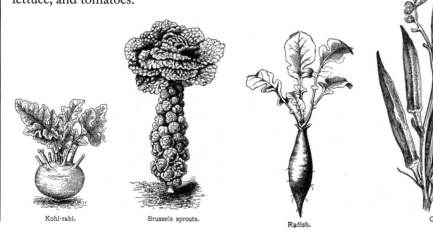

Kohl-rabi.   Brussels sprouts.   Radish.   Okra.

Cabbage.

Cauliflower.

Victoria spinach.

Savoy leaved spinach.

Loose-leaved lettuce.

Head lettuce.

VEGETABLE CULTIVATION

Vegetable fields were small, especially by modern-day standards—for most market garden crops, ten acres would have been a very large field. Most vegetable cultivation was done by hand, although the initial plowing was usually done with a single-horse walking plow, and horse-drawn seeders were used for crops such as carrots. After that, weeds were controlled by hoeing and the use of the hand cultivator. Picking, of course, was a seasonal occupation done almost entirely by hand.

Market farmers could get a jump on the season by starting seeds in hotbeds or cold frames very early in the spring and then transplanting the seedlings to the fields when the ground was warm enough. Farmers prosperous enough to invest in greenhouses could provide hothouse produce to the luxury market nearly year-round.

The preferred method for making a hotbed a century ago was with large amounts of fresh horse manure. To make the bed, fresh manure was combined with equal amounts of chopped straw and piled up to start the heat-producing composting process.

The rotting manure was shoveled into deep trenches; a thick layer of soil was laid on top. Glass frames over the trench kept the heat and moisture in. Permanent hotbeds, heated by underground steam pipes, were sometimes constructed. Cold frames were similar to hotbeds, but they depended solely on sunlight for heat.

SOWING SEED EVENLY

These drawings show the construction of a wheel seeding device that can be easily made at home. The axle is tightly fitted into the wheels so that it turns when the wheels do. This agitates the grain or other seed and helps to keep the seed running out of the holes at the lower back side of the box. The quantity of flow may be regulated at pleasure by making the holes large or small and increasing or diminishing the number of holes.

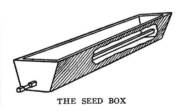

THE SEED BOX

A SOWING MACHINE

Fig. 163.—WHEELBARROW

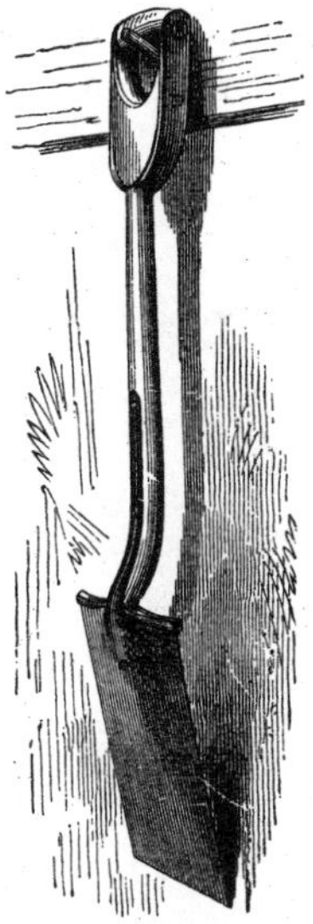

THE SPADE

The best kinds of these in use are Ames' cast-steel; excellent, strong, light articles. They work clean and bright as silver. There are several sizes. For heavy work, trenching, draining, raising trees, etc., the largest should be used.

THE SHOVEL

This is used in mixing, loading, and spreading composts and short manures. The blade should be of cast-steel.

Fig. 164.—SPADE.

THE FORKED SPADE

This resembles a fork. It has three to five stout cast-steel tines, at least an inch wide, and pointed. It is used instead of a spade to loosen the earth above the roots of trees, to turn in manure, etc., being much less liable to cut and injure them than the spade.

Fig. 165.—SHOVEL.   Fig. 166.—FORKED SPADES.

THE DUNG-FORK

There are several kinds. Those of cast-steel, cut out of a solid plate, with three or four tines, are the best, light and durable; they are sometimes made with six tines. It is the only implement proper for loading, mixing, or spreading fresh rough manures with facility and dispatch.

THE PICK

This is a useful, and even indispensable implement in the deepening or trenching of soils with a hard subsoil that cannot be operated upon with the spade. It consists of an ash handle, and a head composed of two levers of iron pointed with steel, and an eye in the centre for the handle.

THE GARDEN-LINE AND REEL

The line should be a good hemp cord, from one eighth to one fourth of an inch in diameter, attached to light iron stakes about eighteen inches long. On one of the stakes a reel is attached. This is turned by means of a handle, and the line neatly and quickly wound up.

THE HOE

This is a universal instrument in this country. In some cases, all the gardening operations are performed with it. Its uses in tree culture are to open trenches for seeds, to cover them, to loosen and clean the surface of the ground from weeds, etc. There are two kinds,

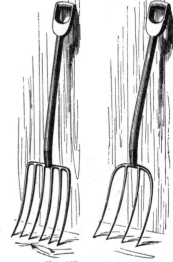

Fig. 167.—DUNG-FORKS.

the draw hoe (fig. 169, 170, 171) and the Dutch or thrust hoe (fig. 172); this we do not use at all. Of the two different kinds and forms of the draw hoe, the most generally useful is the square, a cast-steel plate, about six inches long and four wide, with a light, smooth handle. The semicircular and triangular hoes may be advantageously used in certain cases.

Fig. 168.—LINE AND REEL.

THE POINTED GARDEN HOE

The pointed garden hoe (Fig. 173) is useful among borders and small plants.

THE RAKE

The rake is used to level, smooth, pulverize, and clean the surface of the ground after it has been spaded or hoed, or to prepare it for seeds, etc. They are of different sizes, with from six to twelve teeth. The best are those of which the head and teeth are drawn out of a solid bar of steel. Those that are welded and riveted soon get out of order.

Fig. 170.—TRIANGULAR DRAW-HOE. Fig. 171.—SEMICIRCULAR DRAW-HOE.

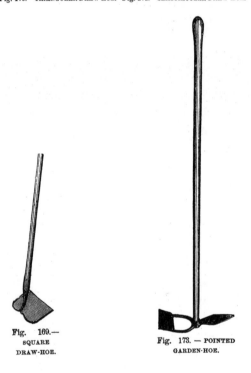

Fig. 169.—
SQUARE
DRAW-HOE.

Fig. 173. — POINTED
GARDEN-HOE.

An attractive trellis is shown. Three strips of wood, pointed at the lower end and finished with a knob at the top, are provided, the length being a matter for individual taste. A trellis for tomato plants will need not more than two hoops, while one for sweet peas may require a half dozen. The strips of wood should be of inch board, 2 inches wide. The hoops are secured to the uprights by small staples made for putting up wire fencing. The wooden posts may be oiled or painted some attractive color. This trellis will be greatly appreciated both in the vegetable and flower gardens, for its strength and attractiveness.

THE TRELLIS

EASY WAY TO POLE BEANS

Set posts at convenient distances apart and stretch a wire at the top. This may be done as soon as ground is plowed. Plant and cultivate one row each side of line until beans begin to vine, then set poles slanting, tying them together where they cross at the wire. This braces the whole row and beans can be cultivated with hoe. Hills 3 feet apart in row with one vine to hill are better than two vines.

TRELLIS FOR BEANS

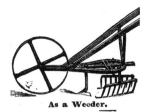

POTATOES

Easy to grow and easy to store, the potato was a staple food for both the farmer and his livestock (unsalable small potatoes were fed to the pigs, for example). They were also a market crop. By the 1880s, potato crops could yield anywhere from 100 to 150 bushels to the acre and bring in anywhere from fifty cents to a dollar a bushel, making them fairly profitable.

Digging the potatoes by hand or by plowing them up was a wasteful and backbreaking method of harvesting. Because potatoes were usually dug in the late fall, the harvest became a race against the first winter freeze, and all available hands were pressed into service. The potato digger, a specialized plowlike device with a shovel that ran underneath the potatoes, came into use by the 1860s. The potato digger left the potatoes on the surface, but they still had to be picked up and loaded into sacks by hand. More elaborate potato diggers that not only raised the potatoes out of the ground but also shook off most of the soil and stones and separated the tubers from the vines were in use by the end of the century. By the 1890s several manufacturers were offering potato planters that would furrow, drop the cut seed potatoes, and cover them all in one operation.

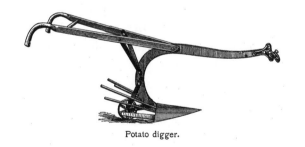

Potato digger.

PRINCIPLE OF OPERATION

The wide steel shovel, set to run at a safe depth below the potatoes, raises the potatoes, dirt, vines and all, onto the elevator. Depth is regulated by adjusting the lifting lever, and by adjustment of beams.

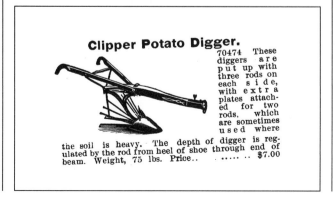

Clipper Potato Digger.
70474 These diggers are put up with three rods on each side, with extra plates attached for two rods, which are sometimes used where the soil is heavy. The depth of digger is regulated by the rod from heel of shoe through end of beam. Weight, 75 lbs. Price.. ...... $7.00

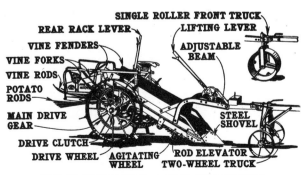

SINGLE ROLLER FRONT TRUCK
LIFTING LEVER
REAR RACK LEVER
VINE FENDERS
ADJUSTABLE BEAM
VINE FORKS
VINE RODS
POTATO RODS
MAIN DRIVE GEAR
STEEL SHOVEL
DRIVE CLUTCH
DRIVE WHEEL
AGITATING WHEEL
ROD ELEVATOR
TWO-WHEEL TRUCK

Figure 166—Elevator potato digger with important parts named.

The main object of the potato digger is to deliver clean potatoes on top of the soil. As stated above, the shovel, digging under the potatoes, loosens the soil and, by the forward motion of the digger, the soil, potatoes, and vines are carried onto the elevator. The elevator is a continuous chain moving toward the rear of the machine. The earth drops through the elevator, aided by the agitating or up-and-down movement of the elevator. This agitation can be increased or decreased according to soil conditions by interchanging the smooth rollers and oblong agitating sprockets provided.

The potatoes and vines are carried to the rear of the machine where they are deposited on top of the soil. There are three kinds of rear racks for diggers. The extension elevator is constricted similarly to the main elevator except that it is operated separately. The continuous elevator, as its name implies, is a continuation of the main elevator, extending to the rear. The agitating rear racks, shown on the digger illustrated in Fig. 166, separate the vines from the potatoes, placing each in a separate row. Having the potatoes in a narrow row, separated from the vines, is an advantage in picking them up.

SORTING POTATOES QUICKLY

The sketch shows a homemade potato cleaner and sorter. It consists of a number of hoops to which are fastened 1/2-inch slats so as to make holes 1 1/2 inches square. Two heavy

POTATO SORTER AND CLEANER

pieces, *a*, are placed inside the cylinder to hold the axle, *b*, which extends entirely through the machine and is turned by a crank, *c*. The frame made is 4 inches lower at the opening end of the cylinder so that the potatoes will run through freely.

At the crank end is a hopper, *f*, into which the potatoes are poured. The cylinder is 2 5/8 feet long and 3 feet in diameter. It will not bruise the potatoes, and the dirt and small ones run through on to the floor or crate and the marketable ones run out at the open end of the cylinder into another crate. With one man to turn the crank and another to fill the hopper, from 700 to 800 bushels can be sorted in a day.

CUTTING SEED POTATOES

In the principal potato growing sections, medium to large seed is used for planting and cut to two eyes. In the famous Greeley district of Colorado, cutting is done by hand.

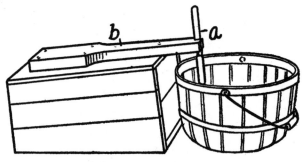

SEED POTATO CUTTER

Potatoes are shoveled into a bin or hopper, made of a dry-goods box raised on legs. The back is made higher than the front, so that potatoes will run down to the opening and the bottom is slatted to let out the soil shoveled up with the potatoes.

The cutting is simple. An old case knife, *a*, is fastened to the end of a plank or board, *b*, in such a way that potatoes can be pushed against the knife and fall from it into the basket beneath. The operator sits on the box to which the board is fastened and can work very rapidly.

CHAPTER 10

FRUITS AND BERRIES

The Agriculturist for January 1870 wistfully suggests, "Were small fruits in abundance, there would be fewer discussions of the question, 'Why do boys leave the farm?'" Whatever their role in keeping boys down on the farm, it is certain that fruits and berries (also known as small fruits) were extremely important for the farmer, both for home consumption and as profitable market crops.

The fruit varieties grown a century ago are startling in their abundance. In 1900 as many as 4,000 apple varieties, some very local, were in cultivation. No single apple dominated the crop. Today, although some 7,000 apple varieties are known in the United States alone, only about 2,500 varieties are in cultivation, and a mere 15 varieties account for 90 percent of the crop.

After the invention of the mason jar by John Mason in 1858, fruits for preserving became an important part of the market. Preserved fruits and pickles gave interest and needed vitamins to monotonous winter diets. The quince, a fruit practically unknown today, was in demand for jelly. Virtually inedible raw, quince, because of its high pectin content, made excellent jelly. Similarly, some strawberry and raspberry varieties were raised primarily for preserving, and crab apples were a market crop.

As the enthusiastic author of *Small Fruit Culturist* pointed out about berries in 1881,

Thousands of bushels are annually preserved for home use by families, both in country and city. One may step into any of our restaurants—even when the snow covers the fields and with the thermometer at zero—and call for a dish of strawberries and cream, and he will be supplied as readily as in the month of June. . . . Not only do private families, saloons, and hotels consume enormous quantities of the Small Fruits which have been preserved in these hermetically sealed cans and jars, but every steamer or sailing vessel that leaves our ports takes with it a supply for use on the voyage, and it often forms a share of the freight. We are not only called upon to produce fruits to supply the home demand, but other portions of the world which cannot or do not produce them, and it can readily be seen that it must be many years before anything like an adequate quantity can be produced, even with the rapid strides we are making.

The demand for fresh fruit was always high, but until rail networks were developed, it could be met only locally. By the 1870s, as the railroad net expanded, so did the number of farmers specializing in fruits, especially in areas along the rail routes. The Georgia peach industry, for example, was rescued from near extinction in the late 1870s by a combination of improved rail service and the development of longer-lasting cultivars that could withstand the journey north. Refrigerated boxcars were developed in the late 1860s. The first long-distance shipment in a refrigerated car was made from California to New York in 1888; it consisted of oranges and berries. By 1900, although home iceboxes and refrigerated rail cars were fairly widespread, frozen food was still twenty years in the future. The farmer raised a number of varieties that ripened in succession over the course of the growing period. Local considerations also played a role: farmers near cities or good transportation could raise varieties that didn't keep as long or couldn't stand much handling. Even so, qualities such as long keeping were important considerations for both the farmer and the consumer.

APPLES

From today's perspective of easy abundance and fresh fruit year-round, the significance of the apple in earlier times is hard to appreciate. The Pilgrims brought the apple with them to North America. By 1741, apples from Long Island were being exported to the West Indies. The legendary Johnny Appleseed, born John Chapman in 1774 in Massachusetts, is believed to have planted over ten thousand square miles of apple orchards. Chapman brought the apple steadily west with him; he died in Fort Wayne, Indiana, in 1845. It was a Captain Simmons, however, who brought apple seeds to Fort Vancouver in Washington State in 1824. Today Washington is the top-producing apple state in the country; the total U.S. apple crop comes to some 145 million bushels.

Apple trees grow easily and yield abundantly. In the age before refrigeration, apples were an essential part of the farm economy, primarily because they could be stored easily in a variety of ways for winter use. Apples could be kept in the cool root cellar for weeks after harvesting; the fruit could also be dried for use in winter pies. Applesauce was used as a condiment, a side dish, a dessert, and an ingredient in baking. Apple butter, an inexpensive and delicious condiment, was particularly important in the winter, when real butter was scarce.

Apples were also made into cider and, often illicitly, into the alcoholic applejack or apple brandy. The apple cider was converted to apple vinegar, an indispensable item crucial for pickling and preserving. Cider mills were a basic item of farm equipment. The apples were fed into a hopper at the top and crushed by a cranked grinder. The pulp fell into a slatted drum, with narrow gaps between the vertical wooden slats. The juice was then squeezed from the pulp by a screw-operated press. Ever-thrifty farmers used the cake of dried apple, or pomace, left in the bottom of the drum as livestock feed.

The Red Delicious apple, the most widely grown variety not only in America but also worldwide, was discovered around 1850 in Iowa by a Quaker farmer named Jesse Hiatt. He noticed a sucker sprouting from the roots of a dead apple tree. The shoot grew into a tree that bore a new type of apple, a natural mutation Hiatt named Hawkeye. As the legend goes, Hiatt submitted the fruit to an agricultural exhibit; when a judge bit into it, he exclaimed, "Delicious, delicious." Regardless of the truth behind the story, the apple was introduced to the world as the Delicious in 1895 and is the dominant apple in today's market.

SELECTION OF TREES

Their Form.—We start upon the principle that, in all cases, tall standard trees, such as are usually planted in orchards, are totally unfit for the garden. This is the chief defect in American fruit gardening. All the trees for a fruit garden should be either *dwarf standards,* with trunks two to three feet high, *pyramids,* branched from the ground, or *bushes,* with stems six to twelve inches high. Trees in these forms are, in the first place, in keeping with the limited extent of the garden, and convey, at first sight, the idea of *fitness.* In the second place, they give a great variety on a small space, for three or four such trees will not occupy more space than one standard.

Fig. 101.—PYRAMIDAL APPLE-TREE.

Fig. 102.—DWARF BUSH APPLE-TREE.

In the third place, they are in a convenient form for management; they are easily pruned or protected, and the fruit is easily gathered, and less likely to be blown off than on tall trees. Finally, they bear several years sooner than standards.

Fig. 105.—PYRAMIDAL PEAR-TREE.
7 feet high ; 4 feet wide at the base.

The Pear as a Pyramid (fig. 105).—The pear is eminently *the* tree for the pyramidal form, either on the free stock or on the quince. On the latter, however, the trees bear much earlier, are more prolific, more manageable, and consequently preferable for small gardens.

FORMS OF APPLES

Round or Roundish (fig. 43).—When the outline is round, or nearly so, the length being about equal to the breadth.

Flat (fig. 46).—When the ends are compressed, and the width considerably greater than the length.

Figs. 43 to 48.—FORMS OF APPLES.
43, round ; 44, conical ; 45, ovate ; 46, flat ; 47, oblong ; 48, ribbed.

Conical (fig. 44).—In the form of a cone, tapering from the base to the eye.

Ovate, or *egg-shaped* (fig. 45).

Oblong (fig. 47).—When the length is considerably greater than the width, and the width about equal at both ends, not tapering as in the conical.

In addition to these forms and their various modifications, some varieties are

Angular, having projecting angles on the sides.

One-sided, having one side larger than the other.

Ribbed (fig. 48), when the surface presents a series of ridges and furrows, running from eye to stem.

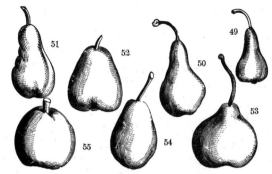

Figs. 49 to 55.—FORMS OF PEARS.

49, pyriform ; 50, long pyriform ; 51, obtuse pyriform ; 52, obovate ; 53, turbinate ; 54, oval ; 55, round.

FORMS OF PEARS

It has been remarked that the pyramidal form prevails in pears; but they taper from the eye to the stem, which is just the reverse of the tapering form in apples. Their forms are designated thus—

Pyriform.—When tapering from the eye to the base, and the sides more or less hollowed (concave) (fig. 49).

Long Pyriform.—When long and narrow, and tapering to a point at the stem (fig. 50).

Obtuse Pyriform.—When the small end is somewhat flattened (fig. 51).

Obovate, or *egg-shaped*.—Nearly in form of an egg, the small end being nearest the stem (fig. 52).

Turbinate, or *top-shaped*.—The sides somewhat rounded, and tapering to a point at the stem (fig. 53).

Oval.—Largest in the middle, tapering more or less to each end (fig. 54).

Round.—When the outline is nearly round (fig. 55).

Improved Cider Mill.

Shipped second-class. 70420 These mills have hard wood frames strongly bolted together. The beams are heavy cast iron; the screws are wrought iron, capable of standing the most severe pressure applied by the lever; have long crushing roller and large crates. Made in three sizes.
Price of Senior, weight, 410 lbs $20.50
Price of Medium, weight, 230 lbs........... .. 17.50
Price of Junior, weight, 165 lbs............. .. 13.75

PROPAGATING AND GROWING

Growing fruit trees from seeds is a cheap but very slow way to start an orchard. The preferred method for trees was grafting buds or scions of desired varieties onto hardy root stock. Root cuttings or layering were used to propagate soft fruits such as raspberries. The various methods allowed for the easy selection and propagation of particularly fine individual plants. New varieties could also be tried out easily.

Orchard work required some specialized tools. Plowing and cultivating, for example, loosened and conditioned the soil, yet the roots and trunks of the trees could be damaged by the process. Narrow equipment with a short turning radius was needed. Also needed were a wide variety of pruning devices and other small tools.

The 1880s saw the introduction of arsenate-based pesticides for use in fruit cultivation. The compounds were generally applied using hand-operated sprayers (see chapter 11 on pests for details). Because orchard trees have deep roots, they don't need frequent watering. When they do, however, substantial amounts of water need to be applied.

PROPAGATING PLANTS BY BUDDING

Budding consists in transferring a bud from one plant and inserting it in the bark of some allied or closely related plant in which it will become attached and develop. Many plants do not produce offspring like the parent stock when grown from seed, but buds always produce fruit like that borne by the tree or plant from which they were taken. Two methods of budding are in general use: (1) the pocket or T-cleft method, (2) the ring method.

THE T-CLEFT METHOD

In this method a horizontal incision is made in the stock to be budded, and just below the center of this cut another incision is made in the bark at right angles to it so as to form a T-shaped cleft. These incisions should be made close to the ground and on the north side of the stock, which should be a hardy one-year-old seedling. Next secure the bud that is to be transferred, taking care not to injure the vascular bundles on its under surface, and insert it in the incision in the stock

T-cleft budding.

previously prepared, and adjust it so that the cambium layer of the bud will come in contact with the cambium layer of the stock. Then press the bark down close and wrap the wound carefully with moist soft twine, cotton yarn, raffia, or other suitable material. In about ten days the bud will unite with the stock if it takes, and the wrapping material should be cut away. At the same time the seedling stock should be cut off at the top to within an inch or two of the bud, so that all the energy of the plant will be directed into the bud. This kind of budding should be done in the fall or spring when the bark will peel easily and mature buds can be easily procured.

THE RING OR ANNULAR METHOD

In this method a ring or loop of bark extended nearly around the stock is removed from the other plant and inserted in this incision in the same manner practically as is done in the case of the T-cleft method. This is the usual method of budding pecans and oranges and is largely used in the South. By budding fine varieties of oranges on hardy seedlings able to withstand cold inclement weather we may be able to grow oranges in many States where formerly it would have been utterly impossible.

PROPAGATING PLANS BY GRAFTING, OR GRAFTS

A graft is a small shoot of one tree inserted in another tree. It is so named from the resemblance of the shoot to a pointed pencil. The word *graft* itself is derived from the Greek word

graphein, which means to write. The young twig or branch which is inserted we call the scion, and the young seedling tree in which it is placed we call the stock. The scions should be cut late in the fall from firm hard wood and should be packed in dry leaves or excelsior and kept in the cellar until needed for use in the spring. With reference to the method of insertion of the scion into the stock, grafting may be divided into (1) cleft grafting, and (2) tongue or whip grafting.

CLEFT GRAFTING

In this method of grafting we saw off or cut off the main limbs of the stock at points where they are sufficiently large to admit of being cleft. Then we cut out a wedge-shaped piece of wood from the center of each branch sufficiently large to receive the scion.

Next, we prepare two scions by trimming them to wedge-shaped points so that they will fit into the cleft of the stock, taking care that each scion when placed in position will have at least two buds pointing obliquely upward. See that the cambium layer of the scion coincides with that of the stock, as

Cleft grafting.

in *d* of the diagram, so that the sap from the stock may flow into the scion and furnish it with proper nourishment. Then apply sufficient pressure to insure that union takes place, and carefully protect all exposed surfaces from the action of moisture and sunlight by covering them with a sufficient supply of grafting wax. If these details are carefully worked out we may reasonably expect success to attend our efforts. Grafting wax may be made by melting together one ounce of tallow or linseed oil, four ounces of rosin, and two ounces of beeswax. If the proportion of beeswax and rosin is increased, the grafting wax will be made correspondingly harder. After melting, the mixture should be poured into cold water, and as soon as it can be handled it should be taken from the water and pulled like taffy until it becomes light-colored and pliable.

WHIP GRAFTING

Secure a scion of the same size as the stock. Trim the scion at the lower end into the shape of a double wedge as shown under *(a)* in the diagram. Then slip the scion into a double

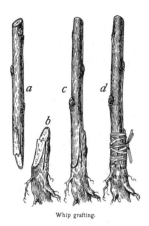

Whip grafting.

wedge-shaped cleft *(b)* as shown under *(c)*, and finally wrap it as shown under *(d)*.

The grafting cloth may be made by coating thin muslin with ordinary grafting wax.

Grafting by the two methods just described is known as Stem Grafting.

ROOT GRAFTING

In this method the roots of seedlings one or two years old are used as stocks, and either the whole primary root or only a piece of the root may be used. The method of procedure is similar to that prescribed for ordinary whip grafting already described.

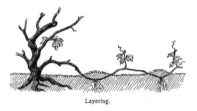

Layering.

PROPAGATING PLANTS BY LAYERING

This is one of the safest and simplest way of propagating plants. The branches while still attached to the parent plant are covered with soil with the exception of the tips of the branches. In a short time roots are developed from the covered portions of the stem and a new plant results. The black raspberry and the strawberry are examples of plants that propagate by layering in nature. The currant and the grape are examples of plants that may be made to propagate by artificial layering.

SECTION 1.—IMPLEMENTS OF THE SOIL

The Subsoil Plow (see fig. 160) is the great reformer of the day in the preparation of soils of all qualities and textures, for nursery, orchard, or garden trees. It follows the ordinary plow in the same furrow; and the largest size, No. 2, with a powerful team, can loosen the subsoil to the depth of eighteen inches. No. 1 will be sufficient in clear land when the subsoil is not very stiff.

Fig. 160.—SUBSOIL PLOW.

The One-Horse Plow.—Similar to the common plow used by farmers. It is a labor-saving implement for cultivating the ground among nursery-trees or orchards closely planted. The horse should be steady, the man careful, and the whiffle-tree as short as possible, that the trees need not be bruised. It should neither run so deep nor so near the trees as to injure the roots.

The Cultivator.—This, with the plow, obviates the necessity of spade-work, and, in a great measure, hoeing. If the ground be plowed in the spring, and the cultivator passed over it once every week or two during the summer, all the hoeing necessary will be a narrow strip of a few inches on each side of the row. The double-pointed steel-toothed, with a wheel in front, as shown in fig. 161, is the best.

Fig. 161.—CULTIVATOR.

The Tree-Digging Plow.—This implement facilitates the work and entirely supersedes the spade in the labor of digging trees of the usual size in the nursery, where an entire plot is to be cleared. It is constructed (see fig. 162) with two beams, one to run on each side of the row of trees, two sets of handles, and a peculiar share, much in shape like the letter U. This share is very sharp, the horizontal part runs under, and the vertical ones on each side of the trees, and the roots are thus smoothly cut off, while the trees remain standing. The plow is of course propelled by horses and guided by two plowmen. It is an admirable implement for root-pruning young trees, especially evergreens, in place of the old practice of removing them in order to cause them to throw out fibres and make balls suited to future removal.

Fig. 162.—TREE-DIGGING PLOW.

MOVING A LARGE TREE

To move a large tree one may find it very satisfactory to use a rig similar to that shown in the picture. Make a three-sided standard of 2 × 4-inch stuff. Loosen the dirt around the roots of the tree and wrap the tree firmly at the base with old carpet or burlap to prevent injury. Place the standard firmly in the

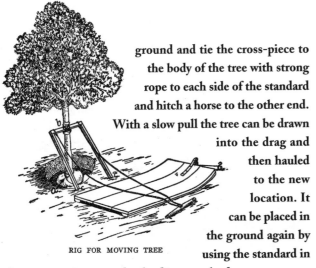

ground and tie the cross-piece to the body of the tree with strong rope to each side of the standard and hitch a horse to the other end. With a slow pull the tree can be drawn into the drag and then hauled to the new location. It can be placed in the ground again by using the standard in the same way it was used to load it upon the drag.

RIG FOR MOVING TREE

TRANSPLANTING TREES

Here is a way to transplant large trees that is not so difficult as such transplanting is by many supposed to be. The first move to make is to dig all round the tree, leaving a large ball of soil, which is carefully wrapped in sacking or canvas to hold it on the roots and prevent drying. When this is well tied in place, a chain is passed round the ball two or three times and hooked, as shown in Figure 1.

FIGURE I—BALLED

Then with a pair of heavy wheels on a short axle and a strong pole laid across it, with a massive iron hook fastened to the pole, it is easy to back up to the tree. The sketch, Figure 2, shows the truck with its lever raised ready to hook into the chain. The rope at the end of the pole brings it down and the tree up, when the pole is fastened under a second pair of wheels. The young trunk must be kept from contact with the machinery by the free use of blankets and bags. The secret of success in transplanting trees is to injure the roots as little as possible.

FIGURE 2—HOOK AND TRUCK

SECTION 2.
IMPLEMENTS FOR CUTTING

The Pruning Saw.—This is used for cutting off branches, either too large for the knife, or so situated that the knife cannot operate. It has various sizes and forms. Some are jointed, and fold like a pruning-knife; others are like the common carpenter's handsaw, but smaller and stouter. Two forms are shown at fig. 175.

The Bow-Saw (fig. 176).—This is the most generally useful form for the gardener or nurseryman. The blade is very narrow, and stiffened by an arch back. It is fastened at both ends by a rivet to the screw on which the back turns, and by which it is adapted to different purposes. It is indispensable in making horizontal cuts close to the ground, as in heading down.

Some are set with a double row of teeth on one side, and the edge is much thicker than the back; these work much easier than those toothed in the ordinary way, and it would be an object to have them where much saw-pruning is to be done. Wherever the saw is used, the cut surface should be pared smooth with the knife, to facilitate its healing.

Long-handled pruning-saws are sometimes recommended, but never should be used in pruning fruit-trees, if possible to avoid it. The branch to be operated should be reached by means of a ladder, if need be, within arm's length, and cut with a common saw.

Hand Pruning-Shears (fig. 177).—There is a kind of these made now, that, having a moving center, as in the figure, make a smooth *draw* cut almost equal to that of a knife, and it is a very expeditious instrument in the hand of a skillful workman. In pruning out small dead branches, shortening in peach-trees, etc., it will perform four times as much work as a knife.

Pruning Scissors (fig. 178).—These scissors cut as smoothly as a knife, and can be easily carried in the pocket, ready to take away a small branch wherever it may chance to be observed.

Lopping or Branch Shears.—These are very sturdily made, with long wooden handles, and are used for cutting thick branches from trees, shrubbery, hedges, etc. One form is shown in fig. 179.

Pole Pruning Shears.—These resemble the hand-shears, but are worked by a string passing over a pulley, and are fixed on a pole of any required length. They are used in cutting scions, diseased shoots, etc., from the heads of lofty standard trees.

Grape Scissors.—These are small, sharp-pointed scissors, as in fig. 180, for thinning bunches of grapes.

The Pruning-Knife.—The best for general purposes are those of medium size, with a handle about four inches long, smooth, slightly hollowed in the back; the blade about three and a half inches long, three quarters of an inch wide, and nearly straight (fig. 181). For very heavy work a larger size may be necessary. "Saynor's" (English) knives of this kind are

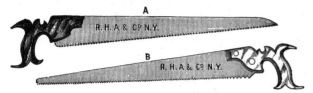

Fig. 175.—PRUNING-SAWS.

unsurpassed in material and finish.

The Budding Knife.—This is much smaller than the pruning-knife, with a thin, straight blade, the edge sometimes rounded at the point. The handle is of bone or ivory, and has a thin, wedge-shaped end for raising the bark. Budders have various fancies about shape and size; one form is given in figure 182.

Fig. 176.—BOW-SAW.

The Grafting-Chisel.—This is used for splitting large stocks; the blade is about two inches long, and an inch and a

Fig. 177.—HAND PRUNING-SHEARS.

half wide, in the shape of a wedge; the edge curved so as to cut, and not tear the bark; the handle eight or ten inches

Fig. 178.—PRUNING-SCISSORS.

long, at the end of which is a narrow wedge to keep the split open until the scion is inserted. (See figure 183.) The whole is of steel. Some are made with the blade in the middle, the wedge at one end, and a hook to hang it by on the other.

Mr. David S. Wagner, of Pulteney, N.Y., has invented an ingenious implement for grafting grapes; as it is patented, those

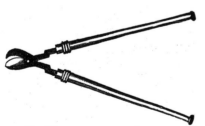

Fig. 179.—LOPPING OR BRANCH SHEARS.

Fig. 180.—GRAPE SCISSORS.

who desire to know about it may inquire of the inventor. *Tree-Scraper* (fig. 184).— This is made of heavy plate-steel, with a long, jointed handle for scraping upper branches, or a short one for the trunks.

Fig. 181. PRUNING-KNIFE.

Fig. 182.—BUDDING-KNIFE.

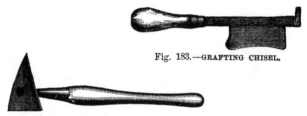

Fig. 183.—GRAFTING CHISEL.

Fig. 184.—TREE-SCRAPER.

The Barrow-Engine (fig. 190) is the most useful for general purposes; it is easily moved from one place to another. The improved kinds are easily worked, and the water-box, being provided with a strainer, excludes anything likely to derange its operations.

Fig. 190.—BARROW-ENGINE.

PICKING AND PACKING

By growing a number of varieties, a good orchardist had a steady supply of fruit, starting with the early-ripening varieties and going on to the late-season keepers. Even so, most of the picking had to be done by hand within a fairly compressed time period. Not surprisingly, a wide range of labor-saving devices were designed to make the picking go as efficiently as possible.

The picked fruit had to get to market quickly. Because it was fragile, and because appearance mattered to the end consumer, fruit boxes and baskets of various sorts were devised both to protect the fruit and to present it attractively.

FRUIT LADDERS

In years of plenty it is only the best fruit that brings good prices. One step towards having good fruit is to secure careful picking, and to this end, it is necessary to have a sufficient

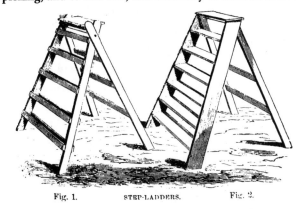

Fig. 1.   STEP-LADDERS.   Fig. 2.

supply of convenient ladders. For low trees, step-ladders will be found serviceable. Fig. 2 gives the ordinary step-ladder used in the peach orchards of Delaware. It is made of two boards 10 feet long, 6 inches wide, and 1 inch thick for the sides; the steps are of the same material, let into grooves in the side pieces. At the top is a board about 10 inches wide,

Fig. 3.—EXTENSION LADDER.

upon which the basket stands. The support is of two narrow strips, strengthened by cross-bars; this is attached to the steps by an iron rod passing through its ends, and through the side pieces.—A cheaper ladder is made of four pieces of shingling lath. Two of these have strips of the same material nailed opposite each other for steps, as in figure 1. The top step has a board nailed to it to receive the basket. The other two pieces are made to serve as supports as shown in the figure. In both these ladders the bottom is wider than the top, in order that they may stand firmly. It is often the case that ladders much taller than these are required. A common ladder, which should have iron points at the bottom of each side piece, may be so guyed with ropes as to be perfectly safe. It takes considerable time to change the position of such a ladder, and it will be found more convenient to support it by means of wooden stays of a proper length. In September 1868, and January 1869, we illustrated two very efficient methods of doing this. Another form of ladder is proposed by Mr. George H. Russel, which is shown in figure 3. It is really two ladders hinged together, and may be used by two persons at once. The dimensions are: side pieces 9 feet long and 13 by 1 1/2 inches. Width of ladder 1 foot 9 inches, distance between the rounds, 1 foot 4 inches. Long hinges of malleable iron are used to fasten the two parts together, as shown at the right hand of the engraving. The basket can be placed upon the upper two rounds. By opening out this, and using it with the hinges down, it will answer as a single ladder.

Orchard Ladders are of various kinds. For pruning or gathering the fruit from lofty trees, a great length of ladder is necessary; it is therefore desirable that the material be as light as possible consistent with the necessary strength. Sometimes these long ladders are composed of several smaller ones, that fit into one another, all mounted on a frame with a small wheel, by which they are easily moved about.

The Folding Ladder is a very neat and convenient article for many purposes. The inside of the styles is hollowed out, and the steps are fastened to them by means of iron pins, on

Fig. 185.—FRUIT-LADDER.

which they turn as on hinges, so that the two sides can be brought together, the steps turning into the grooves or hollows in them, the whole appearing like a round pole—*B*. It is more easily carried and placed where wanted than the ordinary ladder. *A* represents it open, and *B* closed (fig. 186).

There are also Self-supporting Orchard-Ladders, composed of three upright pieces of any required length, and spread widely at the bottom, to give them stability. Two of the sides

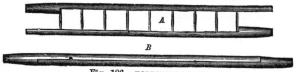

Fig. 186.—FOLDING LADDER.

are fixed, and are furnished with steps all the way up. The third is longer and movable, and can be extended or contracted at pleasure.

A piece of board wide enough to stand upon can be extended from one side to the other, resting upon the steps at whatever hight it is desirable to work. On the movable side a pulley is fixed, by which the baskets of fruit are let down as they are gathered. Two persons or more can ascend and work on a ladder at the same time. Fig. 187 represents one of these; *a, b,* the two fixed sides; *C,* the movable one. It is considerably used in France.

FRUIT LADDERS

The construction is easily understood from the engraving. The use of a common grain bag as a receptacle for picking fruit has some important advantages. One side of the mouth of the bag is tied to the corresponding corner at the bottom, first putting an apple in the corner to hold the string from slipping off. The bag is then hung over the shoulder with the mouth in front. The picker has both hands free and can empty the bag by lowering it into the barrel, without bruising the fruit.

Fig. 187.—SELF-SUPPORTING ORCHARD LADDER.

Fig. 212.—A HANDY FRUIT LADDER.   Fig. 213.—FRUIT LADDER.

Another form is shown in figure 213. To make it, select a chestnut pole, eighteen feet long, or of the desired length. At about four feet from the top, or smaller end of the pole, nail on a band of hoop iron, to prevent splitting, and rip up the pole in the center as far as the band. The halves of the pole are spread apart three and a half feet at the base, and secured. The places for the rungs are then laid out, and the holes bored: those for the lower rungs should be one and three-eighths inch, the upper one inch; drive them in place and wedge fast. The distance between the rungs is usually a foot; when farther apart, they are fatiguing in use. A ladder of this kind, on account of its small width above, is easily thrust in among the branches, without breaking them, and is more convenient to use on large trees, than those of the ordinary shape.

ORCHARD LADDER ON WHEELS

The accompanying sketch shows the manner of construction. Any farmer or orchardist can build it. Secure two old mower wheels and one piece of 2 × 4 scantling for an axle. Place the ladder upon this scantling. To keep it upright use poles, two at the bottom and one near the top of the ladder, extending to the ground. The upper one should be forked at the top so as to hold the ladder firmly. This ladder is 18 feet high, and as the foundation is broad, there is no danger of it

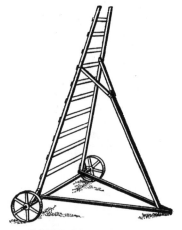

LADDER FOR FRUIT TREES

falling over. The brace is so made that it can be adjusted, thus enabling one to place the ladder at any angle.

VARIOUS FRUIT PICKERS

A good picker is shown in figures 206, 207 and 208. Figure 206 is the picker. The pieces, *a* and *b*, are iron, shaped as seen in the cut. They work on a rivet, and are fastened securely to the end of the pole. Holes are punched through *a* and *b*, and

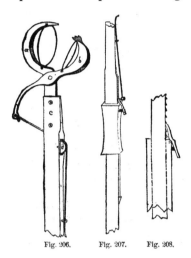

Fig. 206.   Fig. 207.   Fig. 208.

stiff wires inserted, forming a cage for the fruit. The toothed end of piece *b* is sharp, and slides over the end of *a*, which may be sharp or not. A small hole is bored through the pole, and a notch cut in the front edge for a small pulley, *d.* A

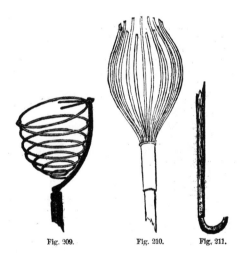

Fig. 209.   Fig. 210.   Fig. 211.

strong cord is attached to the lower end of *b*, and passes through the hole over the pulley, and down the pole through screw-eyes placed a short distance apart. Figure 207 is a section of the lower end of the pole. Eighteen inches from the end, the pole is squared for about fifteen inches. Over this squared portion is fitted a sliding-box handle. A thumb-stop is fastened to the upper end, as shown in figure 208. The

thumb end is held up by a small spring, which presses the upper end into notches in an iron rachet-bar fitted into the pole. A screw-eye is inserted in the upper end, and a cord attached. The pole may be of any desired length.

To pick apples, grasp the pole at the lower end with one hand, and by the sliding-box handle with the other. Press the thumb-piece and slide it up, and the weight of piece *b* opens the jaws of the picker. When the apple is in the cage, draw the slides down until the points of the picker meet on the apple stem. The thumb-stop will hold it secure. Turn the pole slowly without pulling, pushing, or shaking the limb, and the apple will come off easily. The cage of the picker should be large enough to contain the largest apple, and enough wires may be attached to hold the smallest. The jaws should not be over one-eighth of an inch thick, flattened on the inside, to prevent bruising the ripe fruit. They may be wrapped with cloth, if thought necessary.

A cheap and simple picker may be made by bending a stiff wire into the form of a circle six inches in diameter, with one side of the circle prolonged three inches into a V-shaped projection. Upon this wire sew a cloth bag a foot or so deep, and fasten it on to a pole by the end opposite the V-shaped extremity. This V-shaped projection will serve as a corner, in which to catch the apple and pull it off, allowing it to fall into the bag. An excellent picker, as shown in figure 210, can be made from stiff wire by a tinner. The span across the top should be about six inches, and the depth from eight to ten inches. The wires should not be more than a half-inch apart at their tips. The wires being more or less flexible, the apple is apt to draw through them, if they are not close together. Care should also be taken to have the implement made as light as possible. A bungling mechanic will probably use too much solder. Another good picker is pictured in figure 209. It is light, durable and pleasant to handle. When, however, an apple, being very short stemmed, lies close to a limb, it is much more easily removed by the former device than by this. A simple, flattened hook, with a thin, almost cutting edge, secured on the end of a pole, figure 211, is often handy for pulling off stray apples. This is the best implement for thinning.

HOMEMADE FRUIT PICKER

This is a device that is hard to beat for reaching fruit at the top of tall trees. After a little practice, a man can operate it rapidly, far outstripping hand pickers and at the same time not injuring the fruit. The construction is shown in the drawing. The main frame is of heavy copper wire, to which is attached the strong spring, *d.* The end, *a*, is inserted into a

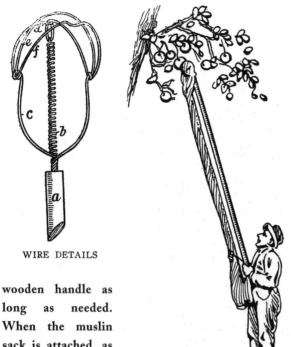

WIRE DETAILS

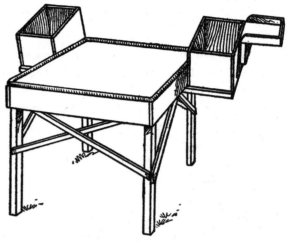

THE PICKER IN USE

wooden handle as long as needed. When the muslin sack is attached, as shown in the picture of the picker in use, the jaws of the picker are easily closed by pulling slightly on the cloth. The fruit falls through the sack or long cloth tube into the hand of the operator. Many devices have been made for this sort of service, but it will be hard to find one that works better than this one if constructed in the exact shape indicated.

CONVENIENT SORTING TABLES

Where fruit is packed from the trees a sorting table will always be found convenient. It generally saves time and labor to do the packing right in the orchard. A handy table is one mounted on wheels which may be of any size desired and should be large enough to hold at least four barrels. The wheels can be picked up from discarded machinery or quickly made by nailing together crosswise two boards to prevent them from splitting, boring a hole in the center for the axle and rounding them off with a key hole saw. One end of the table should be made several inches higher than the other, so that the culls will roll into a pile at the lower end.

In the Hood river district of Oregon a table such as shown above is commonly used. This is made to accommodate two packers. To make such a table take four standards about 3 feet high. It is made 3 × 4 feet in size, the top covered

with strong burlap or canvas and allowed to hang rather loosely. Saw off the tops of the legs on a bevel so as not to have the sharp corners push into the burlap, and make points that will bruise or cut the fruit.

OREGON SORTING TABLE

A piece of old garden hose is generally nailed around the top of the table to protect the fruit. Besides the braces shown in the cut it is also well to wire the legs and braces together firmly, as there is a heavy load to support. The shelves on each side are for holding the boxes, as all the good fruit in this region is boxed. The height is only relative, the point being to construct it so each packer can work with the greatest comfort, avoiding back bending in all cases. The top should not be greater than 3 × 4 feet, as anything larger would not allow two packers to reach all points of it without unnecessary stretching.

SMALL FRUITS

Because the market for small fruits was so profitable a century ago, growers were always interested in new varieties. Nursery owners, horticulturists, and other growers offered a surprisingly large range of berry varieties. The search for new kinds of marketable berries in this period led, on the one hand, to the first commercial blueberry plantings, and on the other down some blind alleys. Attempts to promote dwarf cherries, Cornelian cherries (a type of dogwood), buffalo berries, barberries, and dewberries as market crops never really came off. Gooseberries, currants, and mulberries were more successful, but today they are very limited specialty crops. Not even the prestige of Luther Burbank, the great hybridizer, could make his wonderberry, a cross of two nightshade species, into a popular fruit.

STRAWBERRIES

Berries, especially strawberries, were an extremely valuable market crop. Indeed, the first new variety of fruit created in the United States by crossbreeding was a strawberry. In 1838, Charles Mason Hovey, a horticulturist from Boston, crossbred several strawberry varieties to create the variety that was eventually named for him. The Hovey had a rich color, fine flavor, and juicy texture; it quickly became very popular. By the 1880s, when refrigerated railroad cars expanded the market opportunities for berry farmers, the ongoing hunt for high-yielding, flavorful, hardy varieties had led to hundreds of strawberry varieties.

By the end of the 1800s, the ideal growing conditions in southern California led to a rapid increase in year-round strawberry cultivation. Today California provides more than 80 percent of the fresh strawberry crop in the United States and about 25 percent of the world total. About 25,000 acres in the state are planted to strawberries each year; each acre produces between twenty and thirty tons of strawberries annually.

DESCRIPTION OF VARIETIES

The following are varieties of *Fragaria grandiflora* and *F. Virginiana*. Some of them show more of the peculiar characteristics of one species than of the other, while with a few it would be difficult to tell to which they were related, and it is very probable that they are a mixture of both. They were all produced in this country, and are called native varieties:

Agriculturist.—Very large, irregular, conical, with long neck, large specimens often flattened or coxcomb shaped; color light reddish crimson; flesh deep red, moderately firm,  sweet, rich and good; plant a very strong grower; leaves large, thick, dark green, with reddish petiole; hardy and productive, and succeeds remarkably well on light sandy soils, as well as on those that are heavy. A valuable variety. Figure 30 shows a fruit of medium size in ordinary field culture. Originated with Seth Boyden, Newark, N. J.

Fig. 30.—AGRICULTURIST.

Crescent Seedling. (Figure 31.)—Medium to large, somewhat irregular conical; bright scarlet; flesh rather soft for a market berry, but will do for short distances, or when carefully handled; quality fair, not rich; the plants, however, are of such a vigorous growth and so productive that this variety has become quite a favorite among cultivators for market. Originated with Mr. William Parmelee, New Haven, Conn. This is quite a different berry from the old and long since discarded "Crescent Seedling," which originated at the South.

Fig. 31.—CRESCENT.

Durand's Seedling.—Large, oblong, or oblong-conical, sometimes flattened; seeds but slightly sunken; color scarlet; flesh firm, solid, nearly white of good flavor. Originated with Mr. F. W. Durand, near Irvington, N. J. Figures 33 and

Fig. 33.—DURAND. Fig. 34.—DURAND.

34 give a fair representation of two of the berries, showing its variableness in form.

Forest Rose.—Large, irregular, obtuse-conical; bright scarlet; flesh firm, of good flavor; a superior market berry,

Fig. 35.—FOREST ROSE.

but unfortunately it does not appear to be well adapted to all kinds of soils and locations. Where it succeeds it will rank high for market purposes as well as for home use. An accidental seedling, introduced by a Mr. Fetters, of Lancaster, Ohio. Figure 35 gives a good idea of the size of this variety. From "American Agriculturist," 1878.

Golden Defiance.—Large, obtuse-conical; bright scarlet; flesh moderately firm and of excellent flavor; ripens quite late; plants very vigorous, hardy, and productive. Promises to be a valuable acquisition to our list of good sorts. Pistillate. Originated with Mr. Amos Miller, of Pennsylvania. (Figure 36.)

Fig. 36.—GOLDEN DEFIANCE.

Fig. 39.—LADY FINGER.   Fig. 40.—LADY FINGER.

Lady Finger.—Medium, elongated, conical; color brilliant dark scarlet; seeds set in a deep open cavity; flesh very firm, sub-acid, good; plant hardy, vigorous and prolific. An excellent market variety. Originated with the late Benjamin Prosser, Burlington, New Jersey. Figure 39 shows a berry of this variety of medium size, and figure 40 one of the largest.

Fig. 41.—NEW JERSEY SCARLET.

New Jersey Scarlet.—Medium; conical; light bright scarlet, with long neck; moderately firm, sprightly flavor, and good; very early and productive; the plant a strong and vigorous grower. Succeeds admirably on the light sandy soils of New Jersey. An excellent market variety. See figure 41 for size and form. Originated near Burlington, New Jersey.

Satin Gloss.— Medium to large; rather long-conical; calyx very large; bright glossy vermilion; flesh firm, of good flavor. The large calyx and firm flesh of this variety make it an excellent fruit for shipping, as it is not likely to become bruised during transit. Originated with Mr. Oscar Felton, from seed of the Lady Finger. Figure 43— from "American Agriculturist," 1880.

Fig. 43.—SATIN GLOSS.

RASPBERRIES AND BLACKBERRIES

Raspberries and their close cousins, the blackberries, were raised for use as fresh fruit and also for preserves and wine. These thorny plants grow well in dry, sandy, or poor soil; rich soil, in fact, leads to excessive foliage growth and poor fruit production. Raspberries and blackberries were easy to grow. The hardy, vigorous plants required only annual pruning to get rid of old canes. Farmers often grew them—or encouraged the growth of naturally present plants—in waste spaces along fences and in areas too steep to plow. The berries were valuable for home consumption and as a seasonal cash crop.

Fig. 67.—PHILADELPHIA.

DESCRIPTION OF VARIETIES

Philadelphia.—Medium to large, globular, dark red, scarcely any bloom, moderately firm, sub-acid, not rich, nor very juicy; grains large, adhere more firmly than those of the Purple Cane; canes erect, strong, and stocky, dark red or purple, branching; spines very small, straight, and scattering, almost spineless; leaves large, dark green above, lighter beneath, very thick and tough, have a peculiar wavy appearance on the upper side, finely serrated. Figure 67 shows a cluster of fruit of the average size under common field culture. The canes do not bend over and root from the tips, like the Purple Cane, but produce suckers, although rather sparingly; very hardy and wonderfully productive. Found growing within the present limits of the City of Philadelphia, some thirty or more years ago. It has lately become very popular as a market variety, and for some soils and locations is unexcelled. This is particularly the case in the sandy soils of New Jersey, where all of the finest foreign varieties fail, and no amount of care will enable the growers to secure a remunerative crop. It has been widely disseminated in the past few years, and very favorable reports are being received from all parts of the country in regard to its hardiness and productiveness.

R. fruticosus.—Stems straggling, arched, angular and rather tomentose; prickles recurved, fruit dark purple with a peculiar mawkish flavor. Common European Blackberry or Bramble.

There are several species of the Blackberry found in South America, West Indies, and Mexico, but we have no

Fig. 79.—EUROPEAN BLACKBERRY.

cultivated varieties of them, neither do they possess any qualities superior to those found in the United States.

Very little attention is paid to the cultivation of this fruit except in this country; consequently we have no superior foreign varieties, nor can we find any practical information in regard to their cultivation, in any European work on gardening. The Blackberry has no separate history from that of the Raspberry, as they are both called *Brambles* in the old works; and it is evident that it has never been considered worthy of any special care in any country except our own.

Kittatinny.—Large to very large, slightly conical, deep shining black, moderately firm, sweet, rich and excellent; figure 84 is a fair representation of a well grown cluster; leaves ovate, with rather a long point, as shown in figure 85,

Fig. 84.—KITTATINNY.

finely and unevenly serrate; plant a strong and vigorous grower, and very productive. The fruit begins to ripen a few days earlier than the New Rochelle, and continues for four or five weeks. This is an old variety, although new to the public, as it was not extensively disseminated until last year, but so far as known, it is very hardy, and promises to be one of the very best varieties known. Found, about twenty years ago, by a Mr. Wolverton, growing wild in the woods near the Kittatinny Mountains, in Warren County, New Jersey.

Fig. 85.—LEAF OF KITTATINNY.

BLUEBERRIES

In 1881, the author of *Small Fruit Culturist* wrote of the huckleberry: "I do not think it necessary to enter into any minute details of the history or cultivation of this fruit, from the fact that there is nothing connected therewith which would make the subject interesting." At that time, huckleberries (as blueberries were then called) were exclusively a wild-picked crop. The blueberry is native to North America, but it was domesticated only in 1910 by the pioneering propagation work of Frederick V. Coville of the Department of Agriculture. Coville then worked in New Jersey's Pine Barrens region with Elizabeth Coleman White to improve the varieties and develop blueberries into a commercial crop, an endeavor that finally succeeded in 1916. Until the 1930s, New Jersey was the prime blueberry-producing state. Michigan entered the market in the 1930s. Today more than half of all commercial blueberries are still grown in these two states, but Maine, North Carolina, Georgia, Florida, Oregon, Washington, and New York also produce the fruit. Imports come primarily from Canada, Mexico, and New Zealand. The annual yield in the United States is now some 145 million pounds.

Fig. 104.—SWAMP HUCKLEBERRY.

V. CORYMBOSUM

Swamp Blueberry, or High-bush Huckleberry.—Leaves oval or oblong, variable in size and color. Shrubs four to ten feet high, common in low, wet places. Fruit black, covered with bloom, sweet but sprightly; the best Huckleberry; ripens late in the season, August and September.

Fig. 104 shows a small branch, with bunch of fruit of natural size. This species assumes various forms and colors; sometimes the fruit is oval, approaching an oblong, while others are globular or slightly compressed.

CRANBERRIES

Another native American fruit, the cranberry, was in cultivation by around 1810, when Captain Henry Hall of Dennis, Massachusetts, noticed that the wild cranberries in his bogs grew better when sand blew over them. Captain Hall began transplanting his cranberry vines and spreading sand over them. By the 1820s, cranberries were being exported to Europe, and by the 1840s horticulturists were developing new varieties. By the 1880s, cranberries were a big enough business for the Cape Cod Cranberry Growers Association to be formed. Yields and profits seem to have varied quite a bit. In 1881, yields were anywhere from 150 to 400 bushels to the acre, and profits were based on a price of somewhere between $2 and $6 per bushel.

The real growth in the cranberry industry came later, in 1912, when the Hayden cranberry separator was patented and the first commercial cranberry sauce was marketed. The famed Ocean Spray cooperative wasn't formed until 1930.

VARIETIES

Like other fruits, the Cranberry varies considerably in its wild state; besides, when cultivated, new variations are constantly occurring. All the varieties in cultivation at the present time in this county, belong to one species, the *V. macrocarpon*.

These vary in size, from a half inch up to an inch or over in diameter. Fig. 100 shows a variety usually called the Cherry Cranberry, and fig. 101, one of the largest of the Bell variety. Fig. 102 illustrates the Bell form, and in fig. 103 we give an exact

Fig. 100.—CHERRY CRANBERRY.

Fig. 102.—BELL CRANBERRY.

representation of some remarkably fine specimens, raised by Mr. Orrin C. Cook, of South Milford, Mass. There are many other shapes intermediate between these, but we have given the principal ones.

Fig. 101.—BUGLE CRANBERRY.

In color, the varieties vary from a greenish-yellow or white to dark, rich purple. New varieties are being produced, and, doubtless, in a few years, great improvements will be made in the size, if not in the quality, of the Cranberry.

Fig. 103.—LARGE CRANBERRY.

GATHERING AND MARKETING

Picking the berry crop and getting the fragile crop to market called for some ingenious developments. Because the work was often seasonal but urgent, labor for picking was sometimes scarce. Women and children were often employed. In New Jersey in the mid-1880s, pay rates were generally three to five cents a quart for strawberries, raspberries, and blackberries. Expert pickers could make two to three dollars a day.

All fruit was shipped to market in pint or quart boxes or baskets, which were generally packed into crates for transport. The grower sent the fruit on to a commission merchant and expected most of his boxes and baskets to be returned eventually. The round trip could take days if not weeks, however, and growers needed to have thousands of units on hand.

BERRY CRATE CARRIER

One of the most convenient appliances for use in the strawberry field is illustrated in the picture shown herewith. It shows a novel use for the old-fashioned yoke used so commonly on the old-time farms. The picture is so readily understood that no description need be given. This also suggests the many purposes for which a yoke may be used on

YOKE CRATE CARRIER

a farm. Every farmer ought to have one, to make more easy the task of carrying things. In some places yokes may be found for sale, but if you cannot buy one, make one yourself. Take a piece of strong, tough wood, shape it out to fit around the neck and shoulders and taper off the ends to what you consider the right size. Usually a groove is cut around about 1 1/2 inches from each end and a rope is securely tied. At the other end of the rope a hook is attached the right size to go around the bail handle of any ordinary pail. The hook may be iron or may be formed from a strong, branched stick.

The most common basket used for the New York market is what is called the Jersey Strawberry basket, figure 108; it requires from five to seven to hold a quart. Of late years this basket is less used than formerly, except for the smaller varieties of the Strawberry. They are usually made by the fruit growers

Fig. 108.—JERSEY BASKET.

themselves in winter, but sometimes they are made for sale, and the price varies from ten dollars to fifteen dollars per thousand.

Fig. 125.—BASKET STAND.

At the time of gathering, each picker is furnished with a stand (figure 125), holding ten to twenty-five baskets. When all are filled, they are carried to the tent and put into the crates, ready for sending to market. The small Jersey baskets are put into crates holding from one hundred and fifty to two hundred each, but when pint and quart baskets are used, from thirty to sixty go in a crate.

AMERICAN BASKET

Fig. 109.—AMERICAN BASKET.

This basket is made of two sizes, quarts and pints, and of the form shown in figure 109. They are very strong, of neat appearance, and one of the best baskets with which I am acquainted. Their peculiar form admits of their being very compactly nested for transportation, as shown in figure 110.

The manufacturers also furnish crates to those who desire them. A thirty-two quart crate is shown in figure 111, each one being furnished with lock attached with a small chain. The fruit grower keeps a key to lock the crate, and the one to whom the fruit is consigned, has a duplicate, with which to open it when received.

Fig. 110.—STACK OF BASKETS.

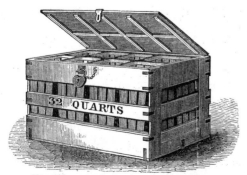

Fig. 111.—CRATE OF AMERICAN BASKETS.

SQUARE CHIP BASKET

Fig. 116.—SQUARE CHIP BASKET.

Here we have an improvement on the common Jersey basket. The slats are reversed, the wide one passing around the basket, and the small ones forming the uprights, thereby giving a comparatively smooth surface, allowing the baskets to be lifted out or put back into place in the crates, without catching upon those adjoining, and upsetting them, as is often the case with the common one. These baskets are made square, consequently packed very closely together, leaving no vacant spaces between them. An excellent basket for Raspberries.

GOTHIC FREE FRUIT BOX

Fig. 117.—GOTHIC FREE FRUIT BOX.

This box is intended to be given away with the fruit. They are of an octagon shape, as shown in figure 117, made of veneer, and can be sent in flats and put together by the fruit grower, thus saving much expense in transportation. The material, all ready to be put together, costs ten dollars per thousand.

COOK'S BASKET

This is a very neat and pretty basket, very strong and durable. Some of our fruit growers object to it on account of the small strips of which it is made, because, as the berries settle, they are injured, by being cut by the sharp edges. It is, however, an excellent basket, but probably on account of its cost is seldom, of late years, seen in our markets.

Fig. 118.—COOK'S BASKET.

THE PARAGON BASKET

Figure 119. Another neat, light box, of more recent introduction than the above, and much liked by the commission men. Three strips of thin whitewood form the bottom and sides of the basket; the bottom hoop is dispensed with, as well as the extra bottom piece. There is ample provision for ventilation, and the shape of the top is round, thus enabling the fruit to show at its best.

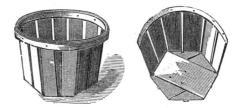

Fig. 119.—PARAGON BASKET.

BEES

The honeybee was not native to North America. These valuable insects were brought by the earliest colonists as a source of honey and for pollinating fruit crops. Before sugar and molasses from sugarcane became cheap and easy to get in the 1850s, honey was the chief sweetener.

Beekeeping became a practical business in the 1850s after the great bee innovator Lorenzo Langstroth invented a practical hanging-frame beehive with removable frames.

Another important invention of the same period was the bellows smoker, an easy and safe way to control bees and gain access to the honey.

Bee plants varied from place to place, which affected the taste of the honey. White clover and raspberries were considered ideal honey plants, producing a honey that was very pure and clear. All fruit trees, but especially the apple, were good for honey; tulip trees, locusts, and lindens (basswood) were also excellent. Composite flowers such as goldenrod, aster, and others were also all desirable honey plants.

Several attempts were made, in the first half of the nineteenth century, to invent a practical hanging-frame hive; that is, a hive in which each comb, hanging in a separate frame, could be readily taken out and replaced without jarring the hive, or removing the other frames. Propokovitsch, in Russia, Munn, in England, Debeauvoys, in France, tried and failed. At last, in October, 1851, Mr. Langstroth invented the top-opening movable-frame hive, now used the world over with slight variations, in which the combs are attached to movable frames so suspended in the hives as to touch neither the top, bottom, nor sides; leaving, between the frames and the hive walls, a space of from one-fourth to three-eighths of an inch, called bee-space. (Fig. 59.)

By this device the combs can be removed at pleasure, without any cutting, and speedily transferred to another hive. Our congenial friend, Prof. A. J. Cook, author of "The Beekeeper's Guide," says of it: "It is this hive, the greatest apiarian invention ever made, that has placed American Apiculture in advance of that of all other countries." And no one knows, better than the revisers of this work, that such is the plain truth, as they have watched the progress of beekeeping in Europe, through its French, Italian, Swiss, and German bee-papers, for forty years past.

A bee-smoker is indispensable to any Apiarist, and should be properly filled, when used, with dry wood, lighted at the bottom by a few hot coals. With a good smoker any kind of wood may be used. When the bees are located in an orchard, dead limbs of apple-trees are handiest and will make good smoke. Shavings, leaves, rags, can also be used, if no wood is at hand. By setting the smoker upright, when not held in the

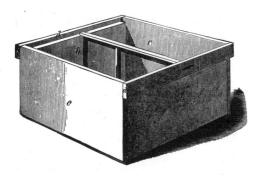

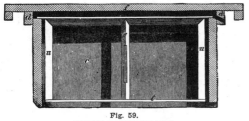

Fig. 59.
ORIGINAL LANGSTROTH HIVE.
b,b, front and rear of hive; d,d, pieces forming the rabbets for the frames to rest upon; c,c, sides of hive; f, movable cover; u,u,t, movable frame.

hand, so as to create a good draft, and refilling it from time to time, a good smoke can be kept up from morning till night, if necessary.

Fig. 71.
HIVE, WITH EXTRACTING SUPERS SET BACK FOR VENTILATION IN VERY HOT WEATHER.
The cap is thrown back to show the straw mat.

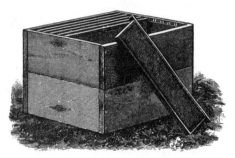

Fig. 204.
TWO HALF-STORY SUPERS FOR EXTRACTING.

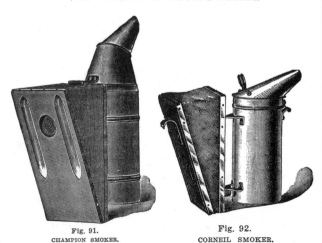

Fig. 91.
CHAMPION SMOKER.

Fig. 92.
CORNEIL SMOKER.

Of all the sources from which bees derive their supplies, white clover (fig. 154), is usually the most important. It yields large quantities of very pure white honey, and wherever it abounds, the bee will find a rich harvest. In most parts of this country it seems to be the chief reliance of the apiary. Blossoming at a

Fig. 154.
WHITE CLOVER.
(From Vilmorin-Andrieux, Paris.)

season of the year when the weather is usually both dry and hot, and the bees gathering its honey after the sun has dried off the dew, it is ready to be sealed over almost at once.

It is at the blossoming of this important plant that the main crop of honey usually begins, and that the bees propagate in the greatest number.

The flowers of red clover also produce a large quantity of nectar; unfortunately its corollas are usually too deep for the tongue of our bees. Yet sometimes, in Summer, they can reach the nectar, either because its corollas are shorter on account of dryness, or because they are more copiously filled.

The linden, or bass-wood (*Tilia Americana*, fig. 158), yields white honey of a strong flavor, and, as it blossoms when both the swarms and parent-colonies are usually populous, the weather settled, and other bee-forage scarce, its value to the bee-keeper is great.

> "Here their delicious task, the fervent bees
> In swarming millions tend: around, athwart,
> Through the soft air the busy nations fly,
> Cling to the bud, and with inserted tube,
> Suck its pure essence, its ethereal soul."
> —Thomson

This majestic tree, adorned with beautiful clusters of fragrant blossoms, is well worth attention as an ornamental shade-tree. By adorning our villages and country residences with a fair allowance of tulip, linden, and such other trees as are not only beautiful to the eye, but attractive to bees, the honey-resources of this country might, in process of time, be greatly increased. In many districts, locust and basswood plantations would be valuable for their timber alone.

Fig. 158.
LINDEN OR BASSWOOD.
(From Vilmorin-Andrieux, Paris.)

CHAPTER 11

WEEDS AND OTHER PESTS

The battle against crop-damaging weeds, fungi, blights, insects, and other pests was endless for the nineteenth-century farmer, as it had been for his ancestors and would be for his descendants.

WEEDS

The weeds against which the farmer battled were numerous. A number were accidentally imported by settlers, who inadvertently carried weed seeds from one region of the country to another or who brought weed seeds with them from overseas. Dandelion, which was brought by the Pilgrims, is perhaps the earliest example. Escaped imported ornamentals also became a problem. The most notorious is kudzu, the weed that continues to eat the South to this day. This plant from Japan was exhibited at the 1876 Philadelphia Centennial Exposition. Adopted as an ornamental and later recommended by agricultural experts as a method of erosion control, this hardy plant soon covered fields, telegraph poles, and fences and remains a major pest virtually impervious to any form of control.

In the days before chemical farming, a number of techniques were used to keep down the weeds—techniques that today are still the foundations of organic farming. First and foremost was careful and frequent cultivation, by hand or horse. Crop rotation was also important. Pastures usually turned weedy from overgrazing; by putting the pasture into a crop for a few years the weeds were exchanged for a different set, but rotation to a different crop or seeding the land back to pasture kept any one weed species from becoming well established. Clean seed that was free from weed seeds was important, as was the proper composting of livestock manure to destroy weed seeds. Smothering out the weeds was also an effective technique. Rapeseed was particularly valuable for this purpose, because the plant grows very quickly. It could then be fed to the livestock or plowed under and a grain crop could be planted in the now mostly weed-free field.

The number of plants considered noxious weeds over a century ago was extremely large. Some of these weeds are today's treasured wildflowers and are now even cultivated flowers, but from a farmer's perspective, they were all pests.

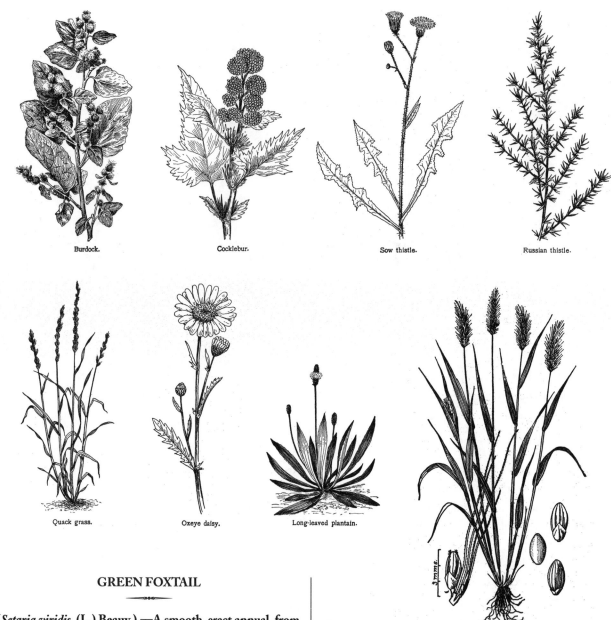

Burdock.   Cocklebur.   Sow thistle.   Russian thistle.

Quack grass.   Oxeye daisy.   Long-leaved plantain.

Fig. 90. Green foxtail *(Setaria viridis).* (U. S. Dept. Agrl.)

GREEN FOXTAIL

(*Setaria viridis*, (L.) Beauv.).—A smooth, erect annual, from one to three feet high, with leaves long, rough margined, greenish, more or less compound, cylindrical spikes from one to six inches long, with few bristles; spikelets shorter than the bristles, about one-half inch long, the chaff of the second and third glumes equaling the minute chaff of the fourth glume, which is faintly transversely wrinkled below or only striate and pitted; blooms from July to September. A single head of the green foxtail produces an enormous number of seeds, which appear to have considerable vitality, hence when the plant once becomes established in a field, it is very difficult to remove it. This difficulty is increased by the habit of the grass of forming tufts. The species common in the northern states and a troublesome weed in corn fields.

COUCH GRASS OR QUACK GRASS

(*Agropyron repens*, (L.) Beauv.).—An introduced grass already becoming troublesome in Iowa; culms one to three feet high, arising from an extensively creeping, jointed rootstock; sheaths usually smooth; leaves from four to twelve inches long,

Fig. 93. Quack grass or couch grass *(Agropyron repens)*. The running "roots" (rhizomes).

Fig. 97a. Sour dock *(Rumex crispus)*. A troublesome weed in fields, meadows and along roadsides. (Harrison and Lockhead.)

smooth, scabrous or somewhat downy above; erect spikes from three to ten inches long, bearing four to eight-flowered spikelets; empty glumes from five to seven-nerved, sometimes notched and short-awned or acute; flowering glume nerved near the apex, awnless or short-awned. Blooming period from August to October. This grass has become naturalized on lawns and cultivated grounds and is a very common wayside pest.

WINGED PIGWEED OR WESTERN TUMBLEWEED

(Cycloloma atriplicifolium, (Spreng.) Coult.).—An annual, diffusely branched, smooth or occasionally pubescent, alternately petioled, occasionally petioled, flowers in panicles and interrupted spikes; calyx five-lobed, stamens five, styles

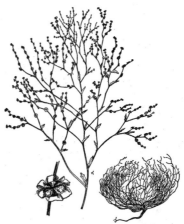

Fig. 102. Winged pigweed *(Cycloma atriplicifolium)*.

three, seed horizontal, flat, coats crustaceous; the winged calyx incloses the fruit, the lobes not entirely covering the summit of the atricle. Common in the sandhills west of the Missouri River, and also eastward around the great lakes. Plant grows in spherical form and at maturity separates from the roots close to the surface of the ground. A well-known western tumbleweed.

TUMBLING MUSTARD

(Sisymbrium altissimum, L.).—A leafy, branched annual, growing from two to four feet tall, lower leaves runcinate, pinnatifid, irregularly toothed or wavy margined; upper leaves smaller, threadlike; flowers with four green sepals, four pale yellow petals; in older specimens only the long, slender pods show with small brownish seeds. This weed has spread with great rapidity in the United States, the first specimen having been observed on ballast ground in Philadelphia, in 1878. It seems to have been distributed largely by railroads and is found frequently along the right of

Fig. 117. Tumbling mustard *(Sisymbrium altissimum.)*

Fig. 121. Black medick *(Medicago lupulina)*, a troublesome weed in alfalfa and clover meadows. (Ada Hayden.)

Fig. 130. St. John's-wort *(Hypericum perforatum)*, common in **fields of** the North. (Ada Hayden.)

way. It is injurious to cattle, seed containing it often causing inflammation and external irritation.

COMMON ST. JOHN'S-WORT

(Hypericum perforatum, L.).—A much-branched perennial with numerous sterile shoots at the base; leaves sessile, oblong or linear, punctate with black dots; flowers borne in cymose clusters, and have five green sepals shorter than the five yellow and black dotted petals; stamens many, in several clusters. Common in the eastern states, but rarely found west of the Mississippi or in the southern states. It is believed in some localities to be poisonous.

Fig. 132. Cowbane *(Cicuta maculata)*. A dangerous poisonous weed of the North. (Ada Hayden.)

Fig. 134. Wild carrot *(Daucus Carota)*. A troublesome weed of the East. (After Harrison and Lockhead.)

Fig. 140. Horse nettle *(Solanum carolinense)*. A most troublesome **persistent** weed with deep perennial root. (C. M. King.)

Fig. 142. Rugel's plantain *(Plantago Rugelii)*.

Fig. 154a. Ox-eye daisy, so-called *(Chrysanthemum Leucanthemum)*. A most troublesome weed in eastern meadows. (Ada Hayden.)

Fig. 159. Canada thistle *(Cirsium arvense)*.

INSECTICIDES AND FUNGICIDES

Insect pests caused a huge amount of crop damage. The larva of the codling moth, for instance, caused serious damage to the apple crop. The potato bug was another serious pest, as were the boll weevil, the tent caterpillar, the cabbage moth, the army worm, the tobacco worm, the chinch bug, and many others.

Traditional methods of pest control—such as crop rotation; spraying with liquid soap, kerosene, tobacco juice, and other substances (alone or in combination); hand destruction of insects; and good cleanup practices in fields and orchards—were labor intensive and barely kept the pests in check. The 1880s saw the introduction of the first chemical insecticides and fungicides. The discovery of bordeaux mixture, a fungicide, was announced in France in 1885. Bordeaux mixture was generally made of five pounds copper sulfate (also known as blue vitriol) and five pounds unslaked lime mixed into fifty gallons of water. It was used primarily to attack the various fungus disease of fruit trees, but it was also used to attack insects. Copper sulfate by itself was also used as a fungicide; iron sulfate was used as an herbicide. A number of highly toxic arsenic-based compounds such as Paris green (made from arsenic and copper) and London purple also came into widespread use around this time as fungicides and insecticides. Paris green, for example, was used against the codling moth. Sprayers were used to apply the chemicals as liquids or powders. Frighteningly, illustrations from the time show absolutely no protective gear for the worker. By 1908, one of the first reports appeared on crop injury believed to be caused by insecticide accumulation in the soil.

Myers' Brass Spray Pump.
WITH 8 GALLON TANK.

43998 The tank is made of galvanized iron and is equipped with one of Myers' powerful brass spray pumps, as shown in cut 44000 Price, complete with 8 gallon tank, each. $4.80

The "Model" Hand and Garden Pump or Fire Extinguisher.

43999 For pumping from pail or tub for spraying fruit trees and bushes, sprinkling lawns and flowers, washing windows and carriages; will force a ¼-inch stream from 40 to 60 feet; is furnished with a spraying attachment in the shape of a flat piece of brass; when attached to nozzle may be twisted so as to spray or to convert the stream into small drops. It is not intended for heavy work, such as extinguishing large fires, etc., but may often prove useful in putting out small blazes, thereby preventing large fires. The piece of hose which comes with pump is 28 inches long and ½ inch in diameter; cannot attach any more than this; is plenty long enough to do the work mentioned; weight, 5 pounds.
Price, each $2.00

The Meyers' Bucket Brass Spray Pumps.
AND FIRE EXTINGUISHER, WITH AGITATOR.

Farmers' and fruit growers' friend. Is constructed of material that is not affected by the poisonous arsenites used in the different formulas for spraying fruit trees, vines and shrubbery. The cylinder and all the working parts are brass; has rubber ball valves and is equipped with our Combination Spray Nozzle, and will throw a spray as fine as mist. The pump differs in construction from the old-line pumps of this class and is arranged so that the heavy work is done on the down stroke of the plunger and nothing on the up.

The operator is enabled to keep a constant pressure on the nozzle of from 50 to 100 lbs. with very ordinary exertion. It will throw a solid stream 50 feet, and is of unusual value for washing windows, etc. For spraying it is arranged so it discharges a fine jet in bottom of bucket to keep the solution thoroughly mixed and agitated, a feature peculiar to this pump. Will throw a solid stream 50 feet.
44000 Price of Brass Spray Pump, with agitator, complete with hose, combination, fire and coarse spray and solid stream nozzles, each............$2.65

The Myers' Fountain Spray Pump.

Is constructed of galvanized iron, with round corners, built with tight lid to prevent liquid from splashing on operator. It is fitted with adjustable straps so as to be carried on the back, or it may be carried by the ball. The hose and bulb are made of the best white rubber and protected at each end by coiled wire to prevent breaking. The valves are made of brass and will not corrode, have large openings, which permit the free flow of water and shut off instantly when under pressure. The nozzle is made of brass, nickel plated, has fifty small openings, and throws a spray six feet wide at a distance of twelve feet.

OPERATION.—The pump is operated by grasping the bulb in the hand and compressing it, which causes a spray to be thrown any distance from three to fifteen feet, as desired, on relaxing the pressure on bulb it expands, refilling instantly, when the same operation can be repeated. To shut off flow of water entirely, use valve on hose for that purpose. The operator can cover one or two rows of plants or vines as desired, and do the work at a rapid walk, thus covering a large amount of territory in a very short time.

CAUTION.—Always mix Paris green or London purple in a separate vessel, forming into a paste before adding water. In this way everything will be dissolved and will not need to be agitated. Holds 5 gallons. weight, 52 lbs. when full.
44001 Price, each, complete, with 1 tube, rubber bulb and rose...... ....$3.00
44002 Price, each, complete, with 2 tubes, rubber bulb and roses to work with both hands. 4.00

LEGGETT'S PARIS GREEN OR DRY POWDER GUN.

For Orchard, Vineyard, Garden or Potato Field. Distributes Paris Green, Sulphur, "Fungiroid," (a powdered Bordeaux Mixture) or any dry powder. THOUSANDS IN USE Illustrated Circular on application.

A Wonderful Invention Light, Swift, Easy, Safe, Strong and Cheap.

70441 Supplied with necessary tubes, nozzles, neck and body straps for dusting trees, shrubs, vines or plants; will apply paris green, hellebore or any dry powder quicker, easier and cheaper than by other methods; weight when in use, 5 lbs., boxed for shipment, 20 lbs.; circulars mailed. Price...................................$7.50

Spray Pump--The Advance.

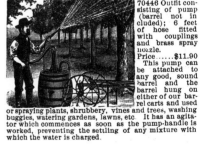

70446 Outfit consisting of pump (barrel not included); 6 feet of hose fitted with couplings and brass spray nozzle. Price......$11.90 This pump can be attached to any good, sound barrel and the barrel hung on either of our barrel carts and used or spraying plants, shrubbery, vines and trees, washing buggies, watering gardens, lawns, etc. It has an agitator which commences as soon as the pump-handle is worked, preventing the settling of any mixture with which the water is charged.

PART IV

Dairy

CHAPTER 12

THE DAIRY

By the turn of the century, record grain harvests on huge farms may have gotten the most attention, but the dairy industry had become extremely important to the American farmer. A growing urban population was demanding more fresh milk, cream, butter, cheese, and other dairy products. The demand could no longer be met by dairy products produced as a part-time activity or sideline. Fortunately, important technological improvements made specialized dairy farming possible and profitable.

Pasteurization, the process of sterilizing milk by heating it, began to improve the wholesomeness of milk and dairy products by the 1870s. The introduction of the cream separator in the early 1880s was a major improvement in dairy efficiency. By 1900 the widespread adoption of silage made dairy farming a year-round, instead of three-season, proposition. Growing demand, better transportation networks, improved sanitation, selective breeding, and farmer cooperatives all began to turn dairy production from a farm sideline that brought in small, steady amounts of needed cash into a large-scale operation. So successful were these innovations that by 1910 there were nearly 22 million dairy cows in the country. Dairy products in that year had a total value of nearly $800 million, greater than any farm crop except corn.

WOMEN IN THE DAIRY

Caring for the cows and milking them were chores generally done by the farmer, but the dairy was traditionally the province of his wife. She was in charge of the value-added operations that turned milk into cream, butter, and cheese; the skim milk went to feed calves and pigs. (Whole milk wasn't as worthwhile a product, especially for farmers more than a hundred miles from a big city.) The farmer's wife was also in charge of the henhouse and the egg production. Her butter-and-egg money was often the only steady source of hard cash on the farm. As dairy production became increasingly large scale and as butter and cheese production moved off the farm and into central creameries, the farmer's wife played less of a role and lost a degree of financial independence. Many a farmer's wife, however, was doubtless glad to exchange the backbreaking labor of dairying for higher farm income and a little less personal autonomy. Here's how the male (of course) author of *American Cattle* put it as early as 1878:

> Dairy factories, aside from improving the quality of their products, and increasing their prices over the old household way of making them, have accomplished a most beneficent and merciful mission, in relieving the wives and daughters of our dairymen of a routine of slavish and most wearing labor. The life of a household dairywoman is toilsome in the extreme. Perpetual watchfulness, anxiety, and work throughout the dairy season, frequently beyond her physical endurance, has been her destiny—over the cheese tub, and shelf, the churn, and butter bowl—to say nothing of her labors in the milking yard, over the wash kettle, and scrubbing brush. No relaxation whatever is permitted. Necessity knows no law, nor mercy for those patient, over-worked solaces of the household.

THE DAIRY BARN

The crucial importance of an airy, well-ventilated, spotlessly clean dairy barn was recognized early on. Fresh air and cleanliness kept the cows healthy, contented, and free of the dreaded tuberculosis. Keeping the barn clean involved more than just good ventilation and sunlight. A tight floor of poured concrete or solid wooden boards, plentiful straw bedding, frequent removal of manure, and annual whitewashing were all important. All cleaning activities had to be done in between milkings to avoid stirring up dust that would land in the milk.

A MICHIGAN DAIRY BARN AND SILO

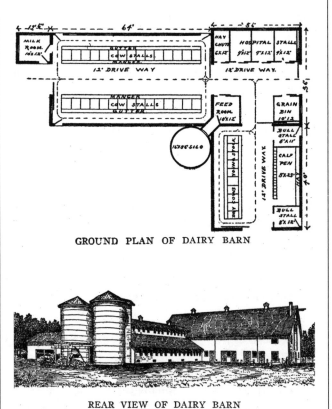

GROUND PLAN OF DAIRY BARN

ELEVATION OF DAIRY BARN

REAR VIEW OF DAIRY BARN

MILKING THE COWS

Cows were milked twice a day, day in and day out, early in the morning and again in the late afternoon. The first milking machines didn't appear until around 1910, but they weren't particularly effective. Truly practical milking machines didn't come in until the 1920s. In 1900 and for the foreseeable future, milking was done by hand.

Milking by hand was laborious and had its risks, particularly from kicking cows. As the cows were milked, they were fed a ration of silage, sometimes mixed with supplemental feed. To keep the cow in place (and to keep her from butting the milker), stanchions or ties were used. The arguments pro and con for each method, and for the best methods within each method, were extensive and endless.

CHAIN CATTLE TIE

Various methods have been devised for coupling cattle in their stalls in a more humane manner than by stanchions. The common chain tie passes about the animal's neck, and slides up or down upon a post or iron rod, attached to the stall or manger. The tie, figure 108, is similar, except that the neck-chain is connected with two posts or rods, upon which it slides. The improvement consists in using rings upon the posts, and connecting the side-chain with the neck chain by means of snap-hooks, attached to the central ring as shown in the engraving. This enables one to adjust the tie to any width of stall, say from three to four feet, and have it reasonably taut. The advantage of this method of fastening cattle over any other is, that while great freedom is given the head, so that a cow can lick both sides and lie down with her head upon either side, she has no more backward and forward motion than if she stood in stanchions, hence must leave her droppings in the gutter—if the stall is of the proper length. There is a constant tendency to give cow stalls too long a floor. Every cow should lie with her rump four to eight inches beyond the floor. The only object to this is that the cows' tail will sometimes become wet from lying in the gutter. If, however, this is given a pretty sharp fall and considerable breadth, water will not accumulate, and there will be no inconvenience experienced on this score.

Fig. 108.—AN IMPROVED TIE FOR CATTLE.

Cow Ties.

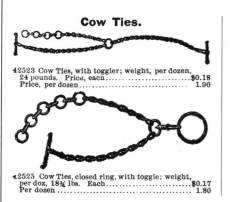

42523 Cow Ties, with toggler; weight, per dozen, 24 pounds. Price, each.....................$0.18
Price, per dozen.............................. 1.90

42525 Cow Ties, closed ring, with toggle; weight, per doz, 18¾ lbs. Each.......................$0.17
Per dozen 1.80

Newton's Improved Cow Ties.

42526 The boss of all other ties. No feed is wasted. Better than swinging stanchions. The tie is made of wood, and bent in the shape of a bail or three sides of a square. It is provided with a swivel that is fastened in the center by two iron pins, and made so that one part turns with the neck piece, and the other part revolves around the wooden tie, making it impossible for the animal to get it twisted. The end of the wooden tie is riveted, so that it will not split where the bolts go through that fasten it to the manger. It will keep the cows cleaner than any other mode of fastening, because it pushes them back when standing, and draws them forward while lying down. We furnish the wooden tie, with neck piece, complete, and bolts to put it up. Full directions for making the manger and putting up furnished with each tie.
Price, in lots of 1 to 5 ties, complete, each.........$1.65
Price, in lots of 6 or more ties, complete, each.... 1.50

CLEANLINESS

Cleanliness was important when milking cows. The cow herself was kept clean with brushing; the udder and teats were wiped clean with a damp cloth and checked for diseases such as mastitis before milking began. The milker was required to wash his hands and dry them thoroughly before beginning. Milkers who were sick themselves were not supposed to go near the cows, although it's unclear how often this general rule was really enforced. The goal was quick, careful, complete milking that didn't hurt the cow. The milker sat on a low stool on the cow's right side and drew the milk as rapidly as possible, using both hands. An experienced milker could take care of eight to twelve or even more cows in a hour. The milk was kept cleaner if small-top milking pails were used.

Bacteria-harboring wooden dairy utensils were already antiques by 1900. The metal of choice, in the days before stainless steel, was pressed tin. Implements made of tin were far easier to keep clean and could be sterilized in boiling water or with steam.

TWO KINDS OF MILKING STOOLS

The construction of a very good milking stool is readily seen in figure 111. Upon a hard-wood board, twelve inches wide, one inch thick, and thirty inches long, fasten at right angles a board to serve as a rest. This should be eight inches wide,

Fig. 111.—MILKING STOOL.

and as long as the width of the back-board. Strengthen the seat with stout braces. Cut a narrow opening in the long board, to admit the fingers, by which to carry the stool, or hang it up when not in use.

The other stool, figure 112, is designed for a man who has a good many cows to milk, and desires to carry his stool around with him, while his hands are left free. The seat consists of the bottom of a peach basket; the single leg is made of

Fig. 112.—MILKING STOOL.

a round piece of wood securely fastened to the center of the seat. The latter may be padded and covered as one chooses. Leather straps to reach up and around the waist of the milker, as shown in the illustration, should be firmly attached to the seat.

A HANDY MILKING STOOL

Milkers who have trouble with restless cows that invariably either upset the pail or get a quantity of dirt in it will find the stool shown here a remedy for their troubles. It is also very serviceable in fly time. The upright pieces forming the legs and ends of stools are made of 2 × 8-inch pieces about 1 foot long. The supports for the bucket and the seat are made of

STOOL TO HOLD PAIL

inch boards. To secure rigidity it is well to put three-cornered blocks under the seat and bucket board as brace stays. The most restless cow is not likely to upset the bucket from this stool.

THE EVER READY STOOL

A very convenient stool for use in milking the cow in yard or field is shown in the cut. It is merely a one-legged stool to

MILKING STOOL

which is attached four straps connecting with a broad strap that is buckled around the waist. The stool is quickly fastened to the milker and is always in a position so one can sit down anywhere. Such a stool with a short leg would also be useful in the garden. Of course, if one preferred four legs instead of one, the stool could be so made, but experience proves that the one-legged kind serves well.

CHEAP MILKING STOOL

A cheap and very useful milking stool is made of the reel from which barbed wire has been removed. Saw off the ends so it will set level and cut a board to fit on top. Make a hand hole through the board as shown in the illustration and the stool is ready for use.

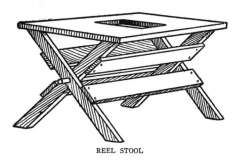

REEL STOOL

KEEP STOOLS CLEAN

Much milk contamination is undoubtedly due to the careless handling of the milk stools. When the milker is through milking one cow he gives the stool a toss, then he picks it up again when he starts to milk the next cow and his hands

become more or less contaminated from the stool and from them the dirt drops into the milk pail during the milking.

When the milking is over, the stool is left in the yard or on the barn floor. It is so easy to make a small rack and to

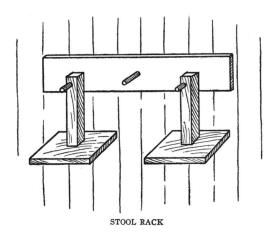

STOOL RACK

bore holes in the legs of the stool, so that they may be hung up. This keeps them out of the dirt and it is only necessary to brush them off carefully once in a while to keep them scrupulously clean.

FIG. 3—DIFFERENT STYLES OF SANITARY MILKING-PAILS

Perfect Milk Pail.

56925 Pail, milk stool and strainer in one. The milker sits on the pail and milks into the funnel. Cannot be kicked or knocked over by the cow. Price..... ....$1.75

Strainer Pails, Tin.

56929   56931

They will not hold as much as represented.
56929 10 quarts ....$0.25 14 quarts $0.30
56931 Milk Pail, with strainer, extra heavy tin, stamped seamless, holds 12 quarts.
Each ....$0.90 Per dozen.......... 9.72

The Dairyman's Favorite.

56933 The accompanying cut represents an article having all the essential points of a perfect Strainer Pail. Among its points of excellence we mention the breast and front half of the pail being formed in one piece, making but two up and down seams in the body. It will be noticed that the breast is funnel-shaped, and will not slop over in pouring. Besides the wire gauze strainer there is a brass spring clamping around the mouth to hold a cloth, thus making a double strainer without extra labor or loss of time. Another important feature is—there is no part but what can be thoroughly washed, and no rough and unsoldered seams in which dirt can accumulate and sour.
12 quarts, per dozen. ..$5.40 Each................$0.50
14 quarts, per dozen 6.05 Each............... .56

The Chicago Milk Pail Holder.

56934 Milking made easy and rest while you milk. The above cut represents a new and useful article for holding a milk pail. So simple that any person can use it without a moment's waste of time. Saves the pail from being kicked over and keeps it up out of the dirt and filth. Fits any size or style of pail and holds it perfectly without cramping the limbs, by simply hanging the holder over the knees with hoop in front, and placing the pail inside. By allowing the holder to rest against the foot the pail can be placed in any desirable position. Made of 1½ inch band iron, enameled or galvanized.
Enameled, each..........$0.25 Per dozen......$2.70
Galvanized, each.......... 0.30 Per dozen...... 3.24

In 1890 Stephen M. Babcock, a professor of agricultural chemistry at the University of Wisconsin and chief chemist of the Wisconsin Agricultural Experiment Station, perfected what came to be known as the Babcock test. Using simple glass tubes, a dairy farmer could sample the milk from each cow and check the percentage of butterfat in it. (The Babcock test kept farmers informed about the production of their cows. It also kept them honest—the Babcock test could detect watered milk.)

Curtis Babcock Farm Tester.

56926 Every dairyman or farmer who keeps a half dozen cows ought to provide himself with one of these milk testers, if he cares the snap of his finger to know whether he has a cow in the herd that is worth keeping. (More than one cow "eats her head off" every year she is kept.) This tester is designed express- ly for farm use, and so low a price put on it that every man who owns two cows can have a four bottle machine.

4 Bottle Tester, complete. Price.......$5.00
6   "   "   "   "   ......:. 6.00
8   "   "   "   " 7.00
With each machine there is a pipette acid measure, a bottle of acid and directions for operating.

Babcock Milk Test.

With Roe's improved swing- ing heads.
56927 4-Bottle Tester, complete. Price......$8.00
8-Bottle Tester, com- plete. Price.......... 10.00
12-Bottle Tester, com- plete. Price 14.00
24-Bottle Tester, com- plete Price.......... 21.00
ith each machine is included testing bottles, pip- ette acid measure and acid for 50 to 200 tests, accord- ing to size, and full directions for operating.

Instruments For Testing Milk.

57057 These instruments are used very largely by factory- men to find out who puts the most water in his milk. They are very good detec- tives. Directions showing how to operate sent with each set.
Per set................$1.90

Heavy Milk Test Glasses.

57058 These tubes are used by factorymen to test their patrons' milk; showing the relative value of each by the cream thrown up. 5 x 1¼ inches.
Per doz..$0.65

Glassware for Babcock Milk Tester.

57059 Babcock bottles, each.......................$0.40
57060 Milk pipette, each............................ .10
57061 Acid measure, each.......................... .10
57062 Test churn tube, each,...................... .10

COOLING AND SEPARATING

The fresh milk was immediately strained through a fine brass wire strainer and several thicknesses of cheese-cloth to remove any animal hair, bits of straw, dust, and other debris. The next step was immediate cooling, which removed the "animal" or "grassy" taste from the milk and helped it to keep considerably longer. A variety of mechanical milk cooling and aerating devices were in use by the 1880s. In 1900, electric refrigeration units were still far in the future.

The next step after cooling was separation, to remove the cream from the milk. Setting the milk, or letting it stand in pails in a cool place or in cold running water while the cream rose to the top, was the usual method up until the 1890s. The process of raising the cream could take anywhere from twenty-four to thirty-six hours. Ideally, the setting was done in a springhouse or dairy house, a separate structure with cold running water either diverted from a spring or pumped in. Where available, ice was used to help in the cooling. For smaller amounts of milk, or where springhouses were too expensive or too impractical, setting troughs were impro-vised in a cool place. Manufactured creameries, compact units designed to handle the output of a small dairy herd, were popular.

Two setting methods were used: deep setting, in deep pails or milk cans set into troughs fifteen to twenty inches deep, or shallow set, in shallower pails or pans. The optimal water temperature was around forty degrees or less for rapid separation.

The springhouse also functioned as a place to churn butter and make cheese, activities that were best done in a cool environment. By 1900, farm-made butter and cheese were becoming less common. Farmers were more likely to sell their milk on a regular basis to a commercial or cooperative processing factory than to keep it for home processing.

Some farmers, however, practiced what today would be called vertical integration: they pasteurized, bottled, and sold their own milk to local consumers. For farmers close to large towns or cities, increasing mechanization and the introduction of motor vehicles made this a viable proposition, even though it was both labor- and capital-intensive.

FIG. 4

FIG. 5

A quick way of cooling milk. The milk in a thin layer runs over a surface made cold by running ice-water. The same water can be used repeatedly by adding ice each time. This method should be used only when the surrounding air is pure.

The milk contained in these long "shot-gun" pails or cans, placed in ice-water is stirred occasionally to insure even cooling.

Curtis' Improved Milk Strainer.

56922 This strainer is adapted for use in all kinds of vessels where milk is set to raise cream. It sets in a tin pan or in an 8-inch deep setting pail. The metal cone shields the strainer from getting jammed. The strainer is made from superior silvered wire cloth, while the tube which projects below has a band, where a cloth is readily put on, straining the milk twice at one operation. The bowl of the strainer is stamped from one piece of heavy plate and then retinned, making it smooth, and as near perfect as a strainer can be. Price $1.30

Howard Patent Milk Cooler.

56923 This valuable implement is made to fit any can. As the milk is poured into one side it is strained and runs in very fine streams into the can below. It cools the milk in the operation, and takes from it the animal odor.
Each.............. ....$2.40

Milk Cooler and Aerator.

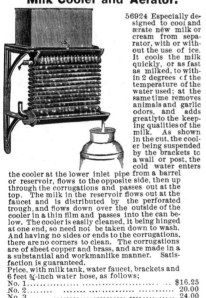

56924 Especially designed to cool and aerate new milk or cream from separator, with or without the use of ice. It cools the milk quickly, or as fast as milked, to within 2 degrees of the temperature of the water used; at the same time removes animals and garlic odors, and adds greatly to the keeping qualities of the milk. As shown in the cut, the cooler being suspended by the brackets to a wall or post, the cold water enters the cooler at the lower inlet pipe from a barrel or reservoir, flows to the opposite side, then up through the corrugations and passes out at the top. The milk in the reservoir flows out at the faucet and is distributed by the perforated trough, and flows down over the outside of the cooler in a thin film and passes into the can below. The cooler is easily cleaned, it being hinged at one end, so need not be taken down to wash. And having no sides or ends to the corrugations, there are no corners to clean. The corrugations are of sheet copper and brass, and are made in a substantial and workmanlike manner. Satisfaction is guaranteed.
Price, with milk tank, water faucet, brackets and 6 feet ¾-inch water hose, as follows;
No. 1.. $16.25
No. 2........ .... 20.00
No. 3...... .... 24.00

Cooley Creamer.

56826 The above is an illustration of the Cooley system of setting milk in submerged cans. These cans are 20 inches deep and 8¼ inches in diameter; the covers are fastened down, and the air under the rims of the covers prevent the passage of any water into the cans. The cans are set in the water coolers, which are lined with metal and fitted with inlet and overflow for using flowing spring water. A thermometer is inserted in the front of each cooler, in order that the temperature can be ascertained without raising the cover. This apparatus is very simple, dispensing with costly milk rooms, as but little room is required.

If the temperature of the water in the cooler is kept at 45 to 50 degrees in spring and summer, and at 40 degrees or below in winter, the cream will rise in 12 hours, in which case only cans enough to hold a single milking are required. By this system of setting milk we have sweet cream from sweet milk, raised in the shortest possible space of time. Prices include cans with bottom faucet, and glass panel in the side of can, showing depth of cream.

SIZE, CAPACITY AND PRICES.

No. 0, for 1 can, milk of 1 cow, 18 quarts........$15.10
No. 00, for 2 cans, milk of 2 to 4 cows, 36 quarts 21.00
No. 1, for 3 cans, size, 25x32 inches, milk of 6 to 9 cows, 51 quarts.................................. 23.50
No. 2, for 4 cans, size 28x38 inches, milk of 9 to 12 cows, 68 quarts.................................. 25 20
No. 3, for 6 cans, size, 28x49 inches, milk of 12 to 18 cows, 102 quarts................................ 33 60
No. 4, for 8 cans. size, 28x61 inches, milk of 18 to 24 cows, 136 quarts....................... 42.00
No. 5, for 10 cans, size, 28x72 inches, milk of 24 to 30 cows, 170 quarts................................ 50.00
No. 6, for 12 cans, size, 28x84 inches. milk of 30 to 36 cows, 204 quarts............................. 58.80

In connection with the Cooley Creamer, if Boyd's Automatic Fermenting Can and Automatic Ripening Cream Vat are used, nothing can be more simple for making prime butter every day in the year. It is making butter by rule. No process in the world like it.

Skimming Bench.

This cut shows a simple device to be used with Cooley creamer upon which to place the cans when drawing off the milk and cream, by the Cooley process of skimming. This bench should be set with one end against the creamer, so that the cans, as they are lifted out, can be readily placed upon it, thus avoiding any drip on the floor. This is an inexpensive arrangement and can easily be made by any one who can handle a saw, plane and hammer.

Tank for Deep Setting Cans.

56827 These tanks are made from two-inch lumber, the ends securely clamped and fastened with rods and have a hinged cover not shown in cut. It is fitted with an inlet and overflow. Painted both outside and inside. It is made strong and substantial and will hold Cooley or any deep setting can.
Sizes and prices.
To hold 4 cans...$5.50
To hold 6 cans 6.65
To hold 8 cans 7.50
To hold 10 cans.............................. 8.45

The Peerless Creamery.

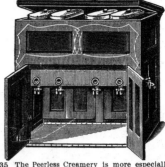

56835 The Peerless Creamery is more especially intended for water alone. The cans are oblong, 14 inches long, 5 inches wide and 14 inches deep, thus giving larger cooling surface. We have a large ice space in rear of and also between the cans; in the No. 4 we have the space between the two middle cans, 7 inches; also, in all the other sizes we have a large space between the second and third, fourth and fifth, and sixth and seventh. In these, as in the round can creamers, we use a straight faucet underneath, which is easily cleaned. The glass to observe the cream is in the nut and not in the can, so is easily repaired if accidentally broken. In the No. 3 and larger sized creameries the faucet for drawing water from the tank is placed outside of creamery, as shown in illustration Where ice is not used, we would suggest emptying tank of water about a half hour after milk has been placed in cans, and refilling tank with cold water. This will save a few hours' time in the gathering of cream. Furnished complete, with cream pail, strainer and dairy thermometer.
PRICE LIST.—Capacity of cans, 18 quarts each.

No.	No. of cans.	No. of cows.	Height, inches.	Length, inches.	Width, inches.	Weight, pounds.	Price.
2.....	2	4 to 6	35	25	23	100	$17.85
3.....	3	7 to 9	35	34	23	125	21.80
4.....	4	10 to 12	35	41	23	160	26.40
5.....	6	13 to 18	35	61	23	220	34.32
6.....	8	19 to 24	35	77	23	280	42.65
7.....	10	25 to 30	35	80	23	320	49.40
8.....	12	31 to 36	35	96	24	440	56.30

Our prices on these creameries are 40 per cent. below factory prices.

Cream Setter.

56935 This Cream Setter has tinned iron bottom, glass panel in graduate case. The glass panel in can is graduated so that if parties are buying cream two degrees will make one pound of butter. Thousands of them are in successful and satisfactory operation. They are easily cleaned and raise as much cream and as quickly as any other cream setting can in the market. The can has a bail on it so that a man can carry two of them at a time. Size, 8¼x20 inches. Weight, 4¼ lbs.
Each........$0.60 Per dozen.....$6.48
56937 Cream Setters, same as above, without gauge. Each.$0.55 Per doz.$5.95
For dairy thermometers, see Index.

Plain Cooley Can.

56938 The submerged system of setting milk for gathered cream is recognized everywhere as a superior way of raising cream. The milk is away from the flies and dust, and any foul odors that may be floating in the air from the barnyard or pig sty. The milk is set in cold water immediately after milking. The cream is all thrown up in twelve hours. The can holds 18 quarts. Each..$1.25

Cooley Can With Bottom Faucet.

56939 For private dairies this can has no equal. The milk is drawn off through the bottom faucet, leaving the cream in the can to be poured into the cream pail. The value of sweet skim milk over sour milk for feeding purposes will more than pay for the cans every three months. All of the Cooley cans are made from the best tin obtainable. They hold 18 quarts. Each..............$1.75

Fig. 173.—INTERIOR OF SPRING HOUSE, WITH ELEVATED TROUGH.

Fig. 174.—INTERIOR OF SPRING HOUSE, WITH LOW TROUGH.

SPRING HOUSES

The main points to look at in constructing a spring house are, coolness of water, purity of air, the preservation of an even temperature during all seasons, and perfect drainage. The first is secured by locating the house near the spring, or by conducting the water through pipes, placed at least four feet under ground. The spring should be dug out and cleaned, and the sides evenly built up with rough stone work. The top should be arched over, or shaded from the sun. A spout from the spring carries the water into the house. If the spring is sufficiently high, it would be most convenient to

Fig. 175.—EXTERIOR OF SPRING HOUSE.

have the water trough in the house elevated upon a bench, as shown in figure 173. There is then no necessity for stooping, to place the pans in the water, or to take them out. Where the spring is too low for this, the trough may be made on a level with the floor, as in figure 174. The purity of the air is to be insured by removing all stagnant water or filth from around the spring. All decaying roots and muck that may be collected, should be removed, and the ground around the house either paved roughly with stone or sodded. The openings which admit and discharge the water, should be large enough to allow a free current of air to flow in or out. These openings are to be covered with fine gauze to prevent insects or vermin from entering inside. The house should be smoothly plastered, and frequently whitewashed with lime, and a large ventilator should be made in the ceiling. There should be no wood used in the walls or floors, or water channels. An even temperature can best be secured by building of stone or brick, with walls twelve inches thick, double windows, and a ceiled roof. In such a house there will be no danger of freezing in the winter time. The drainage will be insured by choosing the site, so that there is ample fall of the waste water. The character of the whole building is shown in figure 175. The size will depend altogether upon the number of cows in the dairy. For a dairy of twenty cows there should be at least one hundred square feet of water surface in the troughs. The troughs should be made about eighteen inches in width, which admits a pan that would hold eight to ten quarts at three inches in depth. A house, twenty-four feet long by twelve wide, would give sixty feet of trough, eighteen inches wide, or ninety square feet. The furniture of the house should consist of a stone or cement bench and an oak table in the center, upon which the cream jars and butter bowls may be kept.

The introduction of the mechanical cream separator around 1880 made setting the milk obsolete. The first cream separator was made by Carl Gustav de Laval of Sweden, whose sturdy, easy-to-use model was sold by the millions worldwide. The basic principle behind De Laval's invention was centrifugal force. The whole milk was poured into a bowl at the top of the separator as the operator turned the crank at a uniform fifty to sixty times a minute. This rotated the bowl and a spindle containing a series of conical disks; the centrifugal force pushes the heavier milk toward the outer part of the bowl, while the lighter cream collects in the center. The

skim milk and cream drain out of separate spouts into milk cans or pails as more milk is poured in from above. Cream separators came with different capacities. For a dairy herd of about fourteen cows, the farmer needed a machine that could handle seven hundred pounds of milk in an hour.

Centrifugal separator.

The cream separator was highly efficient. It could be used immediately on cooled milk, rather than waiting for the cream to rise. The setting method left as much as a quarter of the cream in the milk, while the separator removed all but 1 to 2 percent of it—although the settings could be adjusted for creamier milk. Cranking the cream separator was a chore, one that was lightened where possible by belting the machine to an engine. Later, of course, the separator was electric powered.

Cream separators became so popular that by 1915 there were some two million in use on American farms; some thirty different manufacturers, most prominently the Iowa Dairy Separator Company, were selling variants on the basic idea.

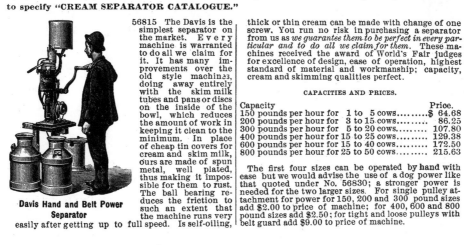

Milk Cans.

The illustration below shows the improved breast used on all our milk cans; the most important feature is to make a breast that is proof against being "jammed in." Our heavy half oval hoop accomplishes this; the hoop is forced on the breast in the block, securely fastened and afterward retinned, which makes it absolutely safe against being knocked off. We have also adopted a new seamless neck on all our cans; this you will observe, is drawn in one piece. The advantages of the New Seamless Neck, as compared with the old style bowl and neck in two pieces are many. There are no seams to come unsoldered, no edges or joints to rust, no bowl to work loose. Adds to weight of your can, being heavier material. Strengthens the weakest part of your can. Is perfectly smooth inside and out.

THE IMPROVED BREAST

NEW SEAMLESS NECK.

56901 Sturges' or Teet's Pattern Railroad Milk Can, with improved breast and new seamless neck.

	Wgt.	Each	Per doz
8 gallons	15½ lbs.	$1.98	$22.58
10 gallons	17½ lbs.	2.10	23.95

56903 Elgin Pattern. All Steel Railroad Milk Can with improved breast and new seamless neck.

	Wgt.	Each	Per doz.
8 gallons	18 lbs.	$2.25	$25.65
10 gallons	22 lbs.	2.45	27.93

56905 Iowa or Dubuque Pattern Railroad Milk Can, with improved breast and new seamless neck.

	Weight.	Each.	Per doz.
8 gallons,	18 lbs.	$1.98	$22.75
10 gallons	21 lbs.	2.10	23.95

56907 Chicago Pattern. All Steel Railroad Milk Can, with improved breast and new seamless neck.

	Weight.	Each.	Per doz
8 gallons,	18 lbs.	2.45	27.93
10 gallons	22 lbs.	2.80	31.95

Milk Can Links and Washers. We always use this washer to strengthen can and prevent its wearing. We can fit any of our milk cans with link and washer at an additional charge of 5 cents per can.

Brass or Copper Milk Can Letters; size, 1⅜ inches, soldered onto can at 1½ cents per letter; when ordering state which is desired, otherwise copper letters will be used.

The above illustration shows ⅜ inch brass faucet fitted to milk can for delivery purposes. When desired it can be put on any of our cans at an additional cost, "including price of faucet and labor," for $1.50.

56909 Milk or Cream Pails, tin, with bails.

	Each.	Per doz.
1 quart	$0.12	$1.30
2 quarts	.15	1.62
3 quarts	.20	2.16
4 quarts	.25	2.70

56911 Milk Peddling Cans. They are made of 4X tin with heavy brass hoop on top and bottom, spout tipped with brass; a very strong and serviceable article. Capacity two gallons.
Each...............$1.56

56913 Milk Measure graduated, made of good quality tin and holds 1 quart.
Each....$0.08
Per dozen.........$0.87

56915 Milk Dippers, made of tin, with long handle.
Price, each............. 1 pint, 10c.; 1 quart, 15c.

BUTTER

With the exception of olive oil, seen as an ethnic specialty, vegetable oils were not in common use at the turn of the century. The primary shortenings were butter, lard, and tallow (beef fat). This made butter one of the most important dairy products, primarily because it was the most profitable. Demand for high-quality, farm-fresh butter was always high. Butter making was labor-intensive, however, and after 1850 butter became increasingly a factory product. After the introduction of the cream separator and the Babcock scale, butter making largely moved off the dairy farm. By 1900, farm butter making was really done only for home use and local sale on small, self-sufficient mixed farms.

Before churning, the cream that was used to make butter needed to stand and ferment so that lactic acid would develop. Otherwise the cream would not churn well—it would be foamy and the resulting butter would have an insipid taste. Fermenting cans stored the cream at a uniform temperature and promoted the formation of lactic acid.

The stoneware churn with its vertical wooden dash was old-fashioned even in the 1870s, even though it continued in widespread use on small farms for years. Later versions of the vertical churn used a crank-operated dash. Barrel churns, operated by a crank, were much more efficient. Smaller churns were hand-turned. In larger operations, dog power or horsepower might be used; later on, the crank was belted to a small engine.

Once the butter came up in the churn, it still needed extensive working to remove the remaining buttermilk (it was fed to pigs and used in baking) and make the butter smoothly uniform. Salt and yellow coloring, if necessary, would be worked in. (The yellow color of butter comes from the carotene in grass. Winter butter was unattractively pale.)

For sale directly to the consumer, the worked butter was packed into decorative molds and pressed into blocks or squares ranging in weight from half a pound to two pounds. Alternatively, the butter was cut into pound or half-pound squares, or prints, so called because they were stamped or "printed" with a decorative wooden stamp, often one that identified the maker. Printing the butter assured the consumer that the product had not been tampered with or improperly handled on the way to market.

Boyd's Automatic Cream Vat and Fermenting Can for Farm Use.

56828 This cut represents Boyd's Automatic Cream Vat for farm use, and it can truthfully be said that no other known process will produce as much and as good butter from a given amount of cream. It accomplishes for butter making what has never been done before. It enables the butter maker to work to a given rule every day in the year, and produces absolutely uniform results. It does away entirely with the necessity of coddling the cream around the stove. This vat is so constructed that when the cream is put into the vat the temperature of the cream will scarcely vary over three or four degrees in twenty-four hours. It is a perfect refrigerator vat with a cover. Quotations are for ripening vats only. Fermenting cans are quoted separately.

	Price.		Price.
10 gallon vat........	$15.10	100 gallon vat......	$35.30
15 gallon vat........	17.65	150 ga lon vat.. ..	40.35
20 gallon vat........	20.10	200 gallon vat......	45.30
30 gallon vat........	22.68	250 gallon vat......	50.40
50 gallon vat..	25.20	300 gallon vat.	55.45
75 gallon vat........	30.25	400 gallon vat......	63.00

Boyd's Automatic Fermenting Can.

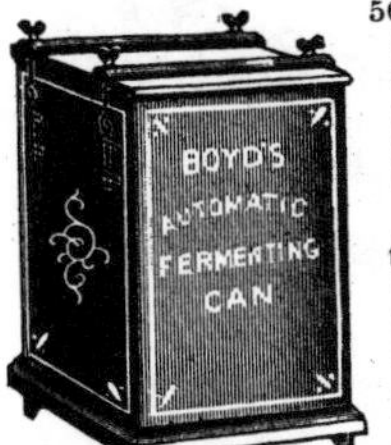

56829 The Boyd process of fermenting is very simple, yet more scientific than appears at first sight. It consists of making a lactive ferment from sweet skimmed milk, dives ed of its butter fat, taken from a fresh cow or cows. The milk is treated to a warm water bath and brought to a certain required temperature, when it is placed in the fermenting can and the vessel closed tightly. In a given time the lactive ferment is ready for use A small percentage of this ferment is placed in the cream at a required temperature, and the cream vat is closed in the same manner as the fermenting can. In so many hours the result is ripe cream, that is, cream of one chemical condition. The operation is uniform; so also is the result. If the rules are strictly obeyed, the operator is at all seasons master of the situation. He has perfect control over the conditions, consequently his work is all down to rule, nothing being left to chance or good luck. The Automatic Fermenting Can and Automatic Ripening Cream Vat are sold only in connection with each other, and are essential to the process.

Fermenting cans holding 1 gallon, price. $3.80
Fermenting cans holding 2 gallons, price........ 4.20
Fermenting cans holding 3 gallons, price........ 4.65
Fermenting cans holding 4 gallons, price........ 5.10
Fermenting cans holding 5 gallons, price........ 5.50
Fermenting cans holding 6 gallons, price........ 5.90
Fermenting cans holding 8 gallons, price........ 6.35

Cedar Box Factory Churn.

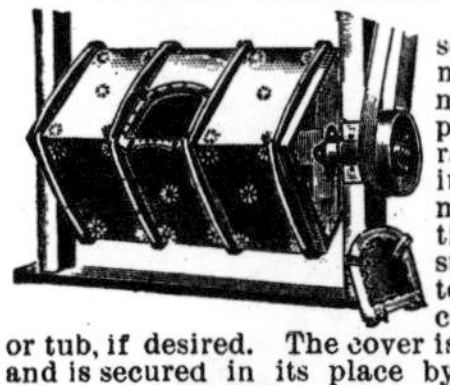

This cut represents our new churn, made of white cedar. The mouth of this churn is placed to one side, or rather at one corner, making it much easier to remove the butter and clean than the usually constructed churn of this pattern; in fact, the butter can be dumped into a tray or tub, if desired. The cover is simple and very strong, and is secured in its place by four bolts, with thumbscrews, two of which only need be loosened to remove or replace the lid, which is done very quickly. This is the most convenient and strongest cover that has yet been made.

The white cedar of which this churn has been manufactured is acknowledged by all who have had experience to be the very best material of which to make vats, tanks, churns, tubs, etc., as the wood is light, will not water-soak, and is the most lasting for such purposes.

All the woodwork is tongued and grooved together, to secure durability and tightness in all the joints. All the ironwork in the cover, and all bolt heads coming in contact with the cream, are galvanized. The flanges and shaft by which the churns are hung, are heavy and substantial.

With each churn is furnished a tight and loose pulley (18x4), with two substantial boxes for the shafting, but no frames, as that must be adapted to the place where the churn is to be used, as may be seen in the engraving; 30x4 pulleys can be furnished for $5.00 extra.

About 50 revolutions per minute is the average speed used with these churns, but that may be varied according to the judgment of the operator, and the thickness and condition of the cream.

No. 56842— SIZES AND PRICES.

Size.	Will hold, gallons.	Will churn, gallons.	Inches square outside.	Inches long outside.	Price.
No. 1	100	50	34	33	$18.15
No. 1½........	150	75	34	44	21.17
No. 2	200	100	34	55	24.20
No. 2½........	250	125	34	66	26.46
No. 3	300	150	34	76	30.24
No. 3½........	350	175	34	86	34.00
No. 4	400	200	34	96	37.80
No. 4½........	450	225	34	106	41.50
No. 5	500	250	34	116	45.36

Sturges Steel Churn.

The latest and best thing out. It is exceptionally well made, being heavily coated inside with chemically pure tin, while the stand, which is also steel, is tastefully decorated in colors to brighten the home of the housewife.

An important feature, and one that cannot but be appreciated by those desirous of keeping their churn sweet and clean, is the diameter of this churn's mouth which is full size. The inside of the churn is perfectly smooth, making it as easy to clean as a crock. The cover has a half inch cork lining around the edge which prevents any possibility of a leak. A glass vent and peep hole adorns the cover for the purpose of determining when butter comes and also to let off the gases.

56845 Five Gallon Sturges Steel Churn, for one to four gallons of cream. Price....................$5.00
56847 Nine Gallon Sturges Steel Churn, for four to seven gallons of cream. Price..................$8.00

The Star Barrel Churn.

This style of churn is old, tried and reliable, easy to operate and keep clean; it is absolutely impossible for this churn to leak as the wear can be taken up as simply as any one can turn a thumb nut. The fastenings are attached to the outside of the churn, and it will be seen from the cut that the bails and cover fastening is a compound "leverage" which increases the pressure ten times more than any other make of churn.

56850 Five Gallon Barrel Churn, for one or two gallons of cream. Each.$3.00
56852 Nine Gallon Barrel Churn, for 1 to 4 gallons of cream. Each......$3.25
56854 Fifteen Gallon Barrel Churn, for 2 to 7 gallons of cream. Each.$3 50
56856 Twenty Gallon Barrel Churn, for 3 to 9 gallons of cream Each.$4.00
56859 Twenty-five Gallon Barrel Churn, for 4 to 12 gallons of cream.... $4,95
56860 Thirty-five Gallon Barrel Churn for 5 to 16 gallons of cream....$6.00

Rectangular Churns.

56861 The Rectangular Churn works the easiest and quickest of any churn on the market. At the Dairy Fair, held in Chicago, December 1878, it received the highest award, a cash premium and diploma in competition with the world. Wisconsin butter won five medals at the Centennial Exhibition, at Philadelphia, and four of these were awarded to butter made in the Rectangular Churn.

No. 0 holding 7 gallons. Price $3.50
No. 1 " 10 " " 4.00
No. 2 " 12 " " 4.35
No. 3 " 20 " " 4.80
No. 3½ " 26 " " 6.00
No. 4 " 40 " " 12.80
No. 5 " 60 " " 18.40

The Nos. 4 and 5 are adapted for use in small creameries and large dairies, and fitted with cranks at both end and so arranged that a pulley can be attached for connecting with power. Full capacity of churns are given; when in use they should be only half full.

Curtis' Improved Square Box Churn.

56862 Its compactness, durability and efficiency make it very desirable for a dairy of one cow or fifty. It is a great favorite and has been improved in many respects, until it is believed to be absolutely the most perfect box churn to be found anywhere. The cover is of heavy tin and securely fastened. The corners are protected with iron caps and are so constructed that when the buttermilk is drawn out and cleansed it will drain perfectly dry.

Holding 7 gal. churns from 1 to 3 gal. Price..$3.50
" 10 " " " 2 to 4 " " .. 4.05
" 12 " " " 2 to 6 " " .. 4.35
" 20 " " " 3 to 9 " " .. 4.80
" 26 " " " 4 to 12 " " .. 6.00
" 40 " " " 6 to 20 " " ..12.80
" 60 " " " 8 to 30 " " ..18.40
" 80 " " " 10 to 40 " " ..20.80

The three largest sizes are adapted to large dairies. They have a crank on one side, a long gudgeon for pulleys on the other; strong bands and rods running around the churn make them very substantial. Light and loose pulleys are worth $6.00 extra.

Union Churn.

The Union Churn. You can make, gather, work and salt your butter without removing from the Union Churn, or without touching the butter with your hands. It churns with ease by the extra power and motion gained by gear wheels.

56863 Union Churn, holding 5 gallons. Each.................$4.00
56864 Union Churn, holding 7 gallons. Each....... ....$4.25
56866 Union Churn, holding 10 gallons. Each............... $4.75

Improved Cedar Cylinder Churn.

56869 This we consider by far the best small, cheap churn on the market It is made from the best Virginia cedar; it has a double dasher, and the crank is locked to the churn with a clamp and thumbscrew, which prevents leakage. Lock cannot break. The top is large and dasher easily removed. The hoops are of galvanized iron and will not rust.

No	1	2	3	4
Will hold. ...	3	4	7	10 gallons
Will churn. .	2	3	4	5 gallons
Price.........	$1.50	$1.90	$2.25	$2.50

Dash Churns.

Common Dash Churns. A long handle goes through the cover at the top, with a dasher at the bottom, which is worked up and down inside the churn.

	Each.	Per doz.
56870 3-gallon dash churn...........	$0.56	$6.00
56872 4-gallon dash churn............	.70	7.56
56874 5-gallon dash churn...	.85	9.18
56875 6-gallon dash churn	.96	10.37

Dash Churns, Striped Cedar, with Brass Hoops.

	Each.	Per doz.
56878 3-gallon....	$0.95	$10.26
56880 4-gallon ...	1.00	10.80
56882 5-gallon....	1.10	11.88
56885 6-gallon....	1.20	12.26

See Index for Stoneware Dash Churns.

DOG AND SHEEP POWER FOR CHURNING

Something has excited the interest of our subscribers in "dog-powers"—that is, in contrivances for utilizing the power of dogs for churning, and, perhaps, other light work—as we judge from the numerous inquiries lately received. This is a good symptom, it shows that there are some people who have waked up to the need of alleviating the drudgery of woman's toil. Where there is much churning to be done, a

Fig. 2.—WHEEL DOG-POWER.

dog-power is truly a labor-saving device. There are several different kinds, the best, perhaps, is a "tread-power," like the ordinary one, or two-horse tread-powers. These, however, are rather costly, and can only be made by experienced mechanics. There are forms, however, which may easily be made by any one familiar with the use of tools.

Fig. 1.—PLATFORM DOG-POWER.

Lamb's Adjustable Animal Powers.
For Churns, Separators, Etc.

The powers are quickly and easily attached to any kind of churn, or can be used for doing a great deal of farm labor, usually done by the man or maid, or the farmer's wife. You can just as well save the wife and maid this ever tiresome task, as well as the time that is expended in churning and like work, by making your dog, goat or sheep do all this labor, as well as the labor required in many of the farm duties. The powers are built with special reference to durability, and they are finished and painted in the best manner; all shafts and bearing are lathe fitted. Special care is given in their construction, that they may be *strong, perfect and durable*

56830 This power is built to be operated by two dogs, sheep or goats, and will furnish sufficient power to run a "Safety" separator, corn sheller, fan mill, sawing machine, churn, pump, washing machine, etc. Balance wheel is banded for 2½ and 3 inch belt; weight, crated, 180 pounds. Price.................$23.00

First Prize Dog Power.

53831 This power can be operated by a dog, goat or sheep; yields 25 per cent. more power from a given weight of animal than any other, and with adjustable bridge to regulate the required power and motion, a 30 pound animal will do the churning; if you keep a dog make him "work his passage." The power can be connected to any churn sold by us. Price.......................$15.00

The illustration above shows how the double dog power can be used in operating a cream separator; when the separator is not in use and you desire to churn connect it to tumbling rod sent with machine. A corn sheller, fan mill or sawing machine, can be connected by belt from balance wheel. Separators require a high gear and for this purpose we recommend our steel pulley, 3½ by 36 inches, this we can furnish at $6.00 extra. If iron coupling rod and coupling as shown in illustration are desired to connect and run **cream separator**, we can furnish them at $3.00 extra.

Fig. 166.—INTERIOR OF THE CHURNING ROOM.

Fig. 167.—INTERIOR OF THE MILK ROOM.

A BUTTER DAIRY

Figures 166 and 167 illustrate a dairy managed upon the shallow-pan system, the pans used being the common tin ones, holding about ten quarts.

AN EXCELLENT BUTTER-WORKER

The farmer of "Ogden Farm" described in one of the "Ogden Farm Papers," a new butter worker he had recently introduced into his dairy. There has been so much inquiry about it we have had engravings made to represent it which scarcely need any other explanation than to give the dimensions. The table is of white oak three feet long, and two feet wide, made very substantially. The side away from the dairy-woman, as shown in figure 1, is the lowest, and a groove runs around three sides of the table to conduct the butter-milk to a drip at one corner. The paddle or knife is shown at figure 2. It is a foot long and five inches wide, with handles six inches long, made from one piece of oak board, worked smooth and true to a blunt edge on each side as shown in the figure.

Fig. 1.—BUTTER-WORKER.

The butter is formed and worked by this knife, which is held in both hands.

Fig. 2.—PADDLE.

HOME-MADE BUTTER-WORKER

The butter worker, figure 114, is made to stand upon a table or low bench, or when of large size, upon the floor. The lever works upon a rod and can be moved sidewise, an arrangement which we have seen in no other butter-worker, but

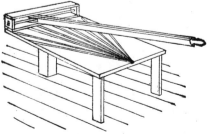

Fig. 114.—A SERVICEABLE BUTTER-WORKER.

which is a very desirable one. The table slopes forward, and has several grooves to carry the liquid down to a pail or a dish placed to receive it. The lever at the under side is leveled to a

Reid Butter Workers.

56887—Size 14 x23 inches, to work 8 lbs. of butter. Each, $3.60
56888 Size 17 x27 inches, to work 18 lbs. of butter. Each... $4.25
56889 Size, 20x36 inches, to work 25 lbs. of butter. Each... 4.80
56890 Size, 23x36 inches, to work 50 lbs. of butter. Each... 5.75

Lever Butter Workers.

56891 The Lever Butter Worker: its simplicity, saving of time, ease of operation and very low price, commend it as an indispensable adjunct to every dairy.
No. 0 size, 20 inches wide, works 15 lbs. Each... $3.50
No. 1 size, 30 inches wide, works 25 lbs. Each... $4.35
56892 No. 2 size, 40 inches wide, works 35 lbs. Each... 5.00

round or sharp edge, as may be wished. The cost of the worker is a mere trifle; it should be made of maple, ash or chestnut.

A HOMEMADE BUTTER WORKER

A butter worker is one of the handy devices that should be upon every farm. A good type is shown in the drawing. It is made of close-grained hard-wood—maple or birch are recommended—tight-jointed, free from knots and perfectly smooth in size. It slopes enough to drain readily at the narrow end through a short piece of lead pipe inserted at the bottom. The working bar has a strong, smooth iron rod or spike at its lower end, which is easily inserted into or removed from the hole in which it works. The part of the bar that comes in contact with the butter is half-round on one side and two flat sides meet at a right angle. Of course, it must be as smooth as possible.

BUTTER WORKER

Fancy Square and Round Butter Molds.

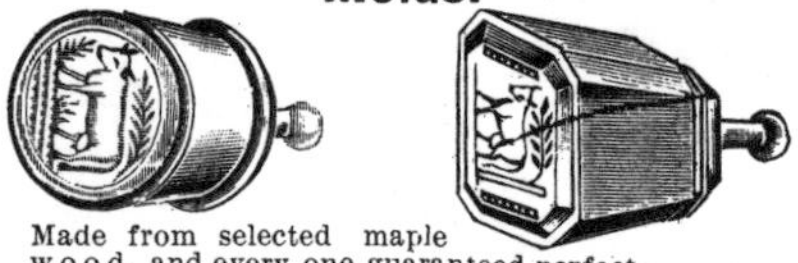

Made from selected maple wood, and every one guaranteed perfect.

	Per doz.	Each
56956 2 lb. mold, fancy carving, round.	$2.16	$0.20
56957 2 lb. mold, Jersey cow, round....	3.40	.20
56959 1 lb. mold, fancy carving, round.	1.70	.13
56961 1 lb. mold, Jersey cow, round ...	2.85	.26
56963 ½ lb. mold, fancy carving, round	1.35	.12
56965 ½ lb. mold, Jersey cow, round...	2.60	.22
56967 1 lb. mold, fancy carving, square	2.85	.26
56969 ½ lb. mold, fancy carving, square,	2.60	.23

	Per doz:	Each.
56971 Individual mold, fancy carving, round...	.75	.08
56973 Individual mold, fancy carving, with any initial letter, round..........	.85	.10
56974 Individual mold, fancy carving, square...	1.55	.14

California Butter Molds.

56976 This cut represents a very popular mould, and is used very extensively in all parts of the country. Made in two pound size only
Price, each.......................... $0.25
Per dozen 2.16

I.X.L. Self-Gauging Butter Printer.

56977 This print is designed not only to print the butter, which it does very neatly and quickly, but also weighs or gauges it into pounds or half pounds, as desired, thus it does in one quarter the time it can be done by hand, making the prints neater and of uniform weight. As the models are square they will be found very convenient to pack for transportation.
Either pound or half pound printer. Price....$ 8.40
Pound and half pound printer combined. 10.95
Two pound printer. Price.............. 8.95
Either initial or monogram can be carved on at an extra charge of $1.00.

The Blanchard Butter Mold.

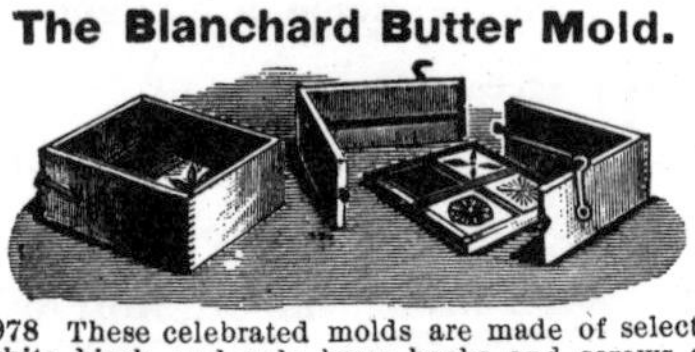

56978 These celebrated molds are made of selected white birch, and only brass hooks and screws are used throughout, so that there is no possibility of rust and consequent discoloration of the wood. The bottom is prevented from warping by strong wooden cleats, while the sides are grooved sufficiently deep to allow for swelling when in use, and are "lock-cornered" together, thus securing the utmost possible rigidity. One great advantage of these molds over most other patterns on the market, is that the prints are released by a single motion, and in perfect shape, instead of being pushed forcibly through a form by a plunger, which injures the grain.
Half-pound size, print 5 inches long, 2¾ inches wide, 1¼ inches deep. Price.................$0.85
One-pound size, print 5 inches long, 4½ inches wide, 1¼ inches deep. Price.................. 1.00
Two-pound size, 10 inches long, 4½ inches wide, 1¼ inches deep. Price..................... 1.40

Reid's Butter Mold.

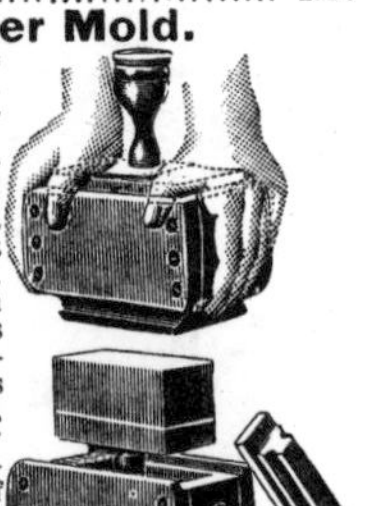

56980 Fig. 1 represents the butter as being in the mold, and the hands of the operator in the act of pressing. Fig. 2 shows the butter *molded* on the print, ready to be taken and turned on to a tray or elsewhere, when it will show the printed face. With this mold very firm butter may be printed. As shown in Fig. 1, the operator can not only put his entire weight on the print, but at the same time he may clasp the base with his fingers, thus add the power of the grip; and, further, by giving the print block a rocking motion by pressing alternately with each hand. The mold with the butter in it may be quickly turned the other side up by lifting it with a finger of each hand in the small depressions in ends of box, when the base may be removed and the butter pushed out as shown in Fig. 2.
Half-pound size, each $1.25
One-pound size, each................................ 1.35
Two-pound size, each 2.10

Mrs. Bragg's Butter Fork.

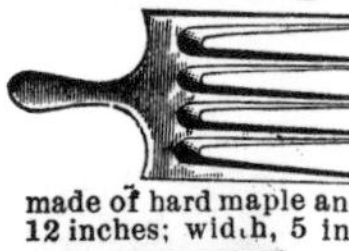

56981 A useful and convenient article to remove butter from the churn. In general use throughout the country in creamery and dairy, and considered almost indispensable; made of hard maple and well finished. Length, 12 inches; width, 5 inches. Each.............$0.15

Butter Tray.

56984 The Butter Tray here illustrated is believed to fill the vacant place in nearly every creamery and dairy. It is designed to hold the butter when taken from the churn to be reworked and packed for market. The oval cover, which increases the capacity of the tray one-third, is made to fit tight, to exclude bad air and dust. They are strong and durable.
To hold 20 pounds, price......................$1.87
To hold 40 pounds, price 2.35
To hold 60 pounds, price...................... 2.80
To hold 75 pounds, price...................... 3.00
To hold 125 pounds, price 3.65
To hold 175 pounds, price..................... 4.65

Curtis' Shipping Box for Print Butter.

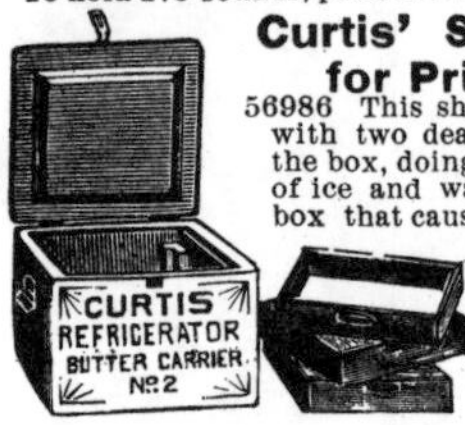

56986 This shipping box is made with two dead air spaces around the box, doing away with the can of ice and water in center of the box that causes such a muss when tipped partly over by careless shippers, often injuring the sale of butter. The butter being thoroughly protected, no ice is needed, and the shipping box need not be so large and cumbersome. In these days of questionable butter, parties who buy are glad to get it direct from the farmer or creameryman, put up in nice prints. A little attention in this matter secures a good customer the year around. The boxes are made in the most substantial manner, the trays being dove-tailed together, and all inside work being of white wood, which is free from taint or smell. Chest handles are put on the ends for convenience in handling. A shipping box will many times pay for itself in three or four shipments.
Capacity 15 pounds, price $3.25
Capacity 20 pounds, price...................... 4.20
Capacity 30 pounds, price...................... 5.00
Capacity 45 pounds, price 6.00
Capacity 60 pounds, price...................... 6.75
Capacity 80 pounds, price 7.65

Lee's Shipping Box for Print Butter.

56987 We offer the above as a low priced shipping box for large shippers; it is made strong and is durable. Price..................................$1.20

Wooden Butter Spades and Ladles

56988	56989	56991
No, 1.	No. 2.	No. 3.
8c. each.	8c each.	8c. each.
Per doz. 85c.	Per doz, 85c,	Per doz, 85c.

Maple Butter Plates.

56992 Oblong Butter Plates, maple.

Size...................	½ lb.	1 lb.
Price, per 1,000......	$2.00	$2.10
Size...........	2 lb.	3 lb.	5 lb.
Price, per 1,000.$2.25	$2.53	$3.07

Butter Packages.

BRADLEY BUTTER BOXES.

56993 2 lb., 24 in crate..........$0.95
56995 3 lb., 16 in crate............72
56997 5 lb., 12 in crate............69
56999 10 lb., 6 in crate............68

Bradley's Bail Butter Boxes.

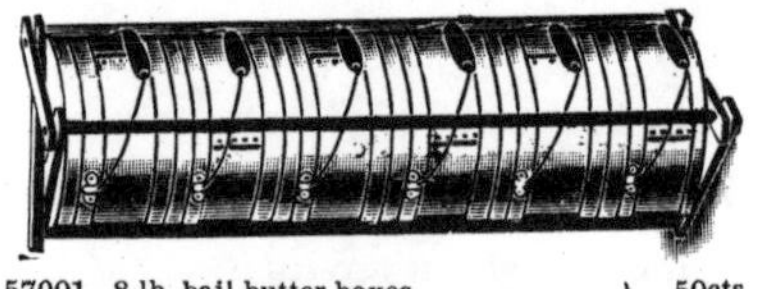

57001 8 lb. bail butter boxes ....
57003 9 lb. bail butter boxes...............
57005 10 lb, bail butter boxes.............. } 50cts. per crate

Creamery Butter Tubs.

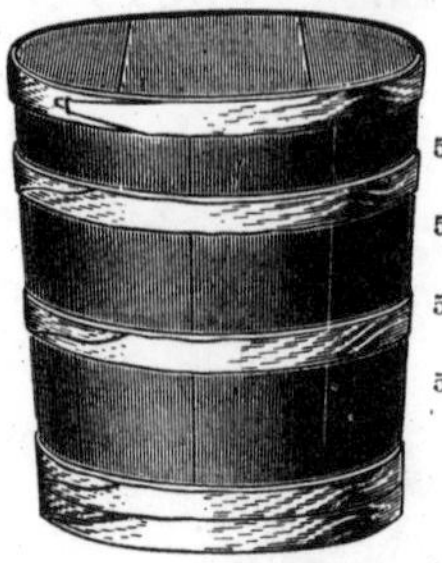

57006 Butter Tubs, spuce, 10 pounds.... ....$0.15
57007 Butter Tubs, spruce, 20 pounds ... .18
57008 Butter Tubs, spruce, 30 pounds... 22
57009 Butter Tubs, spruce, 50 pounds.... 23

Ash Butter Tubs.

57011 60 lbs., 5 hoop $0.24
57013 40 lbs., 4 hoop................................ .22
57014 25 lbs., 4 hoop................................ .19½
57015 10 lbs., 4 hoop................................ .15

Wells, Richardson's Improved Butter Color.

57044 Large, $1.00 size.... ......$0.75
57045 Medium, 50c. size .... .37
57046 Small, 25c. size.............. .18

Fairlambs' Butter Color.

57047 1 Gallon Cans. per gallon....$2.15
5 Gallon Cans, per gallon.......... 2.04
10 Gallon Cans, per gallon......... 1.95
Barrel lots, per gallon............. 1.85

Fairlambs' Cheese Color.

57048 1 Gallon Cans, per gallon...................$1 35
5 Gallon Cans, per gallon.......................... 1.20
10 Gallon Cans, per gallon......................... 1.10
Barrel lots per gallon.............................. 98

Fairlambs' Rennet Extract.

57049 1 Gallon Cans, per gallon...................$1.62
5 Gallon Cans, per gallon......................... 1.50
10 Gallon Keg, per gallon........................ 1.40
Barrel lots, per gallon............................ 1.30

Butter Paper.

57050 Waxed Butter Paper, grease proof, 9x12 inchss, 480 sheets $0.20
12x18 inches, 480 sheets .... .40

Parchment Dairy Paper.

Cut in the sizes as quoted and put up in packages of 1,000 sheets.

57051— Size.	Price, 1,000 sheets.	Price, 5,000 sheets.
12x12	$1.30	$6.28
10x10.....................	.96	4.47
9x12......................	1.05	4.99
8x11......................	.92	4.37
9x 9......................	.87	4.13
8x 8......................	.70	3.33
6x 6	.35	1.67

Write for our prices on large lots.

Parchment Paper Circles.

57052— Diameter.	Price, per 1,000.	Diameter	Price, per 1,000.
4 inches..........	$0.30	11 inches.......	$1.88
5 inches..........	.40	12 inches..........	2.22
6 inches..........	.53	13 inches..........	2.58
7 inches..........	.72	14 inches..........	3.00
8 inches..........	.97	15 inches..........	3.45
9 inches..........	1.25	16 inches..........	3.95
10 inches..........	1.50	17 inches..........	4.28

½-inch sizes between can be furnished at 10 cents per 1,000 extra. Write for our prices on large lots

Cloth Circles.

We guarantee count and every one to be a perfect circle.

57053— Diameter.	Price, per 1,000.	Diameter.	Price, per 1,000
4 inches.......	$0.59	11 inches..........	3 91
4½ inches.......	.70	11½ inches..........	4.33
5 inches.......	.91	12 inches..........	4.78
5½ inches.......	1.07	12½ inches..........	4.95
6 inches.......	1.20	13 inches..........	5.36
6½ inches.......	1.35	13½ inches..........	5.77
7 inches.......	1.65	14 inches..........	6.19
7½ inches.......	2.06	14½ inches..........	6.47
8 inches.......	2.27	15 inches..........	6.60
8½ inches.......	2 47	15½ inches..........	7.01
9 inches.......	2.77	16 inches..........	7 42
9½ inches.......	3.10	16½ inches..........	7.84
10 inches.......	3 46	17 inches..........	8.25
10½ inches.......	3.71		

Write for our prices on large lots.

Butter Cloth, Best Grade.

57054—
28-inch, per piece 120 yards, 3 cents per yard.
36-inch, per piece 120 yards, 3¼ cents per yard.
42-inch, per piece 120 yards, 3¾ cents per yard.
45-inch, per piece 120 yards, 4 cents per yard.

Butter Cloth (Medium Grade).

57055—
36-inch, per piece, 120 yards......3 cents per yard
42-inch, per piece, 120 yards......3⅛ cents per yard
45-inch, per piece, 120 yards......3⅜ cents per yard

CHEESE

Cheese making was a complex and long process. Simple cottage cheese could be made by simply letting milk stand until it soured and coagulated naturally, a process that usually took about two days but could be speeded up by adding starter. The curd was then gently heated to ninety degrees and kept there until the whey ran clear, about half an hour. The curd was then put into cheesecloth or muslin bags to drain off the whey. The end product was lightly salted and formed into balls, at which point it was ready to be sold. It took about a hundred pounds of milk to get about twenty pounds of cottage cheese.

Cottage cheese and similar soft, uncured cheeses were relatively simple to make. Ripened cheeses were more complex and subject to numerous possible causes of poor quality. Because cheese making was not only labor-intensive but also required careful attention to cleanliness, temperature, moisture content, and ripening, it quickly moved off the farm and into the factory.

Small Cream and Cheese Vats.

CURTIS' IMPROVED CHANNEL.

56819 These vats are made to meet the wants of a large class of dairymen who make up their own milk on the factory or creamery plan. The bottom of this vat inclines toward the center channel or groove, which gradually increases in depth throughout its entire length to the outlet, draining the contents from the vat completely. The channel or grooves, being swaged in the bottom tin, stiffen the vat bottom, thus rendering it less liable to move up and down as steam is applied, breaking the joints and causing the vat to leak. The water space underneath the tin vat will be appreciated by everyone who has had any experience in cooling or warming up vats of cream or milk. They are made in a superior manner. Perfection gates are used, and no expense is spared to make them the best vats the dairy public has seen.
Sizes and prices:
25-gallon vat, with ice box on end............$18 00
50-gallon vat, with ice box on end............ 21.00
We can quote prices on large vats, same as above, holding from 100 to 800 gallons.

Curtis' Improved Self-Heating Cheese Vats.

56821— This vat is designed for large and small dairies. It is built same as No. 56819 vat.

Sizes.	Prices.
25 gallon	$21.00
50 gallon	24.50

We can quote prices on self-heating cheese vats holding from 75 to 600 gallons.

Standing Press for Cheese.

The above illustration shows the method of making a good standing press for cheese factory or private dairy. The construction is so simple that any person familiar with the use of saw and hammer can make it. It consists of a frame, which is supported on legs and which are grooved to allow the whey to run off. For making a four-hoop press, as shown, it takes five sets of rods and saddles, four heavy press screws and four hoops and followers. The rods pass up one side of the press and down on the other. Holes are bored through the top timber to allow the screws to project up through when raised to allow the removal of the hoops. The divisions between the hoops are made of two-inch plank and support the upper timber when the screws are raised. The presses can be made any length desired.
56823 Rods, Saddles and Washers, per set......$1.50
56824 Screws, 1¾ by 20 inches long, per set..... 2.75
Prices quoted on all sizes of hoops and followers.

Flat Side Curd Pail.

56943 This is a strongly built pail from the best 4X tin, used for lifting the curd from the vat.
Price.................$0.95

Curd Scoop.

56945 These scoops are made of heavy tin and all seams and wire carefully soldered. Price....$0.50

Family Cheesemaking Apparatus.

56941 This is a very simple apparatus, adapted to the wants of all farmers or dairymen who keep from two to ten cows or more. It will make from two to ten pounds of cheese each operation, according to the quantity of milk; so simple that any boy or girl of average intelligence can learn the process in a very few operations. It makes a perfect cheese each time, whether two pounds or ten pounds.

You will admit that two cows give at least six quarts at a milking, making six gallons a day. A gallon of milk will make a pound of cheese. Six gallons make six pounds—for 30 days is 180 pounds of cheese, which at 10c. per pound is $18 for one month. This is a low wholesale price. The milk is heated by a coal oil lamp, which is easily kept under control. The heating vat is so constructed that the lamp gives all the heat that is necessary. The management of the heat is the secret o' success in making good cheese. The entire apparatus is so light in weight that a lady can move it from one place to another with ease. It does not take up quite as much room as an ordinary kitchen table. A lady can make cheese in the kitchen or pantry and carry on her household work at the same time. With each machine we send simple and full instructions how to make cheese successfully. Each apparatus is complete with heating vat, press, curd knives, lamp and thermometer; made of good material, strong and well finished. The apparatus is guaranteed to do the work exactly as represented. We also include sufficient rennet tablets, bandage and cheese color to make a nice little batch of cheese.
No. 1, holding 10 gals. Weight, 20 lbs. Price, $12.00
No. 2, holding 20 gals. Weight, 30 lbs. Price, 20.00
No. 3, holding 30 gals. Weight, 35 lbs. Price, 25.60

PART V:
Farm Animals

CHAPTER 13

CATTLE

A century ago it was the rare farm indeed that did not have a cow or two to provide milk, butter, and cheese for the family; any surplus butter could be sold for cash or bartered. (Dairying is discussed more fully in chapter 12.)

Any farmer with a milk cow was in a way automatically involved in the cattle business. To stay in milk, cows had to be "freshened" every year to eighteen months by bearing a calf. Few farmers wanted to go to the expense and trouble of maintaining a bull, however. In the days before artificial insemination, the farmer who did keep a high-quality bull could make it pay by servicing the local cows.

If the resulting calf was a bull, however, the farmer had no reason to keep it. Bull calves were slaughtered early for veal or raised for several months and slaughtered as baby beef. Some farmers raised small herds of beef cattle for local sale. The massive tandem growth of western cattle ranching and rail transport in the latter half of the nineteenth century made this unprofitable for most, however.

Old-fashioned wood-and-iron plows needed the strength of a team of oxen to draw them. But the new steel plows that came into widespread use starting in the 1840s needed far less power to pull them. The slow oxen were replaced by faster horses, who also had the speed needed to pull the mechanized cultivators, mowers, reapers, and other agricultural machinery now coming into use. By the 1870s, oxen were almost a curiosity on the farm.

Starting in the 1860s, there was tremendous interest in improving the cattle breeds in the United States. The merits of different meat and dairy breeds were widely discussed. For family use, smaller cows such as the Jersey, Devon, or brown Swiss (Simmental) that gave rich milk high in butterfat were preferred. For larger operations, the Holstein, then as now, was the preferred breed. Holstein milk was less rich than that of other breeds, but it made up in quantity what it lacked in butterfat. Other popular dairy breeds included the Guernsey, Ayrshire, and Dutch belted. The ideal dairy cow had a long, muscular neck, a large, arched rib cage, prominent hips, and a large stomach. The udder was wide, with many large, branching milk veins.

AMERICAN AGRICULTURIST

FOR THE

Farm, Garden, and Household.

"AGRICULTURE IS THE MOST HEALTHFUL, MOST USEFUL, AND MOST NOBLE EMPLOYMENT OF MAN."—WASHINGTON.

VOLUME XXIX.—No. 3.   NEW YORK, MARCH, 1870.   NEW SERIES—No. 278.

THE AYRAULT FAT OXEN.—DRAWN FROM LIFE, BY W. M. CARY.—*Engraved for the American Agriculturist.*

These cattle, said to weigh more than 3300 pounds each, were over six years old, raised and fed by George Ayrault, of Poughkeepsie, N. Y., and slaughtered in February by Wm. Lalor, of Centre Market, N. Y. City.

AMERICAN AGRICULTURIST

FOR THE

Farm, Garden, and Household.

"AGRICULTURE IS THE MOST HEALTHFUL, MOST USEFUL, AND MOST NOBLE EMPLOYMENT OF MAN."—Washington.

VOLUME XXIX.—No. 5.   NEW YORK, MAY, 1870.   NEW SERIES—No. 280.

DEVON CATTLE FROM THE HERD OF HON. E. H. HYDE.—*Drawn and Engraved for the American Agriculturist.*

The above engravings are portraits of animals owned by Hon. E. H. Hyde of Stafford, Conn., and were taken from photographs. The cows were in full milk and the bull in fair working order only. It is impossible to show in any engraving the beauty of this breed which owes so much to its rich, almost cherry-red color and white horns. It is a snug, tightly knit race, very different from any other, showing no indication of intermixture of blood in its origin—and hence by many claimed, with good reason too, to be the original breed of Great Britain. Modern breeders have perhaps introduced a dash of Shorthorn blood to give greater aptitude to fatten and earlier maturity. The Devons are medium-sized cattle, the bulls often rather low in stature; the cows of fair size giving 14 to 20 quarts of rich milk, valuable for both butter and cheese making; the working oxen, both pure Devons and grades, are among the very best in the world, for everything except very slow heavy work. They are spry, intelligent, handy and trusty, fast walkers, and we have known them fair trotters; and they make, when fattened young, the very best beef of our markets. Devons are rather slow in coming to full size and maturity, but they fatten easily, and last in full vigor as cows and oxen until 12 to 18 years old. The cows are docile and quiet, and the steers easily broken. Upon the whole, the Devon probably combines all good points and valuable qualities to a degree not approached by any other breed. These cattle are hardy at the South, and their activity adapts them to pick up a fair living where Shorthorns or Herefords would starve. It is not very unusual to find among the cows deep milkers, giving over 20 quarts of milk, and in quality of the milk takes high rank next to that of the Jerseys.

AMERICAN AGRICULTURIST

FOR THE

Farm, Garden, and Household.

"AGRICULTURE IS THE MOST HEALTHFUL, MOST USEFUL, AND MOST NOBLE EMPLOYMENT OF MAN."—Washington.

VOLUME XXIX.—No. 10.   NEW YORK, OCTOBER, 1870.   NEW SERIES—No. 285.

FRESH MILK.—*Drawn and Engraved for the American Agriculturist.*

Those who live in cities and large towns manage to pass a portion of the summer in the country. The more wealthy have their country residences, while those of limited means content themselves with a visit to a farm-house for a few weeks. With all classes one of the strongest inducements for this change of residence is the ability to procure an abundance of fresh milk for the children. The change from heated streets to open fields is not greater, than that from the liquid dispensed by the milkmen, to the pure milk, fresh from the cow. How the little ones thrive on it, and with what eagerness they watch for milking time! The artist has represented a happy group of these city children in the full enjoyment of their healthful country fare. Milk is the natural food for all young animals, children included, and contains all the elements necessary to growth. The milk of the cow differs from human milk in containing much more caseine, or curd, considerably less of sugar of milk, and more of the mineral constituents; the proportion of all solid substances in the two is nearly the same. The milk of the goat is more nearly identical in composition with human milk, than is that of the cow, though that contains a larger proportion of caseine. While milk forms so important a diet for young children it is liable to become a source of disease from the readiness with which its composition is affected by the health of the animal furnishing it, and the rapidity with which it undergoes change after it is drawn. Nature has indicated in the most positive manner, that the food should be transferred from the mother to the young without change. Whenever we depart from this in any particular, unpleasant effects are likely to follow. Let the milk for children really be Fresh Milk.

AMERICAN AGRICULTURIST

FOR THE

Farm, Garden, and Household.

"AGRICULTURE IS THE MOST HEALTHFUL, MOST USEFUL, AND MOST NOBLE EMPLOYMENT OF MAN."—Washington.

VOLUME XXIX.—No. 12.　　　NEW YORK, DECEMBER, 1870.　　　NEW SERIES—No. 287.

H E A D   O F   P E T T Y P E T.—From Life by Edwin Forbes.—*Drawn and Engraved for the American Agriculturist.*

Pettypet represents, in very high perfection, the very best points of the Channel Island cattle, produced by mingling of the Guernsey and high-bred Jersey blood. She was raised by Mr. James P. Swain, and is regarded by him as one of the best animals he ever bred. On the side of the dam she is nearly pure Guernsey, her dam, Pet, being out of Katie 2d, by a Guernsey bull, of the N. Biddle stock. Katie 2d's dam was Katie, and her sire Echo, imported from Guernsey by Thadeus Davids. Katie was out of Mr. Swain's old imported cow Guernsey, the mother of a line of the greatest milkers and butter makers we ever knew, by a bull called Colt Alderney, whose dam was the Alderney cow Curl-horn, imported by Mr. Swain, and his sire a bull bought of Roswell Colt, which came from the Island of Guernsey. So much for the Guernsey blood with one-thirty-second of Alderney, whatever that may be. The sire of Pettypet was Bashan, imported by R. W. Cameron, a nearly perfect type of the high-bred Jersey. This animal has impressed his characteristics upon his stock to the third and fourth generation with almost unerring certainty, and to-day we think a dash of Bashan blood worth more in a fancy animal than a cross of any other choice strain. His points were great style, beauty of form and carriage, superb head and horns, which were delicate, well set up, pointing forward, and black tipped, fine underpinning, (bony, but strong,) a deep carcass, well ribbed back, a very fine tail, with black switch, black mouth and tongue, very soft hide, with two distinct kinds of hair in his coat, changing his color more or less with the season, but being on the whole of a rather dark fawn, with hairs coming through tipped with gray, with very strong mealy ring about the muzzle.

Cattle　165

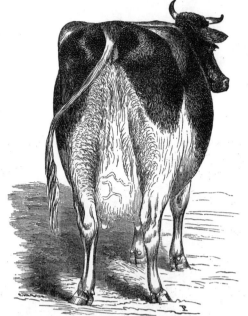

Plate 29. The greatest development of a Milk Escutcheon.

Plate 6. Hereford Cow.

Plate 30. A model Horned Milk Cow.

Plate 17. Alderney Cow.

Plate 3. Devon Cow.

Plate 18. Alderney Bull.

The main beef breeds at the turn of the century were the Aberdeen-Angus, shorthorns, and Herefords. The Hereford was particularly well suited for western range grazing because it could withstand cold weather. (A full discussion of the American cattle industry is subject enough for another book. It is important to note, however, that between 1886 and 1887, overgrazing, drought, and then a huge blizzard brought disaster to ranchers on the Great Plains. The extension of plow agriculture onto semiarid and arid grazing land accelerated after that; by 1890, barbed wire had enclosed the open range and the era of cheap and free land was over. This, according to historian Frederick Jackson Turner, was the closing of the American frontier.)

Breeding stock was imported from Europe to improve American herds, especially the dairy herds. Even the Holstein, the dairy cow par excellence, which had been in America since the days of Dutch settlement, was capable of improvement. A number of Dutch Holsteins were imported in the 1860s and 1870s, with impressive results. Improved breeding greatly increased the milk yield; by 1900 a typical high-quality Holstein could produce between seven and nine thousand pounds of milk annually.

Brown Swiss cow.

Plate 25. Holstein Bull.

Jersey cow.

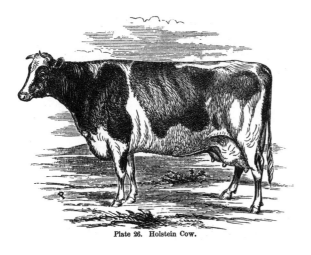

Plate 26. Holstein Cow.

Guernsey cow.

Ayrshire cow.

Dutch belted cow.

CHAPTER 14

HOGS

From time immemorial, farmers have kept pigs. Indeed, pigs were almost a necessity on a farm. Their meat—tasty, abundant, and easily preserved by salting or smoking—was an important food, especially in winter. Pigs foraged on their own and could also be fed cheaply on scraps and very coarse, inexpensive foods such as turnips, cabbage, and corn. They turned waste products on the farm, such as withered apples and small potatoes, into food more efficiently than any other animals, including poultry. Pigs reproduced quickly, in large litters, and their abundant manure was a source of rich fertilizer.

As the nineteenth century drew to a close, the demand for hogs from the meat packers of the Midwest was high. Hog farming as a major side or primary operation became widespread. On dairy farms, pigs were a useful source of additional income. The pigs grew beautifully on leftover milk products—skim milk, whey, buttermilk—mixed with corn, scraps, and whatever else was cheap and easy. And aside from regular feeding and frequent cleaning of the hog house, pigs needed little in the way of attention—certainly not the twice-daily milking of cows.

On grain farms, the pigs were a value-added alternative to shipping the grain to market. By raising hogs, it was said, the farmer had learned how to put fifteen bushels of grain into a three-bushel barrel. Seven bushels of corn was transformed into a hundred pounds of pork. No other farm animal converted food into cash as efficiently or profitably.

PIG BREEDS

The ideal pig breed was one that gave the most meat and fat for the investment in its feed and care. In addition to being well proportioned and meaty, the ideal pig had good behavioral characteristics. First and foremost, it had a vigorous appetite and good digestion. Next in importance was a quiet disposition. As Joseph Harris, the great nineteenth-century authority on the pig, pointed out, "The two great aims of every pig breeder should be to lessen the demands on the stomach for offal or least valuable parts, and for unnecessary activity on the one hand, and on the other to increase the power of the stomach, and digestive and assimilative organs as much as possible."

By around 1900, demand for pork was high and growing higher. For the farmer, the ideal hog was an early-maturing breed that weighed in at between two hundred and three hundred pounds by the age of eight to ten months. Consumers were now starting to demand a meatier hog, one that produced less lard and lighter, leaner ham and bacon.

THE FORM OF A GOOD PIG

The aim of all breeders of animals designed solely for meat, is to have the body approximate as closely as possible to the form of a parallelopiped. In proportion to the size, an animal of this form contains the greatest weight. Hence it is, that farmers who have kept nothing but common pigs, and who look upon a well-formed, grade Essex or Suffolk as "small," are surprised to find, when brought to the scales, that it

Fig. 1.—TESTING THE FORM OF A PIG.

weighs more than an old-fashioned, ill-formed pig of much greater apparent size.

Another advantage of this form is, that it gives a greater proportion of the most desirable parts of the pig.

In a pig of this form the ribs are well-arched. We cannot have a flat, broad, "table-back" without this. And consequently the muscle which runs along each side of the vertebrae, is

well developed, and we have a large quantity of meat of the best quality.

This form also affords abundant room for the lungs, stomach, and intestines; and it is on the capacity of these organs to convert a large amount of comparatively cheap food into a large quantity of flesh and fat that determines the value of the animal.

We annex a portrait of a tolerably well-formed pig, with lines showing how to apply the test above alluded to. The nearer he will fill the rectangular frame, the nearer he approaches to perfection of form. It would be well, for farmers to place a straight cane along the back, also along the sides, shoulders and hams of their pigs to see how near they come up to the desired standard.

The head of a pig should be set close to the shoulders. The broader and deeper the cheeks, the better, as next to the ham and shoulder there is no choicer meat on the pig. A well-cooked cheek of bacon, with roast chicken, is a dish for an epicure.

The snout should be short and delicate, and the ears small and fine. A thick, heavy, pendant ear is an indication of coarseness and is never desirable in a thorough-bred pig. It should be small, fine, soft, and silky. It should be well set on the head and lean a little forward, but not fall over. An ear that is upright indicates an unquiet disposition.

In the 1870s and 1880s, the Chester White was probably the overall favorite breed, but a number of other breeds were raised, each having its own good points. The Berkshire, Chester, Duroc Jersey, and Large Yorkshire remained popular. The Poland China pig, perhaps the most successful breed ever, was just coming into popularity in the mid-1880s. So profitable was this breed that by 1900 it was probably the most commonly bred hog on any farm. Crossbreeding Poland China boars with Yorkshire sows (a breed noted for fecundity and being good mothers) was said to produce an excellent pig, one that was a superior feeder.

In the end, the choice of breed depended in large part on the circumstances of the individual farmer. Where pigs were raised primarily for home consumption and perhaps some local sale, smaller breeds such as the Victoria, Suffolk, Essex, or Small Yorkshire were desirable. The medium breeds such as the Berkshire, Poland China, Duroc Jersey, and Cheshire were good choices for larger hog-farming operations. Large breeds such as the Cheshire White, Improved Yorkshire, and Tamworth, which could weigh in at well over a thousand pounds, were popular for their large amounts of meat.

Harris strongly approved of the tamer breeds popular by the 1870s. He comments:

There is no more docile or tractable animal on a farm than a well-bred pig. There is a good deal of human nature about him. He can be led where he cannot be driven. A cross-grained man will soon spoil a lot of well-bred pigs. They know the tones of his voice, and it is amusing to see what tricks they will play him. We have seen such a man trying to get pigs into their respective pens, and it would seem as though he had brought with him a legion of imps, and that seven of them had entered into each pig. No sow would go with her own pigs, and no pigs would go with their own mother; the store pigs would go into the fattening pen, and the fattening pigs would go where the stores were wanted. Should he get mad, and use a stick, some active porker would lead him in many a chase around the barn-yard; and when one was tired, another pig, with brotherly affection, would take up the quarrel, and the old sows would stand by enjoying the fun. Let no such man have charge of any domestic animals. He is a born hewer of wood, and drawer of water, and should be sent to dig canals, or do night-work for the poudrette manufacturers.

It is not necessary to review the means employed by the breeders of the last century to improve the English breeds of pigs. Suffice it to say that it is generally admitted that much of this improvement is due to crossing the large English sows with the highly refined Chinese boars, and in selecting from the offspring such animals as possessed, in the greatest degree, the form and qualities desired. By continued selection, and "weeding out," the breed at length became established.

The Improved Berkshire is one of the earliest and best known of these Chinese-English breeds.

The old Berkshire hog had maintained a high reputation for centuries. It is described as "long and crooked snouted, the muzzle turning upwards; the ears large, heavy, and inclined to be pendulous; the body long and thick, but not deep; the legs

Fig. 7.—IMPORTED CHINESE SOW

short, the bone large, and the size very great." It was probably the best pig in England, and was wisely selected as the basis of those remarkable improvements which have rendered the modern Berkshire so justly celebrated.

It would be interesting to trace the different steps in this astonishing improvement, but, unfortunately, the necessary

Fig. 8.—BERKSHIRE PIG.

information cannot be obtained. We give four engravings from Loudon's Encyclopedia of Agriculture, the first edition of which appeared in 1825, which will give some idea of the change that has been effected. Figure 8 is the Berkshire pig, as represented by Loudon, which is admitted to represent "one of the best of its kind," and there can be little doubt that it was taken from what was considered a good specimen of the breed at the time the work was written. As compared with the figure of the old original English pig, and also with

Fig. 9.—HAMPSHIRE PIG.

those of Hampshire, Herefordshire, and Suffolk, given by Loudon (figs. 9, 10, and 11), it is easy to trace the influence of the Chinese cross. Loudon speaks of the Berkshire, at that time, as a small breed, and it is undoubtedly true that the first effect of an improvement in the fattening qualities and

Fig. 10.—HEREFORDSHIRE PIG.

early maturity of an animal is to reduce the size. On the whole, this picture of an improved Berkshire, forty-five or fifty years ago, does not give one a very favorable idea of the breed at that time; yet it was then probably the best breed pig in England.

Fig. 11.—SUFFOLK PIG.

Fig. 13.—"SIR ROGER DE COVERLY." YORKSHIRE LARGE BREED.

THE LARGE YORKSHIRES.—(FIGS. 13, 14, AND 15.)

Of the old, unimproved large Yorkshire, Sidney says: "It was a long time coming to full size, and could be fed up to 800 lbs., but whether with any profit, is doubtful. It was and is still

very hardy, and a very prolific breeder. Attempts have been made to improve it by crossing with the Berkshire, Essex, Neapolitan, and other black breeds, which produced a black

Fig. 14.—"PARIAN DUCHESS." YORKSHIRE LARGE BREED.

and white race. Those from the Berkshire are a hardy, useful sort, but fatten slowly; the other crosses have little or no hair, are too delicate for the North, and are fast wearing out.

Fig. 15.—"GOLDEN DAYS." YORKSHIRE LARGE BREED.

"The first step taken in the right direction for improving the old Yorkshire seems to have been the introduction of the White Leicesters. These were a large sort, with smaller heads than the old York, erect ears, finer in the hair, and lighter in the bone."

THE SMALL CUMBERLAND

"The Cumberland small breed," says Mr. Sidney, "are described by Mr. Brown, of Aspatria, who is one of the most noted founders of the modern breed, from whom Lord Ducie purchased some of his most celebrated animals, as not small in reality, but a medium size, short in the legs, back broad, straight, and evenly fleshed; ribs well developed, rumps and twists good; hams well down, and low; breast and neck full, and well formed; no creases in the neck; ears clean, fine, of a moderate size, and standing a little forward; nose short; body evenly covered with short, fine hair."

Fig. 16.—CUMBERLAND YORK BOAR. SMALL BREED.

THE YORK-CUMBERLAND BREED (FIG. 16)

Mr. Sidney classes the Small Yorkshire and Cumberland together, "because, although originally, they somewhat differed in size,—the Cumberland being the larger—they are

Fig. 17.—PRIZE YORK-CUMBERLAND PIG. SMALL BREED.
From Farmers' Magazine.

being continually intermixed, with mutual advantage; and pigs of exactly the same form, the result of crosses, are constantly exhibited under the names of Yorkshire or Cumberland, according to the fancy of the exhibitor."

Fig. 18.—"MISS EMILY." YORKSHIRE MIDDLE BREED

Mr. Mangles writes—"The Small Cumberland is a great deal larger than the Small Yorkshire. By judiciously crossing the two, I have obtained a breed combining size, aptitude to fatten, and early maturity. From the Cumberland I got size, and from the Yorkshire quality and symmetry. I have tried a

Fig. 19.—WHITE LEICESTER BOAR AND SOW. SMALL BREED.

great many breeds of pigs, and, keeping the pounds, shillings and pence in view, have found no breed equal to the Yorkshire and Cumberland cross."

A Warwickshire correspondent of Mr. Sidney writes: "No animal of the pig species carries so great a proportion of flesh to the quantity of bone, or flesh of as fine as quality, as the small Yorkshire, or can be raised at so small a cost per pound. With common store food they can always be kept in condition—with common care, and slight addition to food,

Fig. 20.—SMITHFIELD CLUB PRIZE FAT SOW. IMPROVED BERKSHIRE.

they are ready to be killed, for porklets, at any age; and if required for bacon, take one farrow of pigs from a yelt. You ought to have from seven to ten pigs the first time. I have four sisters, yelts, that have brought me thirty-eight pigs this last January. They are as pure as 'Eclipse,' being descended from the stock of Earl Ducie and Mr. Syley, of Bransby, near York, and are of good size, I killed a sow this winter that weighted 26 score—520 lbs.

"The ordinary weight is from 14 to 17 score—280 lbs. to 340 lbs. In some cases, where very thick bacon is required,

Fig. 20.—SMITHFIELD CLUB PRIZE FAT SOW. IMPROVED BERKSHIRE.

they may be profitably got to 30 score—600 lbs. The Small Yorkshire owes its present superiority to choice selections, and judicious crossing of different families of the same breed; by this means size is maintained with character."

These "Small Yorkshires" which this gentleman called as "pure as Eclipse," are descended from the stock of Earl

Fig. 21.—IMPROVED BERKSHIRE BOAR. MIDDLE BREED.

Ducie and Mr. Wyley; but, as has been already shown, Earl Ducie purchased Cumberland pigs from Mr. Brown, and Mr. Wyley's original stock were White Leicesters.

Fig. 22.—"EMPEROR." IMPROVED ESSEX.

Mr. Sidney says: "The wide extension of this Cumberland and York blood is to be traced wherever the Royal Agricultural Society's prizes for white pigs are won.

"Thus:—Mr. H. Scott Hayward, of Folkington, a prize-winner at Chelmsford, in 1856, in small breeds, with a white sow, states that he has used boars from the following breeders:

Fig. 23.—LORD WESTERN ESSEX.

—The late Earl of Carlisle, Castle Howard; the late Earl of Ducie; the Earl of Radnor, Coleshill; and at present (1860) one from the Prince Consort's stock.

Fig. 24.—ESSEX BOAR.

"The card of Mr. Brown's boar 'Liberator' contains the following pedigrees, and shows a distinct connection between Cumberland and Yorkshire, and all the most celebrated white breeds in the south:—

Fig. 25.—ESSEX SOW.

"'Liberator' was bred by Earl Ducie, got by 'Gloucester' dam 'Beauty' by Lord Radnor's boar, gr.-d. "Julia Bennet' by Lord Galloway's boar, etc.

"'Gloucester' was bred by the Earl of Ducie, got by 'General,' dam 'Hannah' by the 'Yorkshireman;' gr.-d. bred by the Earl of Carlisle, and purchased by Lord Ducie at the Castle Howard sale.

CHESTER COUNTY WHITE PIGS (FIGURE 27.)

The most popular and extensively known breed of pigs in the United States at this time is, unquestionably, the Chester County breed, or, as they are generally called, the "Chester Whites." The rearing and shipping of these pigs has become a very large and profitable business. One firm alone in

AMERICAN AGRICULTURIST

FOR THE

Farm, Garden, and Household.

"AGRICULTURE IS THE MOST HEALTHFUL, MOST USEFUL, AND MOST NOBLE EMPLOYMENT OF MAN."—Washington.

VOLUME XXIX.—No. 4.   NEW YORK, APRIL, 1870.   NEW SERIES—No. 279.

ESSEX SWINE.—*Drawn from Photographs and Engraved for the American Agriculturist.*

Fig. 27.—CHESTER COUNTY WHITE.

Chester Co., Penn., informs us that, for the last three or four years, they have shipped from 2,500 to 2,900 of these pigs each year, and many other breeders have also distributed large numbers of them.

There are several reasons why the Chester Whites are more popular than the English breeds. In the first place, they are a large, rather coarse, hardy breed, of good condition, and well adapted to the system of management ordinarily adopted by the majority of our farmers. They are a capital sort of common *swine*, and it is certainly fortunate that they have been so extensively introduced into nearly all sections of the country.

Fig. 28.—JEFFERSON COUNTY PIG.

THE "CHESHIRE," OR JEFFERSON COUNTY PIGS (FIG. 28.)

This is a breed of pigs originating in Jefferson County, N. Y. For a dozen years or more they have been exhibited at the Fairs of the N. Y. State Agricultural Society, and for the last six or seven years have carried off nearly all of the prizes offered for pigs of the large breed. They were first exhibited, to the best of our recollection, under the names of "Cheshire and Yorkshire," and afterwards as "Improved Cheshires," and in 1868, one of the largest breeders exhibited them as

Texas razor back hog.

Poland China hog.

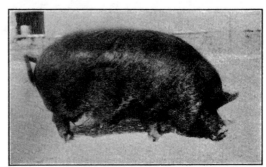

Duroc Jersey hog.

Chester white hog.

"Improved Yorkshires." These different names, in different years, indicate the nature of the breed. They have been very extensively distributed throughout the country, and especially in the West, under the name of "Cheshires." It would be better, we think, to call them the "Jefferson County" pigs, as indicating the place rather than the nature of their origin. The latter is uncertain, while there can be no doubt that Jefferson County is entitled to the credit of establishing a very popular and valuable breed of pigs.

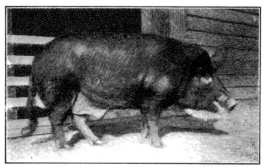
Tamworth hog.

PIGPENS AND HOG HOUSES

Early settlers rarely bothered with pens for their pigs. The animals ran half wild, foraging in the woods and fields and receiving supplemental food from the farmer when it was available. The hogs were often turned out into recently harvested fields to eat what waste grain the harvesters left behind, a practice known as hogging off.

Free-range hogs were ornery and lean and could be very destructive when they got into crops and gardens. In the first half of the nineteenth century there was great interest in pig breeding, especially for size, weight-gaining ability, and docility. A more docile pig was content to live a more sheltered and far less active life, confined to large pens and sleeping when it wasn't eating.

The farmer who kept just a few pigs for his own consumption needed only a simple pen in a corner of the barnyard to house and feed them. Larger operations required purpose-built hog houses, more elaborate feeding arrangements, and special areas for sows with litters.

The importance of good sanitation in the piggery was recognized by the 1880s. Then as now, the copious amounts of manure produced by pigs had to be removed daily and the pens cleaned thoroughly. In the days before chemical fertilizers, however, manure was considered a desirable side benefit of hog farming—indeed, its value was factored into the profit equation.

A PORTABLE PIGPEN

Where a single family pig is kept, provision for changing the locality of the pen is often necessary. It may be placed in the garden, at the time when there are waste vegetables to be disposed of, or it may be penned in a grass lot. A portable pen,

Fig. 115.—A PORTABLE PIGPEN.

with an open yard attached is seen in the accompanying illustrations. Figure 115 presents the pen, the engraving showing it so clearly that no description is needed. The yard, seen in figure 116, is placed with open space next to the door

Fig. 116.—YARD TO PORTABLE PIGPEN.

of the pen, so that the pig can go in and out freely. The yard is attached to the pen by hooks and staples, and both of them are provided with handles, by which they can be lifted and carried from place to place. Both the yard and pen should be floored to prevent the pig from tearing up the ground. The floors should be raised a few inches from the ground, that they may be kept dry and made durable.

The accompanying plan of a piggery (fig. 29) is furnished us by Dr. M. Miles, Professor of Agriculture in the Michigan Agricultural College, who writes:

"It needs but little explanation, except in regard to the backside of the building. The lean-to is a shed, open above the pen partition, that separates it from the yard. This opening may be closed in winter, if desirable. The upright, or main building, is not boarded up below the roof of the lean-to. Figure 30 gives the ground plan. The curved, dotted

Fig. 29.—PIGGERY AT THE MICHIGAN AGRICULTURAL COLLEGE. ELEVATION.

lines, show the swing of the doors, and the straight, dotted lines, mark the position of the low partitions, enclosing the bed. The plan of arrangement can be carried out with a single pen, or it can be indefinitely extended for large establish-

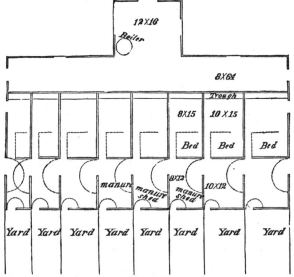

Fig. 30.—PIGGERY AT THE MICHIGAN AGRICULTURAL COLLEGE. GROUND PLAN.

ments. The shed for protecting the manure can be readily cleaned out by a cart or wheel-barrow, running through the open doors, between the shed pens, while the swine are shut out in the yards, or in the front pens. I have not attempted to show the arrangement of the troughs, but simply mark their position. Swine can be easily changed from one pen to another, by shutting out others in the yard, or front pen. The upper story is for storing feed, or bedding, etc."

Paschal Morris, of Philadelphia, an extensive breeder of Chester Whites, describes his plan of a piggery as follows:

"The plan of the piggery, delineated in the accompanying engraving, (fig. 32) is susceptible of reduction or extension, for

Fig. 32.—PASCHAL MORRIS' PIGGERY.—ELEVATION.

a larger or smaller number of pigs, and is intended to supersede the not only useless, but objectionable, as well as expensive, mode of constructing large buildings under one roof, where confined and impure air, as well as the difficulty of keeping clean, interfere greatly with both health and thrift. Twenty-five or thirty breeding sows, farrowing at different periods of the year, can be accommodated under this system of separate pens, by bringing them successively within the enclosure, or an equal number of hogs can be fattened, without crowding or interference with each other.

"The entrance, as seen in the engraving, is on the north side of the building, which fronts the south, as does also each separate pen. The main building is 32 feet long, by 12 feet wide, with an entrance gate, at each lower corner, to the

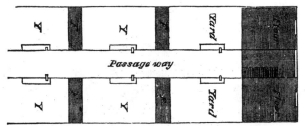

Fig. 33.—PASCHAL MORRIS' PIGGERY.—GROUND PLAN.

yard of two first divisions. The entry, or room, in the center, is 8 feet wide, allowing space for slop barrel, feed chest, charcoal barrel, (almost as indispensable as feed chest,) hatchway, for access to root cellar, underneath the whole building, and also passage-way to second story. This latter is used to storing corn in winter, and curing some varieties of seeds in summer. A wooden spout, with sliding valve, conveys feed to the chest below. The grain is hoisted to the second floor by a pulley and tackle on the outside, as observed in engraving.

"The perspective of main building allows a partial view of platforms, surmounted by a board roof, and divisions in the rear. The ground plan, fig. 33, allows six of these on either side of the passage-way. The first two pens, to the right and left of the door, are 12 × 12 feet each, and attached to them are 25 feet in length of yard, by 15 feet wide.

"All the yards are extended 3 feet wider than the building, which admits of the two entrance gates at the corners."

PLAN OF A PIGGERY

Figure 100 represents the elevation of a piggery. The main building is twenty-two by fifty feet, and the wing twelve by sixteen feet. It is supplied with light and air by windows in front, ventilators on the roof, and by hanging doors or shutters in the upper part of the siding at the rear of each stall or apartment. These last are not seen in the engraving.

Fig. 100.—PERSPECTIVE OF PIGGERY.

Figure 101 shows the ground plan. The main building has a hall, H, six feet wide, running the entire length. This is for convenience of feeding, and for hanging dressed hogs at the time of slaughtering. The remainder of the space is divided by partitions into apartments A, B, for the feeding and sleeping accommodation of the porkers; these are each eight by sixteen feet. The rear division of the apartments, B, B, are intended for the manure yards. Each division has a door, D, D, to facilitate the removal of manure, and also to allow ingress to the swine when introduced to the pen. The floors of each two adjoining divisions are inclined toward each other, so that the liquid excrement and other filth may flow to the side where the opening to the back apartment is situated. Two troughs, S, T, are placed in each feeding room. That in the front, S, is for food, T, for clear water, a full supply of

which is always allowed. This is an important item, generally overlooked; much of the food of swine induces thirst, and the free use of water is favorable to the deposition of fat.

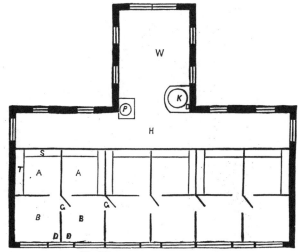

Fig. 101.—GROUND PLAN OF PIGGERY.

A CONVENIENT FARM PIGPEN

Herewith are given the plans and a side view of a convenient pigpen, recently constructed upon the farm of Colonel F. D. Curtis, of Charlton, Saratoga Co., N. Y. The building, shown complete in figures 103 and 104, is forty-eight feet long, twenty-two feet wide, and twelve feet high. There is an upper floor over the pens, which is used as a store room for meal, corn, etc., and a cellar beneath, used for storage of roots, and for cooking and preparing food. There is a cistern in the cellar, into which the water from the roof is collected, and a pump, by which the water may be run into the feed kettle, or to the pens above. The arrangements are made with a view to the convenient handling and feeding of the stock, as well as to most perfect sanitary conditions. The building is warm enough to prevent freezing in the coldest winter weather, so

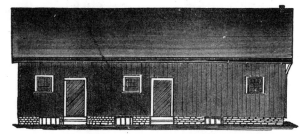

Fig. 103.—SIDE VIEW OF MR. CURTIS' PIGPEN.

Fig. 104.—VIEW OF MR. CURTIS' PIGGERY.

side six and one-half feet high. The pens, see figure 108, are ten by twelve feet, and three feet high, with a four-foot walk at the rear of them. The doors, of which each pen has one opening into the yard, are in halves. The upper half may be left open to admit light and air, while the lower half is kept closed, if it is desired, to prevent egress. At one end of the building is a room furnished with apparatus for steaming food. The feeding is done from the walk, the food being placed in small portable troughs, which can be readily cleaned.

that young pigs, if desired, may be reared without difficulty, even during winter. The outer and inner walls, and the floor of the upper room, are all of matched boards.

MR. CROZIER'S PIGPENS

Mr. Wm. Crozier, of Beacon Stock Farm, Northport, L. I., has a long range of pigpens. The elevation, figure 107, the ground plan, figure 108, and a view of the interior of the

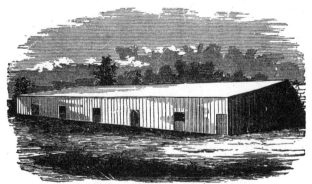

Fig. 107.—FRONT VIEW OF PIGGERY.

building, figure 109, show the simple arrangement. The building is placed against a bank, which has a brick retaining wall that answers as the rear wall of the building, and is nine feet high. The building is sixteen feet wide, with the front

Fig. 109.—INTERIOR OF PIGGERY.

SELF-CLOSING DOOR FOR PIGPEN

A warm dry pen is necessary for the health and comfort of a pig. Cold and damp induce more diseases than are charged to these causes. Neither the winter snow nor the spring and summer rains should be allowed to beat into the pen. But the

Fig. 123.—SELF-CLOSING PEN DOORS.

	Walk				
Steaming room	Pen	Pen	Pen	Pen	Pen

Fig. 108.—PLAN OF PIGGERY.

difficulty is to have a door that will shut of itself and can be opened by the animals whenever they desire. The engraving, figure 123, shows a door of this kind that can be applied to any pen, at least any to which a door can be affixed at all. It is hung on hooks and staples to the lintel of the doorway, and swinging either way allows the inmates of the pen to go out or in, as they please—closing after them. If the door is intended to fit closely, leather strips two inches wide should be nailed around the frame of the doorway, then as the door closes it presses tightly against these strips.

A SWINGING DOOR FOR A PIGGERY

The illustration, figure 124, is of a swinging door for a piggery, which is intended to be used together in connection with a feed trough. The engraving shows a portion of the

Fig. 124.—A SWINGING DOOR FOR A PIGGERY.

front wall, or partition of the pen. The door is hung upon hickory pins set into the frame, one upon each side. It may be easily swung back, so as to permit access to the trough for pouring food into it, and at the same time, closes it against the pigs. The door is held in place by a bolt sliding in a slot,

when in either position, as shown in the engraving. In a piggery, the pens would be most conveniently arranged on each side of a passage way, with feed troughs opening into the passage, by doors of the style here described.

WELL-ARRANGED HOG LOTS

An Indiana farmer keeps his pigs in long houses which are divided into compartments opening into small lots. The sketch shows how they stand. Breeding hogs and fattening shotes are allowed the run of their own lots, as well as occasional changes into the larger field, shown at the bottom of the sketch, which is a timothy and clover pasture. It is better to have pigs in separate quarters in small bunches, for in this way they can be better attended to and the growths are more uniform.

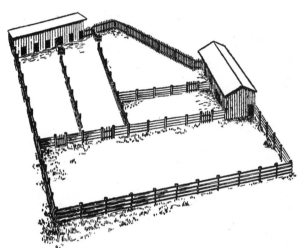

PIG HOUSES AND PENS

FEEDING THE HOGS

Traditionally, pigs raised on small farms for home consumption were fed a fairly haphazard diet. Pigs converted farm products that were very inexpensive to produce or that would otherwise go to waste into valuable meat. They were fed potatoes too small to store or sell, tough root vegetables, pumpkins, carrot and beet

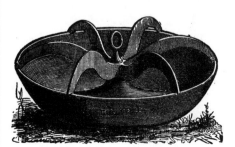

Fig. 51.—CAST-IRON PIG TROUGH.

tops, waste grain, peas, skim milk, whey, sour milk, family slops, and other odds and ends. On dairy farms, the pigs were often fed a highly nutritious mixture of whey or skim milk and corn, along with farm waste and slops.

Once hogs started being carefully raised for market, feeding them stopped being a matter of disposing of waste products and started becoming more of a science. To improve the efficiency with which pigs digested their food, it was often ground, mixed with corn, and cooked in huge boilers.

Fig. 45.—PORTABLE SWILL BARREL.

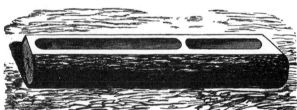

Fig. 46.—HEWN-OUT PIG TROUGH.

Fig. 47.—PLANK PIG TROUGH.

The *American Agriculturist* gives the following plans of pig troughs which allow the food to be distributed along the trough from the outside:

"The pens (fig. 48), being made of horizontal boards, nailed to posts about 6 feet apart, the troughs are accurately fitted between two posts, so as to project a little outside the boarding, and the board above the trough is nailed on a little above it; so that, when the edge is chamfered off a little, any thing may be easily poured into it throughout its whole length. This arrangement admits of putting partitions, nailed to the pen above the trough, and to the floor, dividing

Fig. 48.—A CONVENIENT PIG TROUGH.

the trough into narrow sections, so that each pig shall get only his share. The only objection to this form of trough is, that it must be cleaned out from inside the pen.

"A modification of this arrangement may be made, the trough coming flush with the outside boarding, and the board above it being simply taken off and nailed on the inside of the posts, and stayed by a piece nailed perpendicularly, so as to stiffen and prevent its springing.

"In figure 49 we show an old plan which, after all, is one of the very best contrivances for hog troughs. The trough is set projecting somewhat outside the pen, and placed as in the other pen, filling all the space between the posts. Over the trough is hung a swinging door or lid, some 8 feet wide, and as long as the trough. A wooden bolt is placed upon this lid, so that when it is swung back and bolted, the hogs are shut out completely from the trough; and when it is swung out or forward and bolted, they have access to it again. This style of trough is very easily cleaned out."

Fig. 49.—SWINGING DOOR PIG TROUGH.

KEEP PIGS OUT OF FEED TROUGH

To prevent hogs crowding and getting in the trough with their feet the accompanying plan will be found practical. You can nail the Vs, or rick-rack work, on any shaped trough. They fit on a pointed or flat-bottomed trough equally well.

PARTITIONED HOG TROUGH

Nail a strip lengthwise along the top of the Vs to strengthen them. Stakes driven at intervals and nailed securely to the angles will hold the Vs and trough both solid.

FEEDING CRIB FOR PORK-PRODUCING SECTIONS

To construct the crib shown in the illustration, four forked posts are set in the ground at the corners of a nine foot square. In the forks are placed stout poles and on these are laid the floor and is built the crib. The posts make the pen high enough for the swine to pass under it; hence, any corn that falls through it is eaten. The feeding floor is laid under and around the pen. In the greatest pork producing sections, nearly all the hogs are fattened from October 1st to January 1st, the corn being fed to the hogs as it is husked. In the pen shown fifty to one hundred bushels can be thrown—enough to feed for two or three days—when it is desired to do other work. It is an easy matter to throw the corn from the crib to the feeding floor, and as the corn will never remain in the crib longer than a week, no roof is required. Set the posts

Fig. 12.—CRIB FOR FEEDING LOT.

solidly in the ground, for if the weight of the corn should cause the crib to fall, it would kill any fat hogs that might be under it. The hogs cannot possibly get into this crib. Rats cannot infest it. The materials exist on nearly every farm, and any farmer can make this crib and in a short time.

CHAPTER 15

SHEEP AND GOATS

By the 1860s, the spinning wheel and the days of homespun wool were pretty much over. Raising sheep for wool and meat had become cash operations; both products were sold off the farm. Like cattle ranching, large sheep-grazing operations in the West made smaller operations in the East less profitable. There was still a good market for fresh spring lamb, however, and even small amounts of high-quality wool found a market.

The economic argument for raising sheep was that half a dozen or more sheep could be raised on the same pasture as one head of cattle. Sheep could be slaughtered for meat at six months, as opposed to the eighteen months it took to grow a full-size steer. Sheep were docile and reproduced quickly and easily; ewes often gave birth to twins. The wool could be harvested even from sheep raised for meat. Finally, sheep manure was an excellent fertilizer.

Sheep were also useful for restoring overgrazed or neglected pastures that had become weedy, overgrown, or brushy. The sheep would graze invasive plants such as knapweed down to controllable levels; the pasture could then be reseeded with alfalfa, timothy, or other grasses. Another advantage of sheep was that except in very cold weather, they did not need stabling. Simple three-sided sheds or shelters that blocked the wind were usually enough.

The advantages of raising sheep were offset, however, by some serious disadvantages. Sheep were notoriously stupid and prone to a wide variety of mishaps and diseases. They need to be carefully watched and managed; burrs in the wool, for instance, were almost impossible to remove and sharply lowered the value of the fleece. Sheep were also the most defenseless of all farm animals against predators such as coyotes and dogs—even chickens held their own better.

Fine-wooled breeds such as merinos and rambouillets were raised chiefly for their wool. Merino sheep, originally bred in Spain and considered a state secret by the king,

AMERICAN AGRICULTURIST

FOR THE

Farm, Garden, and Household.

"AGRICULTURE IS THE MOST HEALTHFUL, MOST USEFUL, AND MOST NOBLE EMPLOYMENT OF MAN."—Washington.

| VOLUME XXIX.—No. 8. | NEW YORK, AUGUST, 1870. | NEW SERIES—No. 283. |

THE MAPLE-SHADE COTSWOLDS IN THEIR FLEECES.—Drawn from Life by E. FORBES.—*Engraved for the American Agriculturist.*

Our readers will call to mind a picture we presented of this flock in October of last year, and it would be well for them to refer to that number of the *Agriculturist*. There, they were shown as they appeared soon after shearing —the wool being perhaps an inch long. Shortly after this engraving appeared, the entire flock was purchased by one of the proprietors of the *American Agriculturist*, as was previously noticed. It has had the best of care, and being in fine condition this spring, several of the animals stood for their likeness to Mr. Forbes, who has succeeded in presenting us beautiful and accurate

pictures. The portraits now given show the animals just before shearing, covered with their long, silky fleeces, the staple of which varies from 10 to 14 inches in length. The change in the appearance of the sheep is very striking; and the two pictures exhibit the excellencies of long-wool mutton sheep very satisfactorily. We see in the one the real "Shorthorn carcass" —long, deep, broad, compact, with nothing superfluous,—nothing, which is not either essential to the sheep's well-being, or profitable to the butcher. In the other, the one now shown, we see the immense fleeces of valuable wool which

they carry, and the noble lambs which they bear, and which are a source of such great profit in the spring. The above pictures were taken late in April, just before the shearing, which took place early in May. Such wool, unwashed, is quoted in the open market at 40 to 45 cts.; and grade Cotswold lambs sell in April and May for 20 to 25 cts. per pound on their feet, netting their breeders often over $10 a head. Now-a-days certainly no sheep are more profitable, or better worthy, either the attention of the breeder of thorough-bred stock, or of the farmer who raises mutton and lambs for the market.

were first imported into the United States around 1793. The rambouillets, a very hardy breed, were descended from Spanish merinos brought to France in the 1780s and imported into the United States in the 1840s.

Most medium-wooled breeds such as the Southdown, Shropshire, Horned Dorset, Hampshire Down, Oxford Down, and Cheviot, were English breeds. These were raised primarily for mutton, although their short wool also had value. Long-wooled breeds such as the Lincoln, Leicester, and Cotswolds were also English imports. These hardy sheep were raised mostly for their wool; the meat was considered inferior.

Goats were unpopular as farm livestock, even though there was a small but steady market for the milk as a baby food. Goats were hardy and prolific, but they were also nimble and destructive. They had to be carefully fenced in to keep them out of orchards and gardens.

French merino.

"MAPLE SHADE FLOCK."
THOROUGH-BRED COTSWOLD SHEEP.

This justly-celebrated flock was selected from the flocks of the *most noted breeders in England*, by John D. Wing, Esq., of Washington Hollow, N. Y., who gave personal attention to its collection, with reference to the best wool-producing and mutton qualities. It is pronounced by competent judges to be the finest flock in America; and the present leader, "*Champion of England*" and some of the ewes, are believed to equal the best in any country.

The wool is long, fine, and lustrous, yielding from 8 to 20 pounds per head. They are full and square-bodied, very strong in the loins, and weigh from 200 to 300 pounds at maturity—sometimes exceeding even this weight. They are hardy and vigorous, and for breeding pure or crossing with other breeds, are believed to promise more profit than any other sheep. The wool is in good demand at remunerative prices, and the *thorough-bred* rams crossed with any other sheep produce a good combing wool, and lambs of such size as bring a large price early in the season in market.

Every sheep at present in the "Maple Shade Flock" was either *imported* or bred direct from *imported sire and dam*, and has a perfect pedigree.

This flock took the first prizes in the long wool classes at the New York State and Dutchess Co. Fairs, in 1867 and 1869.

Having purchased of Mr. Wing his **Entire Flock**, we offer for sale Choice **Ewes**, **Rams** and **Lambs**.

Address, LUCIUS A. CHASE, 245 Broadway, New York,

Southdown.

Shropshire.

Hampshire Down.

Oxford Down.

Lincoln.

SHEEP SHEDS AND RACKS

Sheep that are not being prepared for market do not thrive well during winter, unless they have exercise and a well ven-

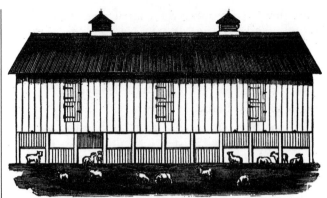
Fig. 67.—FRONT ELEVATION OF SHEEP BARN.

tilated shed. Such a building may be of any hight, but the floor need not be more than six feet from the ground, which gives a large amount of storage room for hay. The floor should be of matched boards, or the cracks should be otherwise closed up to prevent hay seed or chaff from dropping upon the wool. The front of the shed is boarded to within a few feet of the ground, leaving that space open, that the

Fig. 71.—SHED, PEN, AND RACK FOR SHEEP.

sheep may go in or out when they please. The feeding rack is placed round three sides of the shed, and slopes forward so that the sheep can consume the last mouthful of hay contained in it. It is made so high that the sheep cannot reach over the front of it and pull the hay out over each other's wool. Three and one-half feet is the right hight for large sheep. The slats are placed three inches apart, which prevents the sheep from pushing their heads through, and wearing the wool from their necks. Everything about a sheep pen should be smooth, leaving no rough splinters to catch and tear the wool. The pen and yard should be kept well littered. This shed, shown in figure 71, is arranged especially to keep the wool clean and free from hay seed, clover heads, and dust, and that the sheep may be out-doors or in-doors as they wish, and according to the weather.

Fig. 78.—SEMI-CIRCULAR SHEEP SHELTER.

SHEEP RACK AND FEED-BOX

It is often inconvenient to go among the sheep in feeding them, and there is always trouble from scattering hay or feed about the enclosure or from the animals getting out by the open doors or gates. Figure 13 shows how to feed from outside. The boarding of the pen for about eighteen inches in width, and about six inches from the door is

Fig. 13.—FEED-BOX FOR SHEEP.

SHEEP SHELTER ON THE PLAINS

The climate of the Western plains is arid and exhilarating, the soil dry and porous, the herbage short, sweet, and nutritious. Aromatic plants, which are healthful for sheep, abound, and the main obstacle which has hitherto presented itself, to interfere with the complete success of those who have experimented in sheep-raising has been the sudden snow storms which have overwhelmed the flocks. Ordinary buildings are frequently out of the question, both from want of material, and the funds where with to erect them. The flocks may be sheltered from the driving tempest of snow or sleet by means of walls which are semi-circular in shape, and consist of stones roughly laid up, or of sods cut from the plains and piled five feet high. The outside of the curve is always placed towards the north or northwest, the direction from which the prevailing storms blow. Where the flocks are small, a few walls are sufficient, scattered about in convenient and accessible places, generally where the configuration of the ground gives additional shelter, as, for instance, on the southern slope of a hill, or where a grove helps to break the force of the storm. One of these semi-circular shelters is seen in figure 78.

Sheep Shears.

42495 Sheep Shears, common German, bent handles; known as grass shears.....$0.20
Per dozen........ 2.00

Wilkinson & Son's Sheep Shears.
42499 Wilkinson & Son's Sheep Shears, Each. Per doz.
polished blades, swaged, single spring.
5-inch...............................$0.70 $8.10
5½-inch...................................70   8.10
6-inch...................................75   8 70
42500 Wilkinson's Sheep Shears, full polished and etched, swaged, single
spring, 5-inch..........................90   10.26
5½-inch.................................90   10.26
6-inch................................1.00   11.34

Sheep Bells.

Sheep Bells, complete with straps. These bells are made of extra quality of metal and emit a sharp, tinkling sound that can be heard a greater distance than the small sized cow bell that is sometimes used.

42599 Length, 1½ inches; size across mouth of bell, 1⅜ x 1¼, with straps complete. Each.....$0.15
Per dozen............................ 1.60
42600 Length, 2 inches; size across mouth of bell, 1½ x 1⅜, with straps complete.
Each..............$0.20 Per dozen........... 2.00

The Hero Sheep Protector.

Before Taking.
42505 is made of steel galvanized wire formed into links. Each link has two sharp projections. Each collar consists of thirteen links, which, will reach around the ordinary sheep's neck. Links can be removed or more added in a moment's time; by this means you adjust the colars to the sheep's neck. These protectors are made of galvanized wire to prevent them from rusting. They will last for ten years or more. This collar adheres close to the sheep's neck and is not noticeable except for a short time after shearing. What the manufacturers claim and will guarantee: First, that sheep can not hurt themselves on these protectors. Second, that by the use of this protector 95 per cent. of the sheep killed by dogs, wolves, etc., would be saved. You say that a dog does not always catch a sheep by the neck. We say, right you are; but when they catch them elsewhere it is done to check the sheep so that they can get to its neck, and in some instances they do not lacerate the neck to speak of but the object in catching the sheep is to cut the throat and drink the blood. In many instances one dog has killed 30 sheep in one night. In their wrestle with the sheep they are sure to come in contact with this protector. This closes the chase; they will not give blood for blood. If you wil. put the Hero Protector on your sheep, you can pasture them in your remotest field, and you need not lay awake at night for fear of them being molested.

After Taking.
Price, per dozen collars $0.85
" " gross " 8.50
" " .1000 " 54.60

removed, leaving the bottom board in place. Then upright slats are nailed across this aperture inside the fold, allowing twenty to twenty-four inches for each sheep. The slats should be nailed so that an opening eight inches wide is left in the centre of this space for the sheep to thrust their heads through. If much narrower they will rub the wool off their necks.

A tight feed-box with flat bottom and upright sides is made of boards, and placed on the floor outside of and against the slats, and fastened in place. A horizontal swing door, two feet wide and the length of the feed trough, is attached with hinges to the outside upper edge of the feed box. Chains keep it from falling below a proper angle, and a button at the top secures it when closed. The swing door will keep the hay always in reach. With this arrangement one can feed either hay, turnips or grain without going among the sheep, distributing it much more easily than when they are crowding round him. He can also clean out the rack and feed box conveniently from the outside. The sheep cannot crowd each other when eating. When they are through eating, or when the rack is not in use, it may be closed up, shutting off drafts or keeping out dogs. It is desirable to have such an arrangement open under a shed, building or other protected spot, which can generally be provided. It will be found that sheep waste much less fodder and feed than when fed off the ground. The feed trough may be changed so as to come inside the fold, and the rack made so the sheep can put only their noses through, but it makes the trough inconvenient to reach, and will tend to increase the waste of hay and grain in feeding.

A BARREL RACK

The illustration, figure 14, shows a rack for feeding hay or straw to calves or sheep. Procure a crockery cask and cut two thirds of the staves, making holes from which the feed can be obtained. If calves are to feed from it, the holes are made slightly larger than for sheep. The animals feeding from this rack waste no food, and the strong cannot so easily drive the weak from it, as from the ordinary rack or manger. Lambs or

Fig. 14.—BARREL RACK.

calves are disposed to fight over their food, and it may be necessary to drive a stake about a foot from the hogshead and opposite the whole staves; this will effectually prevent the weaker ones being driven from their feed. The rack is easily filled, and the fodder, hay or straw may be fed from it without waste; and if moistened bran or meal are mixed with it, forming a complete ration, it may be fed in an economical manner, and be easily reached.

VAT FOR DIPPING SHEEP

Sheep should be dipped twice a year. They suffer a great deal from vermin, which are destroyed by the dipping. After shearing, the ticks greatly annoy the lambs, upon which they

Fig. 117.—PORTABLE VAT.

gather from the shorn sheep and prevent their growth. The lambs, at least, should be dipped, to free them from these

pests, but it is well to dip the whole flock, as a safeguard against the prevalent scab, and other skin diseases. A very good dipping vat is shown in figure 117. It is made of one and a quarter inch tongue and grooved boards, put together at the joints with pitch, and is furnished with handles, with which it can be moved from place to place. It may be six feet long, three feet wide, and three feet deep. The sloping ends have cleats nailed across them on the inside, by which the sheep are assisted to get out of the vat, upon a draining floor placed to receive them. A good dip is made of one pound of coarse tobacco, and one pound of sulphur, steeped in five gallons of boiling water. It is most effective when used at a temperature of one hundred and twenty degrees, and the sheep should be left in the dip long enough to have the wool saturated, and the skin well soaked by the fluid. A quantity of fresh dip should be kept in a boiler, to renew the old dip as it is diminished by use.

SHEEP-SHEARING BENCH

Shearing benches will be found desirable, as they save the wearisome stooping over the sheep. A bench of this kind is shown in figure 118. It is made of stout strips nailed to

Fig. 118.—SHEARING BENCH.

curved cross-pieces. These are best bent by steaming them, or soaking them in hot water for some hours, or sponging them frequently beside a hot fire, by which the fiber is much softened and the wood is warped permanently. The legs are about twenty inches long. Any dust on the wood falls through the bars.

FEED TROUGH FOR SHEEP

For a sheep trough procure two 6-inch boards, *a*, about 3 feet long and at the bottom of each fasten another board, *b*. Make

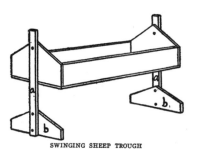

SWINGING SHEEP TROUGH

a flat trough and let the ends project above the top. Bore a hole through each end and also through the standards, *a*, and hang the trough on bolts. After the sheep eat and leave the cobs, or if it rains, the trough can be turned bottom side up and quickly cleaned.

A NOVEL FEED RACK

An overhead manger, as shown in the sketch, is excellent for sheep or calves. It should hang just high enough so that they will pass under without rubbing their backs. When filled

HANGING RACK

with hay from above they will eat of it at their pleasure, and at the same time it will not take up floor space. Such a manger is not suitable for grains or fine cut fodders, as too much may be wasted.

PORTABLE RACK FEEDER

A WHEELBARROW SHEEP TROUGH

It very often happens that one wishes to run the sheep on several different pastures during the season. If heavy feed racks are used it is quite a task to move them. The drawing shows a rack that can be easily moved from one field to another by one person. It is simply mounted upon a pair of wheels and has handles on the other end.

If the rack is made very large, it can be easily attached to a wagon, and thus drawn from place to place. The one shown is mounted on old cultivator wheels.

PACKING THE FLEECE

One of the best ways to pack a fleece is to lay it upon a table, turn in the head and tail, then the flanks. After this roll it up into a neat roll and tie firmly, using such a device as here illustrated.

The tying box is made from light lumber with slits, as shown, through which the rope is passed. The fleece is

FLEECE TYING BOX

placed upon this rope and the roll neatly tied. Wool buyers prefer to have the fleece loose, light to handle and elastic and tied up so that it can be opened if needed.

CHAPTER 16

POULTRY

Chickens were found on every farm. A small flock of chickens provided the family with eggs and the occasional chicken dinner at virtually no cost. The birds ate mostly kitchen scraps, waste grain, and whatever they could forage. A larger flock of chickens was a profitable and steady source of cash income from the sale of eggs and meat. Traditionally, managing the hens—and controlling the income from them—was the job of the farmer's wife. This remained the case where poultry was kept primarily for home use, but large-scale poultry farming became simply a specialized form of agriculture and was dominated by men.

The demand for fresh eggs was always high. In 1900 the farmer could get a wholesale price as high as forty cents a dozen in the late fall, when fresh eggs were scarce, although the usual price was closer to a penny an egg. Even at such an apparently low price, however, raising chickens for eggs and meat was a profitable enterprise. By feeding the chickens on corn raised on the farm, the farmer converted a hundred pounds of grain into roughly thirty pounds of eggs, or about forty dozen (480) small eggs. At the wholesale price of a penny an egg, that translated into $4.80, a greater profit than could be realized by the sale of a hundred pounds of corn.

An additional benefit to raising poultry was the manure from the henhouse, which was particularly valuable to market gardeners.

Egg Cases and Fillers.

Cases to hold 30 dozen.
57100 No. 1, white pine, with fastener, no fillers.
Each ...$0.23
Per doz. 2.63
57102 No. 2, white pine, without fastener, no fillers.
Each ...$0.14
Per doz. 1.60
NOTE.--Above cases, knocked down, at 2½ cents each, reduction
57104 No. 1 Fillers, 10 sections, 8 division boards. Per set.................. $0.09
Per dozen 105
57106 No. 2 Fillers, 10 sections, 8 divisions boards. Per set $0.7½
Per dozen.............................. .85
Get our quotations on large quantities.

CHICKEN BREEDS

Chickens returned their investment quickly. The return was even faster when good breeds were chosen. For meat, the Brahma and Cochin breeds were considered the most economical. For eggs, the preferred breeds were the Leghorn, Minorca, Redcap, and Spanish. For general purposes, the Plymouth Rock, Orpington, wyandotte, and Rhode Island Red were good choices. The Plymouth Rock was a particular favorite. These birds grew quickly; a chick grew to pullet size (about six and a half pounds) in just two to three months and would start laying eggs at six months. They were also good winter layers, an important consideration. Winter egg prices were much higher than at any other time of year—this was when poultry raising gave the farmer real profits. Leghorns were also popular, chiefly because they were very hardy.

Some farmers raised fancy breeds such as bantams and Sultans, as much as a hobby as for the meat and eggs they provided.

Silver-penciled Wyandotte.

White Plymouth Rock.

Barred Plymouth Rock pullet.

Buff Plymouth Rock.

Red Cochin.

White Leghorns.

ROBUST AND INFERIOR TYPES OF FOWLS

A PAIR OF SULTAN FOWLS.

HENHOUSES

The henhouse, chicken coop, or poultry house (the terms were pretty much synonymous) was often an improvised barnyard structure made from scraps. Larger, more solid henhouses were needed for larger flocks, however. The main requirements were that the structure be warm, dry, well lit, and well ventilated. Perches for roosting and nest boxes were needed, as was an open space for feeding.

Warmth and good light in the henhouse were particularly important in the winter to keep the hens laying at a season when egg prices were at their highest. Warmth in winter was also important to keep the chickens' feet and combs from freezing.

A good henhouse had a steady supply of clean water and plenty of roosts at different levels (heavy hens couldn't fly up to high perches), and was secure from marauders such as foxes, weasels, raccoons, rats, cats, and dogs. A fenced yard kept the chickens safely in one place and out of the road or kitchen garden.

A CHEAP AND CONVENIENT POULTRY HOUSE

The plan, figure 80, of a poultry house will be found convenient when two varieties of fowls are kept, yards being made in front of each compartment for an out-door range, when it is necessary to keep them in confinement. The ground plan, shown in the figure, is ten by twenty-nine feet; apartments for

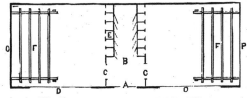

Fig. 80.—GROUND PLAN OF A POULTRY HOUSE.

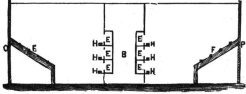

Fig. 81.—VERTICAL SECTION THROUGH THE HOUSE.

fowls ten by twelve feet; A, outside door; B, hall, to provide for storing feed, giving access to the nests without entering the apartments in which the fowls live. Slatted gates, six and one-half feet high, are placed at C; the space above the gates, and above the nest boxes, should be slatted to allow circulation of air. Large windows are in the side at D, D; nest boxes at E, and roosts at F. The back nests are four feet high; front nests, two feet; with large Asiatic fowls, the nests should be made nearer the floor. If but a single variety is kept, the hall and compartment at one end will answer the purpose, and the door, A, figure 80, opening at one side, may be placed at the end. Figure 81 shows a section through the middle of the house—from O to P, in the plan 80. The slats in front of the nest boxes are marked H; other letters as in figure 80. The front elevation, nine feet high, is shown in figure 82. The doors, G, G, for

fowls, are near the main door, A, and within reach from the hall, so that one can readily close them without going into the fowl apartment. An opening with a sliding shutter that can be partly or entirely closed from the alley may be made over the

Fig. 82.—FRONT VIEW OF POULTRY HOUSE.

main door, A, for the purpose of ventilation. The nest boxes may be one foot wide and sixteen inches high. For convenience in cleaning, the nest boxes should be made in sections, so that they can be readily taken apart. The architectural finish of the exterior is a matter of taste, and may conform to that of the surrounding buildings. Poultry houses are frequently made as a lean-to against other buildings, but all things considered, it is best to have them apart, and by themselves. They are not desirable near the horse stable, as vermin are liable to get on the horses unless care is constantly exercised in their extermination.

ANOTHER CHEAP HEN HOUSE

The house, figure 84, is ten feet wide and twelve feet long. A passage way four feet wide runs along the south side, in which are windows; this is formed by a partition three feet high, which extends from near the door to the rear, and supports the lower side of a sloping floor, that rises to the eaves on the north side. The roosts are fixed above this sloping floor, and the droppings of the birds fall upon the floor, which, being sprinkled with plaster, they roll down, or are easily scraped off. There is a ledge at the front edge which prevents their going to

Fig. 84.—SECTION OF HEN HOUSE.

the floor. Under this sloping floor the space is divided by a partition, making a nest room about six feet square, and a setting room five by six feet, which is also used for a store room for grain, eggs, etc. This setting room is entered by another door, and lighted by a pane in the gable end. The nest boxes slide through the partition into the setting room, but there is no access for the fowls, except when sitting. At these times hens are moved, if they happen to be in boxes, against the side building,

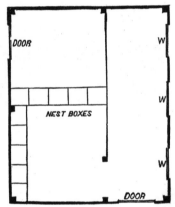

Fig. 85.—PLAN OF HEN HOUSE.

and made to occupy those in the partition. The back end of the four-foot passage way, figure 85, is used as a feeding floor, and here stands the water fountain. The use of plaster on the sloping floor under the roosts is excellent. Nothing can be better, but fine, dry, road dust, swept up on a hot day is very good.

FLOORED CHICKEN COOP

OPEN FRONT POULTRY HOUSE

Fresh-air houses mean cheaper construction, more comfort, no ventilation to worry about, warmth in winter and coolness in summer, more eggs, better chicks and better profits.

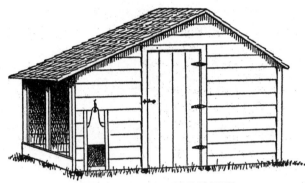

FRESH AIR POULTRY HOUSE

They are believed to be the best and most practical houses that farmers can use, since they save both in labor and money.

Next to the tight or closed house is the curtain front house, with a scratching shed. In this style one is obliged to

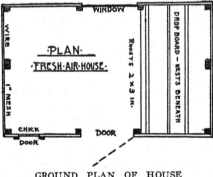

GROUND PLAN OF HOUSE

provide a combination building, which practically means two houses to each flock, an open front shed and a closed roosting house. As the fowls during the greater part of the time are in either the shed or the roosting house, and must occupy the latter at night, one has a house capacity equal only to the size of the roosting house, no matter how large the scratching shed may be. At night it has all of the advantages of the closed house. These fowls spend a very large part of their time on the roost. They need fresh air while there, just as much as they do at other times, probably even more. In closed roosting quarters they have to breathe impure air, and that means loss of vitality and liability to disease.

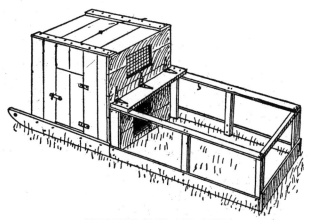

PORTABLE COOP AND RUN

Packing case coop and wire fence covered run.

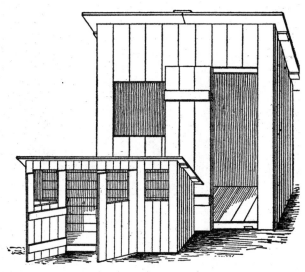

KNOCK DOWN POULTRY HOUSES

A WATERING RACK FOR HENS

Build a crate of lath 2 feet square, 3 feet high, with a slanting cover to keep the hens off the top. Then tack an 8-inch board in front, level with floor of crate. Nail the rack to post or side of henhouse about 2 1/2 feet from floor, and put your water pan in the crate. The hens will quickly learn to fly up and drink by putting corn on the lighting board. This contrivance keeps the hens from spilling their water or scratching dust or chaff into it. Be sure to nail the rack securely to the wall or post where it is put up.

RACK IN PLACE

DRINKING FOUNTAIN

The best drinking fountain, in that it is impossible for small chicks to get drowned, and they cannot stand in the water to befoul it, is made by inverting a can or pail in a pan a trifle larger. Tomato cans with the edges pounded down, leaky pails with the

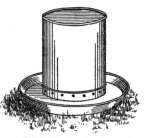

CHICKEN FOUNTAIN

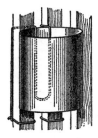

ELEVATED WATER CAN

Wire spring holds can in place.

ears bent up, in fact anything with a smooth top and in which a hole can be made, can be used. Punch a hole or holes in the side just a little less distance from the top than the depth of the pan to be used. Fill with water, invert the pan over the top, and turn over quickly.

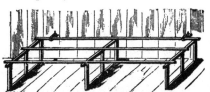

Fig. 88.—LOW ROOSTS FOR HEAVY FOWLS.

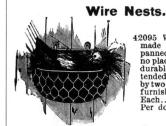

Wire Nests.

42095 Wire Hens' Nests, made of steel wire japanned; are clean, afford no place for vermin, are durable and cheap. Intended to fasten to wall by two screws, no screws furnished.
Each........ ....$0.08
Per dozen .... .75

42096 We also make wire nests with finer mesh, which prevents the eggs from falling through, and prevents the waste of straw. Each........$0.12
Per dozen.... .... 1.00

FOLDING CHICKEN ROOST

This roost is made of 3-inch boards cut any desired length. A small bolt fastens the upright pieces at their top ends, and

MOVABLE ROOST

the horizontal pieces are fastened on with nails. This roost can be kept at any angle, and may be quickly taken out of the house when it is time to clean up. This sort of roost will accommodate more fowls in the same space than the flat kind, but it should not be made very high.

Figures 52 and 53 show lath fences high enough for all kinds of poultry. The posts in figure 52 are eight feet apart. A horizontal bar is nailed to the posts six inches above the ground, a second one eighteen inches, and a third four and a half feet.

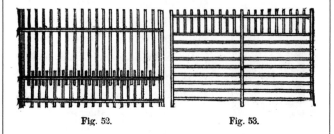

Fig. 52.   Fig. 53.

To two lower strips nail laths that have been cut to half length, first driving the lower part of the laths two inches into the ground. One advantage of this fence is, that the two strips near the bottom, being so close together, sustain pressure from dogs or outside intruders better than any other fence constructed of lath, and dispenses with a foot-wide board, so generally used.

The cheapest lath fence is made with the posts four feet apart, first sawing them in two lengthwise at a saw-mill, and nailing the lath directly to the posts without the use of strips. The two upper laths have short vertical pieces fastened to them with cleat nails, and present points to prevent fowls alighting on the fence. Such a fence (figure 53) will cost, for four feet, one-half post, three cents; twenty laths, eight cents; and the nails, three cents per running foot, six feet high, or one-half cent per square foot.

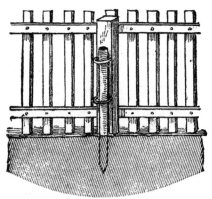

Fig. 124.—PORTABLE POULTRY FENCE.

PORTABLE POULTRY FENCES

It is often very convenient when poultry are inclosed during the growing season, to have a fence for the hen-yard which can be readily moved from place to place. The illustration, Figure 124, shows one of these. Cut the posts the same length as the pickets, and to the inner side of each attach two strong iron hoops bent into a semi-circle, one near the bottom and the other half way up. Through these hoops drive stakes fitted to fill them closely, with sharpened points for easily entering the ground. When removing the fence the posts can be slipped off.

Galvanized Steel Wire Poultry Netting.

Can be used for poultry fence, bird and game cages, vine trellises, pea brush, tree guards, lawn borders, etc. Our netting is made from best wire and galvanized after being woven, making it more durable than if made of plain galvanized wire. Made of No. 19 wire with 2-inch mesh, and has a 3-standard twisted selvedge.

42085 Width.	Bale of 150 running feet	Less than bale, per running foot.
12 inches.	$0.60	$0.01
18 inches.	1.00	.01½
24 inches.	1.35	.02
30 inches.	1.75	.02½
36 inches.	2.00	.02¾
42 inches.	2.40	.03
48 inches.	2.70	.03½
54 inches.	3.05	.04
60 inches.	3.50	.04½
72 inches.	4.10	.05

Galvanized Steel Wire Netting.

For lawn, garden and farm fencing; 1-inch mesh No. 20 wire; excellent for bottom of poultry fence to keep young chickens in.

42086	Price per bale of 150 running feet.	Cut bales. Price per running foot.
12 inch wide.	$1.65	$0.02
18 " "	2.48	.03
24 " "	3.30	.04
30 " "	4.12	.05
36 " "	4.95	.06
42 " "	5.77	.07
48 " "	6.60	.08

42087 1½ in. mesh, No. 19 wire.	Price per bale of 150 running feet.	Cut bales. Price per running foot.
12 inch wide.	$0.90	$0.01½
18 " "	1.35	.02¼
24 " "	1.80	.03
30 " "	2.05	.03¼
36 " "	2.70	.04½
42 " "	3.15	.05¼
48 " "	3.60	.06
60 " "	4.50	.07½
72 " "	5.40	.09

RAISING CHICKENS

On a small, self-sustaining farm, the chicken flock was largely self-perpetuating, augmented or improved by the occasional swap with a neighbor. As poultry farming grew larger and transportation improved, a commercial business in raising and selling eggs for hatching and chicks developed. Day-old chicks could be safely shipped to buyers, who used the newly developed incubators and brooders to keep the chicks warm and fed until they were old enough to manage on their own. The average selling price of a day-old chick at the turn of the century was between ten and fifteen cents.

DAY OLD CHICKS

During the past few years the shipment of day old chicks has grown greatly in popularity. Much that has already been said concerning the sale of eggs for hatching applies to this branch of poultry raising—all that relates to quality of stock, advertising, etc. Next in importance to good stock is ability to secure large hatches of strong chicks in incubators at times when customers are in need. Until the poultry raiser has become proficient in artificial hatching he should not attempt to branch out in this line, nor should he begin to advertise widely until he can care for a considerable volume of business. The development of a local business will usually pay well enough and with less risk and expense than an advertised business of this kind. Where he has worked up a good utility strain of fowls he can thus probably do much better himself as well as be of far greater help to his neighborhood.

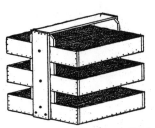

CRATE FOR CHICK SHIPPING
Each tray in four partitions. Burlap lined and surrounded when in use.

The wide increase in numbers of a specially good strain of utility fowls that are doing well for him should be a source of greatly increased income to any locality. Far from working against the owner, as some may suppose, such a development should help. It might easily be the foundation of a special trade for the district in dressed poultry or eggs, or both, a trade that could command higher prices in the market.

A HOMEMADE BROODER

The material costs about $2 and a handy person can build one in a day. The gas from the lamp does not go into the chick apartment at all, but filters around under the floor, making it dry and warm. The lamp flame is about 3 inches from the sheet iron. The heat flows up gently through the drum, f, which is perforated with holes in the side, thus letting part of the heat out into the hover and the balance in the brooder above. The heat reservoir, g, between the sheet iron,

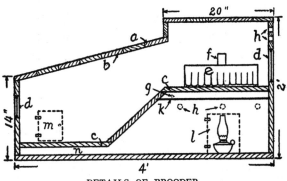

DETAILS OF BROODER

k, and the floor, c, is about 1 inch deep. The tube, f, should not touch the sheet iron, merely extending through the floor, c. It takes very little oil.

In the cut, a, is the paper roofing over inch-matched boards, b; c is board floor of same material; d are small windows, e id the hover, h are holes in each side of the brooder for the escape of gas and fumes, l shows door to reach the lamp, n air space below the floor.

MOVABLE BROODER HOUSE

The type of house shown in the cut is one of the best for raising poultry. It may be built on runners, with a tight board

HOUSE ON RUNNERS

floor of matched boards. A convenient size is 6 feet wide and 10 feet long, 6 feet high in front and 4 feet at the rear. The door is in the middle, and there is a window on each side, with two openings below. The roof should be covered with a good quality of prepared roofing. The same material used to cover the sides will make the house warmer. Roosts may be put in after the brooders are taken out, and the chickens easily protected from foxes and other animals.

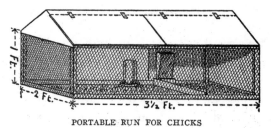

PORTABLE RUN FOR CHICKS

Frame of light wood 1x2 inches; netting sides; light wood top; hinged. Grass and earth divisions.

TURKEYS

Raising turkeys for the market had become a profitable business by the 1890s. The census of 1890 enumerated some 10 million turkeys; the turkey business, including the sale of eggs and breeding stock, was valued at over $12 million annually.

Turkeys were a bit tricky to raise during the first few weeks of life and required more care than chickens. After that, however, they were said to be less trouble. Turkeys were profitable even on a small farm. A single tom and three to five hens were enough to build a substantial flock of seventy-five to a hundred turkeys in just a few years. A large flock could easily bring in $300 in cash every year. Prices for dressed turkeys varied considerably by location and time of year. In 1894 at Thanksgiving time, turkeys retailed at ten to twelve cents a pound. The profit to the farmer worked out to about seventy-five cents to a dollar a head.

All turkey breeds were descended from the North American wild turkey. A number of breeds had become popular by the 1880s. The Mammoth Bronze was the largest and most profitable; toms weighed in at thirty-six pounds, hens at twenty pounds. The White Holland was very popular, though small, because the females were good layers. Toms generally weighed twenty-six pounds, hens sixteen. No matter the breed, certain qualities were always desirable, as the author of *Turkeys and How to Grow Them* explained:

> The male bird should be proud, stately, haughty, ready to resent the presence of a stranger, yet seeming to attract attention to his plumage by the display of its beauty. His voice, as he "gobbles," should be strong and rapid. He should always be gallant to his wives, insisting that they shall admire him, and nothing and nobody else, as doubtless they do.
>
> The female turkey should be of modest demeanor, yet with a quick, alert, bright eye; read to respond to the gentle ministrations of the good woman who has charge of the flock; solicitous for the welfare of her young; willing and able to roost high in some tree near the house, where the proprietor may think them safe from thieves; she should have a soft flute-like voice, as she utters her peculiar cry, that so charms her lordly master; these qualities, combined with a graceful form and carriage, as she quietly and gently moves about foraging for food, make her an object of interest to every one.
>
> No wonder that the raising of turkeys has such fascination for many people. Lords and ladies of high degree in Europe; people in all ranks in life, in nearly all parts of the world, engage in this charming pursuit; some for pastime, more for what money the work brings them; but all with an enthusiastic love for the beautiful birds.

In addition to their market value, turkeys had two other benefits. Like chickens, they produced valuable manure for the kitchen garden. Turkey feathers were also in demand for feather dusters, for decorating hats, and for stuffing cheap pillows and mattresses. The strong quill of the tail feathers was used in making dress stays, a use that thankfully went out of style in the early twentieth century. Feathers required careful handling and tedious sorting, but the prices made the labor worthwhile, at least for a large grower. Choice turkey tail feathers brought between fifteen and twenty-five cents a pound in the 1880s.

FIG. 3. THE PRIZE BRONZE TURKEY.

This bird won the grand prize offered by the New York fanciers' club some years ago. He was two years old, weighed forty-five pounds, and was bred by Sherman Hartwell, of Connecticut. With seven fine hens, he was bought by William Simpson, and exhibited at numerous poultry shows in England, capturing prizes in every case, and proving superior to any English-bred turkeys. The fine picture we present is from an instantaneous photograph by Smalls taken for the *American Agriculturist*, and drawn by Keeler.

FIG. 4. "PURE-BLOODED" BLACK TURKEYS.

FIG. 5. PURE-BRED WHITE HOLLAND TURKEYS.

FIG. 6. BUFF TURKEY COCK.

FIG. 7. NARRAGANSETT TURKEYS.

FIG. 14. A MISSOURI PRIZE-WINNING BRONZE.

A portrait by Sewell for *Farm Poultry*, of the first-prize bird at the Mid-Continental (St. Louis) show. On this bird "was a plumage with a luster like burnished copper; with saddle tips almost pure white, on a body with lines truly thoroughbred, and as a thirty-six pound yearling was a most shapely Bronze gobbler. He carried a deep, round breast, and thick thighs; heavily meated, with fine-grained flesh. He was a quick-maturing tom of twenty-eight pounds at six months and two weeks of age."

PART VI:
Moving Machinery

CHAPTER 17

LIFTING, HAULING, PULLING

A lot of time on a farm is spent lifting, carrying, hauling, pulling, and generally moving objects, both animate and inanimate. Because horsepower or human muscles provided most of the motive force, farmers developed any number of ingenious devices to make these tasks easier.

Derricks and slings were used to handle heavy sacks, barrels, and bales. (See chapter 7 for clever ways to handle hay.) Wheeled barrels, wheelbarrows, sack holders (sacks were widely used as cheap, easily handled containers), stump pullers, and other devices all helped speed the task at hand.

Horse-powered stump pullers were in widespread use by the 1850s and continued to be sold well into the twentieth century. In pioneer days, large stumps were simply left on cleared land to rot away, a process that could take years. Smaller stumps were laboriously dug out by hand. For large stumps, the stump puller was eventually replaced by dynamite or tractor and chain.

The farm wagon (discussed further in chapter 18) often needed to be lifted with a wagon jack for work on the wheels, axles, or tongue.

Small stationary or movable steam engines were in use on farms by the 1870s, often to operate pumps or mills. Machinery such as feed cutters and corn shellers could be belted to the steam engine. (Larger steam-powered equipment such as threshers usually had self-contained engines.) Steam engines were cumbersome. Raising steam could take fifteen minutes or more and required a good supply of bulky coal or wood. Because of the heat and sparks steam engines generated, they had to be used with great caution in and around the barn.

After the Otto four-stroke engine was perfected in 1876, small gasoline- or kerosene-powered internal combustion engines began appearing on the farm. These engines generated noxious fumes and required store-bought fuel, but they were smaller, more efficient, and safer than steam engines. Small, single-cylinder engines known affectionately as Johnny Poppers were in widespread use by the 1890s. Like the steam engines they replaced, gasoline engines were generally independent of the equipment—power was transmitted from the engine to the machinery by belt or rod. The internal-combustion automobile made its first appearances on American roads in this period, but very, very few farmers had the money or interest to invest in one. The age of motorized farming was just beginning to dawn.

THE WHEELBARROW (FIG. 163)

Every man who has a rod of ground to cultivate should possess this machine. In small gardens it is sufficient for the conveyance of all manures, soils, products, etc., and in larger

Fig. 163.—WHEELBARROW

places it is always needed for use, where a cart cannot go. The handles or levers should be of ash or some tough wood, and the sides and bottom of any light wood. The wheel is soft wood, shod with iron.

A CHEAP WHEELBARROW

The construction of this barrow is very simple. Get a pair of old plow handles, two gate hinges about 1 foot long, and a wheel, which may be found at the junk dealer's. The legs of the wheelbarrow are those of an old chair, braced with a piece

MADE FROM OLD MATERIAL

of iron. These articles in themselves are worthless, but in their combination we create something very useful.

A WHEELBARROW CHEAP AND STRONG

Here is a picture of a handy, strong wheelbarrow that any farmer can make on a rainy day. Take a dry-goods box 30 inches long, 24 or 26 inches wide and 20 inches deep, and two sticks 5 1/2 to 6 feet long and 3 × 3 1/2 inches for handles. Nail or screw on crossbrace in front and rear, and pieces with brace as shown for legs. Cut four half circles from inch

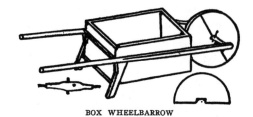

BOX WHEELBARROW

Garden Wheelbarrow.

This Barrow is neater, stronger and easier to put together than any other garden barrow made. It is folded for shipping, including wheel it takes a space 5x24x60 inches; weight 40 pounds. The frame is made of japanned steel, body and handles are of wood, nicely painted. Size of bottom 21x27 inches, sides 12x28 inches, size of front 12x19 inches. It has a steel wheel 16 inches in diameter, with tire ¼ x 1½ inches.
43443 Price, each...$2.25 Per dozen 26.00

Stone Barrow.

Made very strong and especially adapted to heavy work. Bent handles, thoroughly bolted, well ironed, painted brown; size of bottom, 28x28 inches, front 9x28 inches; weight, 65 pounds.
43447 Price, each.............................$2.50

43449 Columbus tubular steel mining and general purpose barrows. No. 6 size, tray made of No. 14 steel; capacity 3 cubic feet of earth. Weight of barrow, 80 lbs.
Price each......$5.82 Per dozen... ....$63.00

Shipped first-class.
70447 Combination Barrel and Utility Cart. Weight, 100 lbs.
Price, with box and irons for 1 barrel......$6.00
Irons for each additional barrel..... 1.00
Barrels have iron gudgeons bolted to each side. Cart will pick up barrel or body in a moment; change instantaneous. One cart answers for any number of barrels required

Barrel Carts, for use in the garden and for feeding purposes; can be attached to any good sound barrel; one cart required for each barrel used.
Height of wheels, 3 ft. axle stubs bolted direct to barrel. Wood or iron frame. Wood wheels and frame probably strongest. Weight, 65 lbs.
70448 Barrel Cart, steel wheels.
Price...............$3.25

70449 Barrel Cart, wood wheels. Price $3.25

Hand Carts.

70450 36-inch wheels, box 24x36, 10 in. ches deep. Weight, 85 lbs. Removable end boards, bent handles, iron foot rest, iron hubs, well painted and striped. A first-class job. Very useful about barn, stable or garden. Price.... ....$5.00

hardwood board and a notch in center to fit around axle. Nail these securely together for the wheel.

For the axle, take a stick 3 1/2 inches square. Trim and band each end or wrap with wire. Bore holes and drive a 6d. wire nail in each end. Just 2 inches apart in center, bore two 1-inch holes on opposite sides to hold the wheel in place. A band of hoop iron around the wheel will make it last longer. When it is put together, you have a very substantial wheelbarrow that cost but little.

DERRICKS FOR FARM USE

Where there is much handling of heavy barrels or sacks, one man, with some simple, mechanical contrivance, can easily do the work of two or three, working by main strength. A boom derrick, figure 178, hung high, so that the weight shall be lifted from the ground ordinarily, when the derrick swings horizontally, is very convenient. A post is banded,

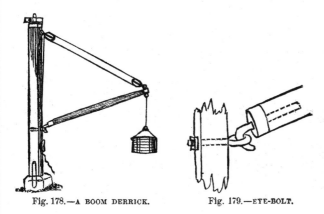

Fig. 178.—A BOOM DERRICK.   Fig. 179.—EYE-BOLT.

and has a strong dowel at each end. The lower dowel is set in a stone fixed in the ground, close to the building where it is to be used, the upper one in a strong oak cleat, bolted to the building. At the height of about five or six feet from the ground, an eye-bolt passes through the post, and another is fixed at the top. The boom is fastened to the lower eye-bolt by a three-quarter inch hooked iron, attached as shown in figure 179, while the other end of the boom has a band with two eyes. This boom is a spar or pole, stiff enough to bear the strain without doubling up or breaking, and may be ten or fifteen feet long. The end of the boom is raised or lowered by a pair of single pulleys, or by a double block tackle, which will exert much greater power. When the weight is lifted, as out of a cellar-way, it may be swung around over a wagon and lowered into it.

A convenient derrick for raising slaughtered animals, for suspending heavy hogs in scalding, and dressing beeves, and for sundry other purposes, can be cheaply and quickly made

thus: Take three scantlings two by six inches, and fourteen feet long, or any other desired length and strength. Round poles will answer, by hewing flat on two sides a small portion of the upper ends. Bore corresponding holes in the top of each, and insert a strong iron bolt, with large head on one end, and large nut and screw on the other. Let the bolt fit loosely, to allow a little play. These pieces can fold together for storage, and be raised to any desired height short of perpendicular. Bore a series of small holes along the upper sides of two poles, for movable iron pins, or larger ones for wooden pins. These may be fastened in, or better, have two loose pins for moving to higher or lower holes. By placing the feet of these two poles against firmly driven stakes, and drawing the third and rear pole inward, the center will be elevated with considerable force, the power required decreasing as the timbers approach a perpendicular, when a beef carcass, for instance, is nearly lifted from the ground, and hangs more heavily. If desired or necessary, horse power can be applied by using a rope with a clevis or otherwise, attaching it to a double-tree or to a whiffletree. A single horse will be sufficient for raising a large carcass by means of this tripod derrick.

SLINGS FOR HOISTING HEAVY OBJECTS

When one has bags to hoist by a block, or simply by a fall, from the barn floor to the loft, rope or chain slings are almost essential. The simplest sling to operate is formed on the end of the fall-rope, as shown in figure 180. This consists simply of an oak stick, half an inch thick, two inches wide and six inches long, having two three-quarter inch holes bored, one near each end. Through one of these the end of the rope

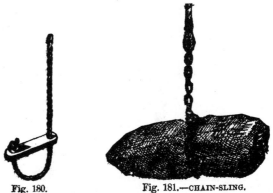

Fig. 180.   Fig. 181.—CHAIN-SLING.

passes, then it is drawn through the other and knotted strongly. The mouth of the bag being caught in the bight of the loop, it may be safely hoisted, for the greater the weight the tighter will be the hold.

Next to this, and still more convenient, is the chain-sling, figure 181. The fall-rope is terminated by a chain with

Fig. 182.—ENDLESS ROPE-SLING.

twisted links, which ends in a ring, and so a loop is made to take the bag, or simply the bag's mouth. Like the rope-sling, it will hold fast all the bags that it can be made to surround. For hoisting many bags at a time, nothing is more convenient and safe than an endless rope, figure 182, cut eighteen to twenty feet long, and the ends spliced together. This is laid upon the floor, forming a long, narrow loop; the bags are laid upon it, resting evenly on both side ropes, then the ends are brought together, one is passed through the other, so as to act like a noose, and hooked over the fall-rope, which should terminate in a strong hook, as shown in the engraving.

LEVER APPARATUS FOR LIFTING

The implement shown in figure 184 is very useful for many purposes on the farm. Mortise a post of three by three-inch stuff into a piece of two-inch plank. In the top of this saw a slot, one and a half inch wide, to receive the lever of the same thickness, four inches wide, and with the short arm, three feet long, and the long arm, six feet long. To the long arm is

Fig. 184.—CONVENIENT LIFTING APPARATUS.

fastened a piece of chain, and to the short arm another piece, provided with a hook at the free end. Having the long arm of the lever twice as long as the short arm, one can easily lift a weight twice his own. It is surprising how often there is use for this. It can be used to lift sacks of grain into the wagon; logs on the sled or saw-horse; the bed off the wagon; the

mower over an obstruction when putting it in the barn; and for some other things nearly every other day. By making the chain on the short lever long enough, it can be passed around a log or sack, and hooked very quickly.

Fig. 185.—IMPROVED LIFTING APPARATUS.

The improvement shown in figure 185 consists in having the long arm of the lever longer and the short arm a very little shorter, giving a greater advantage. As the short arm of the lever is brought up, the free end of the chain is shortened; hence, it will lift the weight a greater height. With the first device one can lift a weight only three feet conveniently.

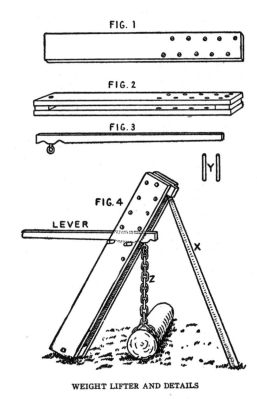

WEIGHT LIFTER AND DETAILS

The drawings show the differnet parts and one of the many uses of this device.

HANDY LOADING DEVICE

Here is a rig simple and strong that works well for loading corn in the field. The picture shows the construction of the

LOADING RIG IN USE

rack and hoisting device with pulley attachment. Such a rig will be found useful for loading many things on a farm.

PORTABLE HAY DERRICK

A very satisfactory derrick for stacking hay is shown in the sketch. The base pieces are 6 × 6 inches by 16 feet. For the center pole we use a straight round pole 7 inches in diameter at the base and 5 inches at the top about 24 feet long. We put an iron band around the base and insert the peg upon which it turns. About half-way to the top is an iron collar, which has three loops to it that form an attachment for the braces, which are fastened about 15 feet from the bottom of the

HAY DERRICK

central pole. This allows the pole to turn readily when in upright position. The top frame work is made of 2 × 6-inch pieces 12 feet long. The rigging, consisting of three pulleys and the hay rope, is attached as shown in sketch. By having the lower pole attached near the base of the upright the arms will make half a turn when the hay fork is lifted, thus swinging around from the ground or wagon onto the stack.

STUMP-PULLERS

Figure 175 shows a very powerful machine for pulling stumps. The woodwork is made of well-seasoned oak, the winding shaft being eight inches in diameter and five feet long. The lower block, in which it revolves, is sixteen inches square and three inches thick, having a hole cut just large enough to receive the winding shaft, and is fastened securely to the middle brace at the bottom. To prevent the splitting of the winding shaft, two stout iron bands are shrunk immediately above and below where the lever or sweep is inserted. An old gear-wheel, with the spokes knocked out, is fastened to the top cross-piece or head-block, to receive the traveling ratchet attached to the shaft. The upright pieces of the frame are of two by eight inch oak, three and a half feet high; the top cross-piece or head-block two by sixteen inch oak, narrowing to twelve inches at the ends, and three feet long. The frame is set on runners four feet long, two by ten inch oak, so the implement can be quickly moved from place to place; the entire frame is mortised together. The anchor is of one-inch round iron, and attached as shown in the illustration, and a strong iron pulley-block is used on the opposite side. In pulling large stumps, a chain is more reliable than a rope. A single horse furnishes the motive power at the end of the lever or sweep, which is ten feet long.

Figure 176 shows a cheaper and lighter stump-puller. The only expense is for the chain, links of one and a half to two inch tough iron, or tough-tempered steel; ring, ten to twelve inches in diameter, and the hook, all of which any blacksmith can make. The point of the hook must be formed so that it will strike in toward the heart of the stump and not tear loose on partially decayed wood. The lever may be twelve to twenty feet long, its size depending on the quality of the wood and the force to handle it. A lever twenty feet long on a stump two feet in diameter, would exert a force of ten tons for each one thousand pounds of direct pull by the

Fig. 175.—HOME-MADE STUMP-PULLER.

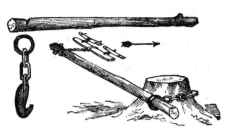

Fig. 176.—A SIMPLE STUMP-PULLER.

team. Though many durable, long-rooted stumps would not yield to this, the large majority of ordinary stumps, after decaying a year or two, can thus be cleared out, with most of the roots.

Figure 177 shows a stump-puller used in New Zealand. The thread of the screw works both ways and gradually draws each chain nearer the center, where the screw is turned

Fig. 177.—NEW ZEALAND STUMP-PULLER.

by a movable bar. One end of the chain is fastened around one stump, and the other around a second; then when the screw is turned, whichever stump is the less firm in the ground is bound to be pulled out. The screw is readily worked by a man, though it will, as a rule, require two persons to work it on heavy land.

ONE WAY TO PULL STUMPS

A Connecticut man has a very handy device for pulling peach stumps from old orchards, and can pull 200 or more a day by this means. The limbs are cut off and the stumps, E,

TACKLE FOR STUMP-PULLING

left as long as possible. A short rope or chain with a single pulley is attached to the top of the stump. The anchor rope, B, which runs through the pulley, is fastened to the bottom of a stout stump A.

A pair of steady horses is attached to the rope and always pull toward the anchor stump. With a steady pull there is no jumping or jerking, and they will walk right off as if pulling a loaded wagon. Use about 60 feet of 1-inch rope, which costs $2.40, and the pulley, $1.75, making a total cost of $4.15.

PULLING FENCE POSTS

An easy and practical method of pulling fence posts, by which all digging and hand labor is eliminated, is here shown. Take a plank 4 feet long, 1 foot wide and make a V-

POST PULLER IN POSITION

shaped notch in one end, nailing on several crosspieces to prevent splitting. This plank is used to change the horizontal draft to the vertical.

Place one end of chain around the post close to ground. Incline the plank against the post so the lower end of the plank will be about 1 1/2 or 2 feet from the base of the post. Place the chain in the notch of the plank, start the team and the post in a few seconds will be clear of the ground.

In moving fences the chain should be attached to the rear axle of the wagon, so the posts may at once be loaded and hauled to the new location of the fence.

BAG HOLDERS

There is an endless variety of devices for holding a bag upright, with the mouth open. One of the simplest, figure 63, consists of a piece of hickory or white oak bent into a half-circle, and the ends passed through a somewhat larger rod of the same kind of wood, and wedged fast. A screw is driven into each end of the rods, and filed to a point. To use it, the mouth of the bag is put through the half circle, and the edge is turned down over the holder, and over the sharp points, which hold it firmly. The bag is then held while it is filled, or it may be hung upon two hooks, or the holder may be fitted in a frame on a stand, so that one can use it without any help to hold the bags.

A very good form is shown in figure 64 for farmers who sack their grain in the granary, one side of the room being used

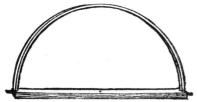

Fig. 63.—CHEAP BAG HOLDER.

as a passage-way. It is swung by staples to the posts, and can be changed readily from one post to another by having staples arranged in each post. Three-quarter inch round iron is used, all in one piece the rod being bent or welded to make the circular shaped opening for the hopper. The hopper is made of common sheet iron, funnel-shaped, turned and wired on the upper side to add to its strength and to reduce the sharpness of

Fig. 64.—GRANARY BAG HOLDER.

the edge. Four small hooks can be riveted to the hopper, to attach the sack when filling it. When not in use, the holder can be swung back out of the way. If desired, the hopper can be permanently attached to the iron rim or holder by a couple of

Fig. 65.—A BETTER BAG HOLDER.

small rivets passing through both. This will prevent the hopper from being displaced by the weight of the bag.

The holder illustrated in figure 65, has the advantage of being built almost wholly of wood, and can be made by any

ingenious farmer. It can also be adjusted to various heights by moving it up or down a notch. The back is of inch board, about one foot wide and of any desired length, from fifteen to thirty inches. The arms are an inch thick and an inch and a half wide, fastened by screws into the notches in the back and supported by wire rods which may be held by screws through the flattened ends, or may pass through the back and arms and clinched. The cross-piece is of tough wood, three-fourths of an inch square. For holding the bag there is

Fig. 66.—PORTABLE SACK HOLDER.

one hook on the back piece, two on each arm, and one under the cross-piece. The whole is supported on two strong spikes driven into the wall of the barn or other building, and projecting far enough to fit the notches on the side.

The bag holder shown at figure 66, is portable and may

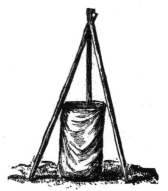

Fig. 67.—A SIMPLE BAG HOLDER.

be taken wherever it is to be used. The sack to be filled is brought up inside of the frame and turned over and hooked on the underside of it. The hooks are put here because they are not in the way and the sack is not torn by the weight of the grain, as would be the case if the hooks were put on the top of the frame. The frame must be somewhat smaller than the sack. The sack can be filled to the top of the frame, as the part drawn over will be enough to tie by. The material used is inch stuff. The length of the legs must be such that when the sack is put on the hooks the bottom will rest on the floor.

Another form of portable holder, shown in figure 67, is so compact and light that it can be carried into the field if desired. The apparatus consists simply of three light poles about six feet long, and loosely fastened together at one end with a small carriage bolt, and three screw-hooks at the proper height for holding the bag when stretched out, as seen in the illustration.

TAKES A MAN'S PLACE

In most cases it takes two men to fill a sack of grain, but by using the sack holder one man can do it alone. Make a platform, *b*, 20 inches square, and fasten to it a 2 × 4, *c*, with

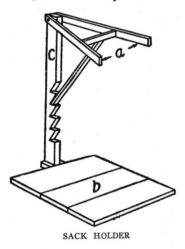

notches cut in. The arms, *a*, should be 18 inches long. Make the upright piece 3 feet long so that long bags can be handled. Some bags will require a still longer upright piece. A device that takes the place of a man or enables a man to work twice as fast as he could without it is worth while.

SACK HOLDER

A HANDY BAG HOLDER

It is constructed with two good boards 1 inch thick and 15 inches wide. The perpendicular one is 3 ½ feet long, and the horizontal one 2 feet long. These are joined together and braced as shown in the drawing, and the hopper is attached, wedged out from the perpendicular board so the bag may wrap it all the way round. The hooks for holding the bag in place can be secured at a hardware store. As the whole affair, if composed of thoroughly seasoned lumber is light to handle, it can easily be carried to any

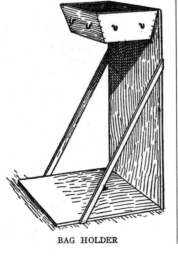

BAG HOLDER

spot where grain is to be put up. Here is another scheme that saves time and labor and makes it possible for one man to do the work that usually requires two. This one is as good and perhaps better than any device that has been invented in the bag-holder line. In making it, an important point is to attach all parts very securely where they come together, especially the hopper and the braces. Otherwise, with hard usage the holder will get loose and break down.

HOW TO TIE A BAG

Figure 97 shows a simple and easily made bag-tie which effectually prevents any slipping, if properly adjusted. Take any strong cord about eighteen inches long and double it as herewith seen, passing the ends through, making a loop

Fig. 97.—BAG TIE.

around the mouth of the bag. Now pull as tightly as possible; then take an end of the string in each hand and pull again in opposite directions; pass the string completely around, make a knot, and double or single bow-knot, and the work is done. A very little experience will make one expert, and he can then make sure the bag will not come untied.

APPARATUS FOR LIFTING A WAGON-BODY

To lift a heavy wagon-body from its truck is tedious work, if to be done by main force only. The use of pulleys facilitates the operation materially, but not as much as the apparatus shown in figure 37. It is simple, very convenient, and may be easily made by any farmer handy with tools. *b*, in the engraving, is a wooden roller, about three inches in diameter, and

Fig. 37.—APPARATUS FOR HOISTING A WAGON-BODY.

resting on the joists *a*, which are over the wagon in its shed. *d* is a rope which winds around the roller, and is fastened at its lower end to the cross-piece *e*. Through each end of the cross-piece passes a half-inch round iron bar, *f*, with bar on top of *e*. The lower ends terminate with square bends of three inches, which hook under the box, and when turned half round will slip off, and may be hoisted up and put out of the way. The handles, *c*, are four feet long and are mortised into the roller. A man or boy standing on the ground can turn the handles with ease, and raise the box from its bed in half the time four men could do it by hand.

JACK FOR WAGON BOX

A cheap method of removing a wagon box is shown in figure 38. A platform to receive the box is made by driving stout stakes into the ground and nailing cross-pieces to them. The platform should be as high as the top of the wagon standards. The lifter consists of a stout piece of timber, which will reach two feet above the wagon box, the top rounded,

Fig. 38.—JACK FOR WAGON BOX.

and a pin, driven into it, which passes through a slot in the lever. Two chains, provided with hooks, are fastened at the short end of the lever, and a rope at the other. One arm of the lever is three feet long, and the other nine feet. The wagon is driven close against the side of the platform. The lifter is placed, as shown in the engraving, on a line midway between the wagon and the platform. The hooks on the end of the chains are caught under the box, or the rod which passes through the rear end of the box, and by pulling on the rope, the box is easily lifted out and swung around on the platform. Then lift the front end over. The jack can be used to return the box to the wagon. The pieces need not be large, and when made of seasoned wood, the jack is easily handled.

SERVICEABLE WAGON-JACKS

Take a scantling two and a half feet long, one inch thick, two and a half inches wide; rip it with a saw from top, to within five or six inches of the bottom, like a tuning fork, figure 39.

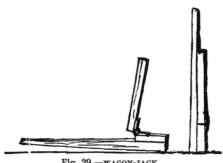

Fig. 39.—WAGON-JACK.

One prong is the lever, saw the other prong off at top, one inch higher than the bottom of the hind axle; then saw it off at the shoulder five or six inches from the bottom; fasten it on again with a hinge exactly where it was sawed off, and it is ready for use. Set it under the axle, lowering the lever enough

Fig. 40.—HOME-MADE WAGON-JACK.

to allow it to go there; then raise the lever past the balance, and it will go together of its own weight, and stay there. At the left of the engraving it is seen as lowered, at the right as raised. This jack is very cheaply made, and varies in dimensions according to the weights to be raised. In the one shown in figure 40, the lever *a* is made of one-inch stuff, and the post *b* and the bearing-piece *c* of two and a half by two and a half. The latter two are slotted to admit of the lever working freely in them. The bearing-piece is held to the lever with an iron or a wooden pin, a little behind the post or fulcrum, so that when in use the jack will support the wagon without any other fastening.

STRONG AND SIMPLE WAGON JACK

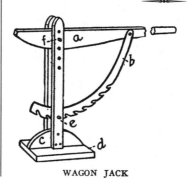

WAGON JACK

Here is a good, practical wagon jack suited to almost all kinds of vehicles. The whole thing is made of wood with the exception of the curved piece, *b*, which is of iron and hooks over an iron bolt, *e*. It is well to have a strong ¹/₂-inch bolt at *f*, so as to support the heavy weight on the lever, *a*. The bottom, *d*, and the piece, *c*, are each 2 inches thick. In using the jack, the axle is lifted by simply pressing down on the handle of the lever. The teeth of *b* catch and hold on *e* automatically. The height of lever is regulated by moving *f* up and down.

A JACK FOR HEAVY WAGONS

Many lifting jacks which are designed for light vehicles would not work well in the case of a heavy log wagon. Here is one that will stand a lot of hard usage and is simple and effective. Make the base and upright of heavy 2-inch oak plank and insert a ³/₄-inch bolt through the lever for a sup-

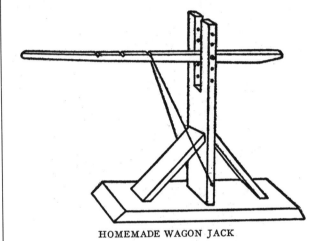

HOMEMADE WAGON JACK

port. Have a good, strong hemp rope attached to the base, passing over the handle of the lever, so that as it is drawn down and the wagon is lifted it can be hooked in a notch to hold it in position.

Agricultural Engine, Six to Twenty Horse Power.

Light Agricultural Engine, Five to Ten Horse Power.

FARM ENGINES

In most agricultural sections, the majority of farms have one or more engines that handle any number of power jobs. This situation requires a general knowledge among farmers of the principles that govern engine operation.

The average engine is not difficult to operate, and its adjustment is mainly a matter of using good judgment. The following text is designed to give the student the basic facts necessary to an understanding of engine operation and adjustment, using the engine shown in Fig. 219 as a basis. Other farm engines are similar in design, and operate on the same principles.

The engines shown in this chapter are of the four-stroke cycle, water-cooled, internal-combustion type. Practically all engines, with the exception of marine engines, are of this type.

The main points in the operation and care of stationary and portable farm engines are not radically different from those given for the engine unit of the tractor described in the preceding chapter.

The engine is composed of four units—the fuel, oiling, ignition, and cooling units. The perfect functioning of each shows a cross-sectional view of a gasoline engine with the name and description of each of the important working parts beneath the illustration.

FUEL SYSTEM. The fuel system is simple, yet it may be the cause of much trouble if a few simple rules are not followed. Only clean fuel should be used, the operator being careful

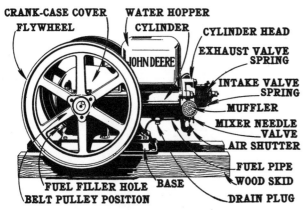

Figure 219—Typical style of gasoline engine with parts named.

that dirt or dust does not get into the supply tank when the tank is being filled.

Nos. 9, 11, 12, 13, and 14, in Fig. 220, show the important parts of the fuel system. When starting the engine, the air shutter (see Fig. 221) is closed to cause the intake stroke of the piston to fill the fuel line with gasoline and the combustion chamber with fuel vapor. The check valve, No. 11, Fig.

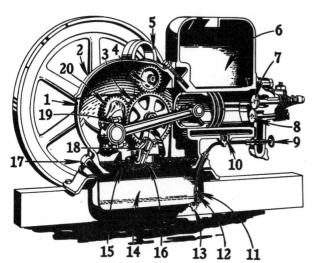

Figure 220—Cross section of a gasoline engine, parts and their purposes being described as follows:

1. Crank case contains all important operating parts.

2. Crank case cover prevents dirt or foreign matter from getting into operating parts. Removable without disturbing magneto or other operating parts.

3. Cam gear drives cam shaft which governs ignition and valve timing. It also drives magneto and governor.

4. Magneto gear drives magneto at the same speed and same direction as crankshaft.

5. Magneto furnishes hot, fat spark for starting and continuous running.

6. Water hopper.

7. Exhaust valve.

8. Intake valve.

9. Mixer needle valve for adjusting amount of fuel.

10. Drain plug for removing water.

11. Check in fuel line keeps gasoline at mixer.

12. Strainer screen prevents foreign matter from entering check, fuel line, or needle valve.

13. Drain plug for flushing water and sediment from fuel tank.

14. Gasoline tank.

15. Oil reservoir—capacity for many hours' continuous running. Note maximum oil level shown.

16. Oil pan—revolving governor (18) splashes oil to all parts of crankcase thoroughly lubricating operating parts. Oil pan governs oil supply.

17. Large gasoline filler hole. Convenient oil-filler on opposite side of engine. (See Fig. 221.)

18. Governor runs in oil.

19. Connecting rod bearings die-cast, removable and replaceable. Metal shims for adjustment.

20. Main bearing fitted to crank case. Replaceable die-cast bearings with metal shims for adjustment.

220, holds the fuel at the mixer needle while the engine is operating. The mixer needle controls the amount of fuel entering the cylinder.

If the engine does not get gasoline, the fuel line and the strainer should be removed and cleaned. Trouble may also be caused by the check, if a piece of dirt lodges beneath it and permits the fuel to flow back into the tank. The check must hold the fuel line full of gasoline.

IGNITION. Gasoline engines are operated either with a magneto or battery. The former is preferred, as the maintenance cost is lower.

The magneto is properly set when it leaves the factory and should give a long period of service without much adjustment. Most important of all is proper timing, which may be disturbed by removing the magneto or by moving the trip bracket unintentionally.

The igniter must trip to produce the spark within the cylinder when the mark "spark" on flywheel is level with or slightly above the exhaust rod (see Fig. 221) and the exhaust rod is clear back toward the flywheel, just starting ahead. If the igniter trips before this point, loosen the clamp bolts that hold the trip bracket and adjust it back toward the flywheel. If it trips later than this, adjust the bracket ahead. The face of the igniter trip must set flat against the igniter hammer when the bolts are again tightened.

Electro Vapor Engine.

GAS OR GASOLINE FOR FUEL.

70612 No fire; no boiler; no engineer; no danger. You turn the switch, engine does the rest. Engine run by spark from small battery. The cost of running: In computing the cost of running, the following facts should be taken into consideration.
I. No expense until started.
II. No necessity of starting until the power is required.
III. Expense while running always in exact proportion to amount of power used.
IV. The moment engine stops all expense stops. When running at maximum speed and power, our engine consumes about one-eighth gallon of gasoline per horse-power per hour, or, when illuminating gas is used, twenty cubic feet of gas per indicated horse-power per hour.

PRICE OF ENGINE ALONE.

No.	Size. Actual H. P.	Floor Space.	Revolutions per Minute.	Shipping Weight.	Price.
1	½	25 x 40 in.	250	600	$127.00
2	2	31 x 51 "	250	876	187.00
3	3	38½ x 55½ "	250	1,201	262.00
4	4	40 x 64 "	225	1,654	337.00
5	6	57 x 82 "	200	2,203	450.00
6	8	61 x 90 "	200	3,097	525.00
7	10	76 x105 "	200	4,402	600.00

Engine and Pump combined on one base.

No.	Size. Actual H. P.	Floor Space.	Shipping Weight.	Capacity Gallons. per Hour.	Price.
1	½	25 x40 in	700	500	$131.00
2	2	31 x51 "	1,127	1,000	225.00
3	3	38½ x55½ "	1,501	2,500	300.00
4	4	40 x64 "	2,054	4,500	375.00
5	6	57 x82 "	2,703	10,000	525.00

CHAPTER 18

HORSES, HARNESSES, AND WAGONS

Horses and mules supplied the primary motive power on American farms until well into the twentieth century. The first gasoline-powered tractor in the United States was built in 1892, but by 1907, only about 600 tractors were in use. By 1920, there were 246,000 in use; by 1930, that number had grown to 920,000. By 1939, the number had grown to 1,445,000—still only about two tractors for every nine farms. By 1945, there were 2,354,000 tractors in use, or about two for every five farms. Five years later, in 1950, there were almost 3,400,000 tractors in use. By 1970, every farm had an average of 1.6 tractors.

As the above statistics show, the days of the farm horse began to be numbered by about 1920. A major reason was the invention of the power takeoff in 1918. A significant improvement in tractor design, the power takeoff used a shaft to transmit power from the tractor's engine directly to whatever machinery was in use. The machinery thus operated at the higher speed of the engine, not the slower speed of the moving tractor. An equally significant development was the all-purpose three-wheeled tractor. This design raised the body of the tractor high enough off the ground so that the tractor could be used to cultivate row crops.

In 1900 and for the foreseeable future, however, the horse still ruled. In 1909, the author of *Practical Agriculture* told young men studying modern farming, "It is true that steam and electricity and the gasoline engine may be made to do much of the work formerly required of animals, but these utilities will never entirely supplant the use of animals. There will always be a demand for animals in plowing, hauling, driving, and as the source of power for driving farm machinery, in spite of the great advances made in cheapening the use of steam and electricity." In 1913 the author of *Management and Breeding of Horses* confidently stated in his introduction: "Though he has been threatened by the steam car, the bicycle, the electric street and suburban car, by the automobile and the like, he has steadily increased in numbers and value. As a source of power and as a substitute for human labor in combination with machines, the horse's economic place is more strongly established than ever before."

In fact, the number of horses in 1913 was substantially higher that it had been in earlier years. According to census figures, in 1870 there were 8,249,000 horses and 1,180,000 mules on farms in the United States. The numbers rose every decade. In 1900 there were 13,538,000 farm horses, valued at nearly $604 million; in 1912, there were 20,509,000 farm horses, valued at nearly $2.2 billion.

DRAFT HORSES

The ideal farm horse was strong and intelligent, with a placid temperament. The vast majority of farm horses were undistinguished, sturdy animals trained to pull not only the plow but also the farm wagon and the buggy. Small farmers could make do with heavy-boned saddle-type horses that could not only pull the plow but were also suitable for lighter work, such as hauling logs. Farmers with bigger farms and heavier machinery needed large draft horses. Optimally, a high-quality draft horse weighed in between 1,600 and 2,400 pounds and stood between sixteen and seventeen hands. While pulling a moderate load at a walk, the ideal draft horse moved at about four miles an hour, with a steady, smooth action.

HORSE LABOR AND MAN LABOR

The horse, properly directed, is equal in productive energy to ten men, and it will cost about one-half as much to keep him as one man. Hence a horse intelligently handled may be made to cheapen labor twenty fold over the old hand method. Here lies the secret of success in America. The American farmer is not, as a rule, contented to direct the energies of but one horse at a time. He usually harnesses two, sometimes three or four and even more, to a single implement or machine. Where the fields are large we frequently see two 16-inch plows mounted on wheels and drawn by four large horses plowing as much as six and even more acres in a single day, more than a hundred laborers could do in a day of the severest toil. A very striking illustration of the economy of horse over man power may be seen in the great wheat fields of California and the Northwest where 14 teams, 28 horses or even more, are attached to a combined machine which cuts, thrashes, cleans and sacks one thousand or more bushels of wheat in a day. One man drives the horses and three others tend the machine and sew up the bags. It would require at least sixty men to accomplish this task in one day with cradle and flail.

FIG. 2.—SAVING HUMAN TIME. PLOWING THE SOIL

FIG. 3.—SAVING HUMAN TIME. FITTING THE SOIL

FIG. 8.—HEAVY DRAFT TYPE

DRAFT HORSE BREEDS

Few farmers could afford expensive blooded draft horses—they made do with local horses, often bred from their own mares. Even so, heavy horse breeds such as the Percheron began to be imported to the United States in the early 1800s. Serious interest in the heavy breeds didn't develop until the 1850s. Interest in heavy horses accelerated rapidly from the 1870s onward. By the 1890s, American breeders were producing champion Percherons, Clydesdales, Belgian draft horses, and others. Today practically all the remaining draft horses in America are either Belgian or Percheron.

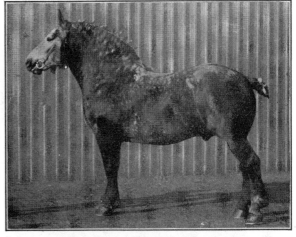

FIG. 52. DRAFT BREED. PERCHERON STALLION "INTITULE"

TABLE GIVING NAME, NATIVE COUNTRY, HEIGHT, WEIGHT, USES AND COLOR OF EACH OF THE BREEDS OF DRAFT HORSES

Name of breed	Native country	Height, hands Weight, pounds	Uses	Most frequent color
Percheron	France	15.2 – 17 1,800 – 2,300	Heavy hauling	Black, gray
French Draft	France	15.2 – 17 1,800 – 2,300	Heavy hauling	Black, gray
Clydesdale	Scotland	16 – 16.2 1,800 – 2,300	Heavy hauling	Light bay
Shire	England	16 – 17 1,800 – 2,300	Heavy hauling	Light bay
Belgian	Belgium	16 – 17 1,600 – 2,300	Heavy hauling	Bay, black, brown
Suffolk	England	16 – 17 1,600 – 2,000	Heavy hauling	Chestnut

FIG. 96.—PERCHERON STALLION "KLAQUEUR"

FIG. 95.—PERCHERON STALLION "CALYPSO"

A CLYDESDALE STALLION.
(Drawn on Wood, by H. W. Herbert.)

FIG. 134.—PERCHERON MARES OF EXCELLENT TYPE FOR BREEDING

FIG. 102.—CLYDESDALE STALLION "SILVER CUP"

FIG. 104.—CLYDESDALE MARE "NUNAS NUMICE"

FIG. 153.—SHIRE STALLION "DAN PATCH"

FIG. 109.—BELGIAN STALLION "MELON"

FIG. 135.—BELGIAN MARES OF GOOD CONFORMATION

FIG. 158.—BELGIAN STALLION "LUDIA"

FIG. 113.—SUFFOLK STALLION

FIG. 116.—SUFFOLK STALLION

FIG. 186.—BELGIAN STALLION "FRANK BRISER"

Horses, Harnesses, and Wagons   219

MULES

The mule in many respects was far superior to the horse as a working farm animal. Mules were stronger, hardier, and lived longer. They needed less food and could get by on food of lower quality. They walked faster and pulled more steadily than horses. In general, they did more work for less outlay than horses. Even so, except in the South, they never became as popular as the horse. The mule did have a somewhat undeserved reputation for stubbornness, but there were some real reasons for its lack of popularity. In part, mules were just scarce. A mule is a sterile hybrid, the product of the mating of a jack (male ass) with a mare. Because the mules themselves can't reproduce, mules must be deliberately bred, which reduced their availability. Sterility also made them less attractive to many farmers, who bred their own horses for replacements and for cash sale. Farm mules were a bit lighter and smaller than horses. They generally weighed between 1,000 and 1,300 pounds and stood between fifteen and sixteen hands. Although they pulled harder, they were less capable of handling the heavier farm machinery that had come into use. Mules were also much in demand by the military, leaving fewer high-quality animals on the market for farmers.

Fig. 127.—Span of Prize Mules

FIG. 142.—SPAN OF PRIZE MULES

HORSE CARE

Horses were expensive but vital to the smooth running of a farm. They were also subject to an amazing variety of ills and injuries, even when gently treated—and farm horses were not pampered. The hard labor of pulling caused sore shoulders, skin sores, and leg injuries. A harness that fit properly and was well maintained, regular grooming, and well-fitted shoes helped prevent injuries and kept a horse in good condition.

What to feed the horse was a matter of serious discussion and few firm conclusions. There was general agreement that oats and ground corn were crucial and that timothy hay was preferred above all others. Beyond that, however, the best food for the horse depended in part on the individual animal, in part on what was available and inexpensive, and in part on tradition and perhaps a certain amount of superstition.

FITTING THE SHOE

In fitting the shoe to the hoof care must be exercised not to rob the hoof or leave too much horn, as either mistake may lead to injury. Of the many factors to be considered in preparing the hoof, perhaps the most important is to keep the foot perfectly level, thus preventing undue weight being thrown on any part, with all the attending injuries. The frog should not be touched further than to remove tags or layers that are so loose as to form no protection. The object sought is to make the foot normal, and then make the shoe fit the foot. In leveling the hoof, carefully note the wear of the old shoe. It

FIG. 164.—WELL-FITTED SHOE

gives evidence of the manner in which the hoof has been set to the ground since the shoe was nailed to it. The shoe should be fitted cold. Never place a hot shoe against a freshly pared sole, as it not only causes the animal pain but may lead to injury.

NAILING AND CLINCHING THE SHOE

In nailing the shoe to the foot the nails should not be driven too near the edge of the sole, for in such cases it is necessary to drive the nails too far up into the wall to make them hold.

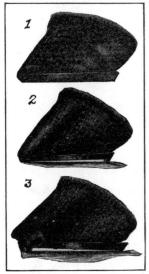

FIG. 165.—METHODS OF SHOEING
1, Normal position; 2, hasten the action; 3, retard the action.

If driven high, when the shoes are reset or the horse reshod, the former nail holes are near the edge and serve to weaken the hoof and interfere with driving the new nails. On the other hand, if the nails are small in size and set well back, they can be driven so as to come out well down on the hoof, say an inch and one-half above the shoe. Nails thus driven destroy the least possible amount of horn and have a wide, strong clinch, thus giving the strongest possible hold on the wall, because the clinch holds more nearly at right angles to the grain of the wall, than if driven high. After driving the nails they are clinched in a small groove fitted for the purpose. Smooth with a rasp, but never rasp the outside of the hoof, as it will remove the natural protective covering. It is of the utmost importance that this natural covering be not removed, as the hoof will absorb water in the wet season and dry out much more rapidly during the dry season.

GROOMING THE HORSE

The work horse should be thoroughly groomed each evening after the day's work is done as well as in the morning before the work begins. In some respects this is almost as essential as feeding and watering. The cleaning and rubbing of the skin stimulates the secretions and improves the tone of the entire system. More important than this, however, is the good effect upon the feet and legs. Cleaning and rubbing the feet and legs are very important factors in preserving soundness.

In grooming the horse, the principal tools needed are a currycomb, body brush, flannel cloth, mane and tail comb, a hoof hook and a half-worn broom for use on the legs. The currycomb is used to loosen the hair which has become mat-

FIG. 161.—GROOMING TOOLS
1. Common currycomb. 2. Body brush. 3. Reform currycomb. 4. Mane and tail comb.

ted with sweat and dirt, and to remove splashes of mud, thus preparing the way for the body brush, which it also serves to keep clean. In currying and brushing the horse with a sensitive skin, great care should be exercised, as carelessness often provokes kicking, striking, biting, and the like. After currying and brushing, rub the hair free from dandruff with the cloth. Straighten out the snarls and tangles in the mane and the tail with the comb. The hoof hook, which is somewhat similar to a hay hook, is used to clean foreign materials from the sole of the foot. The half-worn broom is a very convenient tool for removing loose mud from the horse's legs when he first arrives at the stable.

When the horses are worked in the mud, their legs should be clipped as far up as the knees and hocks, for by so doing the limbs may be kept clean with much less difficulty. Much difficulty is often experienced in keeping the legs of horses that possess "feather" free from disease, especially when the footing is muddy and the weather cold. In case the legs are clipped, it is all the more important that they should be thoroughly cleaned and rubbed each evening after work.

RACKS AND FEED-BOXES FOR HORSES

There are various forms of racks, mangers and feed-boxes for horses. One of the worst devices is the old-fashioned hay-rack, extending from the manger high above the head of the horses, which are compelled to push up for their hay. This is a most unnatural position for a horse, which does not, when out of the stable, take its food like a giraffe from trees, but from the ground. Aside from this, a high rack causes the double peril of getting dust into the lungs and

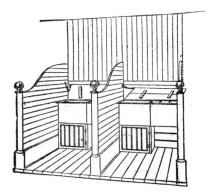

Fig. 1.—FEEDING RACK FOR HORSES.

other objects into the eyes of the horses. The above engraving shows an arrangement for hay and cut feed, or dry grain, which prevents waste, and is very convenient for the horse and its owner. The manger extends across the whole stall (a single one) and is reached through a falling door in the feeding passage. The hay box goes to the bottom, and has a barred door, through which the waste chaff may be removed, if it does not work out. The feed-box is protected by a barred cover, made of half-inch round iron, having spaces through which the horse can feed; but the bars prevent him from throwing out the feed or grain, in the attempt to pick out the best. The halter is run through a hole in the top of the manger, or a ring bolt in the side of the stall, and has a block of wood at the end, by the weight of which it is kept drawn tight, leaving no slack for the horse to get entangled with.

When the horses are fed, the feeding door is shut and fastened by a button.

A HANDY FEED BASKET

Provide a feed basket like this to strap upon the nose of a horse when giving the animal feed while away from the stable. It is simpler to make than the round basket, and has an added advantage. When not in use, the two sides press together and occupy scarcely any room. Cut out two semi-circular pieces of wood from a 3/4-inch board in the shape suggested in the cut. Setting them at the proper distance apart, tack a strip of canvas, or other stout cloth, around

FEED BASKET

the curved partition, as shown in the accompanying picture. Nail a strap and a buckle at the sides, to go over the head, and the feed basket will be complete.

The form of this basket more nearly fits the shape of a horse's head, and besides, because of its oblong shape, gives the horse more freedom in opening his mouth than does the close-fitting round basket.

Horse Powers.
Shipped first-class freight.
When ordering machinery to be run by horse power state the number of revolutions the tumbling rod makes to one turn of the horses, and whether the rod turns against or with the team; also size of hole in coupling.

70400—The New Deal Horse-Power, complete with 4 levers and one long and one short tumbling rod with knuckles. Speed, 32 and 10. Power can be taken from fast or slow motion; weight, 1100 pounds. Price......$35.00
70402 The New Deal 2-Horse Power, same in construction as the 4-horse power, but lighter. Has two sweeps, two lead poles, one long and one short tumbling rod, with couplings; weight, 800 pounds Speed, 33 to 10. Price......$26.00

70404 One-Horse Power, for churning, pumping water, grinding feed, shelling corn, etc., one 9 and one 5 foot length of tumbling rod, 24 revolutions to one turn of the horse; weight, 400 pounds. Price $18.00

HORSE POWERS

Horse powers, also known as tread powers, railway powers, sweep powers, or just powers, were used to provide the power to operate machinery such as threshers, corn shellers, silage cutters, and the like. The horse or horses (or more rarely the dog or even sheep) either walked on an endless moving belt or walked in circles attached to a shaft (sweep power). Horse powers were first developed in the 1830s and became more common with better designs starting in the 1850s. By the 1880s, the sweep power, which could operate with four or more horses and do quite a lot of work, was popular as an alternative to a steam engine.

WAGONS AND HARNESSES

Next to the plow, the wagon was perhaps the most important apparatus on the farm. It was crucial for transporting loads around the farm, for getting farm products to the market, and for basic transportation off the farm.

A good farm wagon was durable, lightweight, and easy for the horse or horses to pull. Although a handy farmer could build a simple cart, wagons involved a high level of craftsmanship and specialized materials; they were always purchased. A standard one-horse farm wagon cost around $50 in the 1880s.

A standard wagon body was unsprung, which made for a rough ride; the driver's comfort was generally slightly improved by springs on the seat. A light, one-horse farm wagon would have a capacity of about 1,500 pounds. Heavier wagons meant for larger teams had a capacity of up to 5,000 pounds. The standard track, or width from the centers of the wheels on the ground, varied. Narrow track wagons were four feet eight inches; wide track wagons were five feet two inches. Confusingly, in some parts of the country one or the other track prevailed, but in many places, both were common. It was crucial when ordering to specify the width of track.

The box or wagon bed was generally removable from the basic wagon frame; the box could be removed and replaced with a hay rack or other specialized equipment as needed. A standard narrow-track box was three feet wide and ten feet long on the inside and three feet two inches wide and ten feet six inches long on the outside. The depth of the box was about three feet. Flareboards, extra boards that flared outward at the top, could be attached to the top of the wagon box to increase the carrying capacity.

With thinner, lighter wheels and springs for a more comfortable ride, buggies were designed for passengers; they had little cargo room and were found only on the more prosperous farms. There were as many styles available as automobile models today. Indeed, some old buggy terms, such as *coupe* and *landau,* are still used by the automotive industry.

In colder climates where snow regularly covered the ground for a portion of the year, sleds were almost as important as wagons. Although farm work was at its slowest during the winter months, slow is only a relative term—the farmer still needed a way to transport hay, feed, and materials around the farm and still needed a means of transportation. Some heavy jobs were actually saved for winter, because sleds had a major advantage over wagons. Because the friction on the runners was so low, the horses could pull heavier loads, provided they could get them started. A brake of some sort was extremely important on a sled to hold it back during descents and to hold it in place when the team was stopped to rest on ascents. Numerous sled models were developed for local use.

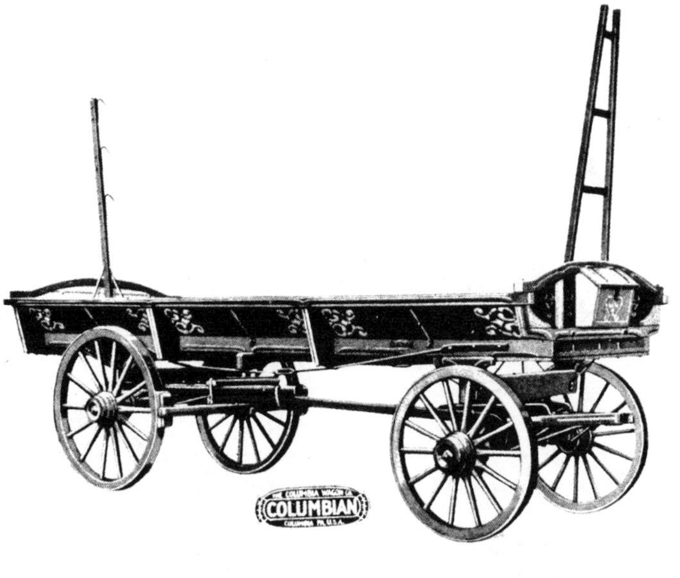

Top Buggy, Elliptic Springs.

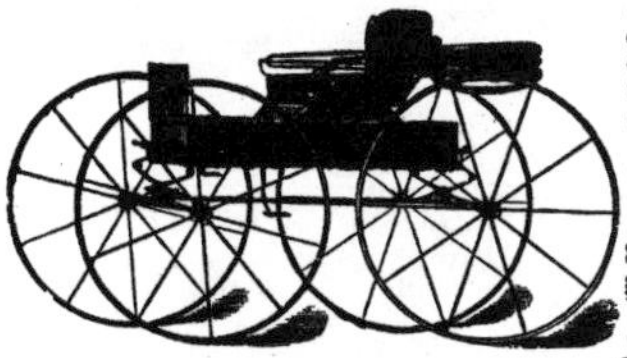

70002 Price, F.O.B. cars, crated. medium grade, $47.60 Standard grade .....$54.40 Standard ExtraGrade ......$58.90 Special grade$69.50 Without top (open buggy) Standard grade $44.50

ELLIPTIC SPRINGS. PIANO BODY.

Weight, crated, 425 pounds. Price

Indiana Piano Box, End Spring. Indiana Piano Box, Brewster Spring.

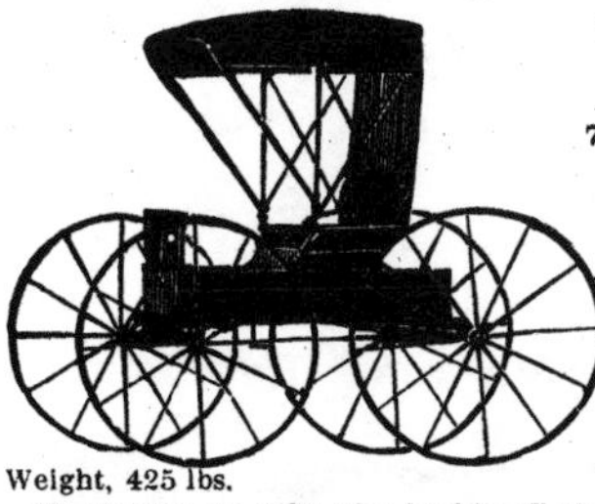

70004 Indiana Piano Box, end springs.
70005 Indiana Piano Box, Brewster springs. Price of either of these buggies, $45.75 Silver hub bands and silver dash rail $2.00 extra.

Weight, 425 lbs.

We propose to take the lead in offering the largest and best variety of buggies ever catalogued, and at prices from which any of our customers can make a satisfactory selection. These two Indiana buggies are a new addition to our list. Vehicles both alike, except style of springs; weight and price the same.

Best leather quarter top, heavy English cloth trimming.

Back of body covered with a good rubber boot.

Furnished only according to these specifications. No changes made.

AXLES—Double collar, swedged, made of steel, $\frac{15}{16}$ inch, ⅞ inch boxing.
BODY—25x50 inches; made from the best of materials and superior workmanship.
DASH—No. 1 Patent Leather
FORGINGS, CLIPS AND BOLTS are all of Norway iron.
GEAR—Made from best second growth hickory, ironed with Norway iron: double reach.
Bodies black; gear dark green.
TOP—Best leather quarter, lined with broadcloth. Always shipped with 3 or 4 bowed top, as ordered.
TRACK—4 ft. 8 in., or 5 ft. 2 in., whichever is ordered.
TRIMMING—Cushions and back, English body cloth; upholstered with hair; Brussels carpet; boot and storm apron.
WHEELS—Sarven or Shell Band, bolted between each spoke; 3 ft. 4 in. in front, 3 ft. 8 in. in rear, ⅞ in. tread.

Brewster Springs, Corning Buggy.

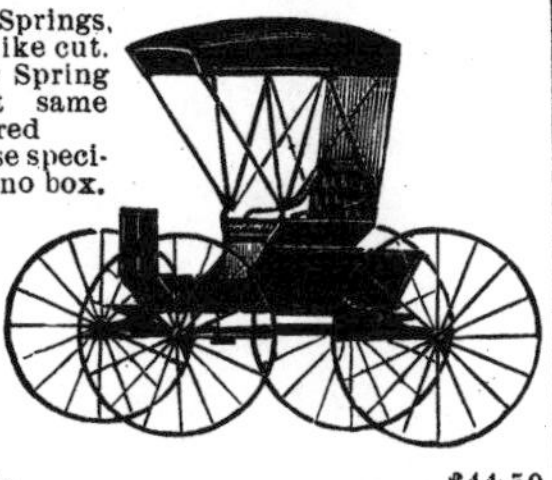

70006 Brewster Springs, Corning Body, like cut.
70007 Brewster Spring Piano Box at same price, if preferred
Unless otherwise specified will send piano box.
Medium Grade.. $47.60
Standard Grade.. $54.40
Standard Extra Grade 58.90
Special Grade, $69.50
Without Top (open buggy)
Standard Grade..$44.50
Weight, crated, 435 lbs. Weight, crated, open, 400 lbs

Top Buggy, Cross or Timken Spring.

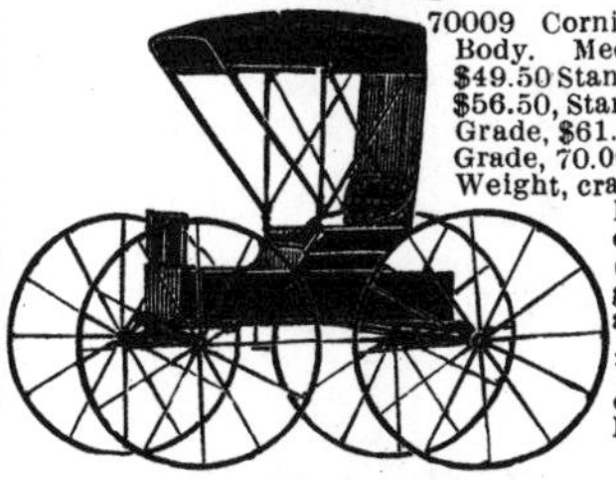

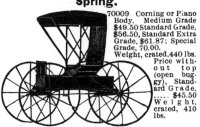

70009 Corning or Piano Body. Medium Grade $49.50 Standard Grade, $56.50, Standard Extra Grade, $61.87; Special Grade, 70.00.
Weight, crated, 440 lbs. Price without top (open buggy), Standard Grade, ... $45.50 Weight, crated, 410 lbs.

Montgomery Ward & Co.'s "Silver Star."

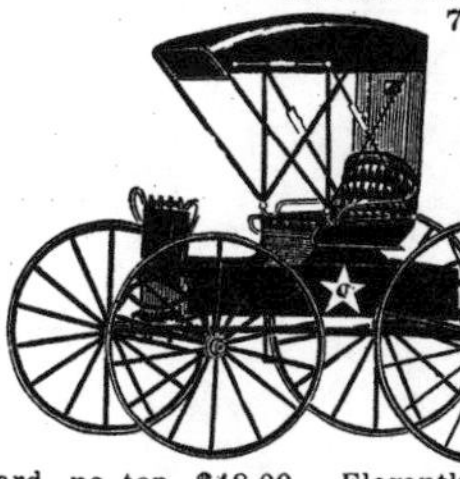

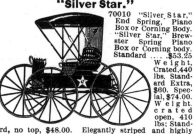

70010 "Silver Star," End Spring, Piano Box or Corning Body. "Silver Star," Brewster Spring Piano Box or Corning body. Standard ..... $53.25 Weight, Crated, 440 lbs. Standard Extra, $60. Special, $74.00. Weight, crated open, 410 lbs; Standard, no top, $48.00. Elegantly striped and highly ornamented; has silver hub bands, silver axle nuts silver dash rail, silver handles on seat, silver whip socket, silver trimmed boot on back, silver joints on brace irons to top, silver top nuts, silver fastenings to back curtains. Ornamental silver star and monogram showing initials of purchaser on both sides of body. Be sure to give initials wanted, and make them plain.

Top Buggy, Maud S Springs.

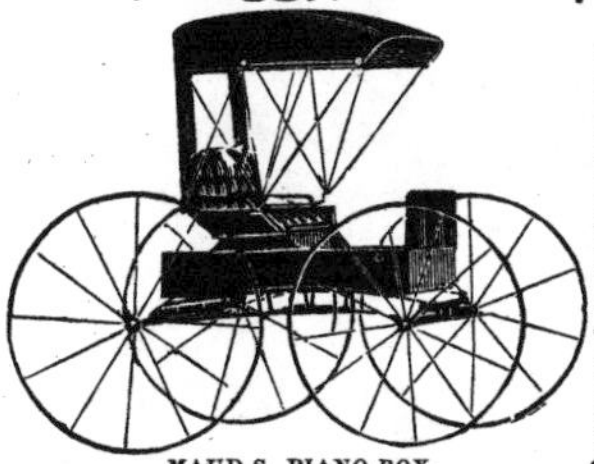

MAUD S. PIANO BOX.

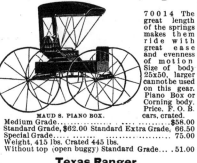

70014 The great length of the springs makes them ride with great ease and evenness of motion Size of body 25x50, larger cannot be used on this gear. Piano Box or Corning body. Price. F. O. B. cars, crated.
Medium Grade...$58.00
Standard Grade, $62.00 Standard Extra Grade, 66.50
Special Grade... 75.00
Weight, 415 lbs. Crated 445 lbs.
Without top (open buggy) Standard Grade... .51.00

Texas Ranger.

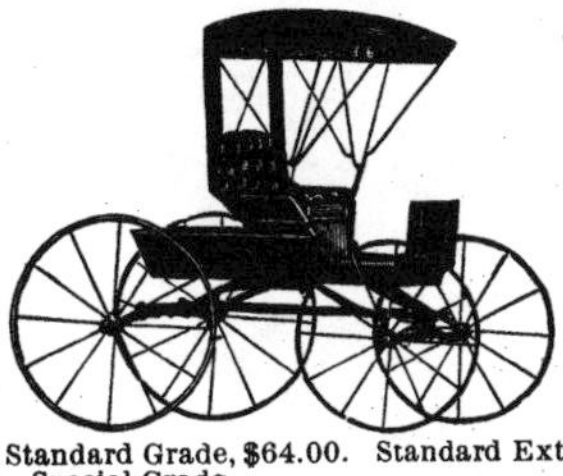

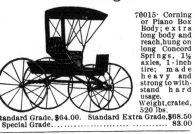

70015 Corning or Piano Box Body; extra long body and reach, hung on long Concord Springs, 1⅛ axles, 1-inch tire; made heavy and strong to withstand hard usage. Weight, crated, 520 lbs.
Standard Grade, $64.00. Standard Extra Grade, $68.50
Special Grade.. 83.00

Heavy Concord, Piano Box.

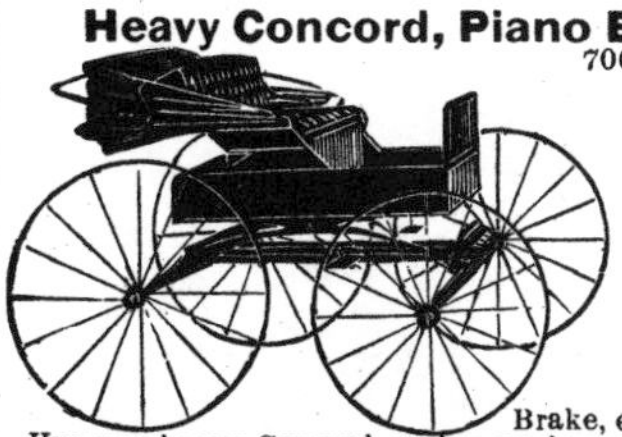

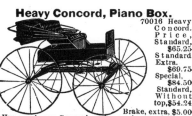

70016 Heavy Concord. Price, Standard, $65.25 Standard Extra. $69.75 Special, $84.50 Standard, Without top, $54.24
Brake, extra, $5.00

Hung on heavy Concord spring made especially for drummers' and livery use. Springs, 1½ inches, 5 plate, with equalizers, body of extra width and length and extra roomy seat. Height above ground, 34 inches; will carry 600 pounds. Body length, 54 ins; breadth, 28 ins.; depth, 8½ ins.; width of seat inside at bottom, 29 ins.; between axles. 56 in.; wheels, front, 42 ins.: rear, 46 ins.; 1 inch tire; axles, 1⅛ ins., with 1⅛ spindle; hub, 7x3 in.; actual weight, 425 lbs.; shipping weight, crated, 500 pounds.

Economy Business Wagons.

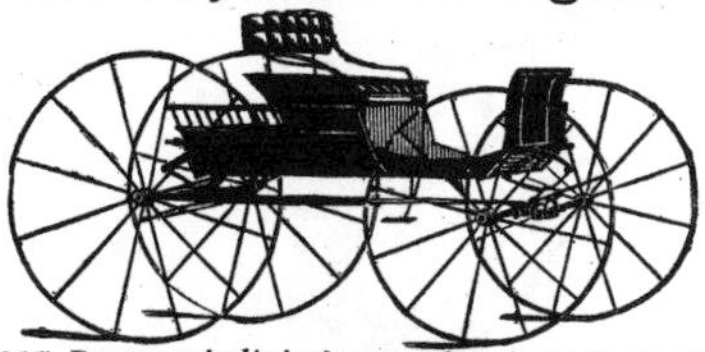

70017 Roomy spindle body on end springs. Sarven patent wheels. Medium Grade, Price, $32.50, Standard Grade, $37.50. f.o.b., Chicago. For description of grade see Vehicle Catalogue C. State whether narrow track, 4 feet 8, or wide, 5 feet 2, is wanted. Price is with shafts. Pole, whiffletrees and yoke adds $3.00 to price. Weight, crated, 350 lbs,

Road Wagons.

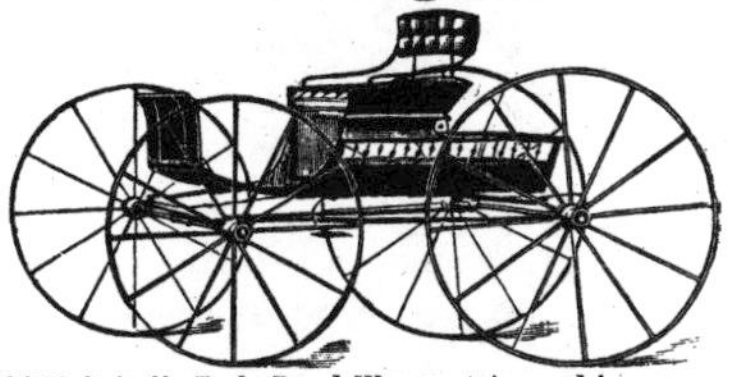

70018 Spindle Body Road Wagon, trimmed in corduroy or imitation leather. Long side springs, end springs, or Brewster springs, as preferred; 1 in. axle, 1⅛ inch spoke, felloe ⅞ inch wide: full width of tire 1 inch, weight with shafts 300 pounds. Price, medium grade $31.00
Common Grade.. 28.00
With rubber top, add to price.......................... 8.50
With lined leather quarter top, add to price.... 13.50
Pole in place of shafts adds $3 to price

Jump Seat Buggy.

Weight, boxed for shipment 500 lbs. (Cut shows vehicle with two seats.)
Jump Seat, Three Springs.

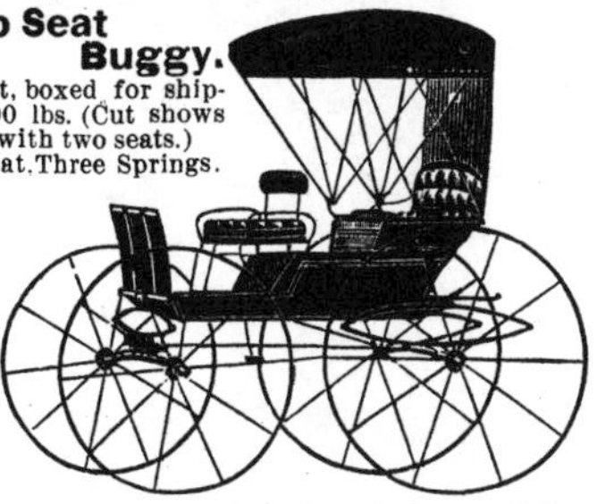

The back seat swings on wrought prop iron and does not mar the body like those moved on slides. 1⅛ axle and shafts are furnished with this buggy at following price:

price:	Medium.	Standard.	Standard Extra.	Special
70019 Jump Seat, three springs, Corning body.	$70.25	$76.00	$80.50	$91.50
70020 Jump Seat, side bar	70.25	76.00	80.50	91.50
Pole in place of shafts..................				4.00

Elliptic Spring Road Wagon with Top.

70021 Medium grade imitation leather or corduroy trimming, low hung steel axles with wood beds, shafts; weight, 400 lbs. Price, with rubber top, Medium Grade $40.00
Common Grade........................ 36.00
Price, with leather quarter top 45.00

Phaetons.

Brewster Phaeton, superior in style of body and strength of gear to any in the market. Body is hung low, making it very easy of access. Very popular with ladies elderly persons and physicians. High, full back and very roomy.

Three-Spring Phaeton,

	Standard.	Standard. Extra.	Special.
70022 Two-Spring Phaeton..	$70.00	$75.00	$87.00
70023 Three-Spring Phaeton.	75.00	80.00	92.00

Weight, crated, 525 pounds.
Fine wing dash and silver rail, extra... ..... 4.00

Three-Spring Phaetons.

70025 Three-Spring Phaeton, with wing dash and lamp-holes and lamps.
70026—Two-Spring Phaeton, with wing dash lamp holes and lamps.

70025 Standard, 3 springs $82.50
70025 Standard Extra 87.50
70025 Special...... ....100.00
70026 Standard, 2 springs.................. 77.50
70026 Standard Extra " " 82.50
70026 Special " " 95.00
Weight, crated, 537 pounds.
Above prices are with shafts; pole, extra, in place of shafts.... .... 4.00
State whether narrow track, 4 ft. 8; or wide, 5 ft. 2, is wanted. Delivered free on board, Chicago.

Canopy Top Surrey.

70027—Canopy Top Surrey, straight sills on end springs.
70028—Canopy Top Surrey, straight sills on Brewster springs

Price same for either style.
Medium grade, with pole.......................$78.75
Standard grade, with pole................... 99.00
Special grade, with pole....... .... 122.00
Weight, crated, 775 pounds.
A very nice carriage. State whether wide or narrow track is wanted. 1¼ in. axle in place of 1⅛ in., adds $3.00. 1½ in. wheels instead of 1 in., adds $1.50.

Family Carriages.

70029 Four-Passenger Extension top Carriage, substantial, light and durable. The body hangs low and is easy of access. Very roomy; light enough for one horse, furnished with lamps, leather fenders and pole, three spring gear, best construction. Full back on front seat if preferred. Standard grade. $140.00
Special grade.................. .... 155.00
Shipping weight, 650 lbs.

Spring Wagons.

70033 Two-Seated Platform Half-Spring Wagon, pole, whiffletree and yoke, two full backs, leather trimming throughout. Price, ...$49.50
The very best wagon for the money ever offered, drop end gate, round-cornered body; 1⅜ springs, 1¼ tire. This is a special vehicle, built in standard grade only. The best wagon of this pattern made. Best Sarven patent wheels. Weight, crated, 625 lbs., intended to carry 1,000 lbs.; body, 88 inches long, 33 wide; body from ground, 32 inches.

Two-Seat Business Wagons.

70034 Price, with shafts, $32.00 Pole, whiffletrees and yoke in place of shafts, adds to price, $3.00 Weight, 500 pounds, crated.
Made in the common grade only.
Drop axles and single half-end springs. Sarven patent wheels. For full description, see our Special Buggy Catalogue.

Light Delivery Wagons.

70035 Price, with shafts, $32.00. Pole, whiffletrees and yoke in place of shafts, adds to price $3.00 Weight, 500 lbs, crated.
Drop axles and half-end springs. Sarven patent wheels.
Has side boards or wings on body; very handy for light or medium delivery up to 600 lbs. Made only in the common grade.

Studebaker Spindle Body "Clipper."

70044 Length of body, 5 feet 3 inches; width, 2 feet 4 inches; depth of box, 4½ inches. The axles are 1 inch double collar steel; wheels, Sarven patent, with steel tires; Studebaker's veneer seat, nicely trimmed. Wine, carmine or green, gearing, natural wood finish body and seat. For cut see our Buggy Catalogue. This is a standard grade job, finely finished, and should have a large sale, as price is low considering quality. Price, with shafts $32.00
Weight, crated, 300 lbs.

Road Carts.

Road carts are usually shipped crated at one and one-half first-class freight. Wrapped, not crated, double first-class. Light carts can often be wrapped and shipped cheaper than if crated.

General Purpose Cart.

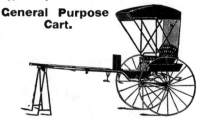

70045 "General Purpose Cart," with three bow top. Price, rubber top $39.50
Leather quarter top.... .... 40.50
Full leather top 45.00
Weight, crated, 319 lbs.
Spring heavy, to carry top. One of the most popular top carts made.

The Eureka Two Wheeler.

70048 Absolutely without horse motion.

Easier to ride in than a buggy A more useful cart would be hard to find. It has the utility of a road cart, and is as roomy as a buggy. Made and finished in best buggy style. Weight, 250 pounds; with top, 300 pounds. Price, open...$30.00
Price, with rubber top........................ .40.00
Weight, crated, 305 pounds.

The Favorite No. 3 Cart.

70050 Our Improved Favorite Road Cart. This is one of the most popular low-priced carts made; built light and neat; Sarven patent wheels, double collar steel axle braced throughout. Long oil tempered spring hung over the axle. Finish natural wood only. Weight, wrapped for shipment, 120 pounds; width of seat, from rail to rail, 30 inches. Price.................................$9.00

The Studebaker Road Cart.

70052 The Studebaker Coil Spring Road Cart. The construction of the cart is of the well-known Studebaker style. Substantial and well made. The frame and seat rests are of angular steel and supported at four points by elastic springs, ⅞ inch axle, painted in wine or finished in natural wood, striped and well varnished; weight, about 125 pounds; crated, 150 pounds. Price, crated, on board car.................. .... $17.00

The "Dream."

70055 Double bent shafts, body mounted on axle only. Width of seat, rail to rail, 32 inches. Easy riding. Weight, 280 lbs.
Price..$29.00
70056 Miniature Dream, for pony............$29.00

Fig. 42.—A JUMPER.   Fig. 43.—REAR VIEW OF JUMPER.

Every horse-powered piece of farm equipment needed a harness. The crucial part of a standard farm harness was the collar, which fitted over the horse's neck and chest—the most powerful parts of the animal. Hames, curved pieces of wood or metal, were fitted to the collar. The horse bore against the hames to draw the implement or vehicle. Traces led the length of the horse's body from the collar to a point just beyond the animal's tail. Breeching, or the part of a harness that attached to the rear part of the horse and then to the traces, was used for slowing down or backing.

Chains attached the traces to the singletree, also known as the whiffletree—a simple piece of wood attached to the drawpole of the implement. The whiffletree was designed for a one-horse hitch. A two-horse hitch had doubletrees or eveners, one for each horse, attached to the whiffletree. The doubletrees could be shifted to bal-

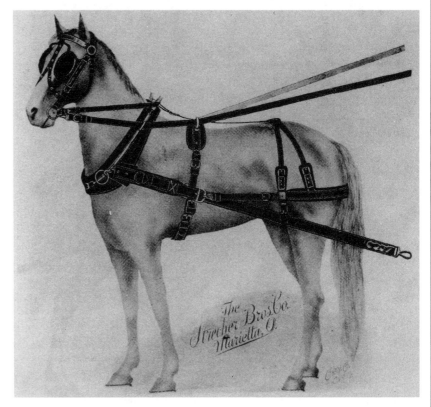

ance the work between horses of different sizes. Various arrangements of doubletrees were used for larger hitches of three, four, or more horses. Wagons and buggies were pulled by harnessing the team to a pole or between shafts, which required a slightly different harness. The ideal arrangement for each team was largely a matter of experience and trial and error.

A harness was always purchased off the farm, and it was pricey—a basic full plow harness for two horses cost, with collars, between $10 and $15 in the 1880s. For maximum efficiency and to keep the horses from being injured, the harness had to fit properly and be maintained correctly. Minor adjustments and repairs were routine. Few farmers could afford the time or expense for repairs, so almost every farm had a harness clamp or horse of some sort to hold the harness in place while repairs were made (they are popular decorative antiques today). The harness horse was also useful for repairing the leather belts used on farm machinery.

Dump Cart Harness.
Hand Made.

37092 Consisting of collar, hames, saddle, breeching, shaft belly band and choke strap, bridle and line, back chain, No. 37190 draft collar, iron over top hames, No. 1 saddle, 3 in. breeching, 2 in. shaft bellyband, ⅞ blind bridle, ⅞ line, single link back chain. All japanned mounted. Per set. $15.25

Ox Harness.

37094 Ox Harness, consisting of two all duck ox collars; two pair of ox hames fastened to collars; four hame straps; two pair of hame tugs with hooks; two 3 in. leather back bands with 4 inch plain leather housings; two 1 inch neck straps with 3½ inch leather housings, and two pair of 7 ft. trace chains. Per set.........$6.75
For all kip leather collars in place of duck collars add $2.00. Weight, per set, 40 lbs.

Plow Harness for Two Horses.
Weight, per set, 40 to 45 lbs.

37096 Double Plow Harness, made up of the following parts: Two pairs of hook hames, two pairs of seven foot trace chains, four pieces of twenty-four inch chain piping, two 3 in. leather back bands with hooks, two 1¼ inch leather loop bellybands, four ⅝ inch hame straps, one set ⅞ inch 18 ft. team lines, two pigeon wing bridles, flat checks. No hitch straps or snaps.
Without collars, per set........ ....$9.00
With No. 37199 collars, per set.................10.00
If collars are wanted, mention size.
Breast straps or neckyoke straps do not go with plow harness No. 37096; if wanted, add $1.56.

37097 Plow Harness or Chain Harness for two horses. Bridles,⅞-inch, Jenny Lind blinds,hook hames, varnished over top; back band, 4-inch leather, with loops; bellybands, 1½-inch; back straps, 2½-inch, hip straps 1¼-inch with snaps; traces, 7 feet chains, 30-inch leather piping; lines, ⅞-inch, 15 feet with snaps; breast straps, 1½-inch with slides and snaps; ⅞-inch, with folded crupper. No pole straps or hitch straps. Without collars. Per set......$11.00
Weight, per set, without collars, 45 pounds.
See our quotations on horse collars.

Short Tug Farm Harness.
FOR TWO HORSES.

37098 Short Tug Farm Harness, traces, 1½ inch, 4 feet long, with 3½ feet stage chain, pads, folded, with loop for back strap; lines, ¾ inch, 18 feet long, with snaps; bridles, ¾ inch, pigeon wing winkers, flat checks, neckyoke straps 1¼ inch, breast straps 1½ in., with snaps and slides; hames, varnished, iron over top, back straps, ⅞ inch, with folded crupper, hip straps ⅞ inch, bellybands flat. Without collars. Per set.....$12.00
With No. 37195 collars. Per set.............14.00
No 37098 Harness weighs 37 lbs. per double set without collars or casing.

37099 Flat Pad Team Harness; for two horses, imitation hand sewed. Bridles, ⅞ inch, sensible blinds; hames red, iron over top; pads flat, folded, 1¼ inch billets; traces 1¼ inch, hip straps 1 inch; traces, 1½ inches wide, 5 ft. 10 inches long, double and stitched, clip cockeyes; lines, ⅞ inch 15 feet with snaps; breast straps, 1½ inch, with slides and snaps; pole straps, 1½ inch. No hitch straps. Without collars. Per set..........................$14.00
Weight, per set, without collars, 40 lbs.

Long Tug Farm Harness.

FOR TWO HORSES.

37100 Traces, 1½ inch, 6 ft. long with hame tugs, Champion trace buckles; hads, folded with loop; lines, ⅞ inch 18 feet, with snaps; bridles, ¾ inch, with sensible blinds; neck yoke martingales, 1½ inch; breast straps, 1½ inch, with snaps and breast strap slides; hames, varnished iron over top; back straps, 1 inch, stuffed cruppers and trace carriers; hip straps, ⅞ inch; bellybands, folded; without collars; either black or white mountings. Per set..................$16.00
Weight, per set, without collars, 41 lbs.
37101 Same style as No. 37100, with 1¾ inch traces, ⅞ inch bridles, without collars.Per set 17.50
Weight, per set, without collars, 44 lbs.
EXTRAS FOR NOS. 37100 AND 37101.
Round lines in place of flat, extra................ 1.25
Breeching, extra................................. 3.50
Above styles are the best value on low priced farm harness that money can buy.
For Horse Collars see following pages.

TEAM HARNESS.

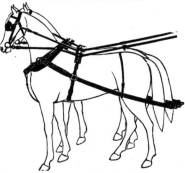

37104 Team Harness, imitation hand sewed.
Bridles, ¾ inch, sensible blinds, round reins and winker stay.
Hames, black clip, iron over top.
Pads, hook and terret, with 1¼ inch market strap tugs.
Back Straps, 1 inch, hip straps ⅞ inch.
Traces, 1½ inch. 6 feet, double and stitched.
Clip cockeyes.
Lines, ⅞ inch, 18 feet, with snaps.
Breast straps and pole straps, 1½ inch, "XC" plate (white) mountings.
Without collars, per set.....................$15.00
Weight, per set, about 40 lbs.
See our quotations on horse collars.
37106 Special Hook and Terret Farm Harness, "X C" trimmed only.
Pads, hook and terret, "Medway," folded skirts, 1 inch back straps with round cruppers and trace carriers.
Bridles, ¾ inch, Concord blinds, round check reins, fancy fronts and rosettes.
Traces, 1½ inch, 6 feet long, two rows stitching, clip cockeyes.
Lines, ⅞ inch, 18 feet long, with snaps.
Hames, black clip X C trimmed, combination loops, long hame tugs with Champion trace buckles.
Bellybands, folded, 1¼ inch billets.
Breast Straps, 1½ inch, with snaps and slides.
Neck Yoke Straps, 1½ inch,with ⅞ inch collar straps.
Hip Straps, ⅞ inch.
Without collars, per set........................$17.00
Weight, per set, about 43 lbs.
We can save you money on horse collars and sweat collars. See our prices.
37108 Team Harness. Imitation hand sewed.
Bridles, ¾ inch, with blinds, round reins and winker stay.
Hames, varnished, iron over top,⅝ inch spread straps.
Pads, hook and terret.
Back Straps, 1 inch; hip straps, ⅞ inch.
Traces, 1½ inch 6 feet, double and stitched.
Lines, ⅞ inch; 18 feet with snaps.
Breast Straps, 1½ inch, with slides and snaps.
Pole Straps, 1½ inch; collar straps, ⅞ inch.
Without collars,
White mountings, per set.......................$18.50
Weight, per set, without collars, 48 lbs.

37110 Traces, 1½ inch, 6 feet long, hame tugs, champion trace buckles, pads, hooks and terrets, folded with layer and fancy housing. Lines, ⅞ inch, 18 feet, with snaps; bridles, ¾ inch with harness leather winkers, round side checks and nose bands. Neck yoke martingales, 1½ inch; breast straps, 1½ inch, with snaps and breast strap slides. Hames, iron over top, combination loops; back straps, 1 inch; round crupper, hip straps, ⅞ inch, sewed in ring; bellybands, folded. Without collars.
Very choice stock used throughout. Either black or white mountings. Per set...........$21.00
Weight, per set, without collars, 48 lbs.
37111 Same style as No. 37110, with 1¾ in. traces and ⅞ in. bridles. Without collars. Either black or white mountings.
Per set.................................... 22.50
Round lines, in place of flat, will cost $1.50 extra. For breeching add $3.50.
Weight, per set, without collars, 50 lbs.
We carry a large line of horse collars at low prices See our quotations.
37112 Farm Harness, same weight and quality as No. 37110, but made "slip tug" in place of "long tug," either blind bridles or open bridles, either black or white mountings, without collars. Per set (two horses)..... .. ...$21.00

Long Tug Farm Harness.
Hand Made.

37114 Traces, 1½ inch, hame tugs, champion trace buckles, pads, hooks and terrets, swelled with fancy housings. Lines, ⅞ inch, 18 feet, with snaps; bridles, ¾ inch, winkers, round side checks. Neck yoke martingales, 1½ inch; breast straps, 1½ inch, with snaps and breast strap slides. Hames, iron over top, combination loop; back straps, 1 inch, with round crupper trace carrier; hip straps, ⅞ inch; bellybands, folded. All hand sewed throughout and made of the best selected oak tanned leather; strictly first-class in every respect. Either black or white mountings, without collars. Per set...$23.50
37115 Same as 37114; 1¾ inch traces, ⅞ inch blind bridles. Per set, without collars..........25.00
Breeching, $4 extra; round lines, $1.50 extra.
Weight, per set, without collars, 48 lbs.
Weight of No. 37115 without collars, 50 lbs.
We keep a large variety of horse collars which we sell cheap.
37116 Farm Harness, same weight and quality as No. 37114, but made "slip tug" in place of "long tug," either blind bridles or open bridles, either black or white mountings, without collars. Per set (two horses).....................$23.50

Breeching Team Harness.

37117 Team Harness, imitation hand sewed. Bridles, ¾ inch, box loops, short round reins, round winker stays, square blinds; Hames, No. 5 Concord, long staples,⅝ inch spread straps, no back pads; breeching, folded, 1¼ inch layer, ⅞ inch double back straps running to rings in hames, ⅞ in. double hip straps, ⅞ inch side straps; traces, 1¼ inch, 6 feet, double and stitched; lines, 1 inch. 20 feet, with snaps; breast straps, 1½ inch, with slides and snaps; pole straps, 1½ inch, with rings, white mountings, without collars. Per set.................$21.00
Weight of No. 37117 Harness, without collars, 45 lbs.
37118 Farm Harness with breeching; bridles, ¾ inch Concord blinds, box loops on cheeks, flat winker braces and nose piece covered with nickel spots, fancy front with nickel rosettes, short check rein; lines, 1 inch 18 feet long with snaps; hames, No. 5 Concord clip, long hame tugs, three loop champion trace buckles; traces, 1½ inch, 6 feet long, two rows stitching and

Harness—Continued.

cockeyes, folded bellybands, 1¼ inch billets; back-bands, folded with loops and eight large nickel concord spots; no hooks or terrets, 1 inch back straps with trace carriers and round cruppers; breeching, folded, 3 feet 6 inches long, with 1⅛ inch layer, ⅞ inch hip straps, ⅞ inch side straps with snaps; breast straps, 1½ inch with snaps and slides; neck yoke straps, 1½ inch with ⅞ inch collar straps and rings for snaps on breeching side straps. Made in good style of first class stock; without collars.
Per set....................................$23.00

We sell horse collars very cheap; look up our prices on following pages.

37119 Double Truck Harness, imitation hand sewed; bridles, ¾-inch sensible blinds, flat winker stays, brass fronts and rosettes, Hames, No. 8, red, Concord bolt, brass ball top; breeching, folded, 1¼-inch layers, side straps 1-inch; back straps, 1-inch, double, running to rings in hames; hip straps, ⅝-inch; traces, 1½-inch, double and stitched with heel chains; lines, 1-inch, 18 feet, with snaps; breast straps, 1½-inch, with rollers and snaps and extension straps; martingales, 1½-inch, with 1-inch collar straps; spread straps, ¾-inch. Without collars. Per set.......................$26.50
Weight, per set, without collars, 60 pounds.

Lumber or Heavy Truck Harness.

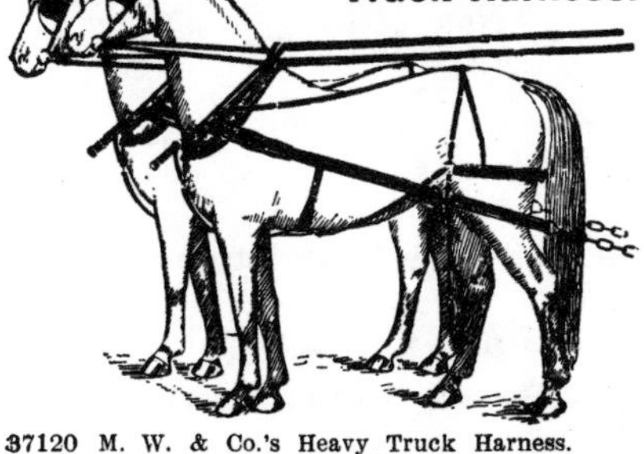

37120 M. W. & Co.'s Heavy Truck Harness. Bridles, ⅞ inch, with Concord winkers, round winker braces, 1 inch brass points, large brass rosettes, short check rein to check over hame tops; lines, 1 inch, 18 feet long, with snaps; hames, No. 8 red Concord bolt, brass ball tops, 1 inch hame straps, ¾ inch spreader straps with brass rings; traces, 1¾ inch, 6 feet long, two rows of stitching, four link and dee butt chain, folded bellybands, 1¼ inch billets on each side, 1 inch double back straps running to sides of hames (no back pads), 1 inch double hip straps sewed in ring with large chafe on rump; breeching, folded, 3 feet 6 inches long from ring to ring, 1¼ inch layer, 1 inch side straps with snaps, 1 inch lazy straps; breast straps, 1¾ inch with snaps and roller snaps; 1½ inch martingales with rings and 1 inch choke straps, 1½ inch pole spreader. All made strong and substantial from No. 1 selected oak tanned leather; without collars. Per set................$28.00

Concord Harness.

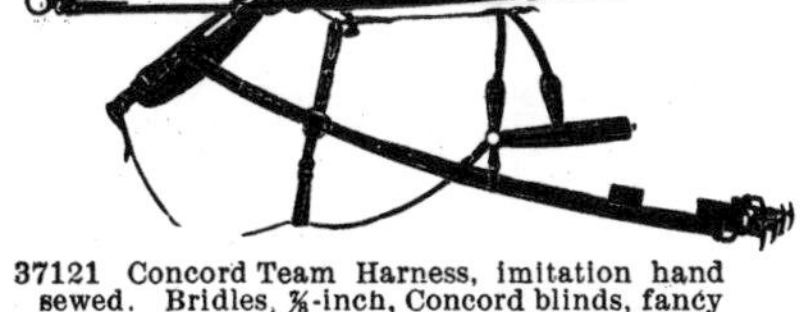

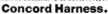

37121 Concord Team Harness, imitation hand sewed. Bridles, ⅝-inch, Concord blinds, fancy face pieces; hames, No. 6 Concord bolt, black; Hame tugs, with box loops; Pads; Concord style, 1½-inch in billets; traces, 6 feet long, 2⅛-inches wide, 1¾-inch fronts; either cockeye or toggle ends; breeching, folded, 1¼-inch layer, 1½-inch back straps 1-inch double hip straps, 1-inch double side straps: lines, 1⅛-inch, 18 feet with snaps; breast straps, 1¾ inch, with slides and snaps; pole straps; 1¾-inch. Without collars. Per set..........................$29.00
For above harness with 2¾-inch traces, with 2-inch fronts add.................................. 1.00
Weight, per set, without collars, 65 pounds.

M. W. & Co.'s Heavy Concord Harness.

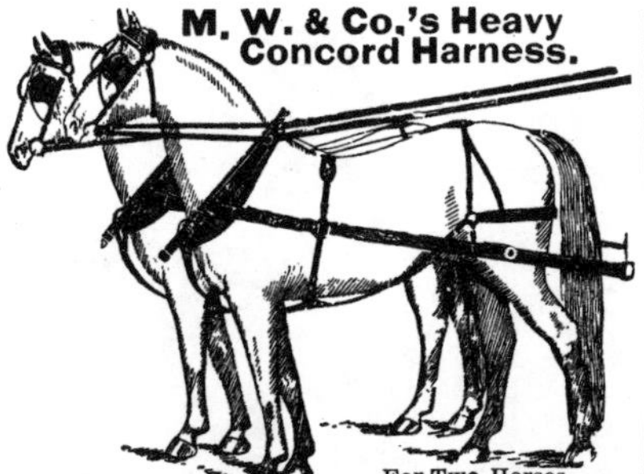

For Two Horses.

37122 Hand Made Concord Wheel or Breeching Harness; traces, 2½-inch single strap, with doubled and stitched points, and either Concord toggles or cockeyes; hame tugs, 1¾ inch, doubled and stitched: pads, Concord style, round loops; lines, 1 inch, 18 feet long, with snaps; bridles, ⅞ inch, with patent leather winkers, flat checks, fancy face piece; choke straps, 1⅛ inch; breast straps, 1¼ inch, with snaps and breast strap slides; hames, polished Concord, bolt No 6; back straps, 1¼ inch, running to ring on rump, with safes; hip straps, ⅞ inch, double and split, bellybands folded; side straps, 1 inch, with snaps; breechings, extra heavy, folded with 1¼-inch layer. All hand made from No. 1 selected oak tanned leather. Without collars, per set...........................$32.00
37122 Harness, without collars, weighs about 63 lbs. Please examine our prices on horse collars

Chicago Truck Harness.

37124 Chicago Truck Harness. Made from selected oak tanned leather, and in keeping with the best custom work. Hames, No. 10 red Concord bolt, with brass plates and balls; traces, 1¾ inch, 6 feet long, three rows of stitching, 4 link and dee butt chain; bridles, ⅞ inch, Concord blinds, round winker braces, fancy face piece with brass spots; 1¼-inch brass fronts and large brass rosettes, short check reins; lines, 1 inch, 18 feet long, with snaps; back straps, 1⅛ inch, double, running to sides of hames; 1-inch double hip straps sewed in rings on rump, padded safes under rings, brass buckle shields; breeching, folded, 3 feet 8 inches from ring to ring, 1½ inch layer, 1¼-inch side straps with snaps; 1-inch lazy straps; breast straps, 1¾ inch, 6 feet long, with 1¾-inch breast strap spreader 2 feet long: snaps and breast strap rollers; martingales, 1¼ inch, doubled and stitched; 1½-inch collar straps; 1½-inch pole spreaders 30 inches long, and rings for breeching, side straps, hame straps, 1 inch; spreader straps, ⅞ inch, with brass rings. Without collars, per set.....$35.00
Weight, per set, about 60 pounds. Our quotations on horse collars follow our harness quotations

Double Hack or Spring Wagon Harness.

37130 Double Hack or Spring Wagon Harness, imitation hand sewed. Bridles, ¾ inch, box loops, flat reins and winker stays, sensible blinds; hame tugs, box loop, oval iron wood coach hames, ½ inch spread straps; pads, hook and terret, with 3¼ inch swell housings, single skirts, double and stitched bearers: turnbacks, ⅝ inch, round cruppers to buckle; hip straps, ¾ inch, with patent leather ornaments; bellybands folded; traces, 1¼ inch, 5 feet 10 inches long double and stitched, with or without cockeyes; lines, round, 1 inch russet hand parts; breast straps, 1¼ inch, with snaps and slides; poles traps, 1¼ inch; "XC" Mountings only. Without collars, per set $16.00
Weight, per set, without collars, 32 pounds.

Road Harness.

37132 This is a double harness and is intended for a light work harness, or for driving in a family spring wagon; it is well made of oak tanned leather and well finished throughout. Low top wood hames, spread straps and rings, short hame tugs with box loops; traces, 1¼ inch heavy, with cockeyes to buckle to tugs; saddles with leather pads; folded bellybands; blind bridles with patent leather coach blinds and box loop; round side check reins and winker stays; breast and neck yoke straps, 1¼ in.; stuffed crupper docks, flat back and hip straps, flat lines, 1 in., 18 ft. long, with snaps; all XC mountings. Without collars. Per set..........$20.00
With No. 37187 collars. Per set......... .... 23.50
Breeching extra.............................. 3.75

We will make No. 37132 harness to order in either full brass or full nickel mountings for $3.00 extra.

No. 37132 harness weighs 40 lbs. per set without collars or extras.

Double Buggy Harness.

FOR TWO HORSES.

37136 Pads, without plates, fancy housings; bridles, ⅝ inch, patent leather winkers, flat winker braces, traces 1⅛ inch, doubled and stitched, clipped to hames; 7 lb. iron hames; lines, flat, ¾ inch fronts, 1 inch hands; bellybands folded; choke straps and breast straps, 1 inch, turn-backs plain, no hip straps, folded cruppers, with buggy collars, all white (XC) mountings.
Per set...$12.50
Weight, per set without collars, 23 lbs.
When ordering Double Buggy Harness, state size of collars wanted.

37138 Double Buggy Harness, special "XC" only. Bridles, ⅝-inch, patent leather winkers, box loops on cheeks, round winker braces ⅝-inch overchecks, white rosettes; lines, ¾-inch, russet leather hand parts; hames, 7-lbs. XC plated, ⅝-inch hame straps, ½-inch spreader straps, hame tugs with box loops; traces 1½-inch, 6 feet 4 inches long, doubled and stitched; coach pads, with iron plates, ¾-inch turn backs with folded crupper docks, folded bellybands; breast straps, 1-inch, 3 feet 8 inches long; choke straps, ¾ inch; no hip straps, with No. 37192 buggy collars. Mention size.
Per set....................................$14.00

37140 Double Buggy Harness, bridles, ⅝-inch, patent leather winkers, box loops on cheeks, round winker braces, round side checks or flat overdraw checks; lines, ¾-inch cross reins, 1-inch hand parts; hames, 7 lbs., 1-inch hame tugs with box loops, ⅝-inch hame straps, ½-inch spread straps; traces, 1-inch, 6 feet 4 inches long, doubled and stitched; coach pads, No. 2 "O. K." doubled and stitched bearers, ⅞-inch turn-backs with stuffed docks, folded bellybands; breast straps, 1 inch, 3 ft. 8 in. long; choke straps ⅝-inch from belly-band to collar; no hip straps. All black (japanned) mountings, with No. 37192 collars. Mention size.
Per set...16.00
Breast Collars in place of Hames and Collars on Nos. 37138 and 37140 harness will cost $1.00 extra.

HARNESS.

Our prices are very low, but our goods are the very best. Chicago is headquarters for leather, so we are able to do more than ordinarily well in such goods.

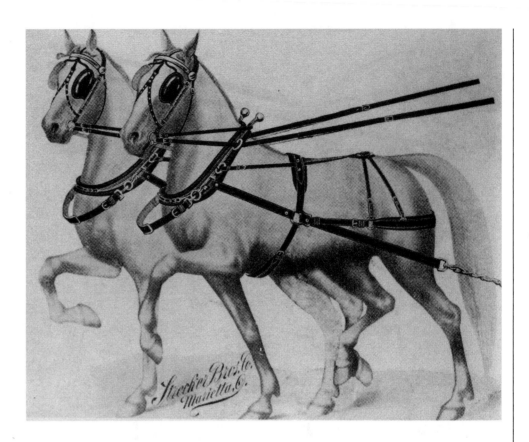

Singletrees and Neck Yokes.
Ironed.

71089 Singletrees, 26 inch plow, hickory, ironed, weight, 3¼ lbs. Each $0.17 Per dozen $1.84
71090 Singletrees, 30 inch plow, hickory, ironed; weight, 3¾ pounds. Each. $0.19. Per dozen 2.00
71091 Singletrees, 36 inch wagon, hickory, ironed with ferrules and hooks; weight, 6 pounds.
Each $0.32 Per dozen 3.25
We can furnish any of the above singletrees with twisted center clip instead of ring, at same price.

Strap End Singletrees.

71092 Have ½-inch strap, riveted on both sides and ⅜ hook, extra strong, 2⅝x36.
Each.................$0.35 Per dozen........$3.60

Davis Safety Singletrees.

71093 With Davis Patent Hooks. Impossible for the trace to become unhooked. Close connection and easily unhooked when desired.
2½x36. Each..........$ .33 Per dozen $3.45
2¼x30. Each .... .21 Per dozen....... 2.18

71095 Neck Yokes, 38 inch; hickory, ironed complete, weight, 6¾ lbs. Each....$0.40 Per dozen$4.50

Perfection Wagon Doubletrees.

71097 Ironed, complete, with stay chain clips and plates, on both sides of evener; woods oiled. Evener 48 inches long. Singletrees 36 inches long. Has adjustable clips. Suitable for wagons, threshers, engines, water tanks, etc. Quality guaranteed. Price, per set..............$1.75

Pefection Plow Whiffletrees.

71098 Ironed, complete, ready for use. Evener 40 inches long. Singletree 34-inches long. Suitable for general farm work. Adjustable clips. Are made of best seasoned hickory, thoroughly oiled, and the best quality malleable clips No holes are bored in the wood to fasten clips, thus preserving full strength of the wood.
Price, per set....................................$1.50

Ironed Evener.

71100 2x4x48 Wrought Iron Plates and malleable clevis, complete as shown in cut, oiled.
Each.......................................$0.42
71101 Evener, Neck Yoke and Singletrees, with clevises, complete sets ironed, and painted one coat; weight, 30 lbs.; per set...... .... 1.50

71102 The Dandy Plow Doubletrees; 38 inches, hickory, evener and hickory singletrees with patent clips and all irons complete. Price, only....... .....$0.90

Iron Hames and Tugs.

38112 Iron Hames. No. 1 full japanned (black), 3½ lb. iron hames with hame straps; box looped hame tugs and 1 inch trace buckles; per pair $1.20,1⅛ in. trace buckles per pair $1.25; 1¼ in. trace buckles, per pair $1.30. Sizes, 17 to 21 inches; mention length.

38114 Iron Hames, No. 1 full XC plated (white), 3½ lbs. iron hames, any size from 17 to 21 ins., with hame straps, box looped hame tugs and 1 in. trace buckles, per pair $1.20. With 1⅛ in. trace buckles; per pair $1.25. With 1¼ in. trace buckles, per pair $1.30

38112-14

Hook Hames.

38120 Hook Hames, iron over-top hook Hames, varnished, with line and breast strap rings. Per pair of two hames for one horse...........$0.40 Weight, per pair, 4 lbs.

38122 Polished Steel Bound Concord Hook Hames, with line rings and breast strap rings (No. 8). Weight, per pair, 5½ lbs. Per pair.... .80

Clip Hames.

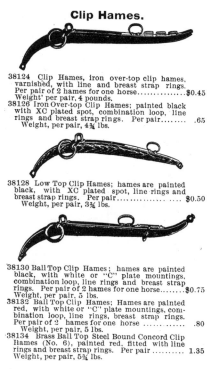

38124 Clip Hames, iron over-top clip hames, varnished, with line and breast strap rings. Per pair of 2 hames for one horse...............$0.45 Weight' per pair, 4 pounds.

38126 Iron Over-top Clip Hames: painted black with XC plated spot, combination loop, line rings and breast strap rings. Per pair........ .65 Weight, per pair, 4¾ lbs.

38128 Low Top Clip Hames; hames are painted black, with XC plated spot, line rings and breast strap rings. Per pair................. $0.50 Weight, per pair, 3¾ lbs.

38130 Ball Top Clip Hames; hames are painted black, with white or "C" plate mountings, combination loop, line rings and breast strap rings. Per pair of 2 hames for one horse.......$0.75 Weight, per pair, 5 lbs.

38132 Ball Top Clip Hames; Hames are painted red, with white or "C" plate mountings, combination loop, line rings, breast strap rings. Per pair of 2 hames for one horse .... .80 Weight, per pair, 5 lbs.

38134 Brass Ball Top Steel Bound Concord Clip Hames (No. 6), painted red, fitted with line rings and breast strap rings. Per pair .... 1.35 Weight, per pair, 5¾ lbs.

Bolt Hames.

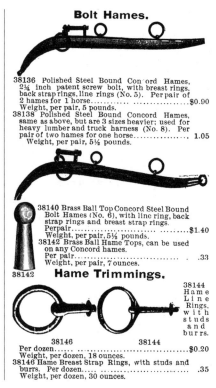

38136 Polished Steel Bound Con ord Hames, 2¼ inch patent screw bolt, with breast rings, back strap rings, line rings (No. 5). Per pair of 2 hames for 1 horse............ ....$0.90 Weight, per pair, 5 pounds.

38138 Polished Steel Bound Concord Hames, same as above, but are 3 sizes heavier; used for heavy lumber and truck harness (No. 8). Per pair of two hames for one horse................. 1.05 Weight, per pair, 5½ pounds.

38140 Brass Ball Top Concord Steel Bound Bolt Hames (No. 6), with line ring, back strap rings and breast strap rings. Per pair.............. ....$1.40 Weight, per pair, 5½ pounds.

38142 Brass Ball Hame Tops, can be used on any Concord hames. Per pair........................... .33 Weight, per pair, 7 ounces.

38142

Hame Trimmings.

38144 Hame Line Rings, with studs and burrs.

38146   38144

Per dozen..... ....$0.20 Weight, per dozen, 18 ounces.

38146 Hame Breast Strap Rings, with studs and burrs. Per dozen..... .... .35 Weight, per dozen, 30 ounces.

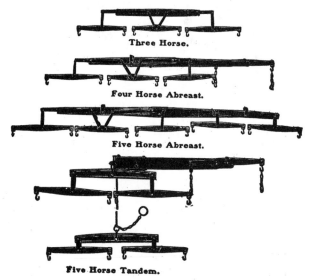

Three Horse.

Four Horse Abreast.

Five Horse Abreast.

Five Horse Tandem.

FIG. 3—GOOD TYPES OF EVENERS WHICH WILL DIVIDE EQUALLY THE DRAFT

CLAMPS AND STOOL FOR REPAIRING HARNESS

The device shown in figure 92 combines a stool and a clamp for holding harness work. The bench or stool, *b*, of any desired size, is supported by two legs near one end. The other end is held up by the foot of the long claw, extending to a convenient height for the operator. A shorter claw, *c*, is fastened to it by a cross-piece, *p*, about an inch thick and three inches wide, passing through a slot in the jaws, in which it works easily but firmly on two iron pins, a little more than half-way up from the bench. In the lower end of the short jaw

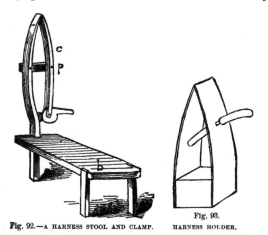

Fig. 92.—A HARNESS STOOL AND CLAMP.

Fig. 93. HARNESS HOLDER.

an eccentric works on a pivot and against a projection on the larger jaw. Depressing the handle to this eccentric or cam closes the jaws at the top with all the force desired.

A simple holder without the stool is shown in figure 93. Two staves of a flour barrel are sawed off at a convenient length for holding between the knees, while sitting on a chair. The sawed ends of the pieces are securely nailed to the opposite sides of a block of wood. A hole is cut through the middle of one side piece, in which a lever is placed for opening and closing the holder. The lever may be readily made of such shape that it will always remain in the hole, ready for use. The curves of the staves will furnish sufficient spring to hold the harness.

HARNESS CLAMP

The accompanying drawing represents a very handy harness mender which anyone who can use a saw and hammer can make in a few minutes. It is made of lumber of the dimensions indicated in the drawing. The clamp is tightened by the worker sitting upon the seat, which should extend at least 2 feet from the clamps. The drawing shows the device with a shorter seat than that. It would doubtless be better to have the seat extended to twice the length shown from the left of the clamps and to have the base extended in a similar manner, so that the device will not tip over too easily. The joint at the upper right-

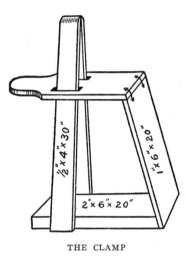

THE CLAMP

hand corner may be hinged with heavy wire run through holes and twisted together underneath, or real strap hinges of iron may be attached.

Harness Mending Outfit.

38048 Harness Mending Outfit. A complete outfit for general harness and belt repairing. Contains the following articles: Lever clamp, sewing awl and handle, round punch, rivet set, ball of thread, ball of wax, package of needles, package of copper rivets and burrs. All sets are exactly alike and we do not break sets. Each outfit securely packed in wooden box with hinged lid. Each..$1.50
Weight, about 10 lbs.

Harness Horse.

38050 Harness Makers' Stitching Horse. This is something every horse owner should have. Any man can do his own repairing and save his time, as well as his money. Made of good sound wood. Without jaw strap. Each.........$2.50
Weight, 18 lbs.
If jaw strap is wanted, add 25c.

INDEX

T